W9-CBE-375

JOURNEY INTO DARKNESS

JOHN DOUGLAS
AND MARK OLSHAKER

A LISA DREW BOOK

POCKET STAR BOOKS

New York   London   Toronto   Sydney   Tokyo   Singapore

The excerpt from *My 8 Rules for Safety* that appears on pages 184–85 is reprinted with permission of the National Center for Missing and Exploited Children (NCMEC). Copyright © 1990 NCMEC. All rights reserved.

The excerpt from *Child Protection* on page 187 is reprinted with permission of the National Center for Missing and Exploited Children (NCMEC). Copyright © 1985 NCMEC. All rights reserved.

The excerpt from *Kids and Company: Together for Safety* that appears on pages 188–89 is reprinted with permission of the National Center for Missing and Exploited Children (NCMEC). Copyright © 1990 NCMEC. All rights reserved.

A Pocket Star Book published by
POCKET BOOKS, a division of Simon & Schuster Inc.
1230 Avenue of the Americas, New York, NY 10020

Copyright © 1997 by Mindhunters, Inc.

All rights reserved, including the right to reproduce
this book or portions thereof in any form whatsoever.
For information address Scribner, 1230 Avenue
of the Americas, New York, NY 10020

ISBN: 0-671-00394-1

First Pocket Books printing September 1997

10 9 8 7 6 5 4 3 2 1

POCKET STAR BOOKS and colophon are registered
trademarks of Simon & Schuster Inc.

Cover photo by Joshua Sheldon / Photonica
Stepback photo by Peter Liepke

Printed in the U.S.A.

To Karla Brown, Suzanne Collins, Kristen French, Ron Goldman, Amber Hagerman, Cassandra Hansen, Tammy Homolka, Christine Jessop, Megan Kanka, Polly Klaas, Leslie Mahaffy, Shawn Moore, Angie, Melissa, and Nancy Newman, Alison Parrott, Nicole Brown Simpson, Shari Fay Smith, and all the other innocents, their families, friends, and loved ones, and the dedicated law enforcement officers who worked tirelessly seeking justice for them, this book is dedicated with respect, with humility, and with love.

Authors' Note

Our special thanks and deepest gratitude go out to all the people who have helped make this work a reality. The first team, as it has been since our first book together, consists of our editor, Lisa Drew, and our agent, Jay Acton, the two people who both shared the vision, encouraged us to see it through, and supported us every step of the way. Likewise, Carolyn Olshaker, our project coordinator, business manager, general counsel, editorial consultant, cheerleader, and to Mark, so much more. Ann Hennigan, our research director, has become an essential part of the operation and has contributed enormously. And we know that with Marysue Rucci handling things at Scribner for us with her amazing combination of efficiency and sunny disposition, everything is going to go smoothly and remain under control. Without these five . . .

We want to express our profound appreciation to Trudy, Jack, and Stephen Collins, Susan Hand Martin and Jeff Freeman for sharing Suzanne with us. We hope, in telling her story, that we have lived up to their faith in us. We are also indebted to Jim Harrington in Michigan and Tennessee District Attorney Henry "Hank" Williams for sharing their recollections and insights with us, and to our intern, David Altschuler, and to Peter Banks and all of the people at the National Center for Missing and Exploited Children for their kindness, as well as giving us the benefit of their research, experience, and good work. We're all a lot better because of them.

Authors' Note

Finally, as always, we want to thank all of John's colleagues at Quantico, particularly Roy Hazelwood, Steve Mardigian, Gregg McCrary, Jud Ray, and Jim Wright. They will always be valued pioneers, explorers, and esteemed fellow travelers on the journey into darkness and back out again.

—JOHN DOUGLAS AND MARK OLSHAKER,
October 1996

Contents

Either man's freedom of decision for or against God, as well as for or against man, must be recognized, or else religion is a delusion, and education is an illusion. Freedom is presupposed by both; otherwise they are misconceived.

Freedom, however, is not the last word. Freedom is only part of the story and half of the truth. Freedom is but the negative aspect of the whole phenomenon whose positive aspect is responsibleness. In fact, freedom is in danger of degenerating into mere arbitrariness unless it is lived in terms of responsibleness.

—VIKTOR E. FRANKL,
Man's Search for Meaning

Down these mean streets a man must go who is not himself mean, who is neither tarnished nor afraid.

—RAYMOND CHANDLER,
"The Simple Art of Murder"

PROLOGUE

In the Mind of a Killer

This isn't the Hollywood version. It isn't sanitized or prettied up or rendered into "art." This is the way it really happens. If anything, it's worse than the way I describe it.

As I had so many times before, I put myself in the mind of the killer.

I don't know who she's gonna be, but I'm ready to kill someone. Right now.

My wife's left me alone for the whole evening, gone out to a Tupperware party with her girlfriends rather than spending the time with me. It probably doesn't matter all that much; we've been fighting all the time anyway and we'd been fighting all day. Still, it's depressing and I'm sick and tired of being treated that way. Maybe she's really out seeing other men like my first wife'd done. She got hers, though—ended up face-down in the bathtub gagging on her own puke. Served her right for the way she treated me. Our two kids ended up with my folks; that's another thing pisses me off—like I wasn't good enough to take care of them anymore.

I sit around watching TV for a while by myself, drinking beer, a couple of six-packs, then a fifth of wine. But I still feel bad. I keep sinking lower. I need more beer or something else to drink. What's it now—9:00, 9:30 maybe—I get up and drive to the mini-mart near the commissary and get another six-pack of Moose Head. Then I drive down to Armour Road and just sit there drinking the beer, trying to sort things out in my own mind.

The longer I'm sitting here, the more depressed I'm getting. I'm here alone, living on the base as a dependent to my own wife, they're all her friends, no friends of my own, don't even have my kids. I was in the Navy myself, you know, and thought it was gonna work out, but it didn't. Now it's just one dead-end job after another. I don't know what I'm gonna do. Maybe I should just go on home and wait, then have it out with her when she comes back, get some things settled. It's all running through my head at the same time. I'd really like to have someone to talk to right now, but there isn't anyone around. Hell, I don't know anyone to tell my problems to, anyhow.

It's dark all around. It's starting to feel . . . kind of inviting. I feel one with the night. The dark makes me anonymous. The dark makes me omnipotent.

I'm over on the north side of the base, parked on the side of the road, still drinking beer, just past the buffalo pens when I see her. Shit, those buffaloes get better treatment than I do.

She's just crossed from one side of the road to the other. She's jogging on the side of the road, all by herself, even though it's already dark out. She's tall and really good-looking, about twenty, I'd say, with long brownish blond hair hanging in a braid. Her forehead glistens with sweat in the moonlight. Yep, very pretty. She has on a red T-shirt with the Marine emblem in gold on the front and little red shorts that show off her ass real nice and make her legs look like they go on forever. Not an ounce of fat on her. Those Marine women keep themselves in real great shape. All that exercise and drilling. Not like the ones in the Navy. They could whip an ordinary man's ass if given half the chance.

I watch her for a few moments, her boobs bouncing up and down with the rhythm of her run. I'm thinking about getting out to run with her, maybe strike up a conversation. But I know I'm not near in the shape she's in. Besides, I'm dead fucking drunk. So maybe I pull up in the car, offer her a ride back to her barracks or something, get her to talk to me that way.

But then I'm thinking to myself, what's she gonna go with someone like me for when she's probably doing those hot-shot Marines? Girl like that thinks she's too good to give my type the time of day. No matter what I say, she's gonna blow me off. And I been blown off enough for one day already. I been blown off enough for one lifetime.

Well, I'm not putting up with any of that bullshit any-more—not tonight, anyway. Whatever I want, I'm just gonna take; that's the only way you get anything in this world. Bitch is gonna have to deal with me whether she likes it or not.

I start up the car and pull alongside her. I lean across to the passenger window and call out, "'Scuse me! Do you know how far it is back to the other side of the base?"

She doesn't seem scared or nothing—I guess 'cause of the base sticker on the car, plus the fact that she probably thinks she can take care of herself, being a Marine and all.

She stops, comes over to the car real trusting like, breath-ing a little heavy. She leans in the passenger side and points back and says it's about three miles. Then she smiles real pretty and turns back to jog some more.

I know this is my only chance with her—another second and she'll be gone. So I open the door, jump out, and run up behind her. I whack her real hard from behind and she goes sprawling. Then I grab her. She kinda gasps as she realizes what's happening and tries to get away from me. But even though she's tall and strong for a girl, I'm nearly a foot taller than her and have to have more than a hundred pounds on her. I hold on to her and whack her on the side of the head as hard as I can, which must make her see stars. Even so, she still puts up one hell of a fight, tries to beat the shit out of me to get away. She's gonna pay for that, all right; no bitch is gonna treat me that way.

"Don't touch me! Get away!" she's screaming. I have to practically smother her to get her over close to the car. I whack her again, which makes her wobbly on her feet, then I grab her and put her in the car on the passenger side.

Just then, I see two men who've been jogging run up toward the car and they're shouting. So I gun the engine and get the hell out of Dodge.

I know I have to get off the base; that is the first thing.

So I head down the road toward the gate near the base theater; that's the only one that's open this time of night. I know because it was the one I came in. I prop her up in the seat next to me to look like she's my date. Her head's resting on my shoulder, real romantic like. In the darkness it must be working because the guard doesn't even react, just passes us through.

We're out on Navy Road when she starts coming to and begins screaming again; she threatens to call the cops if I don't let her go.

No one talks to me that way. It's not about what she wants anymore; it's about what I want. I'm fucking in control, not her. So I take a hand off the wheel and backhand her hard across the face. That quiets her down.

I know I can't bring her home. My old lady could be back by now. What am I gonna do—explain that this is what I really should be doing to her? I need somewhere me and this new bitch can be alone; that we won't be disturbed. I need to go somewhere I feel comfortable. Somewhere I know. Somewhere I know I can do what I have to, where no one'll interrupt us. I got an idea.

I drive down to the end of the road and turn right into the park—Edmund Orgill Park, it's called. I think she might be starting to wake up again, so I whack her good across the side of the head. I drive past the basketball courts, past the rest rooms and stuff toward the other end of the park, near the lake. I stop the car near the bank and turn off the motor. Now we're all alone.

I grab her by the shirt and yank her out of the car. She's sort of half-conscious, moaning. There's a cut around her eye and blood coming from her nose and mouth. I get her away from the car and sling her onto the ground, but she starts to get up. The bitch is still trying to resist me. So I jump on top of her—kind of straddling like—and smack her around some more.

There's this tall tree with spreading branches nearby. It's kind of cozy and romantic. She's mine now. I'm in control. I can do anything to her I want. I tear off her clothes—Nike running shoes, then her fancy Marine T-shirt and her little shorts and the blue sweat belt around her waist. There's not much fight left in her. She isn't so tough anymore. I rip

4

everything off her—even her socks. She's trying to escape or get away, but she can't do much. I am in control. I can decide whether this bitch lives or dies and how she's gonna die. It's all up to me. For the first time tonight, I feel like somebody.

While I press my forearm down on her neck to keep her quiet, I start going for her breast—the left one. But that's just for starters. I'm gonna give it to this bitch like she's never had it before.

I look around. I stand up for a moment, reach up above me and grab a limb from the tree, snap it off—about two and a half, three feet's worth. It's hard because that sucker's almost two inches thick. The end is sharp where it broke off, like an arrowhead or a spear.

She seemed like she was out cold just before, but she screams loud again. Her eyes are wild with pain. God, with all that blood, I'll bet she's a virgin. The bitch just screams in agony.

Here's for all the women who ever shit on me, I'm saying to myself. Here's for all the people who gave me a raw deal. Here's to life—let someone else get shafted for a change! By now she's stopped struggling.

After the frenzy is over and the wildness is done, I start feeling calmer. I lean back and look down at her.

She's completely quiet and still. Her body is pale and empty-looking, like something's gone. I know she's finally dead and for the first time in a hell of a long time, I feel completely alive.

This is what it means to walk in the shoes, to know both victim and subject—how each interacts with the other. This is what you get from spending hours in the prisons and penitentiaries, sitting across the table, listening to the actual stories. After you've heard from them, you begin to put the pieces together. The crime itself begins to talk to you. As horrible as it sounds, this is what you have to do to be effective.

I described this technique to a reporter interviewing me not long ago and she said, "I can't even think about this kind of thing!"

I replied, "Well, we'd better all think about this if we ever want to have fewer of them to think about."

If you understand—not in some academic, intellectual way, but in a visceral, experiential way—then maybe we can begin to make a difference.

What I've just described was my idea of what had happened late on the night of July 11, 1985, and in the early morning of July 12—the day U.S. Marine Lance Corporal Suzanne Marie Collins—an accomplished, well-loved, exuberant, and beautiful young woman of nineteen—had died in a public park near the Memphis Naval Air Station, just northeast of Millington, Tennessee. The five-foot-seven, 118-pound Lance Corporal Collins had left her barracks for a run shortly after 10:00 P.M. and never came back. Her nude and beaten body had been discovered in the park after she missed morning muster. The causes of death were reported as prolonged manual strangulation, blunt-force trauma to the head, and massive internal hemorrhage from a sharply beveled tree limb being thrust so far into her body that it tore through her abdominal organs, liver, diaphragm, and right lung. She had been scheduled to graduate on the twelfth from a four-month avionics school in pursuit of her goal of becoming one of the first female Marine aviators.

It was always a searing and gut-wrenching experience to go through this exercise, but that's what I had to do if I were going to be able to see the crime through the offender's eyes. I'd already put myself through it from the victim's point of view, and that was almost unbearable. But it was also my job, a job I'd created for myself as the first full-time criminal profiler at the Behavioral Science division of the FBI Academy in Quantico, Virginia.

Normally when my group—the Investigative Support Unit—was called in, it was to provide a behavioral profile and investigative strategy to help police hunt down an UNSUB: an unknown subject. By this time, I'd already worked on more than 1,100 such cases since I came to Quantico. But this time the authorities already had a suspect in custody when they called. His name was Sedley Alley—a bearded, twenty-nine-year-old white male from Ashland, Kentucky, six feet four inches tall, 220 pounds, a laborer for an air conditioning company who lived on base as a dependent to his wife, Lynne, who was enlisted in the Navy. They already had a confession from him; in fact, they'd gotten it the next morning. But his version of events was somewhat different from mine.

Agents of the Naval Investigative Service had picked him up from the car description of two male joggers and the base gate guard. Alley told them that he'd been depressed after his wife, Lynne, had gone out to her Tupperware party, that he'd finished off three six-packs of beer and a bottle of wine in the house, then gone out in his old and dying green Mercury station wagon to the mini-mart near the post commissary to buy some more beer.

He said he was becoming increasingly intoxicated as he drove aimlessly, until he had seen an attractive white female in a Marine T-shirt and running shorts cross the street as she was jogging. He said he got out of his car and started jogging with her, exchanging small talk, until after a few minutes he became winded from his drinking and smoking. He wanted to tell her his problems, but didn't feel she would care about them since she didn't know him, so he said goodbye and drove off.

In his drunken state, he reported, he was drifting and weaving back and forth across the road. He knew he shouldn't be driving. Then he heard a thump and felt a jolt in his car. He realized he'd struck her.

He put her in his car, telling her he was going to take her to the hospital, but he said she kept resisting him, threatening to have him arrested for DWI. He drove off the base and headed for Edmund Orgill Park, where he stopped the car and hoped to calm her down and talk her out of turning him in.

But in the park she continued berating him, he claimed, telling him how much trouble he was in. He yelled at her to shut up and when she tried to open the door, he grabbed her by the shirt, opened his door, got out, and pulled her out with him. She was still yelling about how she was going to have him arrested, then tried to break away. So he jumped on top of her and straddled her on the ground, just to keep her from running off. Alley just wanted to talk to her.

She kept trying to get away; he described it as "wiggling."

At that point, he "lost it for a second" and hit her across the face—first once, then once or twice more—with his open hand.

He was scared and knew he was in trouble if she turned him in. He says he got off her, trying to figure out what to do, and went back to the Mercury for the yellow-handled screwdriver he needed to hot-start the car and when he came back, he heard someone running in the dark. Panicked, he wheeled around and flung up his arm, which happened to be holding the screwdriver. It turned out to be the girl he struck, and the screwdriver must have hit her and penetrated the side of the head, because she collapsed onto the ground.

At this point he didn't know what to do. Should he just run away, maybe go back to Kentucky? He didn't know. He decided he'd have to make the death look like something else, like she was attacked and raped. But, of course, he hadn't had sex with her—her injury and death had all been a horrible accident—so how was he going to make it look like a sexual attack?

He removed her clothes from her body—that was a start—then dragged her by the ankles away from the car, over to the lake bank, and placed her under a tree. He was grasping at straws, desperate to think of something, when he stretched his hand out and came in contact with a tree limb, and without even consciously thinking about it, he broke it off. Then he rolled her over onto her stomach and pushed the stick into her, just once, he claimed, just enough to make it look like she'd been attacked by a sex maniac. He ran back to his car, hurriedly left the scene, and left the park at the opposite end from where he'd driven in.

Henry "Hank" Williams, assistant district attorney for Shelby County, Tennessee, was trying to sort the whole thing out. Williams was one of the best in the business—an imposing-looking former FBI agent in his early forties with strong, chiseled features, kindly, sensitive eyes, and prematurely white hair. He'd never seen such a gruesome case.

"As soon as I looked at the file, I thought this was definitely a death penalty case," Williams commented. "I wasn't going to plea-bargain this one."

The problem as he saw it, though, would be to come up

with a motive for such a savage murder that a jury could understand. After all, who in his right mind could do such a horrible thing?

That was the angle the defense was playing. Aside from Alley's account of the "accidental" death, they were raising the specter of insanity. It seemed that psychiatrists examining the subject at the instruction of the defense had proposed that Alley suffered from multiple personality disorder. He had neglected to inform the Naval Investigative Service agents who'd interviewed him that first day that apparently he had been split into three personalities on the night Suzanne Collins died: himself; Billie, a female personality; and Death, who had ridden a horse next to the car in which Sedley and Billie had been riding.

Williams contacted Special Agent Harold Hayes, the profile coordinator in the FBI's Memphis office. He described to Williams the concept of lust murder and referred him to an article my colleague Roy Hazelwood and I had written five years earlier for the *FBI Law Enforcement Bulletin*, entitled "The Lust Murderer." Though "lust," in such cases, is something of a misnomer, the article described what our research into serial killers had shown us about these loathsome, sexually based crimes of manipulation, domination, and control. The killing of Suzanne Collins seemed to be a classic lust murder—a premeditated act willfully committed by a sane individual with a character disorder such that, while he knew the difference between right and wrong, he wasn't going to let that moral distinction get in his way.

Williams asked me onto the case to advise him on prosecutive strategy and figure out how to convince a jury of twelve good men and women who probably had little direct contact with raw evil in their lives that my version of events made more sense than the defendant's.

The first thing I had to do was explain to the prosecution team some of what my people and I had learned during our years of fighting crime from a behavioral perspective . . . as well as the particular price we'd paid to learn it.

I had to take them along on my own journey into darkness.

CHAPTER 1

Journey into Darkness

In early December of 1983, at thirty-eight years of age, I collapsed in a hotel room in Seattle while working on the Green River murders case. The two agents I'd brought with me from Quantico had to break down the door to get to me. For five days I hovered in a coma between life and death in the intensive care unit of Swedish Hospital, suffering from viral encephalitis brought on by the acute stress of handling more than 150 cases at a time, all of which I knew were depending on me for answers.

I wasn't expected to live, but miraculously I did, nurtured by first-rate medical care, the love of my family, and the support of my fellow agents. I returned home, almost a month later, in a wheelchair and couldn't go back to work until May. All during that time, I was afraid the neurological damage the disease left me with would prevent me from shooting at FBI standards and therefore prematurely end my career as an agent. To this day, I still have some impairment on my left side.

Unfortunately, my situation isn't unique in this business. Most of the other agents who've worked with me as profilers and criminal investigative analysts in the Investigative Support Unit have suffered some severe, work-related stress or illness which kept them off the job for some period of time. The range of problems runs the gamut—neurological disease like mine, chest pain and cardiac scares, ulcers and GI disorders, anxieties and depression. Law enforcement is a notoriously high-stress environment to begin with. While I was home recuperating, I did a lot of thinking about what it is in our job that causes the particular kind of stress that's at least different and may even be greater than that of some other FBI agents, detectives, and police line officers—people who face immediate physical danger far more often than we do.

Part of the answer, I think, lies in the service we offer. In an agency long famous for its "Just the facts, ma'am" orientation, we're probably the only group routinely asked for an opinion. Even so, we essentially had to wait for J. Edgar Hoover to die before profiling could even be considered a legitimate crime-fighting tool. For years after the criminal personality program was set up at Quantico, most others within and outside the Bureau considered this witchcraft or black magic practiced by a small group of shamans sixty feet below ground where the light of day never penetrated.

The fact of the matter, though, is that life and death decisions can be made based on our advice, yet we don't have the luxury of hard facts to back them up; we don't have the comfort of black and white. If a police officer is wrong, it means the case might not be solved, but things are no worse off than they were before. When we are called in, it's often as a last resort, and if we're wrong, we can send the investigation off in a completely nonproductive direction. So we try to be very sure about what we say. But our stock-in-trade is human behavior, and human behavior, as the psychiatrists are so fond of telling us, is not an exact science.

One of the reasons police and law enforcement agencies throughout the United States and many parts of the world come to us is because we have experience that they don't. Like the medical specialist who has seen many more cases of a rare disease than any primary-care physician, we have the advantage of a national and international perspective and can therefore pick up on variations and nuances that might escape a local investigator who has only his own jurisdiction as a reference point.

We work on the principle that behavior reflects personality and generally divide the profiling process into seven steps:

1. Evaluation of the criminal act itself.
2. Comprehensive evaluation of the specifics of the crime scene or scenes.
3. Comprehensive analysis of the victim or victims.
4. Evaluation of preliminary police reports.
5. Evaluation of the medical examiner's autopsy protocol.
6. Development of a profile with critical offender characteristics.
7. Investigative suggestions predicated on construction of the profile.

As the final step indicates, offering a profile of an offender is often only the beginning of the service we offer. The next level is to consult with local investigators and suggest proactive strategies they might use to force the UNSUB's hand—to get him to make a move. In cases of this nature we try to stand off at a distance and detach ourselves, but we still may be thrust right into the middle of the investigation. This may involve meeting with the family of a murdered child, coaching family members how to handle taunting phone calls from the killer describing how the child died, even trying to use a sibling as bait in an effort to lure the killer to a particular place.

This was what I suggested after the murder of seventeen-year-old Shari Faye Smith in Columbia, South Carolina, since the killer gave indications of being fixated on Shari's beautiful sister, Dawn. Every moment until we had the killer in custody, I sweated out the advice I'd given the sheriff's department and the family, knowing that if my judgment was flawed, the Smiths could be facing another unendurable tragedy.

Less than six weeks after the killer called Dawn with elaborate instructions on how to find Shari Faye Smith's body in a field in neighboring Saluda County, Lance Corporal Suzanne Collins was murdered in a public park in Tennessee.

There are just so many of them out there for us.

And what we do see, as my colleague Jim Wright characterized them, are the worst of the worst. We live every day with the certain knowledge of people's capacity for evil.

"It almost defies description what one person can do to another," Jim notes. "What a person can do to an infant; to a child less than a year old; the evisceration of women, the dehumanization process that they go through. There's no way you can be involved in the type of work we're doing or be involved as a law enforcement officer or in the investigation of violent crime and not be personally affected. We very often receive telephone calls from surviving victims, or from the loved ones of victims. We even have some of the serial killers and serial rapists calling us. So we're dealing with the personal side of these crimes, and we do personally get involved and take them to heart. All of us in the unit, I think, have our pet cases that we refuse to let go of."

I know what some of Jim's are. One of mine is Green River, which was never solved. Another is the murder of Suzanne Collins, which haunts me to this day.

While I was home recuperating from my illness, I also visited the military cemetery in Quantico and stared at the plot where I would have been buried had I died that first week. And I did a lot of thinking about what I would have to do if I were going to survive to retirement age. I'd considered myself as good at what I did as anyone, but I realized I'd become a one-dimensional person. Everything—my wife, my kids, my parents, friends, house, and neighborhood—had all come in second behind my job, a very distant second. It got to the point that every time my wife or one of my kids got hurt, or had a problem, I'd compare it to the victims in my horrific cases, and it didn't seem like such a big deal. Or, I'd analyze their cuts and scrapes in terms of blood patterns I'd observed at crime scenes. I tried to work off my constant tension through a combination of drinking and a feverish exercise regimen. I could only relax when I was completely exhausted.

I decided while walking through that military cemetery that I had to find a way to ground myself, to set a greater store in the love and support I got from Pam and my daughters, Erika and Lauren (our son, Jed, would come along several years later), to begin relying on religious faith, to try to take some time off, to explore the other aspects of life. I knew this was the only way I was going to make it. And when I moved from managing the profiling program and became unit chief in 1990, I tried to provide ways that everyone working for me could maintain his or her mental health and emotional equilibrium. I'd seen firsthand what can happen, how sapping our work can be.

To do what we do, it's very important to get into the mind of not only the killer or UNSUB, but into the mind of the victim at the time the crime occurred. That's the only way you're going to be able to understand the dynamics of the crime—what was going on between the victim and the offender. For example, you may learn that the victim was a very passive person, and if so, why did she receive so many blows to the face? Why was this victim tortured the way she was even though we know from analyzing her that she would have given in, done anything her attacker said? Knowing how the victim would have reacted tells us something important about the offender. In this case, he must be into hurting his victims. The rape isn't enough for him, it's punishing them that's important to him, that represents what we refer to as the "signature" aspect of the crime. We can begin to fill in much of the rest of his personality and predict his recognizable post-offense behavior from this one insight.

It's important for us to know this about each case and each victim, but it's also among the most devastating emotional exercises imaginable.

Police officers and detectives deal with the effects of violence, which is disturbing enough, but if you're in this business long enough, you do grow somewhat used to it. In fact, many of us in law enforcement are concerned that violence is so much around us that it's taken for granted even by the public.

But the kind of criminals we deal with don't kill as a means to an end, such as an armed robber would; they kill or rape or torture because they enjoy it, because it gives them satisfaction and a feeling of domination and control so lacking from every other aspect of their shabby, inadequate, and cowardly lives. So much do many of them enjoy what they do that they want nothing more than to experience it again at every opportunity. In California, Lawrence Bittaker and Roy Norris made audiotapes so they could relive the sexual torture and murder of teenaged girls in the back of their specially equipped van, nicknamed Murder Mac. Also in California, Leonard Lake and his partner, Charles Ng, produced videos of young women they'd captured being stripped and psychologically brutalized in captivity—offering voice-over commentary along the way.

I'd like to tell you these are isolated practices, or just limited to the exotic perversions of California. But I've seen too much of this, and my people have seen too much of this, to be able to tell you that. And hearing or seeing violence as it happens in "real time" is about as unbearable as anything we deal with.

Over the years, as it became my responsibility to evaluate and hire new people for my unit, I developed a profile of what I wanted in a profiler.

At first, I went for strong academic credentials, figuring an understanding of psychology and organized criminology was most important. But I came to realize degrees and academic knowledge weren't nearly as important as experience and certain subjective qualities. We have the facilities to fill in any educational gaps through fine programs at the University of Virginia and the Armed Forces Institute of Pathology.

What I started looking for was "right-brained," creative-type thinkers. There are many positions within the FBI and law enforcement in general where engineering or accounting types do the best, but in profiling and investigative analysis, that kind of thinker would probably have some difficulty.

Contrary to the impression given in such stories as *The Silence of the Lambs,* we don't pluck candidates for the Investigative Support Unit right out of the Academy. Since our first book, *Mindhunter,* was published, I've had many letters from young men and women who say they want to go into behavioral science in the FBI and join the profiling team at Quantico. It doesn't work quite that way. First you get accepted by the Bureau, then you prove yourself in the field as a first-rate, creative investigator, then we recruit you for Quantico. And then you're ready for two years of intensive, specialized training before you become a full-fledged member of the unit.

A good profiler must first and foremost show imagination and creativity in investigation. He or she must be willing to take risks while still maintaining the respect and confidence of fellow agents and law enforcement officers. Our preferred candidates will show leadership, won't wait for a consensus before offering an opinion, will be persuasive in a group setting but tactful in helping to put a flawed investigation back on track. For these reasons, they must be able to work both alone and in groups.

Once we choose a person, he or she will work with experienced members of the unit almost the way a young associate in a law firm works with a senior partner. If they're at all lacking in street experience, we send them to the New York Police Department to ride along with their best homicide detectives. If they need more death investigation, we have nationally recognized consultants such as Dr. James Luke, the esteemed former medical examiner of Washington, D.C. And before they get to Quantico, many, if not most, of our people will have been profile coordinators in the field offices, where they develop a strong rapport with state and local departments and sheriff's offices.

The key attribute necessary to be a good profiler is judgment—a judgment based not primarily on the analysis of facts and figures, but on instinct. It's difficult to define, but like Justice Potter Stewart said of pornography, we know it when we see it.

In San Diego in 1993, Larry Ankrom and I testified in the trial of Cleophus Prince, accused of murdering six young women over a nine-month period. We'll get into more of the details of that case in the next chapter. During the preliminary hearing to rule on the admissibility of our testimony on linkage based on "unique" aspects of each crime, one of the defense attorneys asked me if there was an objective numerical scale I used for measuring uniqueness. In other words, could I assign a number value to everything we did. The answer, of course, is no. Many, many factors come together in our evaluations, and ultimately, it comes down to the individual analyst's judgment rather than any objective scale or test.

Likewise, after the tragedy at the Branch Davidian compound in Waco, Texas, there was much soul-searching, breast-beating, and attempt at self-critique within the federal law enforcement agencies about what could and should have been done differently. After one such meeting at the Justice

Department in Washington, Attorney General Janet Reno asked me to have my unit compile a list of scenarios for standoff situations and assign each one a percentage success rating.

Ms. Reno is an extremely bright and sensitive individual and I lauded her desire to prepare herself in advance for the next unknown crisis rather than having to respond from a purely reactive mode. But while it might be considered insubordination, I told her how reluctant I was to do anything of the sort.

"If I tell you that a certain tactic worked eighty-five percent of the time in a particular type of hostage situation and any other response has only been effective twenty-five or thirty percent of the time," I explained, "then there's going to be tremendous pressure on you to go for the highest percentage. But I or another analyst may see something in that situation which indicates to us that the lower percentage option is the one to go with. We can't justify it in statistical terms, but our judgment tells us it has the best chance of working. If you're going to go with the numbers, you might as well let a machine make the decision."

That, actually, is an issue which comes up with some regularity in our business—can't a machine do what we do? It would seem that after you have enough cases and enough experience, an expert programmer ought to be able to come up with a computer model that could, say, duplicate my thought processes as a profiler. It's not as if they haven't tried, but so far, at least, machines can't do what we can do, any more than a computer could write this book even if we gave it all the words in the dictionary, their relative usage in speech, all the rules of grammar and parameters of style and models of all the best stories. There are just too many independent judgments to be made, too many gut feelings based on training and experience, too many subtleties of the human character. We certainly can and do use computer databases to quantify material and retrieve it efficiently. But like a doctor making a diagnosis, objective tests only go so far. Since machines can't do it, we have to find human beings who can, who try to balance objectivity and intuition.

And while we can offer the techniques and hone the skills, we can't supply the talent. As with a gifted professional athlete, it's either there or it isn't. Like acting, or writing, or playing a musical instrument, or hitting a baseball, you can teach someone the concept, you can give pointers, you can help them develop the skill. But unless you're born with what my friend the novelist Charles McCarry calls a "major league eye," you're not going to hit the ball consistently in the big leagues; you're not going to be pro material.

But if you are pro material in our field, and if you are at all a decent, normal person—as I hope we all are—you can't see the things we see, you can't become involved with the families and survivors the way we do, you can't encounter repeat, multiple rapists and killers who hurt other people for the sport of it, without taking on a sense of mission and developing a deep and enduring kinship with the victims of violent crime and their families. So you might as well know going in that this is where I'm coming from and that is the perspective from which this book is written. I would like to believe in redemption and I hope rehabilitation is possible in some cases. But from my twenty-five years of experience as an FBI special agent and nearly that long as a behavioral profiler and crime analyst, seeing the evidence, the statistics, and the data, I cannot place more faith in what I would *like* to be true than what I *know* is reality. What I mean by this is that I am much less interested in giving a convicted sexually motivated killer a second chance than in giving an innocent potential victim a first chance.

Please don't get me wrong. We don't need a fascist, totalitarian police state to accomplish this, we don't have to threaten the Constitution or civil liberties; from my experience I'm as aware as anyone of the real and potential abuses of police power. What I do believe we need is to enforce the laws we already have on the books and bring some simple common sense, based more on reality than sentiment, to the issues of sentencing, punishment, and parole. What I think we need more than anything else in our society today is a sense of personal responsibility for what we do. From what I see and hear and read, no one is responsible anymore; there's always some factor in a person's life or background to excuse him. There is a price to the passage through life, and regardless of what's happened to each of us in the past, part of that price is responsibility for our actions in the present.

Having briefly laid out these views, let me also repeat at the outset what almost anyone in law enforcement will tell you: that if you expect us to solve your social problems, you're going to be very disappointed. By the time the problem reaches our desk, it's already too late; the damage has been done. I've often said in speeches that many more serial killers are *made* than *born*. With adequate awareness and intervention, a lot of these guys can be helped, or at least neutralized, before it's too late. I've spent much of my career dealing with the results if they're not.

How do we know this? What makes us think we understand why a killer acts the way he does and that we can therefore predict his behavior even though we don't know who he is?

The reason we think we know what's going on in the mind of the killer or rapist or arsonist or bomber is because we were the first ones to get the word directly from the real experts—the offenders themselves. The work my colleagues and I did, and the work that's still being done in Quantico after me, is based initially on a study Special Agent Robert Ressler and I undertook beginning in the late 1970s in which we went into the prisons and conducted extensive and detailed interviews with a cross section of serial murderers and rapists and violent criminals. The study continued intensively for several years and in a sense is still ongoing. (With the collaboration of Professor Ann Burgess at the University of Pennsylvania, the results were compiled and eventually published under the title *Sexual Homicide: Patterns and Motives.*)

To deal with these people effectively, to get what you need out of them, first you have to prepare extensively—study the entire file and know everything you can about the case—and then you have to come down and deal with them on their own level. If you don't know exactly what they've done and how they've done it, how they got to their victims and the methods they used to hurt and kill them, then they're going to be able to bullshit you for their own self-serving purposes. Remember, most serial offenders are expert manipulators of other people. And if you're not willing to come down to their level and see things through their eyes, they're not going to open up and confide. And both of these factors add to the strain.

I wasn't getting anything out of Richard Speck, mass murderer of eight student nurses in a South Chicago town house, when I interviewed him in prison in Joliet, Illinois, until I abandoned my official Bureau detachment and berated him for taking "eight good pieces of ass away from the rest of us."

At that point he shook his head, smiled, then turned to us and said, "You fucking guys are crazy. It must be a fine line, separates you from me."

Feeling the way I do about victims and their families, this is always a bitter and extremely difficult persona for me to assume. But it's necessary, and after I did it with Speck I was able to start penetrating the macho facade and achieve an understanding of how his mind worked and what made him escalate that night in 1966 from a simple burglary to rape and mass murder.

When I went to Attica to interview David Berkowitz, the "Son of Sam," who had killed six young men and women in cars in New York City during a year-long reign of terror beginning in July of 1976, he held to his well-publicized story that his neighbor's three-thousand-year-old dog had made him commit the crimes. I knew enough about the specific details of the case and I'd seen enough of his methodology that I was sure the killings were not the result of such a complex delusional system. I felt this way not because I made it up, but because of what I'd already learned in interviews we'd previously conducted and analyzed.

So once Berkowitz started giving me the song and dance about the dog, I was able to say, "Hey, David, knock off the bullshit. The dog had nothing to do with it."

He laughed and quickly admitted I was right. This cleared the way to the heart of his methodology, which was the aspect I most wanted to hear about and learn from. And we did learn. Berkowitz, who had started out his antisocial career as a fire-starter, told us that he was on the hunt nightly for victims of opportunity who met his criteria. When he couldn't find them, which was most nights, he would gravitate back to the scenes of his previous crimes to masturbate and relive the joy and satisfaction, the power of life and death over another human being, just as Bittaker and Norris had with their audiotapes and Lake and Ng did with their home movies.

Ed Kemper is a six-foot-nine giant of a man who probably has the highest IQ of any killer I've ever encountered. Fortunately for me and the rest of us, where I encountered him was in the secure visitors' room of the California State Medical Facility at Vacaville, where Kemper was serving out multiple life terms. As a young teen he had spent some time in a mental hospital for killing both his grandparents on their farm in northern California. He had gone on as an adult to terrorize the area around the University of California at Santa Cruz in the early 1970s, where he decapitated and mutilated at least six coeds before getting himself focused and butchering his own mother, Clarnell, the real object of his resentment.

I found Kemper to be bright, sensitive, and intuitive. And unlike most killers, he understands enough about himself to know that he shouldn't be let out. He gave us a number of important insights into how an intelligent killer's mind works.

He explained to me, with insight rare for a violent criminal, that he dismembered the bodies after death not because of any sexual kick, but simply to delay identification and keep investigators off his trail as long as possible.

From other "experts" we got additional nuggets of information and insight which were to prove tremendously valuable in devising strategies to catch UNSUBs. For instance, the old cliché about killers returning to the scenes of their crimes turns out to be true in many instances, though not necessarily for the reasons we thought. True, a certain personality of killer under certain circumstances does feel remorse and returns to the crime scene or the victim's grave site to beg forgiveness. If we think we're dealing with that sort of UNSUB, it can help dictate our actions. Some killers return for different reasons—not because they feel bad about a crime but because they feel good about it. Knowing this can help us catch them, too. Some inject themselves directly into an investigation to keep on top of things, chatting up cops or coming forward as witnesses. When I worked on the Atlanta Child Murders in 1981, I was convinced from what I saw that the UNSUB would actually approach the police with offers to help. When Wayne Williams was apprehended after he'd thrown the body of his latest victim into the Chattahoochee River (as we predicted he would), we learned that this police buff had offered his services to the investigators as a crime scene photographer.

And others we interviewed told us that they had taken a companion, generally a woman, on a trip to the general area of the crime, then made some excuse to leave her long enough to actually revisit the scene. One killer told us of taking his sometimes girlfriend on a camping trip, then leaving her briefly with the excuse that he had to relieve himself in the woods. That was when he would go back to the body dump site.

The prison interviews helped us see and understand the wide variety of motivation and behavior among serial killers and rapists. But we saw some striking common denominators as well. Most of them come from broken or dysfunctional homes. They're generally products of some type of abuse, whether it's physical abuse, sexual abuse, emotional abuse, or a combination. We tend to see at a very early age the formation of what we refer to as the "homicidal triangle" or "homicidal triad." This includes enuresis—or bed-wetting—at an inappropriate age, starting fires, and cruelty to small animals or other children. Very often, we found, at least two of these three traits were present, if not all three. By the time we see his first serious crime, he's generally somewhere in his early to mid-twenties. He has low self-esteem and blames the rest of the world for his situation. He already has a bad track record, whether he's been caught at it or not. It may be breaking and entering, it may have been rape or rape attempts. You may see a dishonorable discharge from the military, since these types tend to have a real problem with any type of authority. Throughout their lives, they believe that they've been victims: they've been manipulated, they've been dominated, they've been controlled by others. But here, in this one situation, fueled by fantasy, this inadequate, ineffectual nobody can manipulate and dominate a victim of his own; he can be in control. He can orchestrate whatever he wants to do to the victim. He can decide whether this victim should live or die, how the victim should die. It's up to him; he's finally calling the shots.

Understanding the common background is very important in understanding a serial killer's motivation. After spending many hours with Charles Manson at San Quentin, we concluded that what motivated him in inspiring among his followers the butchery of Sharon Tate and her friends one night in Los Angeles in 1969 and Leno and Rosemary LaBianca the next was not the apocalyptic blood lust of "Helter Skelter" as had been widely thought. Born the illegitimate son of a sixteen-year-old prostitute who had grown up with a fanatically religious aunt and sadistic uncle until he began living on the streets at age ten and in and out of prisons thereafter, Manson craved fame, fortune, and recognition, just like the rest of us. What he really wanted to be was a rock star. Short of that, he could set himself up as a guru and would settle for a free ride through life with susceptible followers providing the food, shelter, and drugs. His "family" of social misfits and middle-class dropouts provided him with enough opportunity for manipulation, domination, and control. To keep them in line and interested, he preached apocalypse, an ultimate social and race war symbolized by the Beatles' song "Helter Skelter" in which he alone would emerge victorious.

Everything was okay with Charlie until August 9, 1969, when Manson follower and would-be usurping leader Charles "Tex" Watson broke into the Beverly Hills home of director Roman Polanski and his eight months pregnant wife, movie star Sharon Tate. After the brutal slaughter of five people (Polanski was not home at the time), Manson realized he had to assume control, make it seem that he had actually intended these murders as the beginning of Helter Skelter, and direct his family into another killing, or else he would lose credibility and surrender his leadership to Watson. Then his free ride would be over. In Manson's case, the violence began not when he began his manipulation, domination, and control, but when he began *losing* control.

All that we learned from Manson doesn't mean he's any less a monster than what we thought, it only means he turns out to be a somewhat different type of monster. Understanding the differences gives us insight into his type of crime

24

and, equally important, his type of charisma. What we learned from Manson we were later able to apply to an understanding of other cults, such as the one led by the Reverend Jim Jones, David Koresh's Branch Davidians at Waco, the Weaver family at Ruby Ridge, the Freemen in Montana, and the entire militia movement.

Through our interview and research efforts we came up with a number of observations which have had significant bearing on our ability to analyze crimes and predict behavior of criminals. Traditionally, investigators have given great weight to a perpetrator's modus operandi, or MO. This is the way the perpetrator goes about committing a crime—whether he uses a knife or gun, or the method he uses to abduct a victim.

Theodore "Ted" Bundy, who was executed in 1989 in the electric chair of the Florida State Penitentiary at Starke with my colleague Bill Hagmaier not far away, was handsome, resourceful, and charming, well-liked by those around him and the model of a "good catch." He was a perfect example of the reality that serial killers don't often look like monsters. They blend in with the rest of us. He was one of the most notorious serial killers in American history, a man who abducted, raped, and murdered young women all along the way from Seattle to Tallahassee, having developed a ruse in which he would have his arm in a sling and removable cast, making him appear disabled. He would then ask the assistance of his intended victim in moving some heavy object. When her guard was down, he would whack her. Novelist Thomas Harris used this particular MO in creating the character of Buffalo Bill in *The Silence of the Lambs*.

Additional aspects of the character were taken from other serial killers with whom we acquainted Harris during a visit he made to Quantico before writing his previous novel, *Red Dragon*. Buffalo Bill kept his victims in a pit dug in his basement. In real life, this is what Gary Heidnick did with the women he captured in Philadelphia. Buffalo Bill's penchant for using the skins of women to create a female "costume" for himself came from Ed Gein, the 1950s killer in the small Wisconsin farming community of Plainfield. Harris wasn't the first to borrow the idea, though. Robert Bloch had already used parts of it in his own memorable novel, *Psycho,* made into the film classic by Alfred Hitchcock.

What's important to note here is that while using an arm cast and sling to abduct women is a modus operandi, killing and flaying women to use their skins is not. The term I coined to describe that was "signature," because like a signature, it is a personal detail that is unique to the individual. The MO is what the offender does to effect the crime; the signature, in a sense, is *why* he does it: the thing that fulfills him emotionally. Sometimes there can be a fine line between MO and signature, depending on the reason why it was done. Of the three aspects of the Buffalo Bill composite, the cast is definitely MO, the skinning is signature, and the pit could be either, depending on the situation. If he keeps his captives in the pit as a means of holding and controlling them, then I would classify that as MO. If he gets some emotional satisfaction out of holding them down there, of seeing them degraded and pleading in fear, then that would fall under signature.

I have found that signature is a much more reliable guide to the behavior of serial offenders than MO. The reason for this is that signature is static, while MO is dynamic; that is, it evolves as the offender progresses in his criminal career and learns from his own experience. If he can come up with a better means of abducting a victim or transporting or disposing of a body, he'll do it. What he won't change is the emotional reason he's committing the crime in the first place.

Clearly, in a routine crime such as bank robbery, MO is the only thing that matters. The police will want to know how he's pulling off the job. The reason he's doing it is obvious—he wants the money. But in a sexually based serial crime—and virtually all serial murders are sexually based in one sense or another—signature analysis may be critical, particularly in being able to link a series of crimes together.

Steven Pennell, the "I-40 Killer" in Delaware, lured prostitutes into his specially equipped van where he raped, tortured, and murdered them. His methods of getting the women into his van varied; that was his MO. What stayed consistent was the torture; that was his signature, and that is what I testified to at his trial. That was what gave him emotional satisfaction. A defense attorney might claim that various cases are not related and do not represent the work of the same subject because the instruments used or the methods of torture might have been different. But this is insignificant. What is significant is the torture itself, and that remained consistent and static.

One final note here: you've probably noticed that whenever I mention serial killers, I always refer to them as "he." This isn't just a matter of form or syntactical convenience. For reasons we only partially understand, virtually all multiple killers are male. There's been a lot of research and speculation into it. Part of it is probably as simple as the fact that people with higher levels of testosterone (i.e., men) tend to be more aggressive than people with lower levels (i.e., women). On a psychological level, our research seems to show that while men from abusive backgrounds often come out of the experience hostile and abusive to others, women from similar backgrounds tend to direct the rage and abusiveness inward and punish themselves rather than others. While a man might kill, hurt, or rape others as a way of dealing with his rage, a woman is more likely to channel it into something that would hurt primarily herself, such as drug or alcohol abuse, prostitution, or suicide attempts. I can't think of a single case of a woman acting out a sexualized murder on her own.

The one exception to this generality, the one place we do occasionally see women involved in multiple murders, is in a hospital or nursing home situation. A woman is unlikely to kill repeatedly with a gun or knife. It does happen with something "clean" like drugs. These often fall into the category of either "mercy homicide," in which the killer believes he or she is relieving great suffering, or the "hero homicide," in which the death is the unintentional result of causing the victim distress so he can be revived by the offender, who is then declared a hero. And, of course, we've all been horrified by the cases of mothers, such as the highly publicized Susan Smith case in South Carolina, killing their own children. There is generally a particular set of motivations for this most unnatural of all crimes, which we'll get into later on. But for the most part, the profile of the serial killer or repeat violent offender begins with "male." Without that designation, my colleagues and I would all be happily out of a job.

Until that happens—which, if the last several thousand years of human history are any indication, won't be anytime in the foreseeable future—some of us are going to have to continue making that journey into darkness: into the dark mind of the killer and the dark fate of his victim.

That's the story I want to tell here.

CHAPTER 2

The Motive Behind the Murder

I've often said that what we do in analyzing a murder, that what any good homicide detective does, is very similar to what a good actor does in preparing for a role. We both come to a scene—in the actor's case a scene in a play or movie script, in ours, a murder scene—we look at what's there on the surface—written dialogue between the characters or evidence of a violent crime—and we try to figure out what that tells us. In other words, what really happened between the principal characters in this scene? Actors call this "subtext," and what they'll tell you they need to know for themselves before they can act a scene is: What does the character want? Why does he say this particular thing or take this particular action?

What is the motive?

Motive is one of the thorniest issues in criminal investigative analysis. It is also among the most critical. Until you can figure out why a particular violent crime was committed, it is going to be very difficult trying to come to meaningful conclusions regarding the behavior and personality of the UNSUB. Even if you do catch him, it can still be very problematic prosecuting him successfully. That was the problem Hank Williams faced going into the Sedley Alley trial, and that was why he called me in. In the case of bank robbery, the motive—like its related element, the signature—is obvious: the offender wants the money and he doesn't want to work for it legitimately. But let's say you're investigating a breaking and entering in which the resident of the apartment was raped and killed. Was the primary motive burglary, sexual assault, or murder? Either way, the victim is still dead, but it makes a big difference to us in figuring out what kind of person the killer is.

During the fall of 1982, we got a call from a police department in the Midwest investigating the rape-murder of a twenty-five-year-old woman. The crime occurred in the living room of the apartment she and her husband had lived in for about six months. When the husband returned home, he found the place had been completely ransacked, leading police to wonder whether the primary motive had actually been burglary and the rape and murder a secondary crime of opportunity.

The crime scene photos were very complete and well-done. The victim was found face-up on the living room floor, with her dress up around her waist and panties pulled down to her knees. Despite the disarray in the room, there was no evidence of struggle and no defense wounds on the body. The murder weapon was a hammer belonging to the victim and her husband. It was found in the kitchen sink, where it appeared the UNSUB had placed it to wash off the blood. The husband reported that some of his wife's jewelry had been taken.

In interesting contrast to the appearance of the crime scene, the ME's report found no apparent evidence of sexual assault and no traces of semen on the victim or her clothing. However, tox screens did show that she had been drinking shortly before the attack. This was where I said, "Bingo!" The crime was staged to look like what an inexperienced person thinks a rape-murder is supposed to look like.

I told the surprised detective I was pretty sure he'd already interviewed the killer, and that the motive wasn't burglary. It wasn't even sexual aggression.

This is what I visualized having happened:

The victim and the offender had been drinking together in her apartment. They got into an argument, probably a rehash and continuation of one they'd had many times in the past. The tension reached a threshold that the offender could no longer stand. He grabbed the closest weapon of opportunity, which happened to be the hammer in the kitchen, returned and angrily struck the victim several times on her head and face until she collapsed. Realizing he would be the obvious suspect, the offender rushed to the kitchen sink to wash blood from his hands and bloody fingerprints from the handle of the hammer. He then went back to the dead victim and rolled her over into a face-up position, lifted her dress and pulled down her underpants to stage a sexually motivated assault. He then ransacked the drawers to make it appear that the intruder had come in searching for money or valuables.

At this point in my narrative the detective said, "You just told me the husband did it."

I coached him on how to reinterview the husband. During the polygraph, I said, the key thing would be to stress that the police knew he got blood on his hands and tried—unsuccessfully—to wash the bloody evidence away.

Within a few days the husband was polygraphed, failed the test, and then admitted his guilt to the polygraph examiner.

Sometimes you're faced with a case in which the motive should be apparent, but something doesn't quite add up. That's what happened early in the afternoon of January 27, 1981, in Rockford, Illinois.

About 1:00 P.M. someone walked in to Fredd's Groceries and shot and killed the fifty-four-year-old owner, Willie Fredd, and an employee, Fredd's twenty-year-old nephew, Albert Pearson. There were no witnesses.

Fredd was found face-down on the floor behind the counter. Detectives determined that he must have been sitting behind the counter when he was shot twice with .38 caliber slugs—one in his neck, the other in his spleen. The younger victim was found halfway out the swinging doors to the outside. He'd been shot three times in the chest by the same weapon, evidently while backing away from his assailant. Strangely, there was no evidence of anything of value being taken from the store. Fredd and Pearson, it should be noted, were black.

Around 8:45 the following morning, a man coming in for gas at a Clark Oil Company Super 100 service station in Rockford came upon the body of the attendant in the station's supply storage room. The victim was an eighteen-year-old white male identified as Kevin Kaiser. He was propped against the wall where he'd fallen after being shot five times with a .38 caliber weapon, though ballistics tests later showed it was not the same weapon that had killed the two men at the grocery store the previous day. Four of the bullets had passed through his chest. The fifth entered the right side of his face and exited the left side of his neck, clearly shot at close range. The lack of bleeding at either the entry or exit wound meant the heart had already stopped; the young victim was dead before this last shot was fired.

As far as victimology, people who knew Kevin had nothing but good things to say about him, describing him as hardworking and "a real nice kid." And like the incident the day before, nothing of value appeared to have been taken. There was a description of a possible suspect in the area, however: a black male in his late twenties, medium height with short hair and a mustache.

Shortly after 7:00 the next morning, a husband and wife who'd pulled in at the E-Z Go gas station in Rockford found the attendant lying face-up in a large pool of blood in that station's storage room. They'd gone in to try to find someone when the station appeared to be unattended during business hours. The victim this time was Kenny Foust, a thirty-five-year-old white male who had been shot twice—one bullet entering the left side of his face and passing into his brain, the other after he collapsed to the floor, from the right side of his neck to the left. The customers immediately called the rescue squad, which arrived while Foust was still alive, but he died shortly after arriving at Rockford Memorial Hospital without regaining consciousness. It appeared that about $150 was robbed from the station. There were no witnesses, but ballistics tests indicated that the gun that had killed Kenny Foust had also killed Willie Fredd and Albert Pearson—the first real link in any of these three incidents. Rockford police immediately formed a major case task force.

Four days later, on the afternoon of February 2, someone came into a Radio Shack store in Beloit, Wisconsin, and shot and killed both the twenty-one-year-old manager, Richard Boeck, and a twenty-six-year-old male customer, Donald

Rains. Another customer later found them lying next to each other on the floor near the rear of the store. Both had been shot multiple times in the head and chest even though detectives saw no sign of a struggle with the gunman. It seemed that some money had been taken from the store, but they couldn't tell how much. Beloit is just over Wisconsin's southern border, about twenty miles or so north of Rockford.

There were three witness accounts of men seen in the area prior to the killings. One of those was of a black male similar in description to the one spotted in connection with the second shooting in Rockford. The witness accounts and similarity of circumstances suggested this last crime could be related to one or more of the previous three. That gave it an interstate character and meant the FBI could be called in. I got involved right after this when I got a frantic call from the FBI in Illinois.

The problem was, the case didn't add up. There were multiple weapons. The victims were both black and white, a wide variety of ages, and almost nothing of value had been taken in crimes that looked like nothing else but armed robberies. Who was he and why was he doing it?

As I looked at the police reports, the crime scene photographs, and the autopsy protocols, this started looking less like a string of armed robberies gone bad and more like a certain type of serial murder. I still didn't really understand what the motive was, but the style of killing was consistent and I would characterize it as an assassination style. None of the victims appeared to have put up any resistance and most were shot more times and more viciously than was necessary to achieve the purpose of neutralizing them for a robbery. That is to say, the killing went far beyond modus operandi.

The killings were methodical and sequential, but didn't make much sense. You could even think of them as spree murders rather than serial crimes. Nothing of significant value was taken. There was no sexual component to the murders. There was no evidence the UNSUB knew any of the victims, so an attempt at personal revenge didn't seem likely. Quite the contrary, the victims didn't seem to have anything in common with each other.

When you've analyzed what should be the motive based

on the crime scenario and that doesn't make sense, and you go through all the other "logical" ones and you can't make one of them fit reasonably, then you start looking into psychiatric territory. All crimes have a motive, all crimes make sense according to some logic, though that logic may be a strictly internal one with no relationship to any "objective" logic.

This made me think our UNSUB was probably a paranoid individual, delusional but still functional. I thought the multiple weapons spoke to this, too. He only used one type of ammunition; he was familiar with the .38 slug and trusted it. But he had more than one gun. I was willing to bet there were more still. When you're paranoid you can never have too many guns.

To commit this series, he had to be able to get from point A to point B, which meant he had to be able to drive, which meant he probably had a driver's license, which meant he was operating in the everyday world at some level and he had some job, even if it was a menial one. He would have interaction with people around him, but they would know he was "odd."

In any series of crimes that takes place over some distance, we concentrate on the first case, which for our purposes is usually the most significant. In multiple homicides the killer is usually of the same race as his victim. Assuming that the four cases were related, here we had a situation in which the first two victims were black and all the other subsequent ones were white. A killer begins where he feels the highest comfort level. For that reason, I believed the UNSUB was black, and therefore possibly matched the description of the two separate witnesses. For that same reason, I also felt he was likely to live within a relatively close distance of Fredd's Groceries. He would have had some excuse to be in that area.

From our data, paranoid personalities as well as paranoid schizophrenics typically surface in their mid-twenties. Assassin types also seem to surface around their mid-twenties, so I felt pretty secure pegging this guy in his mid- to late twenties.

I expected this type of individual to feel more comfortable at night and in the darkness. The first crime—the one I presumed to be close to home—was committed in the afternoon. But the next two were done late at night or in the early morning hours. It took until the fourth crime for him to be bold enough to go out again in broad daylight. For the same reason, I thought he'd drive a dark-colored car and favor dark clothing. He'd also feel the need of a large "power dog" for protection, either a German shepherd or Doberman pinscher; he might even have two. If I were constructing the same profile today, I'd probably specify a pit bull, the current vogue. But back then, it would be either a shepherd or a Doberman. Along with the police-type dog, he might use a police radio scanner.

He'd also have some sort of record. I wouldn't expect necessarily any homicides, but there'd be some assaultive behavior, reacting against authority figures, possibly institutionalization. Killing every person in each of the holdups spoke of someone who "overcompensated" for everything.

The police circulated the witness descriptions, which eventually led to a man staying in a motel two blocks from the grocery store. Cigarettes which had been sold at the store were found in his room. His name was Raymond Lee Stewart, but by the time police identified him, he had fled.

FBI agents working on an Unlawful Flight to Avoid Prosecution—Armed Robbery warrant arrested Raymond Lee Stewart in Greensboro, North Carolina, on February 21. Stewart was a twenty-nine-year-old, five-foot-six-inch-tall black male. He had lived in Rockford before moving to North Carolina and had returned for the upcoming birth of his out-of-wedlock child. He had stayed at a motel two blocks from Fredd's Groceries. Concerned that he might be harrassed, bothered, or attacked at the motel, he had registered under an assumed name.

On February 4, two days after the Radio Shack murders in Beloit, he returned to North Carolina, his old, dark-colored car pulling a rented U-Haul trailer in which he carried most of his possessions. As soon as the agents approached his car and trailer, they saw Stewart's two Dobermans tied up nearby. After obtaining a search warrant for his trailer and the house of the cousin with whom he was staying, the investigators found a .38 caliber RG 31 revolver, a .38 caliber Smith & Wesson Model 60 Chief's Special, ammunition, and a police radio scanner. He had a history of armed robberies of self-service gasoline stations.

He was charged with four counts of murder in Illinois and two in Wisconsin, though as it turned out he ended up standing trial twice, once for the armed robbery and killing of Willie Fredd and Albert Pearson, and a second trial for the murder of Kevin Kaiser. During the trials, his manner was angry and full of contempt for the system and his victims. He was found guilty of felony murder and sentenced to death by the Circuit Court of Winnebago County, Illinois. He later claimed the murders were spurred by racial hatred, but said he deserved clemency because of childhood abuse.

On September 18, 1996, Stewart was executed by lethal injection at the state penitentiary at Springfield. In his final words he said, "May you all have peace because of this. May my victims' families have peace."

Delineating signature as a separate and distinct element from modus operandi was an attempt to shed light on the critical question of motive. And motive and signature were indeed critical in linking a series of six murders of women in San Diego from January through September of 1990. Former Cuyahoga County, Ohio, prosecutor Tim McGinty, now a judge in Cleveland, who'd used me in the Ronnie Shelton serial rapist case a few years before, recommended me to the San Diego Police Department. When the case reached my unit, it was assigned to Larry Ankrom, who had geographic responsibility for that part of the country.

When we first saw the case, there had been three murders, all at the Buena Vista Garden Apartments in the Clairemont area. The first victim was a twenty-year-old student at San Diego State University named Tiffany Schultz. A boyfriend who found her body was arrested as a suspect, but quickly released. Before long there were two more victims: Janene Weinhold and Holly Tarr.

Because of the high-risk nature of attacking women in such a setting in the middle of the day, we would expect the UNSUB to know the complex well. Violent offenders usually begin where they feel most comfortable and at home. That's why the first crime in the series is so important. We also expected him to have made approaches to other women in the past. These approaches—a warm-up for his later violent crimes—may have seemed innocent but were ultimately unsatisfying to him.

Before the attack on Tiffany Schultz there would have been a real or perceived crisis in the offender's life which would have triggered his acting out. He came to each of these locations with focused anger. It would be a reasonable conclusion that he held a woman, or women in general, accountable for his problems and this was how he dealt with his rage. He would have had a number of failed relationships with women, most of them marked by periodic violent or abusive behavior. He could have taken personal items such as jewelry from one or more of the victims, which he would then give to the woman he was in a relationship with, but not tell her where it came from.

We believed the offender would be employed in some capacity but because of his temper and lack of interpersonal skills, it would not be a high-level job and his employment history would be spotty. He'd be an underachiever who has problems getting along with his peers, prefers to be alone, and has a history of run-ins with authority. He might easily live in a dependent relationship with someone from whom he receives financial support. A conflict with her might have triggered the series of murders.

Like many offenders, this one would likely display changes of behavior after the first killings which would be noticeable to those around him. These could include heavier reliance on alcohol or drugs, change in sleeping or eating habits, weight loss, anxiety, more eagerness to associate with others. He would also closely follow the news of the investigation. We told the police that the public could be extremely instrumental in identifying the killer if these traits were publicized and it was made clear that there would be at least one person close enough to him to have a sense of what he'd done.

Holly Tarr was killed in April. She was an aspiring actress from Okemos, Michigan, who had come during spring break to visit her brother, who lived at the Buena Vista Garden Apartments. After this murder, the UNSUB narrowly missed capture. Several witnesses reported seeing a man with a knife dash outside with a T-shirt covering his face.

The only physical description they could provide was that he appeared to be a dark-skinned man of shorter than average height. In the process of making his escape, he knocked down a maintenance man who was responding to another tenant's report of a "horrible scream." The maintenance man found Holly Tarr in the bedroom under a blood-covered towel.

By this point the media had dubbed him the "Clairemont Killer."

We expected this could signal a cooling-off period in which he'd lie low for a while and recover his nerve. And we expected this to be the end of his activities at this particular apartment complex. He might even move to another city on the pretext of a job offer or visiting relatives or friends. But it was unlikely he'd stop altogether. Most of these guys have no burn-out point.

He did surface again, almost two months later, at a different location, but still an apartment complex in the same general vicinity where he obviously felt most comfortable. Then there were no more similar killings until the middle of September, when two women, Pamela Clark and her eighteen-year-old daughter, Amber, were killed in a house in the nearby area of University City. Even though these last victims had been mother and daughter, Pamela Clark was youthful-looking and very attractive. All of the six women fit a general physical profile, and in photographs Amber Clark looked remarkably like the previous victim, Janene Weinhold.

In the largest manhunt in the city's history, San Diego police worked intensively for thirteen months to find the one subject they were convinced was responsible for all six grisly and sadistic deaths.

The break came early in February of 1991, when Geralynd Venverloth returned home from a Family Fitness Center health club and was going into the shower when she heard her doorknob jiggling. Looking through the peephole, she saw a black man trying to open the door. She managed to slip the dead bolt and he fled. But then several mornings later, Venverloth saw the same man dropping off her associate, Charla Lewis, at work.

His name was Cleophus Prince, Jr. Police arrested him

after staking out the health club and booked him for burglary. They found several knives on the floor of Prince's 1982 Chevy Cavalier. But they had to release him on his own recognizance for lack of evidence. They did, however, get blood and saliva samples, which were sent to Cellmark Diagnostics in Maryland for DNA analysis. Three weeks later, the results came back with a match for Janene Weinhold's attacker.

Police went to Charla Lewis's apartment, where Prince had been living. It was next door to where the fourth victim, Elissa Keller, had lived. Prince had skipped town, and gone back home to Birmingham, Alabama. But at the apartment, detectives found a gold opal ring identical to the one Holly Tarr's father had given her on her sixteenth birthday. The ring's manufacturer told police that only sixty-three such rings were made, none distributed in California.

On Sunday, March 3, 1991, police in Birmingham arrested the twenty-three-year-old black former Navy mechanic, who had lived in the Buena Vista Garden Apartments complex at the time of the first three murders. He had been arrested for theft and had been released on bail just before San Diego PD called. At Prince's residence, detectives found another ring that looked like one described as belonging to Elissa Keller and shoes that matched prints found at several of the scenes. The San Diego Sheriff's Department began investigating him in relation to the unsolved murder of Diane Dahn in May of 1988. And Homewood, Alabama, police wanted to talk to him about the unsolved murder of twenty-three-year-old Toni Lim in March 1990. Both slayings bore some of the same characteristics as the stabbing deaths of the six women in the main series.

The key to the case was the DNA match between semen found on the clothing of the second Buena Vista victim, twenty-one-year-old Janene Weinhold, and blood and saliva samples they got from Prince. But what about the other five murders?

San Diego police asked us to reexamine the six cases to see if it was reasonable to conclude that one individual had committed all the murders. Several people, including prosecutors Dan Lamborn and Woody Clark and Sergeant Ed Petrick of the task force, came to meet with us in Quantico.

If the prosecution could prove that the defendant had committed all six murders, rather than only that of Janene Weinhold, the number and nature of the crimes would qualify as "special circumstances" under California law, which would make it a capital case. They didn't want this guy getting out again.

Looking at six cases now rather than just the original three, based on both MO and signature considerations, we concluded that all the murders were, in fact, related.

All six victims were white females. Except for Pamela Clark, all were brunettes between the ages of eighteen and twenty-one. As far as modus operandi, in each case the killer entered through an unlocked door or window, the crimes were all committed with a knife, and all occurred within the victims' residences, four of which were apartments, and in five of the cases the assault period was late morning to early afternoon. In four instances, the knife was a weapon of opportunity taken from the victim's kitchen. The first three victims were living in the same garden apartment complex in second-floor units, which indicated to us a level of comfort created by the attacker living close by and knowing the area well. There were no signs of forced entry, and in five of the six there was no ransacking, although jewelry was taken from the third, fourth, and fifth victims. This last fact would likely fall in the category of signature, assuming the initial purpose of the offender was not simple robbery.

And we certainly didn't believe that to be the case since nothing apparently was taken from victims one, two, and six and they were all killed by relatively shallow stab wounds, very similar in five out of the six, concentrated in the chest area and indicative of focused anger and rage. The rage, however, was highly and unusually controlled. There was no frenzy as we often see in such situations, and other than the knife wounds there was little physical trauma. All of the victims were discovered face-up on the floor, nude or partially nude, with no attempt made to conceal the bodies.

Equally important as all of this, no other similar homicides occurred within the San Diego area anywhere near the time of this series and a review of our Violent Criminal Apprehension Program (VICAP) database didn't identify any murders matching this wound pattern anywhere else in the country.

Of course, then we had to consider the differences within this supposed series. The last two victims, the Clarks, lived not in apartments but in a single-family house. Two of the six were sexually assaulted before being killed. Holly Tarr was stabbed only once, while the most brutally assaulted one was stabbed fifty-two times. However, as we noted, the evidence at the crime scene suggested that the killer had been interrupted in the process. Most of the victims would be considered low-risk, but two could have fallen into the high-risk classification. Tiffany Schultz, the San Diego State English major who became the first victim, had taken a part-time job as a nude dancer in a San Diego nightclub shortly before her murder. The relative risk of a crime happening to a particular victim and the relative risk taken by each offender in the commission of a particular crime are useful indicators to us in determining both victimology and the personality of the UNSUB.

In the Tarr case, the offender attempted to clean up the scene and the victim was found covered with a sheet. This could have represented a change either in signature or MO, but it could also have been related to the way he felt about this particular victim. Most likely, it had to do with him being interrupted in the process.

Now this all might seem to be a statistical approach to crime scene analysis and it might seem that a computer could do the same thing Larry Ankrom did—crunch the numbers and make an evaluation. But a computer would be unable to give weight to each similarity and difference. There simply is no way of coming up with a numerical value for each piece of information. It can be properly evaluated only by running it through the brain of an experienced profiler like Larry. And putting all of this together, we concluded that all six murders were committed by the same individual and that his motive was the controlled sexualized rage so evident from the knife wounds.

Dan Lamborn, the prosecutor, asked me to testify at the trial. I was already starting to think about retirement and knew that the people who were staying on after me needed to get experience and develop their own independent reputations. Larry had done the key work on the analysis and made a very impressive, credible, and authoritative witness. I suggested that I take the stand to introduce and give background on the discipline of profiling and that Larry should testify on the analysis itself. That was fine with Lamborn and his partner, Rick Clabby.

The defense, represented by public defenders Loren Mandel and Barton Sheela, wasn't thrilled with the idea of our testifying at all, arguing in pretrial motions that, not being psychiatrists or psychologists, we weren't qualified to comment on psychological issues, and that what we had to say about the crimes and their linkage would be prejudicial to the defendant. In other words, if the jury believed us and thought that Prince had committed even one of the murders, they'd have to conclude that he did the other five as well. Lamborn and Clabby countered by pointing out that our testimony could actually put the greater burden on the prosecution, because if the jury believed us that the same individual was responsible for all six murders, then if they didn't feel Prince had done any one of them, they'd have to let him off for all six.

Ultimately, in what had become a growing trend in courts across the country, Judge Charles Hayes ruled that we did have an expertise sufficiently beyond the common sense of the average person that it could be of guidance to the jury. In a complicated logic which tried to balance the concerns of both sides, however, he ruled that we couldn't actually use the term "signature" in our testimony, as the defense felt that implied psychological motivation. Larry and I both felt somewhat hamstrung by this restriction, but we made the best of it.

The jury deliberated more than nine days before coming back with a verdict on July 13, 1993. They found Cleophus Prince guilty of all six murders and twenty-one burglaries. Since they deemed that there were special circumstances present, including murder during the course of a rape and the commission of multiple murders, the crimes were eligible for the death penalty. The next month, the same jury deliberated one day, returning a recommendation that he be sentenced to execution in the gas chamber at San Quentin or by lethal injection. Judge Hayes affirmed the sentence on

November 6. As of this writing, he remains on San Quentin's death row.

In 1986, I was a coauthor of an article for the *Journal of Interpersonal Violence*, entitled "Sexual Homicide: A Motivational Model." By way of introducing the topic, we wrote:

"When law enforcement officials cannot readily determine a motive for murder, they examine its behavioral aspects. In developing techniques for profiling murderers, FBI agents have found that they need to understand the thought patterns of murderers in order to make sense of crime scene evidence and victim information. Characteristics of evidence and victims can reveal much about the murderer's intensity of planning, preparation, and follow-through. From these observations, the agents begin to uncover the murderer's motivation, recognizing how dependent motivation is to the killer's dominant thinking patterns. In many instances, a hidden, sexual motive emerges, a motive that has its origins in fantasy."

Tragically, this motive of uncontrolled anger and the need for sexual domination doesn't always occur against strangers. In the mid-1980s, I was called in on a case up in Toronto in which a Malaysian college student named Deliana Heng had been found in the bathroom of her own apartment, lying face-down with her head next to the toilet bowl and her legs bound at the ankles with a belt. She'd been beaten about the face and head and strangled with the strap of a camera bag. She was nude from the waist down and blood was smeared across her abdomen and left leg. She'd also been sexually assaulted, and a pendant in the shape of a cross that she wore around her neck was missing. There was no forced entry and from all the victimology and evidence at the crime scene, I concluded that the murderer was someone whom she knew and trusted.

Toronto police concurred. In working their way through the people with whom Heng had contact, they had identified a friend of hers named Tien Poh Su as their prime suspect, a bodybuilder who worked out at a nearby gym. The problem was getting proof that would convince a prosecutor and then a jury.

What the police really wanted was a blood sample, but

they didn't want to tip off this guy that he was under suspicion. And without sufficient corroborating evidence, if he refused to give the blood, they couldn't compel a test.

Canadian law is very strict on certain issues such as trial publicity, but police have latitude on searches and information gathering up there that we don't have in the States. For example, we can't bug a jail cell or set up a cop in disguise as a cellmate. And given what they were allowed to do, Toronto officers came up with a creative proactive strategy.

They identified a police officer who was a veteran weight lifter and had him begin frequenting the gym where the suspect worked out. He'd make a point of being there at the same time as Su and working out on machines close by.

Their eyes kind of lock in on each other. Before too long, the two men are exchanging friendly greetings, then comparing techniques and training habits. It's clear that the suspect admires the somewhat older man's physique and definition and the fact that he can outlift him on every exercise. Su starts asking him what he did to get those kinds of muscles.

He says he has a special diet, individually tailored to his system and keyed to the way he metabolizes various nutrients.

Su wants to try the diet, too, but the cop tells him that for it to work, he went to a special doctor who analyzed his blood to see which nutrients he was lacking. Su says he'd like to go to that same doctor, but the cop tells him this is a new technique, not yet regulated, so it's somewhat unkosher.

"Tell you what, though," the cop offers. "If you remind me, I'll get a blood sample kit from him and I'll take your blood and give it to him. Then I'll tell you what he says you should be eating and what supplements you should be taking."

The suspect likes this idea, and keeps reminding him about the blood sample. So before too long, the cop shows up at the gym with a sample kit, sticks Su's finger, and takes some blood. It matches up with blood found at the crime scene, they now can get a search warrant, they find other incriminating evidence and charge the man with murder.

Among the things they find is a book published in the United States entitled *The Rapist Files,* which purports to be a collection of actual rapists talking about their crimes. In one of the cases, a subject describes bringing a victim into the bathroom, where he beats and rapes her. Then he gets her in front of the bathroom mirror, puts a ligature around her neck, and tightens it to the point where she passes out. He loosens it until she revives, then repeats the procedure, making the cord a little bit tighter each time until the victim literally watches herself being killed. This was the fantasy the killer was harboring long before the act itself.

Su was married and police learned that recently he had given his wife a cross-shaped pendant identical to the one missing from the neck of the murder victim.

The Crown attorney asked me to come to Toronto for the trial and consult on prosecutorial strategy. They thought that the defendant might testify, and that if he did, he would prove highly credible to a jury. After all, he knew this woman and sexually sadistic rage and control was a tough motive to get across. When he did decide to testify, we knew there had to be some way of shaking him up.

One of the critical pieces of evidence in the Crown's case was the victim's bloodstained panties. I suggested that the prosecutor take them over to the witness stand and force him to handle them. In several successful suspect interrogations, I'd found that if you can get the guy to focus on some object involved with the crime—something belonging to the victim, the murder weapon itself, almost anything that has meaning to the killer—you can throw him off. In the murder of twelve-year-old Mary Frances Stoner in Adairsville, Georgia, in 1979, we got a confession out of prime suspect Darrell Gene Devier by placing the bloody rock which had been the murder weapon at a forty-five-degree angle to his line of vision. This led to a first-degree murder conviction and Devier's eventual execution, sixteen years after the murder.

The strategy worked here, too. As soon as he was handed the panties, Su became visibly upset. The longer he was forced to hold the evidence, the more shook up he became. From that point on in his testimony, his veneer of sensitivity and innocence was shot and the jury got a sense of what he was really like.

During a break in the case, I happened to run into the

defense attorney in the corridor. He commented to me that it was really a shame how his client was coming across on the stand.

"What are you talking about?" I said.

He said it was a shame the jury was seeing him in such an unfortunate light, almost as if he were lamenting the fact that his client had dressed inappropriately that morning and was therefore giving a bad impression of himself.

"Are you kidding?" I responded. "This is a classic case. You've got an inadequate guy, who goes in and rapes this girl in front of the mirror, showing all this fantasy and anger and hostility. And to keep the fantasy going, he takes the cross and gives it to his wife so he can imagine doing to her what he did to the woman he killed. You're defending a classic killer," I said.

Just as in the prison interviews, if you know your subject and his crimes well, you can often cut quickly to the truth.

Had Su not been caught and convicted, there is no doubt in my mind he would have become Canada's next serial killer.

CHAPTER 3

Candy from Strangers

One spring day when my daughter Lauren was about eight, I took her to a local fair set up in a park not far from where we lived. There were ice cream, hot dogs, and cotton candy, exhibits, all kinds of arts and crafts for sale, and rides for the kids. The mood was festive and everyone seemed to be having a good time.

Maybe it goes back to my days as a lifeguard, but I never quite relax in a crowd. I'm always looking out for the "bobbing head": someone in trouble or something that doesn't seem quite right. And as I'm looking around, I see this one individual about five foot seven or five foot eight, with a potbelly and glasses. He has a camera around his neck and he's watching the children on the pony ride. I'm about fifteen feet away and I can tell by the way he's looking at these children that he doesn't have a child there. He's looking at the kids on the ponies with an expression that borders on lust; that's the only word to describe it.

I figure this is a good opportunity to teach Lauren a useful lesson. I say to her, "Lauren, you see that guy over there?"

"What guy?"

"That guy right over there. You see him? Look how he's looking at those kids. You see that? This is the kind of thing I've been telling you about."

She whispers, "Dad, be quiet!"

I say, "No. Turn around and look at him. Look at what

47

he's doing. You see the way he's looking at that little girl getting off the pony over there?"

"Yeah, Dad, I see him. Now be quiet! You're embarrassing me. He may hear us."

"No, let's watch him, Lauren. He's following these kids. You see the way he's following them?"

So we tail him out of the park as he pursues these little girls, occasionally snapping pictures of them. And Lauren starts to get it, to understand that this man is not just a benign presence at this fair and around these children. What I explain to her, what I warn her about, is that this is not the type of individual who will plan ahead and boldly snatch a child off the street. He wouldn't come up to our driveway and grab her off her bike. But if she were out selling Girl Scout cookies, say, or I let her go trick-or-treating alone and she went up and knocked on his door and he saw there was no adult around, the timing and the setting would be just right. By allowing this scenario to take place, I'd have, in effect, given away my daughter.

Around two years later my little object lesson paid off. Lauren was by herself on one of our town's main streets when she saw this same guy, following her down the block, taking *her* picture. Now to a ten-year-old, he looks harmless, maybe even inviting, like a poor, lonesome soul. But because of our experience two years before at the fair, because of the somewhat uncomfortable exercise I put her through, she recognized what he was up to and was equipped to deal with the situation.

She ducked into the Ben Franklin store, surveyed the situation, then approached and started talking to a female customer, doing a tremendous acting job to make this guy think the woman was her mother. Seeing that, he quickly took off.

This kind of thing happens all too commonly. We'd all pick it up if we were attuned to it. About five years before, my wife, Pam, and I were down in Hampton, Virginia, with our older daughter, Erika, when she was about ten. We were around the harbor, a very pleasant place with all kinds of shops and attractions, and were watching a little girls' dancing class putting on a recital for the public. As I watched, I spotted a guy in the crowd of about 150 spectators. He looked to be in his early forties and had a camera around his neck.

I nudge Pam, who says back to me, "Yeah, yeah, I saw him, too. I know what you're going to say." She was used to this in me because of the kind of work I did. But I can see it clearly in his eyes. He's looking at these young kids as if they're the Rockettes.

Now again, this type of individual isn't going to grab a child in front of a crowdful of witnesses. He probably hasn't even acknowledged to himself that he might act upon his fantasies.

But he's got his camera, and let's say he spots a child who seems to fit his particular profile, coming off the platform after this recital. What would be some of the elements of that profile? Probably a sex preference (in this case, girls), and a general physical appearance, but the behavioral cues she's giving off to a sensitive observer—and our guy is exquisitely sensitive to this—are going to be even more important. He's going to be looking for a child who isn't loud or assertive, who seems shy, without a strong self-image. He's looking for someone naive for her age, introspective, who'll be susceptible to compliments and dreams of recognition. And, of course, he'll be looking for someone without a hovering parent or protector close by.

So maybe he'll approach this child and tell her how good she was on stage, tell her he represents some magazine or dance studio and that he wants to take pictures of her outside where the light is better. And if he's able to lure her away from the crowd, if she willingly goes with him, then one thing's going to follow another, and we might never see that little girl again.

This is what happened to Alison Parrott.

At the end of July 1986, I was up in Toronto speaking before a meeting of the Canadian and American National District Attorneys and Crown Attorneys Association, about five hundred prosecutors from both countries. I had a strong relationship with the Toronto Metro Police. I'd worked with them two years before on the Christine Jessop case—which we will be discussing shortly—and in the deaths of babies at Toronto's Hospital for Sick Children. So while I was there, they asked me to consult on the case of a young girl who had disappeared after leaving her house on a Friday morning and whose body had been found in a local park.

Alison Parrott was eleven years of age, a local track star who was preparing to compete in a meet in New Jersey. This was a big event and the local papers had covered it, accompanied by pictures of her in her school track uniform.

What the police knew was this: Alison's mother, Lesley, said she had been called at home by a man claiming to be a photographer who said he wanted to take publicity photos of her at Varsity Stadium for a sports magazine. She agreed, and at the arranged time, she took the subway alone from her suburban home, got off as planned at the St. George station, and proceeded to the stadium. They knew this because a bank surveillance camera—set to take a photograph every fifteen seconds—happened to record two images of her from the waist down through the front window as she walked past on the street to the stadium. Her mother identified her in these photos from the clothing and shoes.

She never returned home. Less than twenty-four hours later, her nude body was found face down in the mud on the bank of the Humber River by two boys walking through King's Mill Park in Etobicoke. The body wasn't covered, and there were already insect larvae in the nose and mouth and rectal area, which showed evidence of bleeding as a result of sexual assault. The cause of death appeared to have been strangulation.

Toronto police took me to the dump site. From the scenario and the crime scene evidence, I profiled a white male in his thirties, a respectable-looking man, not at all threatening in his appearance. He could have a job that involves being around children, even something as indirect as a custodian or maintenance engineer in a school. He may have had some previous run-ins with the law, but more likely some ambiguous complaints against him involving children. I thought it very unlikely he would have previous murder or violent crime arrests. He would have some connection to photography, at least as an avid amateur. And he would be a local rather than an outsider, possibly a recreational hunter or fisherman.

I felt this would be an older, more sophisticated individual because of several key elements in the story. Having read about Alison in the newspapers, he would begin fantasizing about her and devise a strategy to meet her. Since he wouldn't know her home address, he'd systematically have to make "pretext calls" to all the Parrotts in the phone book, each time asking for Alison until he hit pay dirt. To make himself believable and get her to agree to meet him at all, much less at a location other than her own home or school, he'd have to have a convincing and disarming, carefully rehearsed conversational style. This much planning and sophistication pointed to a more mature, intelligent, organized offender. He'd used this technique before to get to other kids, though the consequences had never been anywhere near this tragic. But this meeting was not spontaneous or haphazard.

Neither was what I believed happened afterward. As I saw it, Alison arrives at the stadium where she's approached by a man who has a camera and looks legitimately like a photographer. But he can't get into the stadium, and even if he could, that's not a controlled situation; there'd be guards or watchmen there and he'd immediately be challenged.

So he has to get her into a location where he feels comfortable. He probably tells her that because of the cloud conditions or the time of day or whatever, the light isn't right so he wants to drive somewhere else, probably the park where her body was found, which is how he gets her into his vehicle.

And what kind of vehicle was it? I believed it would be a commercial style van without windows in the back, and that that was where the assault took place. Everywhere between the stadium and the park has too much traffic during the day for him to have been able to find a secluded location. Therefore, he had to have been able to deal with her in broad daylight but without having to worry about the prying eyes of witnesses. Based on a lot of past experience with MOs in similar cases, this scenario suggested the van.

Despite the apparent degree of planning and forethought, he didn't necessarily intend to kill her. In fact, that was probably not even a part of his thinking. Many times, a van will be the vehicle of choice for a sexual sadist, someone like Steven B. Pennell, who raped, tortured, and murdered

51

women he had picked up in his van along Interstate routes 40 and 13 in Delaware. After a trial in which I testified regarding the signature aspects of his crimes, Pennell was executed in 1992 by lethal injection, a far milder and more humane death than the one to which this monster subjected his innocent victims.

And that was the point. Pennell was a monster, someone who derived his sexual pleasure and satisfaction from hurting, then exercising the power of life and death over his victims. His van was fitted out with a "rape kit," restraints and pliers, knives, needles, whips, and other instruments of torture he knew he would need. A normal sexual "relationship" with these women, even if that were obtainable, wouldn't have satisfied him. His aim was to hurt them, make them suffer, sexually react to their screams and their pain and, ultimately, their deaths.

Alison's killer did not conform to that profile. While the sexual assault was brutal enough, the kill itself was "gentle" and there were no signs on the body of torture or physical abuse for its own sake. Instead, it was my belief that this guy would have developed the fantasy of a real relationship between himself and the attractive, prepubescent young girl. This fantasy would have been solidified in his own mind by her willingness to get in the van, which he would have interpreted as a personal interest in him.

But once he drives to the park, roughly five miles away, then his problems begin. Most of these guys have a very warped sense of how children will react to them. In this man's fantasy, she reacts to his sexual advances the way a consenting adult woman would, rather than the reality, which is a terrified little girl who wants no part of him. She's crying, in pain, wants to go home. Quickly, he's lost control of the situation.

He can't let her go, because if he does, his life is ruined. He's made no attempt to disguise himself. And his victim isn't a three- or four-year-old child who might not be able to relate what had happened to her but an intelligent young lady, almost a teenager, who could easily identify him and his vehicle and who would have high credibility and believability no matter what he said. So now that he's assaulted her, he has to dispose of her.

Which he will do as easily for himself and painlessly for her as he can. He probably doesn't have a weapon; that's not the way he controls his victims. He strangles her in the back of the van, then has to get rid of the body.

Now the placement of the body is as significant as any other single aspect of the crime and told me a tremendous amount about the UNSUB. As soon as the police took me to the park, I knew this had to be a local who was intimately familiar with the area. He had brought Alison somewhere he felt comfortable. He would have had to walk into the dark woods at night carrying this body. There is no way he would have done that unless he knew the area well, knew what to expect, and knew he would not be disturbed.

Once in there, he could have done any number of things with the body. He could have thrown it in the river that runs right through the park, which most likely would have delayed significantly its discovery and neutralized most of the forensic evidence. He could have placed it deep in the woods where it might never have been found, or not found until it was completely skeletized.

But what he does is place her gently near a trail where her body will be found quickly, before it has decomposed. He is not treating the dead body as a used-up piece of trash as some of these guys do. He wants her to be found. He wants her to be properly taken care of in death and to have a decent burial. To me, that's an encouraging sign in terms of getting to him. He does not feel good about himself for what happened.

No one who does something like this can feel good about himself. You can argue that a sexual sadist, even one who gets off torturing children, may take pride in his "work" and look back with satisfaction on his ability so completely to manipulate, to dominate, and to control his victims in carrying out his hideous intentions. But someone who fantasizes about a "normal" love relationship with a twelve-year-old, and who falls apart as soon as he realizes his fantasy is not going to be fulfilled in reality, has to feel extremely inadequate and ineffectual. This individual is not going to feel proud of what he's done; he's going to feel remorseful. This presents an opportunity to utilize proactive techniques that can be designed to play on his psyche. And that is the key to catching him.

While I would not characterize Alison Parrott's murderer as a serial killer, his criminal sophistication shows he is definitely capable of killing again if the situation presents itself, and the insights into behavior we've learned from our study of serial killers can be helpful. With this type of offender, the profile can be useful in narrowing a suspect list or in recognizing a new subject who comes up in the course of investigation. But for me and my people, the profile is most helpful in coming up with proactive techniques, and that is where the emphasis should lie.

The specific details of the profile can be deemphasized here. The only thing we really have to know, and we know it unquestionably from the details of this crime and the crime scene itself, is that the subject does not feel good about what he did. So I told the police we should try to get him to go to the grave site. Our research has shown that offenders tend to do this for two reasons, generally mutually exclusive: one is out of remorse and the other is to relive the thrill of the crime, to symbolically roll around in their own dirt. If this one went to the grave, it would be out of remorse, and there are any number of ways to play on this.

I suggested articles in the newspaper giving details of Alison's life and impressive accomplishments, humanizing and personalizing her to this man who would have done his best to depersonalize her after the fact. I suggested staging a well-publicized memorial service at the grave or body dump site. In the hope that someone could identify or describe him, I suggested getting the word out that he'd probably tried something like this with other children. I thought there was a good chance he'd used alcohol to lower his inhibitions before the crime, and that he might have taken up heavy drinking since the murder as a way to deal with his stress. People around him—friends, family, and co-workers—would have recognized a noticeable change in his appearance and behavior, which would be a tip-off.

And, since I had a pretty strong feeling about the possibility that he used a van, I suggested planting the seed of doubt in his mind by having the police state publicly that a suspicious-looking van had been seen near the stadium or in the park and that anyone who had information about this vehicle should contact police. What this might have done was gotten the UNSUB to come forward to neutralize the van report. He might have identified himself as the owner of a van that could have been the one in question, but offered a legitimate or innocent reason as to why he was in the area. This would have delivered him right into police hands.

Alison Parrott's killer has never been found despite the fact that Toronto Metro Police offered a $50,000 reward for information leading to his arrest. They felt very strongly about this one. It's always been frustrating for me and my colleagues at Quantico in most cases not to be able to stay on scene and help follow up on our own suggestions. I don't fault the Toronto Metro Police Department, which is as good an organization as any I've worked with. At the time of this crime, their murder clearance percentage was in the high nineties, and the previous year they cleared all but one of their cases. They're a fine, dedicated group of men and women. They did check every photography shop in the area, using the profile to describe the man they were looking for. But some of my other suggestions were never instituted. Everyone has their own methods and procedures, and once the profiler leaves, his or her suggestions can easily end up on the back burner. I still believe this guy is catchable, though this many years later, of course, it would be a lot more difficult. In cases we believe to be nonstranger homicides, we can take a more conservative approach; the potential suspect population is limited. In homicides that appear to have been committed by strangers, though, a more radical, creative approach is often the answer.

I'd recommend searching out the weaknesses in the offender. When you have an UNSUB, of course, this can be difficult to ascertain. But in this case, I do believe that his weakness is his remorse and you have to keep up the psychological pressure. For one thing, I'd target Alison's birthdays or the anniversaries of her death to get the guy to come forward. Remind him of the significance of the day. You might think that forearmed with some of my strategy, the killer may be able to avoid the traps we'd set up for him. But I can tell you from long experience, the more he does to avoid them, the more behavior he'd show us and the more we'd have to work with. There is no such thing as a perfect crime or a perfect criminal.

In my mind, there's a double tragedy to Alison's death. Not only was this young life so full of love and promise brutally snuffed out and her killer unpunished, but it was a death that could have been avoided. Had Alison's parents or some other authority figure accompanied her to her meeting with the self-proclaimed photographer, I don't believe anything would have happened. He probably would have taken his pictures, which he would have used not to sell to a magazine but to fantasize over on his own, and then would have been on his way. It's upsetting to think about this degenerate masturbating over pictures of children and happily musing about how close he was able to get to them, but this young girl would be none the wiser and still alive. I believe he was frankly shocked when she showed up alone and therefore felt she was independent and grown-up and that he could go further than ever before.

As parents, we may not always be able to prevent all of the horrible things that I've seen happen to kids. But we can prevent some of them if we just try to understand the nature of the threat and the range of personality types and motivations of the threateners. It's critical that we try. I hate to say that we have to be less trusting of people, I hate to have to give my own kids that message, but we do have to accept the realities of our time. We don't have to become crazy with fear that there's a monster lurking behind every tree because there isn't. The number of child abductions is statistically low and most of them are carried out by noncustodial parents. We don't have to become crazy, but we do have to become cautious and observant.

About forty miles away from the site where Alison Parrott's body was found, a different personality type—a true monster—was responsible for the death of Kristen French and, as it turned out, at least two others.

By all accounts, Kristen Dawn French, of St. Catharines, Ontario, near Niagara Falls and the border with New York, was an exceptional young lady. Beautiful, with long, shiny black hair, she was adored by her family, friends, and teachers at Holy Cross Secondary School where she was an hon-

ors student. She'd been skating since she was a little girl
and now, in addition to everything else, was an accomplished
precision skater. Friends say she was always smiling, always
able to help them over their own problems, a genuinely
happy person in love with her first boyfriend.

Shortly before 3:00 P.M., on a rainy Thursday, April 16,
1992, the day before Good Friday, less than a month before
her sixteenth birthday, Kristie French disappeared on her
way home from school. Doug and Donna French knew their
daughter well enough to know she was always on time or
else would call with a legitimate explanation why she wasn't.
They even briefly entertained the possibility that she might
have been kept after school as punishment, but this would
have been so out of character for Kristie that they dismissed
it. When she wasn't home by 5:30, Donna called the Niagara
Regional Police and reported Kristie missing.

At least there was something to go on. Five separate witnesses reported seeing something related to Kristen's disappearance. A schoolmate noticed her walking from school in
her uniform of green plaid skirt, tights, V-neck sweater with
a white shirt, and oxblood-colored Bass loafers as he approached the corner of Linwell Road in his van around 2:50.
Another reported seeing a cream-colored Chevy Camaro
with rust on the back and primer paint on the side pull over
in front of Grace Lutheran Church about two minutes later.
Three minutes after that, two men in the car were speaking
with Kristen. The car window was down and the driver appeared to be around twenty-four to thirty years of age, with
brown hair. A third witness, on her way to pick up her
daughter downtown, thought she saw a girl struggling with
a passenger in the car, who was trying to shove her into the
maroon-colored back seat, but figured it was probably a boy
and girl fooling around or having a minor argument. The
fourth and fifth witnesses were drivers who nearly collided
with the speeding Camaro just after it pulled out of the
church parking lot around 3:00. Others believed they had
seen a similar car in the area around Holy Cross and next
door to Lakeport High School in the days preceding the
abduction. This led police to speculate that Kristen or other
students might have been stalked and that the abduction
was planned rather than spontaneous.

As the investigation intensified, police psychologists used hypnosis to help potential witnesses evoke memories of that afternoon. More than one described having seen an elderly couple walking by the church as the abduction was in progress and pointing in shock at the car and Kristen. If these people did, in fact, exist, they never came forward.

All of this information is important. However, too many times I've seen information considered that really has nothing to do with the case. If it is irrelevant or out-and-out wrong, it can derail an investigation. Therefore, I always recommend concentrating on the overall crime analysis rather than on any one possible clue.

In the parking lot, crime scene technicians identified tire tracks and found a worn, folded map of Canada and a small lock of hair that appeared to be Kristen's. On Good Friday, as Kristen's close friend and fellow skater Michelle Tousignant drove with her mother along Linwell Road as part of a general community search, she noticed an oxblood right loafer like Kristen had worn. She picked it up and brought it to two Niagara detectives who were conducting a house-to-house canvass along the route Kristen ordinarily took home from school. Donna French identified the shoe, which had an arch support inside, as belonging to her daughter.

A massive search and investigation were undertaken. The students at Holy Cross kept a hopeful but agonized vigil for their friend. They tied green ribbons around trees and poles as symbols of hope and remembrance. And Doug French appealed publicly for the safe return of his beloved daughter as his wife went through unremitting torment at the thought of what Kristie must be going through. Nearly every night she was tortured by dreams of Kristie crying out, but no matter what she did, she was never able to find her.

There was another terrifying prospect associated with Kristen French's disappearance and that was the possibility of a serial killer operating in this relatively peaceful and secure area of Canada. The previous June 14, at 7:00 P.M., Leslie Erin Mahaffy—like Kristen French, a month shy of her sixteenth birthday—left her home in Burlington, just across the western rim of Lake Ontario from St. Catharines. The area is known as the Golden Horseshoe.

The pretty ninth-grader at Burlington High School was

going to the Smith Funeral Home for the wake of Chris Evans, a school friend who had died in an automobile accident with three other teens. Leslie promised her mother, Debbie, a teacher in nearby Halton, that she'd be home by her 11:00 P.M. curfew.

The curfews were indicative of some of the problems and conflicts that had come up between mother and daughter. Leslie had always been a bright, spunky, independent girl, but as she had approached her fifteenth birthday, the traditional teenage emotionalism and rebelliousness seemed to well up within her. She took to staying out well beyond her parents' curfews, sometimes all night. She was once caught shoplifting. The problem may have been compounded by the fact that her father, Robert, known as Dan, often had to be away from home on his job as a government oceanographer.

That night after the wake, Leslie and several friends convened in a clearing in the woods popular with local teens to have a few beers and console each other on their loss. By the time Leslie walked back to her house, accompanied by a male friend who wanted to see her home safely, it was almost 2:00 A.M. and the house was dark. She told him her parents would just yell at her when they saw her, so he might as well leave before she went in. He said good night and that he'd be back for her in the morning to take her to the funeral.

But when Leslie tried all the doors, she found them locked. Her mother had decided to teach her a lesson this time by locking her out of the house. She would have to ring the doorbell and wake up her mom. She wouldn't be able to postpone the confrontation and resulting discipline.

Instead, Leslie walked over to Upper Middle Road and called her friend Amanda Carpino to see if she could stay there overnight. But Amanda was afraid to ask her mother, Jacqueline, knowing the trouble Leslie had been in with her own mom before and Mrs. Mahaffy's complaints to Mrs. Carpino. Coincidentally, Amanda's younger sister was sleeping over at another girlfriend's house but called home to say she was sick. Around 2:30, Jacqueline Carpino got dressed and went out to get her. Knowing of the phone call to

Amanda, she drove down Upper Middle Road to see if she could spot Leslie and take her home.

By this time, however, Leslie had apparently gone home, resigned to facing the music with her own mother.

But she never went inside, and when Debbie Mahaffy woke up that morning, Leslie wasn't there. She'd done this kind of thing before, crashing at friends' houses, so Debbie wasn't overly concerned until Leslie didn't turn up at Chris Evans's funeral. That was totally out of keeping. Leslie would have made sure to be there. At 4:30 and panic-stricken, Debbie Mahaffy called the Halton police and reported her daughter missing. In the next several days, Leslie's family and friends put up more than five hundred missing person posters throughout Burlington and the Halton area, hoping for any lead or word on her.

On June 29, 1991, two weeks to the day after she was reported missing, Leslie's dismembered body was discovered encased in several blocks of concrete in the shallow waters of nearby Lake Gibson. Autopsy reports indicated a brutal sexual attack.

Every parent I've ever encountered whose child has become the victim of a violent crime goes through a harrowing and punishing personal inquisition, agonizing over whether he or she could have done anything to prevent what happened. Debbie Mahaffy was no exception. As soon as Leslie disappeared she was plagued by thoughts that if she hadn't locked her out that night, her daughter would still be with her.

Before Leslie's parents even had the opportunity to bury their daughter, another local girl, Nina DeVilliers, was discovered murdered. There was no clear-cut connection but two violent deaths of young girls in the same area seemed like more than coincidence. The previous November, Terri Anderson, another fifteen-year-old who was a good student and cheerleader at Lakeport High School, next to Holy Cross, had disappeared around 2:00 A.M. from her home on Linwell Road after returning from a party where she reportedly took LSD for the first time.

These, then, were the fears as days dragged on into weeks and Kristen French had still not been heard from. Police put out an all-points bulletin for the cream-colored Camaro.

Before the investigation had taken its course, billboards throughout Ottawa would picture the type of car police were looking for together with a toll-free number to call and as each cream-colored Camaro or similar-looking car was noticed, an officer would question the driver and place a sticker on the windshield to register it.

But on the morning of Thursday, April 30, 1992, two weeks to the day since Kristen disappeared, a forty-nine-year-old scrap metal dealer named Roger Boyer was horrified to come upon a naked body amidst the underbrush by the side of a road while foraging for abandoned farm equipment to salvage. The corpse was folded into the fetal position, as if asleep. The black hair was cut short like a boy's, but from what he could see of the shape of the body and the small size of the hands and feet, Boyer thought it was probably a woman or girl.

As it happened, the site was only separated by a narrow greenbelt from Halton Hills Memorial Gardens in Burlington, the cemetery where Leslie Mahaffy was buried.

Police responded immediately to Boyer's call and cordoned off the area. It wasn't long, however, until the media got wind of the discovery. Speculation as to its significance was rampant and pointed. It was left to Halton Detective Leonard Shaw to confirm everyone's worst fears. As the result of a childhood accident, Kristen was missing the tip of the little finger of her left hand. As soon as Shaw lifted the corpse's left hand, he saw an identical disfigurement.

The medical examiner's report compounded the horror. The cause of death was ligature asphyxiation. Like Leslie Mahaffy, she had been beaten and sexually attacked. And the well-preserved state of the body suggested that Kristen had been alive until a few days ago, maybe even less than twenty-four hours ago, held captive for at least a week and a half by whoever did this to her.

More than four thousand mourners showed up for Kristen's funeral on May 4 at St. Alfred's Church in St. Catharines. So great was the outpouring of public sympathy that the massive church was filled to overflowing. More than a thousand people had to listen to the service from outside. She was buried in the family plot in Pleasantview Cemetery alongside her grandparents. It soon became clear that virtually everyone associated with Kristen's case, from the detectives to the crime scene technicians to the medical examiners, was affected by it in ways these seasoned professionals had seldom been before.

Fear gripped the entire Golden Horseshoe area. The discovery of Kristen French's body led directly to the formation of Operation Green Ribbon, which became one of the largest manhunts in the history of Canadian law enforcement. Named for the campaign of hope launched by her classmates, the multiagency task force was under the direction of veteran Niagara Police Inspector Vince Bevan. The cases became known throughout Canada simply as "the Schoolgirl Murders."

On May 21, Terri Anderson's body was discovered floating in Port Dalhousie harbor on Lake Ontario. Evidence was inconclusive as to cause of death. Police eventually ruled her death accidental, relating to her drug ingestion.

Speculation linking the Anderson, Mahaffy, DeVilliers, and French deaths was rife in the media, even though the police tried to underplay it. Inspector Bevan was a dedicated and serious-minded investigator with little time or patience for the press. This was indicative of the larger problem with publicity and the public that the task force was facing. The Halton force had a long history of going public with information in the hope that someone might come forward with useful tips. The Niagara department, on the other hand, seldom willingly released anything, which tended to encourage the media to launch their own independent investigations of important cases.

My experience has shown me that the public is very often a critical partner with the police in bringing dangerous men to justice. So while it is often a good idea to withhold certain specific facts and pieces of information, my own bias is that you work with the media and let the public help you as much as possible.

In addition to following up leads and following forensic clues, the Green Ribbon task force contacted the FBI, specifically Special Agent Chuck Wagner of the Buffalo, New York, Field Office. Buffalo is right over the border from the southern end of the Golden Horseshoe and the field office had always had a good, mutually beneficial relationship with local Canadian police agencies as well as the national RCMP—the Royal Canadian Mounted Police. Chuck, the profile coordinator for the field office, in turn called Gregg McCrary at the Investigative Support Unit in Quantico. We'd organized the unit so that each agent would have primary responsibility for a particular geographic territory. Gregg, a former high school teacher and black belt in the Asian martial art of Shorinji Kempo, had been a field agent in New York before we brought him to Quantico.

As soon as he took a look at the cases, Gregg was struck by the location where Kristen French's body had been dumped, very near the grave of Leslie Mahaffy. Leslie had been taken from Burlington and dumped near St. Catharines. Kristen was abducted in St. Catharines and left near Burlington. He didn't think that was coincidental. Either the crimes truly were related or the UNSUB wanted the police to believe they were. In any event, Kristen's killer clearly was reacting to the Mahaffy murder.

To Gregg, both murders had all the earmarks of stranger homicide. There was nothing to suggest that the killer or killers knew either girl personally, though both were probably surveilled and stalked beforehand. These were high-risk crimes for the perpetrator. Kristen was grabbed in broad daylight from a church parking lot in view of witnesses. Leslie was taken at her own house from under her parents' bedroom window.

When we see this type of crime, the first thing we think of is a somewhat younger, unsophisticated, perhaps disorganized offender with a highly developed sexual fantasy that he is increasingly desperate to act out. For this reason, when we see a high-risk crime, we expect the victim to be kept alive for a relatively longer period of time, which the medical examiner told us had been the case with Kristen French.

But eyewitness accounts had spoken of two offenders, which changed the profile considerations. If two people were involved in a high-risk, daylight abduction, the evaluation changes and we'd boost the sophistication level significantly. The fantasy aspect remains just as important, but now it appears to be planned, organized, and carried out by older, more criminally experienced individuals. The stalking and surveillance of girls at both high schools spoke to this as well. This type of crime perpetrated by a sole offender would likely be his first. Two people committing the same crime speaks to a more evolved and developed MO.

The body disposal methods in the two main murders under consideration were very different, suggesting the possibility of two separate killers. All things considered, though, Gregg thought this unlikely. More likely, the killer was getting bolder and/or smarter. He'd obviously gone to a lot of trouble and effort to dismember the body, mix and mold the concrete, put the blocks in a car, and drive it to Lake Gibson. In spite of all that work, the body had been found and identified relatively quickly. So next time, why bother? Another possible explanation for the change in this part of the MO was that the killer was growing more confident, flaunting his work to the police, letting them know that he was the same one who had killed Leslie Mahaffy and was therefore "burying" his latest prey nearby. Whichever was the explanation, or if both were correct, what was clear was that he was escalating, that he had begun to act out his fantasies and had convinced or coerced another person into working with him.

The cutting off of Kristen's long hair and the evidence of sexual assaults on her body indicated a man with a hatred or contempt for women, an emotional need to degrade them in order to feel powerful or even adequate. This man would likely have difficulty with normal sexual function and if he had an ongoing relationship with a wife or girlfriend, he'd have the need to sexually dominate or degrade her in a similar fashion.

A couple of years before, Gregg had profiled an UNSUB in a series of murders of prostitutes and homeless women in Rochester, New York. From the facts he knew, Gregg had predicted the man would have some sort of sexual dysfunction, possibly on the order of erectile insufficiency. A further escalation of behavior in later crimes led Gregg to suggest secretly surveilling a newly discovered body dump site to which he felt the killer would return. This strategy ultimately led to the capture of Arthur Shawcross, who was convicted of multiple counts of second-degree murder and sentenced to 250 years to life. Interviews with other prostitutes Shawcross had visited revealed that he was unable to maintain erection or achieve orgasm unless they played dead.

Gregg predicted that if there were two offenders working as partners as seemed to be the case, then one would be the dominant leader and the other would always be a subservient follower. Double offenders in rape and sexual murder aren't common, but we have seen and studied them, going back to Kenneth Bianchi and his cousin Angelo Buono, who together terrorized Los Angeles in the late 1970s as the "Hillside Strangler," and even before that, James Russell Odom and James Clayton Lawson, Jr., who met at Atascadero State Mental Hospital in California where they were both doing time for rape.

Clay Lawson would while away the time describing to Russell Odom the tortures he'd like to inflict on captured women when he got out. He himself wasn't interested in intercourse. But Odom was, and, upon his release in 1974, sought out Lawson in South Carolina. Within a few nights they had kidnapped, raped, killed, and horribly mutilated a young woman working in a 7-Eleven they stopped in. The victim's body was left in plain view and the killers were arrested within days. The terrified, submissive Odom admitted raping the girl but denied having any part in the murder. He was found guilty of rape, unlawful weapon possession, and accessory before and after the fact of murder. The dominant Lawson, who chewed chalk in the courtroom during his own separate trial, adamantly denied taking part in the rape, saying, "I only wanted to destroy her." He was convicted of murder in the first degree and electrocuted by the state of South Carolina in 1976.

If it is possible to conceive of a more depraved partnership, it would be Lawrence Bittaker and Roy Norris. Like Odom and Lawson, they met behind bars, in this case the California Men's Colony at San Luis Obispo, where they discovered their mutual affinity for dominating, hurting, and sexually abusing young women. When they were both paroled in 1979, they got together in Los Angeles and made plans to undertake a project to kidnap, rape, torture, and kill one teenaged girl of each age, thirteen through nineteen. They had successfully carried out their plan against five girls in a brutal and horrifying manner, when the sixth managed to escape after being raped and went to the police. Norris was the submissive one in this team and he was the one who caved in to police interrogation, confessing and fingering his dominant partner to escape the gas chamber. He also led police to the various bodies. One skeleton still had Bittaker's ice pick protruding from its ear opening. The unrepentant Bittaker, among the vilest human beings I have ever come across, became something of a celebrity on California's death row. When asked for his autograph by admiring fellow prisoners, he would sign it "Pliers Bittaker" after one of his favorite instruments of torture.

This is not to say an offender of this type is incapable of deep and genuine emotion. Special Agent Mary Ellen O'Toole and I had the opportunity to interview Bittaker at San Quentin. We thought it significant that during the several hours we were with him, Bittaker never once made eye contact with Mary Ellen. He would not look at her. Yet when we brought up the crimes he cried. Big, tough Lawrence Bittaker shed tears of sorrow. But he was crying not for the lost lives of his victims, but for the fact that his life was ruined by having been caught.

Gregg McCrary saw the dominant one of Kristen French's killers in much the same way. He would be between the ages of twenty-five to early thirties, which squared with witness descriptions. He would be first and foremost a human predator, a born manipulator who would get by in life by exploiting people and systems. Like Lawrence Bittaker or Clay Lawson and unlike Alison Parrott's killer, he would feel no guilt or remorse for the suffering of the victim, her family, or the community. Each successful kill would only fuel his appetite for inflicting more pain and shedding more blood.

This dominance would carry over into his personal life. Many sexual sadists are married or in ongoing relationships with women. If this were the case with the UNSUB, he would probably beat and sexually abuse his own mate. Small, ordinary things like questioning his comings or goings would be enough to trigger his wrath.

There would be prior sexual offenses in his background, beginning either with flashing or being a Peeping Tom, eventually escalating into sexual assaults for which he may or may not have been arrested. But someone, either his wife or girlfriend or partner in crime, would know about this history. Gregg felt he would probably work at some sort of manual skill, possibly with power tools or in a metal shop, and would have his own shop at home. And finally, there would have been some stressor which triggered his initial homicidal rage. Perhaps his wife finally threw him out of the house. Perhaps he lost a job or suffered some serious professional setback. Perhaps both.

As police looked for the cream-colored Camaro and followed up every tip, the investigation dragged on without much progress. Not wanting to let the case grow cold and stale, the Green Ribbon task force decided to go public, which we at Quantico had been advocating for some time.

On the evening of Tuesday, July 21, 1992, television station CHCH-TV in Hamilton, Ontario, broadcast an extraordinary program, which was simultaneously picked up by other stations throughout Canada for a national airing. Entitled "The Abduction of Kristen French," the program featured Green Ribbon chief Vince Bevan and Sergeant Kate Cavanagh, the Ontario Provincial Police Department profiler, as well as Chuck Wagner and Gregg McCrary on a feed from Quantico.

Using police reports, diagrams, eyewitness accounts, and re-creations of the Camaro's reported position at various points in the crime, "The Abduction of Kristen French" had as its goal finally going public with the major details of the case in the hopes that a viewer would recognize something that could get the investigation moving. For the first time publicly, police revealed the witness accounts of the two men seen in the car and presumed to be involved in the kidnapping. A phone bank staffed by trained volunteers took called-in tips throughout the program and in the weeks following the broadcast. Using the clue of the map found at the crime scene, one of the first things Bevan and host Dan McLean did was urge people to call in about any adult male in the area around that time who had aroused their suspicion by asking for directions or help. One of the main focuses was on trying to locate the car, which could then be traced back to an owner.

When Gregg McCrary came on about halfway through the broadcast, he went over the main points of his profile, explaining what the various behavioral clues suggested about this UNSUB in his mid-twenties to early thirties who was already a seasoned sexual criminal. Cutting off Kristen's beautiful dark hair indicated his emotional need to humiliate and degrade women to cover for his own personal and sexual inadequacy. Then he outlined the typical relationship between dominant and submissive partners in sexual crime. He explained what to look for in the offender's behavior and how it would have changed recognizably to those around him in the days and weeks after Kristen was taken.

Essentially, there would be a total disruption in his (or their) normal life from April 16 to at least April 30, the day her body was found. We knew Kristen was still alive up until very close to that date, which meant the UNSUB would have been preoccupied feeding, maintaining, and monitoring her wherever he kept her imprisoned, as well as repeatedly assaulting her according to the dictates of his fantasy. This disruption didn't necessarily mean he'd miss work all during that time if, in fact, he had a steady job, but it would mean that he would be preoccupied, stressed, and his demeanor would be noticeably different to friends and co-workers. He would be following the investigation and press reports very closely, and would engage frequently in discussions of the case and the progress—or lack thereof—the police were making. If he were in an ongoing relationship with a woman, that relationship would also be more stressful than usual; there would be more frequent and severe flare-ups of temper and he would be even more abusive.

The main purpose of our profiles is to let observers recognize behavior and help identify an UNSUB. By increasing the amount of information available to the public, we're potentially letting the people closest to the UNSUB become profilers themselves.

Almost all sexual serial killers, particularly of the organized variety, will follow closely what the media reports about the investigation. When we go in on a search warrant, we're not surprised to see scrapbooks, newspaper clippings, and videotapes of news reports in the offender's possession. We therefore assumed Kristen's killer or killers would be tuned in to this highly publicized broadcast. So at one point Dan McLean asked Gregg what the killer would be feeling.

"Stress," Gregg replied, none of it having to do with feelings of guilt or remorse, but real worry over the possibility of discovery and apprehension.

"And if you are watching," Gregg declared, speaking directly to Kristen French's unknown killer, "I want to tell you that you are going to be apprehended. It's just a question of when."

If someone out there recognized the behavior Gregg and Sergeant Cavanagh described and came through with a tip, then that apprehension would come sooner rather than later. But it would come, Gregg emphasized, and the UNSUB had better not rest easy.

He went on to explain that as the UNSUB's stress level escalated, close friends and family members would be in increasing danger. He would become increasingly angry and erratic, increasingly unable to control his fear and his temper. The two people who would be in the gravest danger would be the two people who presumably knew about his crimes: his submissive helper and his wife or girlfriend. Unlike the primary killer, either of them might be having a problem coping with the guilt of having participated in the killing of an innocent person. Gregg and the police urged either of those two accessories to come forward before it was too late and one of them became the next victim.

Vince Bevan stated, "If you're listening, please, for your own good, give us a call!"

This kind of proactive technique had paid off handsomely for us in the past. In one example, a stenographer named Donna Lynn Vetter who worked in one of the FBI field offices in the Southwest was raped and brutally murdered by an intruder who broke into her ground-floor garden apartment. The Bureau director at the time felt he had to send a strong and immediate message: you don't kill FBI personnel and get away with it. Two of Quantico's best and most experienced agents—Roy Hazelwood from Behavioral Science (the teaching and research side) and Jim Wright from the Investigative Support Unit—were dispatched immediately to the site on the director's jet.

After examining the murder scene and the preliminary forensics, Roy and Jim agreed that it had been a rape gone bad; murder was not the offender's planned or primary intention. They also felt they had a pretty good behavioral image of the assailant—his background and educational level, how close he lived to the apartment, his sustained anger and personal inadequacy. They felt he would have confided the fact of the crime to someone close to him, either a colleague or a woman with whom he was living in an abusive, though dependent, relationship. That individual, the agents felt, would now be in danger. In the short amount of time they had in town before having to return to Quantico, they gave interviews to the local media, giving out most (though not all) of the details of their profile, and urging the UNSUB's confidant to come forward before he or she were hurt or killed.

Within a couple of weeks, the killer's armed robbery partner contacted the police. The subject was arrested, a palm print matched up with one found at the murder scene, and he was charged. The profile turned out to be gratifyingly accurate in nearly every significant detail. He was a twenty-two-year-old male who lived with, and was financially dependent on, his sister. At the time of the murder he was on probation for rape. He was tried, found guilty, sentenced to death, and executed a couple of years ago.

It was a similar result we were hoping for from this program televised throughout Canada.

Kristen French's killer was, in fact, tuned in to and taping the broadcast.

His name was Paul Kenneth Bernardo, and as he watched, he rejoiced in arrogant glee at how inaccurate he thought the profile was. Though he was twenty-eight years of age, he didn't work with his hands or in a metal shop. He was highly intelligent, had majored in accounting in college, and had worked as a junior accountant at Price Waterhouse before failing the rigorous national accounting exam. For the last several years he had made his living, often a good one, smuggling crates of American cigarettes across the Canadian border and reselling them, often to biker gangs. He didn't own or drive a cream-colored Chevy Camaro. Instead, he had a champagne-gold Nissan 240SX hatchback which had been used in the kidnapping in the church parking lot. No two people witness a crime quite the same way, but this underscores why I never accept eyewitness statements as gospel. Moreover, Bernardo didn't have a submissive male partner in crime. The person who had helped him abduct Kristen French and force her into the car was his beautiful blond wife of less than a year, twenty-two-year-old Karla Leanne Homolka.

It was Karla to whom Paul brought Leslie Mahaffy the night she was locked out of her parents' house. He'd been stalking Leslie. He saw her on the porch and struck up a conversation. She'd told him what had happened, bummed a cigarette, gotten into his car to talk. Then he'd pulled a knife on her, blindfolded her, and drove to his house.

The cops were looking for a nonexistent male accomplice and a nonexistent car.

"They'll never catch me!" Bernardo exclaimed to Karla as he watched. Agent McCrary's promise that sooner or later he would be apprehended was laughable.

What Paul Bernardo apparently failed to grasp was all the ways that Cavanagh's and McCrary's profiles were dead on the money. He didn't support himself by working with his hands, but he did have a basement workshop whose tools he had used to cut apart Leslie Mahaffy and encase the body parts in cement blocks molded from cardboard boxes. He did regularly and systematically abuse and humiliate his wife through beatings, nonconsensual sadistic sexual practices, and such demeaning habits as locking her in the root cellar of their rented house and making her sleep on the floor beside his bed. He did require constant phony reassurance to deal with his problem of erectile insufficiency and recurring impotence, demanding that Karla, his previous girlfriends, and all of his victims call him "king" and "master" as he ritualistically choked or sodomized them or otherwise dominated them sexually.

And he did have prior criminal experience. In fact, though the police didn't know who he was, he already had quite a reputation.

He was "the Scarborough Rapist."

The Scarborough Rapist terrorized the northeast suburb of Toronto for which he was named from May 1987 through May 1990. His key modus operandi was coming up behind women as they got off buses, usually late at night, overpowering them and raping them. As he attacked, he mentally tortured them, saying he was going to kill them and calling them slut, bitch, whore, and worse. Gregg McCrary made a trip to Toronto during that time and he and I both worked on a profile of the rapist, coming up with a description pretty close to this individual who watched the television show so gleefully that night.

No one in any official capacity made much of a connection between the Scarborough Rapist and the Schoolgirl Murders because the MO was so different. The rapist had waited at bus stops and blitzed his victims from behind. And he had not killed. The murderer, on the other hand, grabbed his victims in broad daylight or from the steps of their own house. What they didn't factor in was that several years had elapsed between the initial Scarborough rapes and Leslie Mahaffy's murder and one of the things we predicted about the rapist was that he would escalate in his rage and learn from his own experience.

Though Paul Bernardo had no criminal record, the police already had a file on him. On Tuesday, May 29, 1990, the *Toronto Sun* had run a composite drawing of the Scarborough Rapist, based on a description by his most recent victim, the only one who got a good look at him. The drawing looked uncannily like Paul Bernardo, so much so that some of his friends joked that he could be the rapist. One of them took it more seriously and actually contacted police with the tip. This led police to make a visit to Bernardo, in which he was cooperative and charming and agreed to blood, hair, and saliva samples.

Though he was never officially cleared of suspicion, neither was the matter pursued. DNA testing was a laborious and time-consuming process and the police lab had extremely limited capacity, so limited that it would have taken them years to process samples based on every lead or tip. Paul Bernardo, who had no police record of any kind, was never high on the list of suspects. So his sample was never even processed. Had it been, Leslie Mahaffy and Kristen French might be alive today.

And another victim, too, one that the Green Ribbon task force hadn't even considered because no one knew she was a victim. That was Karla Homolka's younger sister, Tammy.

Fifteen-year-old Tammy Lyn Homolka was blond and

beautiful like her older sister. Early in the morning of Christmas Eve 1990, Tammy had died at St. Catharines General Hospital after losing consciousness under mysterious circumstances at her parents' house. Paul and Karla had been in the house at the time, saying they had all fallen asleep watching television. They awoke to the sound of Tammy's wheezing and labored breathing, which quickly became total respiratory distress. They were the ones who called the ambulance. Police ruled the death an accident.

In reality, Tammy was the object of sexual obsession of her sister's fiancé, Paul, who got Karla to help him drug her so he could have sex with her while she was unconscious. Still under the effects of the drug, Tammy aspirated her own vomit. The following June, Paul and Karla were married in an elaborate ceremony and reception. It was the same day the pieces of Leslie Mahaffy's body were found in Lake Gibson.

The obvious question that should occur around now is how, in the name of God, could an intelligent young woman with so much going for her marry the man responsible for the rape and death of her sister, submit to his beatings and physical and emotional degradations, and actually take part in his schemes to kidnap, assault, and kill innocent young women?

I wish there was an easy answer to this question; there isn't, though we've been studying the phenomenon of sexual sadists and their compliant victims for years. What we do know is what does happen, all too often. Through the pioneering leadership of Roy Hazelwood, we've identified the common progressive steps in a sexually sadistic relationship that frequently starts relatively normally.

First, the sexual sadist identifies a naive, dependent, or vulnerable woman. She may, in fact, be vulnerable because she's currently in an abusive relationship and she legitimately sees this new man as rescuing her from it.

Second, the sadist charms the woman with gentleness, gifts, emotional or financial support, physical protection, whatever she needs. She will see him as loving and supportive and she'll love him in return. Paul Bernardo was charming, handsome, and smooth. Women were always falling for him.

Third, once he achieves that goal, the sadist will begin to encourage or persuade her to engage in sexual practices she might consider unusual, bizarre, or kinky. At first this will be an occasional thing. Eventually, it will evolve into the regular routine between them, which will have the effect both of breaking down her will and breaking down her sense of values and the norms with which she was brought up. This, in turn, will help isolate her from her family and anyone she might want to talk to, because she won't want to talk about these sexual activities.

Fourth, the sadist completes this practice of isolation by discouraging her from having anything to do with her family or friends. He needs to approve of everything she does, her comings and goings and everyday activities. He needs to become the center of her existence, to the exclusion of all else. He might take away credit cards, control and dole out cash, insist she be home at a particular time and punish her severely if she isn't. In fact, any perceived disobedience or lapse in loyalty can be met by punishment.

Fifth, when the woman is isolated from everyone else, the sadist becomes her only support system. She strives to warrant his love and affection and avoid his anger and wrath, even though both have little to do with her and all to do with his moods and whims. Everything the sadist does, everything he says to her, confirms her new self-image as bad, inferior, stupid, or inadequate, warranting the anger and punishment which is now regularly visited upon her. There were literally hundreds of cards and letters and notes from Karla to Paul apologizing for all her faults and promising to try to do better.

In every important way, Roy's five-step analysis turns out to be a very accurate characterization of Karla Homolka after she met Paul Bernardo. It later came out that during Kristen French's imprisonment, the bright and resourceful teen tried to convince Karla to help her escape and to go with her. But Karla was so beaten down, with such a bleak, isolated outlook by this point, that all she could think of was Paul's anger and the severity of the punishment she would receive when he found out. This totally overrode her revulsion at watching the rape and abuse of this innocent girl, knowing full well the murder that was to follow.

Though certain family members and friends knew Paul had hit Karla on occasion, no one either recognized or acknowledged the reality of a severely abusive relationship. She always made excuses for the bruises and welts from his beatings. Either she'd fallen down, or she'd been in a car accident, or one of the animals at the veterinary clinic where she worked had turned on her. Even as Karla was undressing one day to try on her wedding gown, two of her friends had noticed large bruises on her too-thin body. But at the time they said nothing.

Paul continually hinted to her that he would kill her someday. During his sadistic role playing, he would even choke her with the same cord he used to strangle the two girls. He blackmailed her into silence by threatening to tell her parents the truth about Tammy. That was the one thing she couldn't stand to think about.

Most sexual sadists are totally self-involved narcissists and Paul Bernardo was no exception. He favored stylish designer clothes, fancied himself an entrepreneur, blamed the world for his failures. He thought he could go on the way he had forever, punctuating his complete manipulation, domination, and control of his once outgoing and exuberant wife with frequent liaisons with other women and adventures with abducted teenage girls. He'd even fantasized about starting a colony of sexual slaves. Before he even began his rapes, he'd already established a long-standing practice of sitting in his car positioned so he could watch young girls through their bedroom windows as they undressed. Often he was able to catch the action on video. As far as we know, no one noticed or came forward to report this behavior. And if they had, would it have been taken seriously?

What finally sank Paul Bernardo was what we in the unit predicted would, though it's doubtful Karla was thinking about Gregg McCrary's words when she went, through intermediaries, to the police. Ultimately, the reality of her situation was unavoidable to her and the evidence of abuse became unmistakable to her parents and friends. Even so, she hesitated several times before she finally left.

A lawyer began negotiating a plea bargain for her in return for testimony against her husband. She checked into Northwestern General Hospital for seven weeks of psychiatric evaluation. The final bargain called for a twelve-year jail sentence, which was then approved by the families of Leslie Mahaffy and Kristen French. Paul Bernardo was arrested on February 17, 1993. Typically for this type of sexual sadist, he also proved himself to be a self-centered coward. Once he got to jail he underwent what Gregg McCrary calls a major "attitude adjustment." He began complaining to authorities he was afraid the other prisoners might give him back some of his own medicine and had to be isolated from the general prison population for his own protection.

The ensuing trial, for which the judge imposed a total news blackout as is legal in Canada, became that country's "Trial of the Century." The crime riveted Canadians to the same degree as the O.J. Simpson case did during some of the same period of time in the summer of 1995.

During weeks of testimony, Karla unfolded the entire story of their relationship, discussing such horrifying details as the videotapes Paul made not only of himself debasing her, but raping and tormenting the teenage girls as well. She testified how Paul had made Kristen watch the tape of Leslie's rape in an effort to control her and make her compliant. She also told how she had been the one to cut off Kristen's long black hair according to Paul's orders. She told how Paul religiously followed the Scarborough Rapist and, later, Schoolgirl Murder investigations, just as we predicted the perpetrator would.

And just as Gregg had outlined in his profile, Bernardo sat through all the grisly testimony without any emotional reaction or the slightest evidence of remorse or human feeling. His only regret was getting caught and the fact that his wife and personal sexual slave had betrayed him. For his own part, Paul admitted he had taken part in the rapes but that Karla had actually killed the girls.

On Friday, September 1, 1995, after a day of deliberation, the jury brought in verdicts of guilty on all nine counts. The two most serious—murder in the first degree in the deaths of Leslie Mahaffy and Kristen French—brought with them an automatic life sentence with no parole possible for at least twenty-five years.

One of the great tragedies of the Paul Bernardo case is all of the missed opportunity: the opportunity to recognize the early signs of a criminal, sexually sadistic personality; the opportunity to catch the Scarborough Rapist through DNA before he escalated into killing; the opportunity for an abused wife to leave her husband before she herself became a felon; the opportunity for her friends and family to recognize what should have been obvious to them; the opportunity for Karla to escape with Kristen; and, most overwhelmingly, the opportunity for two beautiful and intelligent young women to grow up, fall in love, have families, and fulfill their glowing promise.

Did we learn anything as profilers from our own mistakes? Sure we did. Would we make some of the same mistakes again? Probably. Given the forensic evidence and the eyewitness accounts, we'd still be looking for two men—a dominant and a submissive partner. But now I think we'd at least bear in mind that a compliant female victim can also be a partner in unspeakable crime.

As I mentioned, the Toronto police called us in on the original Scarborough rapes and Gregg McCrary and I both went up for firsthand consultations on separate occasions. Among the proactive suggestions we came up with at the time was a plan for "hardening targets" just as you would in a series of bank robberies, forcing the UNSUB to strike next where you want him to. This tactic might have worked here, but it was never implemented. The point of this exercise is not to pin blame on any one person or institution. It's just to suggest that if we could all be more vigilant, more aware of the things that just don't add up or seem quite right, maybe some future tragedy could be avoided.

And one of the elements of that is to know what you're looking for, to know who the real enemy is or may be. Back in the 1950s, when times were simpler and J. Edgar Hoover was portrayed not only as the ultimate square-jawed tough guy against crime but also as the stern but loving father figure to all of American youth, the FBI used a drawing to warn kids away from potential danger. I remember it showed a man coming out from behind a tree, offering a bag of candy to an innocent and trusting child. The metaphor and the message were clear: beware of taking candy from strangers.

While the intent behind the drawing was certainly laudable and the dangers back in the 1950s might have seemed more clear-cut, I'm afraid experience has taught us that we have a lot more to worry about than candy from strangers.

Such was the issue in a third Canadian case in which I was involved. Like the Parrott and Mahaffy and French killings, it involved the rape and murder of an innocent child. Yet its circumstances and lessons were just as different as the first two cases were different from each other.

In January of 1985, while I was up in Toronto advising on prosecution strategy in the murder trial of Tien Poh Su, Detectives John Shephard and Bernard Fitzpatrick of the Criminal Investigative Branch of the Durham Regional Police asked me if I'd drive with them to a recently discovered body dump site and tell them what I thought. I was exhausted; I'd been in court all day and I just wanted to go back to the hotel, have a drink, and crash. They'd already submitted the case to Special Agent Oliver Zink, then profile coordinator of the Buffalo Field Office, and I figured it would eventually make its way back to Quantico. But when I heard the details of the case, it wasn't something I could easily leave alone.

On the previous October 3, nine-year-old Christine Marion Jessop was seen buying bubble gum on her way home from school in the town of Queensville, Ontario, north of Toronto. That was the last time anyone saw her. A massive search for days by police and volunteers turned up nothing, not a clue.

Fear gripped the small, safe town. The assumption was that someone passing through must have abducted her and carried her away. The mayor and city officials urged parents to warn their children to be wary of outsiders, not to accept gifts or to take candy from strangers. The sense of paranoia was equal to the sense of horror at Christine's disappearance. It was a sad holiday season in Queensville.

Then, on New Year's Eve, a farmer and his two daughters were out crossing a field in nearby Sunderland searching for a possible owner of a stray dog they had spotted when they came upon a small human corpse, mostly skeletized, undressed from the waist down except for a pair of white socks with blue trim, arranged in a froglike position. Other clothing, badly decomposed, and a pair of Nike track shoes were found nearby. And in the nearby grass, inside a canvas pouch, was a recorder type of flute, plastic with a piece of masking tape behind the mouthpiece, the same one Christine had been given in her music class the day she disappeared. Forensic examination and dental records confirmed that the skeletized remains were Christine's. She had been stabbed several times, and blood and semen stains on her panties indicated she had been sexually assaulted. My oldest child, Erika, was the same age as Christine.

As we drove to the site in an unmarked police car, the two detectives gave me some of the rundown on the case. The Jessop house had been empty that day. Her mother, Janet, and adoptive fourteen-year-old brother, Kenneth, had gone to the dentist and then to see their father, Robert, who was in prison for a white-collar crime.

We knew that Christine had been given this recorder that day and her teacher confirmed to the police that she was very excited about it. We also knew about her buying the gum, and the clerk at the Queensville General Store recalled seeing a dark car down the street which everyone in town assumed to be that of the suspicious stranger who abducted her. I thought this was a red herring that probably had nothing to do with the case. She wasn't grabbed off the street. We knew she made it home; she parked her bike in the garage. The house was about seventy-five or a hundred yards from the road and I didn't see any way a stranger would go all the way down the drive and risk being seen when he would have no idea whether anyone else was home or not. It's a fact of violent crime investigation that people want to help, and so will bring in anything they can think of that might be relevant. This is important and we encourage it. But we also have to be able to sift through what we hear and try to separate the real clues from the incidental details.

They also brought me to talk to Christine's parents, who gave me a good idea of what their daughter had been like. Later that evening, I remember I was sitting in the back seat of this unmarked car. After viewing the dump site and then going to the house and other relevant areas around town, I said to the detectives, "This is not a stranger homicide. This killer lives in the community. In fact, this killer knew Christine and lived within a short walking distance to her house."

The two officers looked at each other, then they both looked back at me. One of them said, "Can you put this down on paper for us tonight?"

I said, "It's one o'clock in the morning. I'm totally wiped out." But it seemed really important to them, so I asked for a tape recorder, had them drop me off back at the hotel and I stayed up in the room lying on the bed with the pages of the medical examiner's report spread out around me as I dictated my thoughts.

Maybe it was because I was so tired, but I found myself going into a near-trance state as I sometimes do. I saw the crime vividly in my own mind.

What I knew about the victimology, what I knew about Christine, was that she was a bright, inquisitive, enthusiastic child. When she got home from school, I felt, she was excited about this new recorder, but no one was home to share her excitement. So what I believe she did was seek out someone else in the neighborhood, someone she could tell, someone who would appreciate what she was learning in music class. Whoever that person was, I said, was probably the killer.

The UNSUB had to take her away in a car. He'd either have to take a back route or risk driving through town where he could be spotted. Either way, he clearly knew where he was going. He knew the area well. He would have had to, to have arrived at this rural, secluded field in nearby Sunderland.

I believe what happened next would have been in some ways similar to what happened to Alison Parrott. At some point along the way, Christine would have realized they weren't going where the UNSUB said he was taking her, possibly to see her father. She became frightened, at which point he probably took out the knife to control her. But he couldn't even control this slight, skinny nine-year-old girl, which underscored the fact that he was not a professional killer. The situation developed spontaneously when she presented him with the opportunity.

She was a very outgoing and friendly child. He may have misinterpreted her openness and enthusiasm and thought she would welcome his sexual advances since that was part of his fantasy, either with Christine specifically or with pre-teen and young teen girls in general. This is not uncommon among sexually immature offenders. He probably began fondling her or forcing her into oral sex. He was well-known to the family, I believed, and when she started yelling or crying, he knew she'd tell her mother. So he had to kill her. The stab wounds all over the body show that he had a hard time subduing her. Even though she was hurt, she'd tried to escape from him. On one of the ribs, the medical examiner actually found that the knife had hit bone.

The individual I described would probably be in his early to mid-twenties, I said, though in this instance age was hard to predict. Given his difficulty controlling this young girl, not to mention the objects of his fantasy life, he could be somewhat older, a case of arrested emotional development. I said that the police had probably already interviewed him.

The wide pattern of the stab wounds further confirmed for me that she had tried to struggle. It also suggested that this was not an experienced offender. In all probability, this was his first homicide, though I thought he might have a prior record of nuisance type crimes, voyeurism or small arsons. In the case of an older or more experienced UNSUB, I would have expected to see the cause of death as strangulation or blunt-force trauma, which are a whole lot less messy than multiple knife stabs. The body was found many miles from the abduction point, which can tend to point to someone trying to get away from his own area where he is well-known. Also, the condition of the body, spread-eagled and not completely covered up, indicated to me a relatively disorganized offender. For this reason, he'd probably be somewhat disheveled in his appearance, he'd be nocturnal, preferring to sleep during the day, and his job, if he had one, would not be terribly mentally taxing. His car would not be particularly well-maintained and would have high mileage.

I thought there would probably be some major stressor going on in the UNSUB's life at the time. The type and details of the crime didn't lead me to suspect he was married or in an ongoing relationship with another woman, so I didn't think that would be the most likely reason for his stress. Perhaps it was a problem at his job or being laid off from one. Perhaps he was living with his parents or some other older relative and they were putting some sort of pressure on him. Whatever the issue was, it likely related to his overall problem with self-esteem. He might even have physical scars or disfigurement, a speech impediment, bad complexion, or something he feels puts him at a disadvantage with women his own age. I thought he would be someone in the neighborhood who plays with children and associates with people younger than himself.

Undoubtedly, he would have gotten blood on himself during the struggle, which means he would have gone home immediately afterward to bathe, clean himself off, and probably destroy the clothes he was wearing. Anyone observing this post-offense behavior would know something was wrong. They would also notice the change in his normal behavior, which would become tense, overly rigid; he'd have trouble sleeping, rely more on alcohol or cigarettes. If he lived in the neighborhood he would be questioned by the police. To deflect suspicion away from himself he would be overly solicitous and cooperative, and in other ways would attempt to inject himself into the investigation to keep up with its progress. This is not someone who planned to kill, so he would not have had an elaborate plan to avoid detection. He will not leave the area if he thinks he is at all under suspicion because he would perceive this as evidence of his guilt. Someone around him may have noticed his need to go back to the dump site and he would have offered some excuse why he had to do this.

I also outlined a number of proactive techniques I thought might help get the UNSUB to reveal himself. I gave the detectives the tape the next morning and they had it transcribed right away.

The reason Shephard and Fitzpatrick were so interested in what I had to say, I soon learned, was that one of the subjects they had interviewed fit my profile almost exactly. His name was Guy Paul Morin, he was in his late twenties, and he lived with his parents in the house next door to the Jessops'. He was interested in music, played the clarinet in the community band, and Christine knew him well. There was good forensic evidence, too, including blood, paint chips from his house, and fibers from Christine's clothing.

He was arrested and charged in April 1985, though the police weren't able to get a confession during interrogation. I think there was a lot of mixed feeling in the neighborhood, too. Christine had to have been killed by a stranger. No one who knew her could possibly do this to her. Guy Morin just didn't look or act like a monster.

Neither, for that matter, did Paul Bernardo.

In addition to the forensic evidence, police eventually sent an undercover cop into the jail where Morin was being held, posing as a fellow prisoner and his cellmate, a tactic that was legal in Canada. The cop later testified at the first trial that Morin had made statements that strongly suggested guilt, which Morin then denied.

The history of the case from that point forward became strange and unsettling. Ultimately, it led to the divorce of Christine's parents, the financial ruin of Morin's parents, and serious illness for his father. In what turned out to be Morin's first trial in London, Ontario, early in 1986, Morin pleaded not guilty, but in the middle of the proceedings his lawyer stated that if the jury decided he was guilty, then they should find insanity. However, the jury found insufficient evidence and acquitted him.

The Crown Attorney appealed, in itself an unusual move, and in June 1987 the Ontario Court of Appeals overturned the verdict and ordered a new trial. The following year, the Supreme Court of Canada upheld the appeals court ruling.

Late in 1991 a second six-month trial began, the result of which was a guilty verdict after eight days of deliberation. He was sent to Kingston Penitentiary.

But then in 1995, DNA testing, not available at the time of the murder, indicated that Morin's DNA from a blood sample did not match that of the semen found in Christine's underwear. He was released from prison and acquitted of murder. The Christine Jessop murder is an open case once again.

As law enforcement officers as well as parents, we hate to see messy, ambiguous results like this. Do I still think Guy Paul Morin is guilty of Christine Jessop's murder? That's for a court of law to decide, not me. No one in my unit ever claims to be able to deliver up the name and identity of a particular UNSUB. All we can do is describe the type of individual we think did it based on the information we're given and what kind of pre- and post-offense behavior we would expect to see. In that way, we hope to be able to help investigators narrow down their list of suspects. I still believe firmly that her killer was someone who lived in the neighborhood, knew her well, was interested in music, and was an immature loner with a self-image problem who hung around with people younger than himself.

I also believe that so much time has passed, custody of evidence may have been compromised over the years and the crime scene, body, and clothing were in such a poor state to begin with that I would have serious doubts at this point about the infallibility of any scientific testing.

In addition, a number of sordid and very troubling revelations have come to light since the first trial, including the fact that Christine's brother, Kenneth, three years older than she, and several of his friends had been sexually abusing her since she was four. Appalling as it is to contemplate, I don't think we can be certain where the semen deposits in her underwear originated. The DNA evidence might just be a large red herring in this case, as occasionally happens.

Whatever the explanation in the Jessop case, I'm afraid this might be one of those tragic instances in which truth and justice will always be elusive.

Of all the things I've had to deal with in my career, violent crimes against children are unquestionably the worst. Once you've seen the murder scenes and the crime scene photos, it never leaves you. Seeing what I have seen, knowing what I know is out there, my first instinct when my children were younger was to handcuff each of them to my own or my wife, Pam's, wrists and never let them out of our sight.

The problem is how to strike a balance between being overbearingly protective and allowing your children room to mature and develop their independence. I was a nervous wreck the first time Erika took the car out alone or went on her first date. One of my closest friends in the unit, normally a very easygoing guy with a fine sense of humor, practically interrogates his daughter's dates before he lets them out of the house. We've all just seen too much.

The best we can hope for as parents, I suppose, is to remain alert, to remain cognizant, to teach our children well without making them fearful of every shadow. We have to set a standard of behavior and integrity while letting them know that they can always come and tell us anything. And I'll be the first to admit, that's not an easy balance to strike.

CHAPTER 4

Is Nothing Sacred?

Cassandra Lynn Hansen, known as Cassie, was a six-year-old girl from Eagan, Minnesota, a southern suburb of St. Paul. She was a year older than my daughter Erika, and seeing a picture of her with brownish blond hair cascading down below her shoulders made me think at once of an adorable little pixie. Her dimpled smile looked as if it would brighten the darkest day.

On the evening of November 10, 1981, she was attending a family night service with her mother and younger sister in the basement of Jehovah Evangelical Lutheran Church in St. Paul. She told her mother she had to go to the bathroom, then went down the hall and up the stairway to find the ladies' room. On the stairway she was seen by a woman church member. She was not seen alive again. When she didn't return, her mother, Ellen, went to the ladies' room, turned on the lights and looked around. It was empty. She went outside the church and repeatedly called her daughter's name. Other people took up the search. When they still couldn't find Cassie, they called the police.

The next morning, her body, still clothed in the baby blue dress she'd been wearing, was discovered tucked in the corner of a Dumpster behind an auto repair shop on Grand Avenue, about three miles from the church. Her black patent leather buckle shoes were found separately about two blocks away. The only other items not accounted for were the barrettes she'd had in her hair.

The murder of this little girl was among the most heart-rending cases I've ever encountered. It also demonstrated some of the best uses of proactive strategies and involvement of dedicated and courageous citizens I've ever known.

The Twin Cities public immediately reacted to Cassie's murder with horror, revulsion, and sorrow. If a sweet and joyful little child could be abducted from a church service, from a house of God, and have her life snuffed out, then was anything sacred?

The medical examiner found no evidence that she'd been sexually assaulted, though small traces of semen and several pubic hairs were discovered on one thigh of her navy blue tights. The semen revealed blood type O, a good piece of information since Cassie's blood type was B. The cause of death was ligature strangulation, probably with a two-and-a-half-inch-wide belt, based on the bruises on her neck. Abrasions across her chest indicated that another belt had been used as a restraint around her upper body. And there was one more detail the police kept secret as a "control" and to disqualify any false confessions: the six-year-old had been scratched and beaten about the head and face.

Cassie's parents were separated and she had lived with her mother. Police quickly determined that neither parent was a suspect. Ellen told investigators that Cassie had been taught to scream if she felt threatened by a stranger, and she had clearly grasped the significance of this lesson. Not too long before, Cassie had seen her four-year-old sister, Vanessa, talking to someone she didn't know and had pulled her forcefully back into the house.

As is often the case, witness accounts were somewhat contradictory and confusing. The church member who had seen Cassie on the stairs also remembered seeing a white male somewhere between fifty and sixty years of age with "salt-and-pepper" gray hair and dark-rimmed glasses on a rough face. A realtor who was on the street less than a block from the church after Cassie disappeared said he spotted a white male in his twenties carrying a motionless child who appeared to be a female, six or seven years old. Later, a similar description was taken near the alley leading to the Dumpster where Cassie's body was found.

The St. Paul Police Department pursued the case rigor-ously, employed the services of the FBI's Minneapolis Field Office, and developed some promising leads. But through the Christmas holidays and into the new year, they hadn't been able to make an arrest. Everybody wanted this one. Everybody wanted to find the killer of this little girl.

Late in February of 1982, Special Agents Bill Hagmaier and Brent Frost in Minneapolis got in touch with me and asked me to profile the case. This was the first time I'd ever worked with Bill, and it turned out to be a fortuitous meeting. Within a year, he had been transferred to the Behavioral Science Unit in Quantico. When I was near death in Seattle in December of 1983, Bill organized a collection to bring my wife and father out to the hospital to be with me. He later joined my Investigative Support Unit and was a key member until I retired in the spring of 1995. He now heads the Serial Killer and Child Abduction Unit at Quantico.

On March 3, after analyzing all the relevant case materials, I offered my profile in a lengthy conference call with Bill and Brent and the key St. Paul police people on the case: Captain Donald Trooien was chief of the homicide and sex crimes unit and had attended a sex crimes investigation seminar at Quantico in January where he heard a presentation from my Investigative Support Unit. Also on the line were Deputy Chief Robert LaBath, Lieutenant Larry McDonald, and Sergeants Roger Needham and Darrell Schmidt. As was our custom at Quantico, the one thing I did not want from the investigators was any information on suspects they might have developed. I wanted to remain objective, my profile based solely on what the evidence suggested to me.

Given the nature of the crime itself—an abduction in a church—I felt we were dealing with a white male UNSUB with a long history of obsession with children, perhaps a lifelong pattern. This crime was almost certainly committed by someone of the same race as Cassie and was not a casual, opportunistic off-the-street grab, though the abduction itself was a crime of opportunity. This guy was frequenting places where he knew children would be present, where he could freely observe them and be near them, and where parents' guard would be down. Age is always among the toughest points to nail down in a profile because emotional or experiential age doesn't always match chronological years. But although experience had shown us that a predictable time for the manifestation of child obsession disorders was early to mid-twenties, I thought the offender would be in at least his early thirties. I warned, however, that this wasn't necessarily something to go on. Four months before this, I had finished up work on the notorious "Trailside Killer" case, involving the murder of women hiking in densely wooded parks just north of San Francisco. The particulars indicated a white male around thirty or so. When David Carpenter, an industrial arts teacher in San Jose, was arrested for the crimes, he was fifty. But he had first been incarcerated for sex crimes in his mid-twenties, just about the time we would have predicted. At any rate, regardless of his age, I expected Cassandra Hansen's killer to have a previous history of sex offenses involving children, though they'd be far less serious than murder. He was able to get her out of the church quickly and efficiently, which spoke to a certain level of sophistication and maturity. He may have even gotten some thrill out of the challenge of getting her out of there. (I've interviewed a number of child molesters who said that they really got off on the challenge of spiriting a child out of a crowded shopping mall without anyone noticing or stopping them.)

At the same time that the circumstances showed some criminal maturity and sophistication, the choice of a child victim definitely showed an inability to deal with peers in an age-appropriate manner. This type of individual would not have been able to have his way with an eighteen-year-old or someone closer to his own age. He could only do it with a helpless child. He happened to abduct and kill a little girl. I think Cassie represented his victim of choice, but he easily could have done the same to a little boy, if that were the available victim. In spite of this, he still could be married or be with a woman, but it would not be a mature or deep relationship and I wouldn't be surprised to find the woman to be dependent or immature herself. Arthur Shawcross, who raped and murdered prostitutes in Rochester, New York, had served a previous fifteen-year jail term (much too short, in my opinion) for the assault and murder of both a young boy and a young girl. At the time of the prostitute murders, Shawcross was employed, married, and had a steady girlfriend.

I told the investigators I thought the church location had a major bearing on the personality of the UNSUB. He might not even realize why he was at that church; it might not even be his denomination. He may have thought he was there for religious reasons, to communicate with God. He might consider himself highly moral and whatever he does is because God has told him directly to do it. We could possibly be dealing with a paranoid schizophrenic; at least I would expect him to have had hallucinations or delusions. And these religious delusions could be tied up with his fantasies about children. When you finally identify this guy, I said, expect to find elaborate diaries and scrapbooks, possibly even some poetry, related to his obsession with children and possibly even this particular child. You'll also find one or more Bibles with many passages underlined and/or meticulous notes in the margins. He will be something of a loner, with a poor self-image, probably overweight. He could be big and strong since he'd had to get this presumably struggling child quietly out of the church, but he wouldn't be a good-looking guy. If he were in his twenties or (more likely) thirties, he might have some kind of physical disfigurement or speech impediment that made him self-conscious. If he were in his forties or fifties, I'd expect him to be fat or with a prominent gut and probably losing his hair. He won't have a large number of friends or any close friends, and so his diaries and scrapbooks will serve as one of his primary means of communication. Some of these guys will even record their thoughts on audio- or videotape, such as videotaping kids getting off a school bus and recording comments about individual children. If the UNSUB becomes worried that the investigation may be closing in on him, he'll hide his material but he won't destroy it unless he absolutely has to; it represents his lifelong avocation.

This type of individual will be obsessed with the case and the murder investigation. In his scrapbook he'll have every newspaper clipping he can find, particularly those with photographs. The picture of Cassie the police had shown me had also been published in the newspapers and I was confident the UNSUB had kept a clipping of it.

He could easily have gone to the funeral. He might have made repeated visits to the grave site. He probably took souvenirs from the child—I had noted Cassie's barrettes were missing—and some of these guys have been known to return missing items and to "talk to" their victims at the grave. Another possibility for the souvenirs was to give them to another child. In this way, he could "transfer" his obsession with the dead girl.

The disposal site was symbolic. By tossing this little girl in the trash when he was finished with her, he was, in effect, saying that he had the right to do with her what he wanted, that he was justified in his actions. This would tie in with the religious delusions. His direct contact with God would help him rationalize the murder and deal with it. Either God wanted the UNSUB's help in reclaiming this pure soul into heaven, or she needed to be punished or purged and he was God's instrument in this. For this reason, he might be attending church more frequently than before. This would be one way to deal with his stress. Another would be through alcohol or drugs.

When you have this symbolic a scene, you expect the killer to return to it, to the cemetery, or to some location significant to the victim and the crime. Stakeouts can often lead to positive results, which is why I suggested periodic "reminders" in the media as to where Cassie was buried.

This struck me as a serial type offender, and with most of them, you generally see a precipitating stressor in the hours, days, or weeks before the crime. The two most common, as I've said, have to do with jobs and relationships—losing one or the other—but any type of hardship, particularly an economic one, can trigger the violent outburst. The only important qualification is that the stressor represents something with which the UNSUB can't cope, that makes him feel he's been unfairly dealt with, or that the world is out to get him. Then—since I believed this offender had some sort of past with child molestation or sex crimes—when the opportunity presented itself, when he saw a child without anyone else around, where the risks of being seen or stopped were small, he instantly and instinctively sprang into action.

I told the police officers that regardless of whether they

had any good suspects or not, they should state publicly that the investigation was going well. I suggested to Deputy Chief LaBath that he go on television and declare that if it took him his entire career, he was going to make sure that this case was solved and the killer was brought to justice; that would keep up the emotional pressure on him.

Because this UNSUB would be feeling the pressure. As I mentioned, alcohol could be one manifestation of this, but I felt it wouldn't help enough. He might have confided his act to another person, and if he had, that person could easily be in danger as the heat rose. He would be getting more and more desperate as he tried to figure out whether the length of time that had passed since the crime meant he was home free, or whether the investigative case was closing in on him. That desperation could easily take the form of another criminal act.

If and when the police did have a good suspect, I suggested making the pressure more overt. When John Wayne Gacy became the prime suspect in the disappearance of young boys around the Chicago area, Des Plaines police detectives undertook an overt, high-profile surveillance, dogging Gacy wherever he went. At first the rotund construction contractor took it as a joke, even inviting two of the detectives to dinner. Knowing the police would not want to pick him up on anything trivial, he toyed with them by openly defying traffic laws and smoking marijuana. The pressure continued to grow, though, and eventually Gacy cracked. He invited police right into his house, where they smelled rotting flesh. Ultimately, they picked him up on a drug charge, got a search warrant, and found the first of thirty-three bodies concealed in the structure of his home.

I thought a similar tack could work here. If a suspect went to church, the police should go to church with him. If he went to a restaurant, they should go to the restaurant with him. Let him see you knocking on his neighbor's door. I also suggested rattling him by having some female voice call him regularly, sob on the phone, and then hang up. You've got to be imaginative about not letting the subject off the emotional hook.

This kind of offender would probably be nocturnal. If the police went by his residence at night, they would find lights on. He would also be nomadic, driving around after dark. He won't flee the area because he knows that might alert investigators, and anyway, he feels at least partially justified in what he did. At that time, there was a technique known as psychological stress evaluation, or PSE, that was popular in certain law enforcement circles, particularly in the Midwest. Using specific observation parameters and an electronic device something like a polygraph, PSE was supposed to detect deception during interrogation. Personally, I didn't set much store in it, particularly with subjects who had rationalized their acts in their own minds. He wouldn't give them any satisfaction if they confronted him with killing the little girl. The only line of questioning that might elicit some telling response, I thought, would be challenging him on having masturbated on her since we did have the semen deposit on her tights.

Once I'd described the type of individual I objectively thought was responsible for Cassie Hansen's abduction and murder, the police told me that during the course of the investigation they had conducted more than five hundred interviews and considered 108 possible suspects.

One in particular stood out remarkably. "When you described what we should be looking for, you hit this guy on about ten major points," Captain Trooien commented.

The suspect in question was a fifty-year-old, six-foot-tall white male cab driver named Stuart W. Knowlton. He had been approached by the police after being seen driving in the area near the church the day Cassie disappeared but he refused to be questioned and refused to take a polygraph. He was of stocky build, had short gray hair and a receding hairline, and wore glasses. The police told me he was known to frequent area churches and had a history of child sexual abuse, including charges involving his own children. After our consultation, the police concentrated on him as their prime suspect, placing the others they'd been following on the back burner.

Despite police suspicions, however, there wasn't enough to charge him, so he was still free. But coincidentally, about three weeks before this telephone conference, Knowlton had been hit by a car while walking home and lost about half of one leg. It wasn't going to be difficult to keep track of him for a while, because he was still in the Ramsey County Nursing Home rehabilitating.

Someone else associated with Stuart Knowlton was also undergoing rehabilitation and recuperation down in Florida near Orlando. Her name was Dorothy Noga, and at the time of Cassie's death she was working as a masseuse in St. Paul. She didn't much like the work, but it paid an average of $2,000 a week, enough to let her husband stay home and raise their four children. According to the story investigators had pieced together, Knowlton first came into Lee Lenore's sauna where Noga worked on November 11, 1981, the day after the abduction and the day Cassie's body was found. Curiously, he asked her to be an alibi witness for him in case anyone accused him of anything around this time. Noga didn't know what to make of this, but took his business card, on which he wrote his address and phone number.

Noga had been appalled by news of the little girl's death, though she didn't connect Knowlton with it. She did, however, think of another of her clients who had professed fantasies of sex with children. In the intimacy of the massage room, men tended to confide in Dorothy. So she phoned in an anonymous tip to the police.

Several days later, the crime was still preying on her mind and Dorothy Noga decided she had to get more personally involved if she thought she had information that could help. This time when she called, she left her name and agreed to be interviewed by detectives. During the interview, a photograph of Knowlton happened to slip out of the detectives' folder onto the floor. Noga recognized him as the man who had come in for a massage the day after the murder. Was he a suspect, she wanted to know. The detectives confirmed that he was, but that he was refusing to talk to them.

Maybe he'd talk to her, she figured, and offered to call him. The police turned her down on this offer, not wanting to be accused of obtaining information illegally after Knowlton had contacted a lawyer and the lawyer had told him not to talk.

But once the police left, Noga decided that they had no power to tell her what to do, so she called the number on his card. Noga was confident she could get this man to talk to her. The thirty-two-year-old masseuse was a good listener and she could almost always get men to talk to her.

And that's exactly what she did. Before long, she was having almost daily phone conversations with Knowlton, some lasting several hours. He seemed to her lonely and in despair, and inordinately preoccupied with the killing of the little Hansen girl. Noga felt sure she was on the right track.

At the same time, the exercise was draining and depressing. Knowlton often talked as if they were having a romantic relationship and Noga felt queasy leading him on this way. "I would get so depressed talking to him, I wanted to give up. I would just sit and cry," she later told the *St. Paul Dispatch*.

But she had four children of her own and her heart went out to Cassie and her grieving family. If she could, she wanted to spare others the same horror. Then in one conversation, she said, he admitted killing Cassie. That inspired her to continue, and also made her start taping the conversations. She informed the St. Paul police, and gave them the tapes. Seeing the resource they had, the police encouraged her to keep going. But once the taping began, Knowlton never again mentioned any personal role in Cassie's death, though he still continued to talk about the case.

On December 13, a little over a month after the murder, the conversations stopped for good. It was her husband's thirty-fourth birthday and Noga was working at the Comfort Center Sauna. The only thing she initially remembered from that day was waking up in a hospital room at the St. Paul–Ramsey Medical Center—the same facility to which Stuart Knowlton would be brought after being struck by the car—and seeing her agonized mother at the foot of her bed. She had been stabbed repeatedly and her throat slashed. Her attacker had left her on the floor, bleeding and near death. Doctors called her survival "miraculous." She was put under twenty-four-hour guard at the hospital and gave police a vague description of her assailant. They brought her photographic spreads of possible suspects. One man was brought in, but was released for lack of evidence.

The police immediately suspected Knowlton and when they told me what had happened, I agreed. He would have confided in Dorothy to try to relieve his own stress, but as his stress mounted, he would have realized how vulnerable he'd made himself. The only way out would have been to eliminate the threat.

There were no witnesses to the crime, no useful forensic evidence, and Noga could remember nothing more than what she had said. After she got out of the hospital, she and her family moved to Florida to continue her recuperation and try to remove herself from the reach of her attacker, who probably regretted not finishing the job.

But another series of conversations between Stuart Knowlton and a woman he had met only recently were to prove equally critical. Janice Rettman, the same age as Dorothy Noga, was the director of the St. Paul Housing Information Office. It was a high-ranking job with a tremendous amount of responsibility, and the short, vibrant strawberry blond was known in city government circles as an administrator who could get things done.

Rettman met Knowlton on March 16, 1981, eight months before Cassie Hansen's abduction and murder. He came to her agency saying that he was about to be evicted from the Roosevelt Homes public housing project. His wife was leaving him, taking their two children with her, and the welfare payments and food stamps they had been using to make ends meet had been cut off. He'd just begun driving a cab and had been to several churches and social service agencies, he said, but no one seemed able to help. The reason for the eviction, as Rettman discovered, was two complaints filed against Knowlton. The first had been early the previous fall when Knowlton invited two fourteen-year-old girls into his apartment to play cards. Once he had them there, Knowlton reportedly described to them how babies were born and began talking about sex, birth control, and menstruation. He promised to show them his penis. When the girls' parents reported the incident to the police and they, in turn, informed the public housing office, Knowlton was warned that if there were any more such incidents, he and his family would be evicted.

Then in February, Knowlton asked a nine-year-old girl to take her pants off for him. The girl was so frightened and traumatized that she developed recurring nightmares.

At the time, Knowlton was living temporarily in an efficiency apartment a couple of blocks from the women's shelter where his wife and children were staying.

In speaking to Rettman, Knowlton had no hesitancy talking about his sexual involvement with children. Though she'd never done anything like it before, Rettman instinctively decided not to give him her real name, introducing herself as Janice Reever. She said she was obligated to report any suspected instances of child abuse to the proper authorities and told him, "I think you need help."

The child protection authorities told her there had been other reports about Knowlton but that they'd never been able to get sufficient proof for prosecution.

When Rettman heard on the news that Cassandra Hansen's body had been found, she immediately thought of the man she had dealt with in March. He said he'd been going to various churches and the efficiency he'd been renting was only ten blocks from Jehovah Evangelical Lutheran Church. A few days later she called Stuart Knowlton to follow up on his housing situation. She found him distraught and unwilling to talk. A couple of days after that, though, he called her back. With the same candor he had demonstrated at their first encounter, he told her the police had just searched his apartment when she'd called and he was so upset he couldn't talk. He told her he was going through hell, was very lonely, and needed someone to talk to and to visit him.

Knowing that the police were trying to put together information on Knowlton, but that they were having difficulty doing it, Rettman, like Noga, decided to get involved.

"No child should be hurt," she later told Linda Kohl of the *St. Paul Dispatch*. "Every adult is responsible for the children's welfare. If I could assist the police in bringing that person to justice, or assist in making sure that person never touches a child again—then it was right, it was important. We are responsible for our children, whether it's yours or somebody else's."

I firmly believe that if Janice Rettman's attitude was more widely held and acted upon, we'd all be living in a lot safer, more humane society.

Being a fellow municipal official, Rettman went directly to Police Chief William McCutcheon and offered to help. As he had with Dorothy Noga, Knowlton began pouring out his soul on the telephone to Janice Rettman. He talked about the child molestation charges that had led to his eviction, he talked about his marital problems and inability to hold a steady job, and he told about his religious conversion the previous year while listening to Johnny Cash. Rettman took notes during each conversation, then typed them up and delivered them to the police. Much of the information the police had on Knowlton, much of the way they knew he conformed so closely to my profile, came from Rettman's compiled dossier.

The near-fatal attack on Dorothy Noga upped the ante considerably. Though fearful, Rettman kept at it, now making copies of her notes for safekeeping if anything similar happened to her.

What made Rettman take the physical and emotional risks to become involved? What made her so different, say, from the thirty-eight neighbors who listened without lifting a finger as Winston Mosely stabbed Kitty Genovese to death outside her apartment house in fashionable Kew Gardens, Queens, on the morning of March 13, 1964? We could come up with some glib, superficial answers: She had a degree in social work. She had spent six and a half years as a VISTA volunteer. She was naturally adventuresome, having left her Texas home at eighteen in quest of an education. But none of this really speaks to the core values that made her part of the solution rather than part of the problem. The fact is that she got involved because she felt it was the right thing to do, just as Dorothy Noga had.

I have spent my career studying the complex motivations of criminals, but basically, all the prior influences on an individual resolve down to one key element: the *choice* to commit the crime. Likewise, doing the right thing resolves down to a simple factor: the choice to get involved. We're all responsible for our actions.

Knowlton never admitted the Hansen murder to her, but he seemed obsessed with it in their conversations in ways that chilled Janice Rettman to her core. He said he had had a "vision" about the case and had a "sixth sense" that the murder of Cassie Hansen and the attack on Dorothy Noga were related. He discussed all sorts of details, including the method of disposal of the body.

And in one of these conversations, he made his crucial slipup.

He mentioned that Cassie Hansen had been beaten before she died, the fact police had kept confidential as a control.

It was shortly after this revelation that Knowlton suffered his automobile accident, losing the lower part of his leg. Rettman visited him in the hospital, and later at the Ramsey County Nursing Home. For some of these visits, she brought a tape recorder, hidden in her handbag. For later ones, she was wired with a police body mike. Going impressively proactive, she wore a pair of black patent leather shoes on several occasions because they were similar to the ones Cassie was wearing when she was taken. I wish I'd thought of this, but it was purely Rettman's idea.

When the police told me about her activities, I told them that this was absolutely the right way to proceed with such an elusive and "uncooperative" suspect, and suggested some other types of approaches that might be fruitful. For example, Rettman might give him a nice journal in which he could record his thoughts and feelings.

Though he claimed to have nothing to do with the murder and murder attempt, he told Rettman he might have a "perfect double" somewhere in the city. This was a key piece of information, signifying another mechanism for trying to cope with the crime. This would be in my mind three years later as I sat in the office of Sheriff Jim Metts in Lexington County, South Carolina, interrogating a dark-haired, pudgy, bearded electrician's assistant named Larry Gene Bell. A solid combination of good profiling, good proactive technique, first-rate police work and forensic analysis, and wonderful and courageous families had led to the arrest of Bell for the heartbreaking murders of seventeen-year-old Shari Faye Smith and nine-year-old Debra Helmick. I knew the chances of a confession were slim to none. South Carolina was a capital punishment state and there aren't many sales tools available to convince a subject to buy a one-way ticket to the chair. The only real possibility is to offer him some face-saving justification or explanation for the crime.

So I spoke to him about how everyone has a good side and a bad side. The only thing the judge and jury in court were going to know about him was that he was a cold-blooded killer. I was giving him the opportunity to tell me about the other side.

"Larry, as you're sitting here now," I said, "did you do this thing?"

With tears glistening in his eyes, he replied, "All I know is that the Larry Gene Bell sitting here couldn't have done this, but the bad Larry Gene Bell could have."

I knew that was as close as we'd ever get to a confession. But the state's case, directed by County Solicitor Don Meyers, was convincing. After a nearly month-long trial, the jury took less than an hour to find Bell guilty of kidnapping and first-degree murder. He was sentenced to death by electrocution. More than eleven years after the killing, Bell was finally executed early on the morning of Friday, October 4, 1996.

In May 1982, after the police had keyed on Stuart Knowlton as their primary suspect and instituted the types of proactive techniques we'd discussed, Dorothy Noga showed up at St. Paul police headquarters and told detectives she was beginning to get back some memory of the day of her attack. She said that Knowlton came to the sauna where she was working and angrily accused her of betraying him. He told her he had stopped in Jehovah Evangelical Lutheran Church to use the men's room and saw the little blond girl going by herself to the ladies' room.

He waited for her to come out, Noga reported from his account, asked her to play a game with him in the hallway, then took Cassie out to where his taxicab was parked. He made advances to her, made the child touch his penis, then rubbed it between her thighs. This gave him feelings of euphoria, Noga said, but the little girl kept crying so he put his hand over her mouth and the next thing he knew she wasn't breathing. At least, that's the way he reportedly told her it had happened.

After this confession, according to Noga, he brought out a knife, chased her around the room, then began slashing at her throat. Then she lost consciousness.

On May 26, St. Paul police believed they finally had sufficient cause for a search warrant, which they applied for and received. Up until then, they had kept the details of the investigation of this highly publicized case as quiet and out of the media as they could.

Knowlton's account did square with the finding of semen on the thighs of Cassie's tights and Al Robillard of the FBI Laboratory confirmed that the pubic hair found on her body and head hair found on her turtleneck sweater were consistent with Knowlton's. Under microscopic examination, both reflected an unusual disease condition known as "ringed" or "banded" hair which makes various parts of the individual hair strand appear light or dark. His blood type also corresponded with that of the semen stains on Cassie's clothing.

Stuart Knowlton was charged with the kidnapping and first-degree murder of Cassandra Hansen. He was placed in a state mental facility, examined and found competent to stand trial. At his own request, his case was heard by a judge rather than a jury. Ramsey District Judge James M. Lynch presided at the trial. Thomas Poch led the prosecution. Philip Vilaume and Jack Nordby defended Knowlton, and offered to plea-bargain to second-degree murder, but without an admission of guilt.

"That was totally unacceptable," Poch recalled.

Dana McCarthy, a mother who took her son to the same family night service from which Cassie disappeared, testified that she saw a man going up a flight of stairs just after the little girl had. In court, she identified that man as Stuart Knowlton.

When it was Janice Rettman's turn to testify and she was asked, "Do you swear to tell the truth, the whole truth, and nothing but the truth?" she gave the bailiff a thumbs-up signal and responded, "You bet." Her notes and the level of her organization were very impressive.

The opposite was true for Knowlton. He said he was driving his taxi during the time Cassie had been abducted. As a cab driver, he was supposed to have trip logs which at least could have given some weight to his alibi claim. But he said his logs were in a briefcase that he believed had been stolen by a customer and he couldn't remember where he'd been that night.

Donald Whalen, Jr., Knowlton's taxi dispatcher, testified that he tried to radio the driver several times that evening but couldn't raise him. Patricia Jones, general manager of a competing cab company, stated that Knowlton tried to buy blank trip sheets from her on the day Cassie's body was found, even though Whalen told the court there were plenty available for the asking at his own company.

It also came out in court that Knowlton had spent time in a mental hospital in Traverse City, Michigan, after molesting a seven-year-old girl.

The trial lasted thirteen days and involved forty-eight witnesses and more than a hundred exhibits. Knowlton did not choose to testify. At the trial's conclusion, Judge Lynch found Knowlton guilty of first-degree murder and second-degree criminal sexual conduct and sentenced him to life imprisonment. Under Minnesota law, that made him eligible for parole in 2001.

Knowlton listened impassively, then in a ten-minute rambling statement, asserted his innocence. "As God is my witness, I swear to you this day, I did not abduct Cassandra Lynn Hansen from the church she was attending," he told the judge. Interesting to note, he did not deny killing her, all of which could have amounted to a complex psychological defense mechanism on his part.

Without admitting anything he also reasserted the religiosity that I thought would be a part of his personality when he said, "I had no reason to take anyone's life for God had not given me that right. I have had no reason to have any vengeance against Cassandra Lynn Hansen or Dorothy Noga."

Defense attorney Vilaume, who seemed more devastated by the verdict than his client and made a public statement professing his belief in Knowlton's innocence, still said he believed Judge Lynch was fair and conducted a good and impartial trial.

Cassie's mother, Ellen, who also testified at the trial, came away from her ordeal dedicated to educating others about dangers to children and urging tougher enforcement of laws aimed at protecting them. Noting that Knowlton had been beaten and abused by his father, she called in media interviews for putting abusing parents in prison so that their victims didn't become abusers themselves. Only if the vicious circle of incest is broken, she said, will child molestation decrease, and one of the most important things was that children who've been abused be made to feel comfortable opening up to parents or other relatives, teachers, or family friends.

Ellen Hansen and her husband, William, had done a good job of preparing their children, Cassie and Vanessa, to deal with threats to their safety. They were taught not to speak with or go with strangers who approached them and that if they were afraid, to scream loudly and run. The Hansens therefore have no idea how their daughter was lured or forced away.

Knowlton was first incarcerated in the mental health unit of Oak Park Heights State Prison, but then transferred to St. Cloud Reformatory because correctional officials feared for his life. Even other convicts won't tolerate child killers in their midst.

I don't want to give the impression here that girls are the only victims of child molesters, or even that crimes against boys are confined to youngsters. While not in the same danger as females, males the age of Alison Parrott or Kristen French can become targets.

That's what happened to thirteen-year-old Shawn Moore. The case is another good example of how profiling can help investigators focus their efforts on the right type of suspect.

Shawn was somewhat small for his age—only four foot ten and about eighty-five pounds—but very good-looking, with straight, longish blond hair, bright hazel eyes, and an infectious smile. He was, according to my colleague Special Agent Jim Harrington, "a kid who had everything going for him." On the afternoon of Saturday, August 31, 1985—Labor Day weekend—he was helping his dad mow the lawn of their house in Green Oak Township near Brighton, Michigan, about thirty miles northwest of Detroit. It was hot for that time of year—almost ninety—and the weather was taking its toll. Shawn asked his father if he could ride his bike down to the local convenience store. The Pump 'N Pantry was not quite two miles from the house, but it was near old U.S. Route 23, and there was often a lot of traffic, particularly on a holiday weekend. But Shawn really wanted to get a root beer, so after characteristically telling his son to be careful, Bruce Moore, promotions director for the *Ann Arbor News,* reluctantly agreed to let him go.

Shawn never came back home. His maroon and silver Huffy ten-speed touring bike was found later that day near the convenience store, on the side of the road where the gravel shoulder met the grass embankment, about a mile from the state police post. The twenty-six-inch bicycle was big for him, but he was hoping to grow into it, and had worked hard to pay half its cost. He was very proud of that bike, according to his father, and never would have willingly abandoned it. He also wouldn't have wandered off for a long period of time because the family was going to the movies that night. Reconstructing the time of the disappearance, we noted that a Livingston County sheriff's car would have been about a block away.

There were conflicting witness accounts. One woman thought she saw a blond man in his twenties drive away in a Jeep with "Renegade" in blue letters on the side of the hood. Another saw a man in his forties driving a truck. A third spotted a "heavyset, out-of-shape" man in his forties running after the boy. There was also contradiction on whether the young boy seemed to be afraid or in distress, and whether the man was actually pursuing him or merely talking to him, perhaps asking directions. Each of these potential suspects could take the investigation in an entirely different direction.

It was the Tuesday after Labor Day Monday when the FBI was called in to the presumed kidnapping. By that time a multiagency task force had been established which already included the Michigan State Police, Brighton City Police, and the sheriff's department. The state police was the lead agency. When they requested the assistance of Ken Walton, the special agent in charge of the Detroit Field Office, he handed the case to Jim Harrington, who was the field office's profile coordinator. A number of the people who worked with me in the Investigative Support Unit over the years had first been profile coordinators.

The Detroit Field Office had been my first assignment in the Bureau, directly out of New Agents Training. There was always a lot of action in Detroit, and the Detroit police were among my best teachers. Much of my experience with profiling began with my informal interviewing of serial bank robbers we arrested while I was working a bank robbery unit. Jim Harrington called me as soon as he had gathered the facts on Shawn Moore's disappearance.

He gave me the details on the phone and together we came up with a profile which we elaborated to the task force in a phone conference. There were two prevailing theories of the case which we tried to dispel. One was that Shawn had been the victim of a stalker who had been targeting him for days or weeks before he finally struck. The other theory was that a close family member was involved. As horrible and unnatural as it is to contemplate, parents do kill their children, for a variety of reasons. And normally when they do so, they report them missing or abducted, leaving a staged scene. As dispassionate investigators, we always have to consider parents, children, spouses—whoever was closest to the victim.

Some of the police felt that Bruce and Sharon Moore, an elementary school teacher, weren't reacting properly; they didn't seem sufficiently grief-stricken and seemed overly optimistic about the prospect of their son's safe and speedy return. This raised red flags. But when Jim went to see the Moores, he saw a loving, caring couple with strong, solid values. Their lack of overt grieving struck Jim as their attempt to be unwavering beacons of hope for everyone throughout the ordeal. He came away touched and impressed by both of them. Studying the victimology, everything Jim found that was so solid about Shawn appeared to be a reflection of his nurturing parents.

The stalking scenario didn't make much sense to us, either. A grab of a thirteen-year-old kid on a bike in broad daylight near a major highway was too daring and high-risk for that. Anyone who'd been stalking this young man with the idea of eventually abducting him would have had many less obvious and personally dangerous opportunities to take him. We were convinced this was a crime of opportunity committed by a stranger.

So what did this abduction scenario tell us about the UNSUB here? For one thing, he knew the area. He wasn't someone passing through who just happened to be there. For another thing, he was probably under the influence of alcohol or drugs at the time. He would have needed something to lower his inhibitions even to attempt so foolhardy a snatch.

Not surprisingly for this type of crime and this type of victim, we pegged him as a white male in his early to midtwenties. He would not be happy with himself—an inadequate type personality with a low self-image for which he was constantly trying to compensate. This could include a macho, kick-ass kind of car, guns, hunting, or fishing. But these would all be a mask to hide his preoccupation with young boys; so would a girlfriend if he had one. That would be a cover, a purely platonic relationship to make him appear more "normal" to himself and the rest of the world. I would doubt that he'd ever had heterosexual relations, and if he had, the experience would have been intimidating, incomplete, or unsatisfying to him. His real relationships would be with younger males, with whom he would feel more comfortable than with his own peers. Even so, he would use money or material possessions as gifts to keep them interested in him. He'd be soft and weak. Even in his choice of a thirteen-year-old to abduct, he chose a small one who would seem easier to intimidate and control.

This would not be someone with a sophisticated job or education, but he would be employed because he had the means to maintain and operate an automobile. He'd be blue-collar and not highly skilled, would probably have graduated from high school but not gone to college. Along with his macho aspirations, he might have thought about joining the service, but would probably realize he couldn't cut it. If he did have a service record, I expected to see a dishonorable discharge. Another consideration which led us to the conclusion about his job was that since we were convinced this type of daylight snatch would have been accomplished with the inhibition-lowering aid of drugs or alcohol, he would have been used to drinking during the day. This would also point to a suspect who didn't have a high-powered job as well as to someone from the area.

Even emboldened by some artificial substance, the UNSUB had to have had experience to pull off this crime so well. We told the police they should be looking for someone with a history of sex charges against him and at least some experience with similar abductions. The charges might have resulted in either imprisonment or hospitalization or both. In any event, there would be a record.

If he abducted this boy, he probably knew the area pretty well and had someplace specific in mind to bring him that was secluded and afforded a measure of privacy. This type of individual would be dependent: though his relationship with his parents would have been a troubled one, we expected him to be living with them or some other family member, perhaps an older sister or aunt. Therefore, he couldn't bring Shawn back to his house. Where he would bring him was a place in the woods he had found that he knew no one else was likely to come to, or, since we thought it possible that he hunted or fished, there might be a cabin within an easy drive that either belonged to one of his friends or family or was abandoned. Despite the Moore family's optimism that Shawn would be returned safe and sound, Jim and I were preparing for the worst. If he hadn't been released the first day, or even the second, we were afraid the kidnapper wasn't intending to release him at all. Eventually the body would be found, and it would likely be found by the side of a road or in the woods a short car ride from wherever the UNSUB had taken him.

As far as I was concerned, this would be a pretty solid, unambiguous profile. Again, the factor we're usually most unsure about is age, but in this case I was pretty confident even about that. Somewhere around here, we told the police, there had to be a suspect who fits this description, and you may even have spoken to him already.

From our research and experience, we believed the abduction was the result of some precipitating event or other stressor, probably related to one of the two most common triggers: job or personal relationship. Either was certainly possible here, but since this was a holiday weekend, we were giving more weight to the relationship one. People of the type we thought we were dealing with are often lonely, frustrated, and depressed on holidays, and if he were, he might have needed to vent it on someone. My guess was that the individual who rejected him would be someone he perceived to be very much like the young boy he abducted. Shawn, therefore, was a surrogate, a displacement for anger or rage against whomever the UNSUB felt he'd lost.

Each day that passed without Shawn's safe return made us more and more pessimistic about a happy outcome. But with the profile as a guide, the police began concentrating their investigation in the direction of the type of individual we'd described. They gave greater weight to the witness report of a blond or light-brown-haired man in his twenties, driving a Jeep. They disseminated the information to surrounding police jurisdictions and the media. They also put out a wanted flyer with a photograph of Shawn, a police artist's sketch of the suspect, and a photograph of the car they thought he'd been driving based on the description. This turned out to be a Jeep Renegade hardtop, white or a light metallic color, with the word "Renegade" or "Cherokee" printed in large blue letters on the side of the hood. Two phone numbers were printed on the flyer: one directly to the investigative team and another for people wishing to leave an anonymous tip.

We were sure this guy was from somewhere in the general area and there couldn't be too many people who matched this description. That's why I've always been such an advocate of involving the public in the search. In almost all cases, someone out there knows something and is willing to cooperate if he or she only knows they have information to contribute and that we need their help.

In this case, it was a member of the law enforcement community who recognized the profile and came forward. He was a police officer in Livonia, a town about halfway between Brighton and downtown Detroit. He called the task force command center and mentioned a young man named Ronald Lloyd Bailey.

"You've got to look at this guy," he said. "We've had him in before on these sexual fixations with young boys and he sounds just like the guy you're describing."

The task force checked him out. Jim and I were almost stunned by how well he fit the profile. He was a twenty-six-year-old white male high school graduate who lived in the general area—Livonia—and had a blue-collar job as a delivery man. He lived with his parents, with whom he had never gotten along well. His father, Alfred, was strict and career-oriented, and from the time he was young, his mother had always warned him about girls. In fact, it later turned out that when Shawn Moore disappeared, Al Bailey worried that Ron might be responsible. Recently, Ron had bought a silver Jeep Renegade hardtop. He was soft and slightly built, had straight, longish blond hair like Shawn's, and was known as a loner who'd been in trouble with young boys. In fact, he'd been institutionalized on three separate occasions.

A team of state police investigators went to talk to Bailey on September 10, but he had an alibi. The day Shawn Moore disappeared, Bailey said, he was up north in Caseville boating and fishing with a young boy he knew. The fishing wasn't any good, so they'd cut their trip short and come back on Labor Day Monday. It was the next morning when Al Bailey told him about the Moore boy's disappearance and said police had a description of a Jeep that sounded similar to his son's. Ron did have access to a rustic hunting and fishing cabin near Gladwin that belonged to the family of his professed girlfriend, Debbie. He and Debbie's brother were scheduled to go up there the next week and Ron knew it would be empty until then.

But when the investigative team approached the boy Bailey said he was with, the young man reported that while he did know Ron Bailey and was supposed to go away with him for the weekend, his mother had found out about the trip and had forbidden him to go.

How did Ron take this rejection, the police asked.

He was very upset and disappointed, the boy replied.

The next day, police went back to Bailey and confronted him with the inconsistency. Bailey stuck to his story and at that point demanded a lawyer. The lawyer refused to let him answer any more questions, and when he was placed in a lineup, witnesses didn't identify him. So the police had to release him.

But they didn't give up on him. He was still the strongest suspect and the only one who conformed to the profile. What's more, his alibi didn't square and the details provided by the young boy suggested a triggering event of the type we'd predicted. So a surveillance team was set up to keep an eye on Bailey and see what he'd do next. I was convinced he'd revisit the body dump site and we were hoping he would lead police right to it.

What he did do was visit an ATM machine and withdraw several hundred dollars in cash. Then he drove to the airport, bought a ticket for Delta Flight 807 to Florida, and boarded the plane without any luggage. On the other end, Florida police tracked him into the woods.

In the meantime, on September 13, Shawn Moore's nude body had been discovered by the side of a road, covered with a tent of twigs, leaves, and brush. The entire skull and most of the rib cage showed through. The body was already so badly decomposed from exposure, hot weather, animals, and insects that the medical examiner couldn't determine an exact cause of death, other than that it was a homicide. Witnesses came forward who had seen a Jeep matching Bailey's near the cabin the weekend Shawn had disappeared. The investigators now felt they had enough to move and gave instructions to their colleagues in Florida to try to bring Ron in.

They searched, and eventually found him in a tool shed where the bugs were eating him alive. He turned himself in peacefully.

The ongoing investigation into Ron Bailey turned up some interesting information. His sexual experience with boys his own age and younger was extensive. He had also, apparently, had two sexual encounters with women, the first a nurse at a mental hospital to which he had been sent. She was in her twenties when he was in his mid-teens.

During interrogation sessions with Ron, detectives were able to piece together the key elements of the story.

He had been planning a big, fun weekend up at the cabin and was sorely upset when his young friend canceled on him. In fact, he slammed down the phone in a rage. He then asked virtually everyone else he knew to go with him, but for one reason or another, no one could make it. Debbie had to baby-sit. A friend wasn't feeling well. One cousin had a wedding, another had to go back to school. He started driving around in his new car, looking for parties, drinking beer, and smoking marijuana. He drove around for several hours, going from one friend's house to another, occasionally stopping for gas or to buy more beer or more of the cigarettes he smoked almost continuously.

He stayed at a party in Brighton for a while, then left and got back in his car. He noticed that he had passed the Brighton post of the Michigan State Police. He stopped at a convenience store just off U.S. 23 and bought two packs of cigarettes. Like many smokers, he had the idea that if he only bought a couple of packs at a time rather than an entire carton, he might cut down.

It was in front of the convenience store that he spotted the young boy who turned out to be Shawn Moore. He was dressed in a tan T-shirt, gray jogging shorts, and blue sneakers, sitting on the curb with his bike drinking a bottle of soda. He was slim and blond and handsome and reminded Ron of his idealized self. He described Shawn as "the best-looking of them all," and thought he seemed lonely. He sat in his Jeep watching him for several minutes.

Ron then drove away across the freeway, thinking about maybe going to Cincinnati for the weekend. No, maybe he would just go to Ann Arbor, but wasn't sure how to take the back roads to get there. He was back near Brighton, on the service road for Route 23, when he spotted Shawn riding his bike and recognized him as the beautiful boy from the convenience store. He stopped the Jeep about thirty feet behind him and walked up to him.

"Hey, I want to talk to you," Ron called out. Shawn stopped. He talked to him for about a minute or so, asking if the road he was on went to Ann Arbor.

Then he said sharply, "Come with me! I've got a knife." He did actually have a knife, but it was in the Jeep.

Fearfully, Shawn went with him, saying he couldn't be gone too long. Ron put his arm around the boy's shoulder. Leaving Shawn's new bike, Ron started the Jeep. First he drove south, then turned around and headed north. He tried to make conversation, asking the boy about school.

Between Flint and Saginaw he decided to go to the cabin. He'd asked for and been given the key. He said he considered Shawn a friend and at no time was he concerned the boy would run away, even when they stopped for cigarettes at another convenience store. Ron waited in the Jeep while Shawn went to the men's room. When asked if he worried about what Shawn's parents would be going through, he replied, "I didn't even think about it."

The cabin was rustic, a bedroom and kitchen with an outhouse in the back. Inside the cabin, he drank more beer and smoked more cigarettes and marijuana and got Shawn to indulge, too. He said he let Shawn play with his loaded .22 rifle and 12-gauge shotgun. He opened some canned food and heated it on the stove. They slept together in the lower bunk of the cabin's bunk bed. The next morning, he had a hell of a hangover, complicated by the mescaline and Valium he downed regularly. Shawn asked, "Are you sure you're gonna take me back and not hurt me?"

"Sure," Ron replied. "If I wanted to hurt you, I would have done it by now."

Late in the afternoon, Ron had them drinking again, then performed oral sex, masturbating to climax on his belly. He kept Shawn in something of a stupor induced by a potent combination of alcohol, marijuana, and fear. Later, he escalated his behavior, though he said he felt badly that he had done to Shawn what an older guy had done to him. When he instituted sex again, it was with a slide-lock belt tightened around Shawn's neck, which he explained would heighten the sensation.

That was when he said he began "feeling really weird," not thinking straight. He went outside for a walk to try to clear his head, then came back in and straddled Shawn on the bed, gradually tightening the belt. At first Shawn struggled and Ron held him down. Then he stopped struggling and was still. Ron passed out, flooded with relief, and slept next to him that night in the bed.

When he awoke Monday morning, he felt Shawn's thigh. It was cold. His naked body was already stiff. The belt was still tight around his neck. He said he freaked out, jumping up and banging his head on the upper bunk. He ran out of the cabin and threw up. He was "hungover like hell," crying and trying to piece everything together. He couldn't bring himself to look at Shawn's face. He had a few beers and smoked a joint to steady his nerves.

Still panicked, he went for a ride in the Jeep, trying to think what to do. He stopped for breakfast and coffee, hoping it would make his light-headedness go away. He drove around some more and went out to sit by the lake before coming back to the cabin. He picked up the rigid body by an arm and a leg and lugged it to the back of the Jeep. He found a place by the side of the road to dump it, then gathered sticks which he placed over it and covered it with leaves and ferns. Then he drove the twenty miles back to Saginaw.

As we'd predicted, this was not the subject's first sexual crime involving young boys. In September 1973, when he was fourteen, Bailey abducted a fifteen-year-old boy at knifepoint, tied his hands, carried him off on his bicycle and then sexually assaulted him before finally letting him go. The victim identified him from a school yearbook picture. Bailey was first admitted to the Hawthorne Center as a result.

He was let out after fourteen weeks, and by June of the next year he'd been picked up again for threatening a twelve-year-old boy with a knife and fondling his genitals. This resulted in a second stay at Hawthorne. He was discharged after eight weeks as "a model patient throughout his hospitalization."

In May of the next year he accosted a ten-year-old boy with a fishing knife, took him on his bike to an open field where he drugged the boy, pulled down his pants, forced him to take several pills, and choked him for sexual gratification. When the boy came to, Bailey was gone, but the boy was able to identify him. Ron's father, Al, asked that he be readmitted to Hawthorne but he was sent instead to Wayne County Youth Home. The authorities there decided Ron needed long-term care and recommended he be sent back to Hawthorne. In the meantime, he was released to his parents. Apparently, though, that didn't work out and in August, Al called the police, reporting that his son had "flipped." That same day, Ron was admitted to Hawthorne for the third time.

After seven weeks there, during which he was found fondling a younger boy, Ron ran away. When he was apprehended, he was again sent to the Wayne County Youth Home. A couple of months later he was transferred to the Northville Regional Psychiatric Hospital. He tried to escape, and bounced back and forth between the youth home and the hospital.

There was a recurring pattern to Ron's treatment. After an incident and his arrest, he would initially deny any responsibility, constructing an alternate scenario which absolved himself of guilt. For one of the crimes, he said he had choked the boy to keep him quiet so they wouldn't be attacked by nearby construction workers. Eventually, he would admit his responsibility and swear he had changed and that it would never happen again.

By 1977, his primary therapist, Dr. José Tombo, reported that he was making excellent progress. When he was caught using drugs and sexually approaching another patient, Dr. Tombo characterized this as "a normal growth pattern," given the defendant's past psychosexual history. He was released in October 1977 with a discharge diagnosis of "adjustment reaction of adolescence." He was put on five years' probation for the charges outstanding against him and instructed to continue outpatient therapy with Dr. Tombo.

In February 1980 he moved with a friend to Summerfield, Florida, where he stayed until May 1983, working in the tire delivery business. While there, he admitted to accosting and kidnapping several fourteen- to sixteen-year-old boys. His victim of preference was thin and blond and looked like he had at that age. He liked using belts or elastic bands around his or his partners' necks to create an erotic high. He estimated this had happened three to five times, around the Hernando and Daytona Beach areas. On one occasion, he accosted a boy in a mobile home park, saying, "Why don't you suck my dick?" The boy's family called the police and Bailey was charged with contributing to the delinquency of a minor and again put on probation.

On Wednesday, July 18, 1984, two boys found the partially clothed body of fifteen-year-old Kenny Myers of Ferndale, just over the Wayne County line north of Detroit, close to the Middle Rouge River bank in Edward Hines Park, in Westland, just southwest of the city. They flagged down a passing Wayne County sherriff's car. Kenny's mother had reported him missing two days earlier when he didn't return home after dinner. His blue Columbia ten-speed bike was found in Detroit the same day. The blue jersey he'd been wearing was found the next day near a tennis court just outside of the park. He had been strangled with a belt and toxicology tests revealed the presence of alcohol and marijuana in his system.

A witness in Detroit reported she had seen a dirty and damaged brown station wagon with a white top approach a young white male on such a blue bike. The car's driver got out, pushed the boy off the bike, threw him in the car, and sped off. She thought the driver was the boy's father and that the boy had done something wrong. Still concerned, though, she tried to note the license plate number but couldn't read it.

The Myers case remained unsolved, with little progress made until Ronald Bailey was arrested for Shawn Moore's murder. The similarity of the two cases—the abduction from bicycle to car of a slightly built, five-foot-tall, ninety-pound white male, forced to ingest drugs and alcohol, strangulation with a belt—made police think Bailey might be good for this one, too.

Through a name and address found in Bailey's possession, Michigan State Police contacted a young man who admitted he knew Ron, that Ron had had a damaged brown station wagon with a white top the year before, and that Ron had given him beer and marijuana on several occasions. Police traced the car. It turned out to be a 1970 Buick station wagon that Bailey had owned until December 10, 1984, when he traded it in on a 1985 Toyota pickup truck. At the time of Kenny Myers's murder, Ron had been working for Hank Greenfield, owner of A.R.A. Systems Coffee Service in Livonia, and had parked the Buick behind the building and left it there for a month until Greenfield got tired of looking at it and told him he had to move it.

A teenage boy told Livonia police that he had been abducted by someone driving an old Buick station wagon whom he identified as Bailey and driven to Hines Park where this individual performed fellatio on him before driving him back and releasing him near his home. Similar reports came from other teens.

When Kenny Myers's body had been found, something was apparently missing: a black plastic watch Kenny's mom said he had bought at a flea market about a month before he disappeared, with five dollars she had given him. Lieutenant Mike Smith of the Livingston County Sheriff's Department told a task force meeting he thought it strange that after being brought back from Florida on murder charges, Ron Bailey's main concern seemed to be where the cheap black plastic watch that had been taken from him was and whether he could get it back. He later admitted that he had to kill the most beautiful of all the boys—the ones who reminded him of himself.

Now, there are a couple of points to this whole story, though I'm afraid they're repeatedly missed by many supposed professionals.

In preparation for trial, Bailey was examined by a number of psychiatrists and psychologists, some appointed by the prosecution and some by the defense. The defense lawyers thought they had a pretty good case for insanity. After all, he'd been in and out of mental institutions since he was a teenager, and his psychiatric records reflected his claim that he had the classic parental situation of stern, aloof father and domineering, disciplinarian mother who was continually punishing him and warning him about women, and there was his assertion—supported by the claims of other patients—that his psychiatrist at Northville, Dr. José Tombo, had engaged in sex with him on numerous occasions. The story Bailey gave was that he considered these young boys he had abducted his friends, that he hated himself, and when he was killing Shawn, he really believed he was killing his younger self, thereby ridding the world of the harm his adult self would cause.

Okay. But while Ron originally claimed (in keeping with his past history of not owning up to his actions) that Shawn's death was "an accident," the prosecution's psychological team—Harley Stock, Ph.D., and Lynn Blunt, M.D.—got him to admit that as early as when he was driving up to the cabin in Gladwin, Ron knew he would have to kill the boy, that he would not be able to return him alive. As to why he didn't kill Shawn the first night, he replied that they "had not had sex yet." He further admitted that one of his motives for the murder was that he was jealous and killing Shawn would prevent him from having sex with anyone else; presumably, he meant women. While this all certainly points to mental instability, this is not insanity. He had the ability to plan, to organize, to think ahead to his crimes. His reasons for murder betray no lack of appreciation for the difference between right and wrong; rather, they demonstrate a self-centeredness and narcissism which is at the basis of sociopathic—not psychotic—behavior. There is confusion over the difference between insanity and character disorder. A legally insane person cannot distinguish between right and wrong. Someone with a sociopathic character disorder knows the difference but chooses to do what he wants to anyway, out of anger, jealousy, or just because it makes him feel good.

What about the alleged abuse by Dr. Tombo—couldn't that contribute to "insanity"?

Well, if it was true (Dr. Tombo denied it), then it certainly didn't help a boy who already had severe personality problems and feelings of self-loathing. Such action would be a gross and despicable breach of patient-healer trust and should be dealt with in the most vigorous way possible. But something else must be kept in mind, as the prosecution psychiatrists pointed out. By the time Bailey came into contact with Tombo, his pattern of sexual aggression was already well established. We might have hoped for more constructive therapy. We might have hoped for a different home life and upbringing. And we might have hoped for a more effective and discriminating juvenile justice system.

But none of this justifies or explains the willful and premeditated killing of one human being by another. "In all of the defendant's psychiatric history," the prosecution psychiatrists concluded, "there is absolutely no indication that he behaved in any way that would be characterized as representative of an underlying mental illness."

Apparently, the jury in the Livingston County courtroom agreed. Though Bailey took the stand and tried to conjure up the proper emotional responses indicative of contrition and remorse, he fell rather flat. The defense psychiatrist, Dr. Joel Dreyer, diagnosed Bailey as suffering from "pseudopsychopathic schizophrenia." Dr. Stock countered with his own diagnosis: borderline personality disorder, homosexual pedophilia, and sexual sadism that led him to inflict pain on others in order to sexually gratify himself. He said that Bailey had a character disorder which still allowed him to distinguish right from wrong and he had the ability to decide whether or not to harm someone. "The ones who were more resistant got hurt," Stock said. "Those who were compliant were released and sometimes recontacted." This no longer seemed to hold true by the time Bailey encountered Shawn Moore.

In the final analysis, most jurors said it was the use of the belt that convinced them of Bailey's rationality and premeditation. It took over a minute to choke Shawn to death with it, during which time Ron had to hold his hands down and keep him from resisting. The jury found Bailey guilty of kidnapping and premeditated murder. He began serving his sentence in Michigan, but, as with Stuart Knowlton, there were continual threats against his life from other prisoners. He was transferred to a prison out of state for his own safety.

In the aftermath of any violent crime, particularly murder, we try to take away whatever lessons we can from it, essentially by examining the various tragedies.

And in fact, there are a number of tragedies relating to the crimes of Ronald Bailey. For one, authorities did not recognize his earliest actions as serious enough to warrant decisive action. For another, there was little publicity in the Kenny Myers case, which might have encouraged critical information from some member of the public. If there had been more publicity about such details as the type and description of the vehicle the UNSUB was thought to be driving, Bailey's boss, Hank Greenfield, would have reported the car parked behind his office, which he saw and which rankled him every day for a month. And if that had happened, perhaps Shawn Moore would be alive today.

In my opinion, the police did all of this correctly and well in working up Shawn's murder, consulting us at the right time and using our profile to focus their investigation. And certainly I am convinced that because of the way the Moore task force went about their job, other young men are alive today who could have been Ron Bailey's next victims.

The other lesson I take away from the Bailey case is that however noble the callings of psychiatry, psychology, and social work may be, and no matter how hard they strive to help each troubled individual brought before them, from my own long experience I believe you can't simply look at someone like Ron Bailey in isolation as a patient without looking at the totality of his actions. By that I mean that while it's the mental health professional's job to try to help this person, it's just as important to think of the people he's going to interact with if he's allowed back out into the world. (Ron was usually institutionalized for only weeks or months at a time and then released to go back to whatever he'd been doing before.)

There is a natural tendency to want to empathize with the subject, which is why so many psychiatrists don't want to read the crime scene reports or know too much about what the person is accused of. It might bias them, they fear, make them lose their objectivity. To me, this is like an art historian not wanting to see any of Picasso's paintings because it might bias his evaluation of the artist.

Dr. Joel Dreyer, who analyzed his problem as "a post-traumatic stress disorder on top of an already disarrayed mind," went so far as to write, "His encounters in Northville State Hospital, I believe, were as heinous, or more so, than the crimes he committed because the hospital took him in to help him, and as the Hippocratic Oath says, 'Do no harm.'" A page earlier he had written, "I understood at that moment I was sitting not with a victimizer, but with a victim."

Excuse me, doctor, but let's keep our eye on the ball here. Ron Bailey may very well have been victimized in various instances, as many people are, in various ways. But Ron Bailey killed. He took lives that can never be retrieved. No one did that to him. And once we lose sight of the fact that this young man and others of his ilk are very much victimizers, we also lose sight of the Kenny Myerses and Shawn Moores and Cassie Hansens of the world—the true innocents.

The problem with psychiatry in a forensic setting is that it is based on self-reporting. If you go to a therapist as a private patient, it is presumably because you are unhappy or mentally troubled and therefore have a vested interest in telling that therapist the truth so he or she can help you. If you see a therapist as an offender, your goal is to get out of whatever institution you've been placed in and therefore have a vested interest in telling that therapist whatever you have to in order to accomplish your goal. A psychiatrist might hope his patient is getting better; naturally, that will make him feel more effective as a professional and better as a human being. He will want to believe what the subject is telling him and give him a shot back in normal life. But if by doing so, he's possibly putting the lives of more potential victims at risk, then that's a price I, for one, am not willing to have us pay.

Ultimately, we've got to ask ourselves as a society if there's still anything sacred. And if the answer to that question is yes, then I hope the lives of innocent children are always at the top of the list.

CHAPTER 5

For the Children

Walking into the National Center for Missing and Exploited Children in Arlington, Virginia, just outside Washington, D.C., you're at first struck by how normal the reception area seems. It could be the lobby for a business or a law office. The friendly people you meet seem like regular professionals, an image that's hard to reconcile with the horrors you know they deal with every day. But if you look at the walls, covered by posters, photos, and plaques, you start to get a sense of the deep level of commitment and involvement these people give to their work.

Moving down the corridors the mood changes. These walls are covered with photos of smiling, childish faces, many of them with toothless six- or seven-year-old grins, posed in front of a fake forest or pasture in the classic school photo setup. The faces are happy, but you know those children are now in a very different place from the day that picture was taken. Surrounded by these faces, NCMEC staff still smile and greet you, but the atmosphere in here is different: people walk quickly past, or they're on the phone, typing on a computer, taking notes by hand, doing at least two things at once. From them you feel the urgency surrounding their mission: there are so many faces on the walls!

I think to myself that these people face the same overwhelming stresses I faced just before my near-fatal collapse in Seattle: every case is first priority; in every case, time is critical. How can you triage when so many innocent young lives are at stake? How can you stand to take the time for lunch, or go home at the end of the day and unwind, maybe spending time with your own small children? These kids looking out at you—and these are only the small *reported* fraction of all cases of missing and/or abused children—represent the most unspeakable of horrors.

Look at one specific photo—pick any at random—and imagine what that child's been through. Wonder if he or she is still alive, and how long loved ones have been waiting for word. Looking at these faces one by one, you're struck by the fact that these are normal kids. We speak of how beautiful little Cassie Hansen was, or what a promising track star Alison Parrott was, but the fact is child molesters don't prey only on the most attractive or talented.

Many of the children on the wall are victims of opportunity more than specific targets: this little boy went to the bathroom alone; this little girl disappeared walking home from school; this one was born to a woman who, abused as a child herself, lacking self-esteem, vulnerable and lonely, turned to the wrong man for companionship.

There is another wall of smiling faces under the heading "Recovered." When you first see it, you might get goose bumps thinking of emotional reunions. Then they explain: "Recovered" simply means located and returned. It doesn't necessarily mean located and returned alive.

The National Center for Missing and Exploited Children is a private, nonprofit organization that was established in 1984 under the mandate of that year's Missing Children Act. The Center works in cooperation with the U.S. Department of Justice's Office of Juvenile Justice and Delinquency Prevention and has branch offices in California, Florida, New York, South Carolina, and Virginia. In 1990, it merged with the Adam Walsh Child Resource Center, founded by John and Reve Walsh after their six-year-old son was abducted and murdered in Florida in 1981. Today, as described in one NCMEC brochure, it "spearheads national efforts to locate and recover missing children and raises public awareness about ways to prevent child abduction, molestation and sexual exploitation."

Through the Adam Walsh Children's Fund, it also provides assistance to missing children's families, works toward legislative reforms that would protect children, and educates and motivates families and concerned citizens to get involved personally in protecting our nation's children.

Since there is no federal law requiring police or other agencies to report cases of missing children to the NCMEC, and since the stigma attached to the crimes—and the fear and embarrassment of victims—is so great, there is only sketchy data on how big the problem really is in this country. According to the National Committee to Prevent Child Abuse, there were about 350,000 reported cases of sexual abuse of children in the United States in 1995, about ninety percent of which were perpetrated by someone the children knew—usually a family member. In its first ten years of operation, the NCMEC's hotline, 1-800-THE-LOST, took more than 900,000 phone calls from people who wanted to make reports on lost or potentially exploited children. In approximately the same time period, the Center assisted in the recovery of more than 28,000.

The best way to protect your children, though, is to know your enemy. Because of my job and the things I've seen, I probably went a little overboard with Pam and my kids, but it's important to be aware.

Even more than with other violent crimes, people are always asking me what kind of person could do this? What kind of monster could abduct, molest, and/or take the life of an innocent child? Since we know now that the image of the scary-looking stranger in the trench coat is not representative of the bulk of child molesters or abductors, how can we recognize them?

As with perpetrators of other types of offenses, these subjects exhibit behaviors—both before and after committing their crimes—that can help reveal their secret identity.

We'll start with sexual predators, considered even by other violent criminals to be the lowest of life forms. Just as we talk about the different types of rapists (so-called gentleman rapist versus a sadistic or power assurance rapist), there are different types of child molesters. Special Agent Ken Lanning, my associate for many years at Quantico and among the world's leading experts on crimes against children, has studied and published extensively on this subject. He gives the definition of a child molester, from a law enforcement perspective, as someone who "engages in illegal sexual activity with children." Children are defined as individuals who are under eighteen years old when the criminal activity takes place. Beyond that broad definition, a host of experts including Ken and Dr. Park Elliott Dietz—the noted forensic psychiatrist who has served as a consultant to my unit—define different types of child molesters.

First, there are the true pedophiles—people who prefer sex with children and have them as the subjects of their fantasies—and then there are those whose primary sexual drives and fantasies are directed at adults, but who will have sex with a child to fulfill some other need: perhaps they feel too inadequate to approach the true object of their desires, using a child as a substitute. Dietz and Lanning classify these two types of offenders as preferential child molesters (true pedophiles who molest) and situational child molesters (the child is more a victim of opportunity than a preferential victim).

It is possible for a pedophile to go through his whole life without molesting a child, even having a sexual relationship with an adult, satisfying his urges in other ways: fantasizing about children, masturbating with dolls, or perhaps picking an adult sexual partner who is childlike in some way. His lover may be a flat-chested woman, small in stature, or someone who engages in baby talk, for example. There is nothing criminal in these activities. A pedophile may also hire adult prostitutes to act out his fantasies. Again, at this point, no child has been victimized or exploited. Like someone with a foot fetish, as long as the fetishist's lover doesn't mind parading around in high heels, letting him paint her toenails, or whatever, no harm has been done.

But as Ken points out, a lot of these guys are also heavily into pornography featuring children: photos, videos, magazines. They collect and trade child porn the way kids collect baseball cards. Now, from my research and experience, I know that a lot of violent offenders buy and collect pornography, particularly bondage and sadomasochistically related. It's one of the elements we routinely look for when preparing affidavits for search warrants of the residences of sexually sadistic rape and murder suspects. But I'm not going to tell you that pornography fuels the desires of someone who wasn't already thinking in that direction. I have often seen an offender stage a scene to resemble something he's read or seen, as Tien Poh Su did when he killed Deliana Heng up in Canada. But these guys would have done it one way or another if the desire was there. The fact of the matter is that most people who buy and read pornography are not at all dangerous and never commit antisocial offenses. So I'm not about to advocate restricting the First Amendment for the sake of the small percentage of men who consume pornography to bolster their violent and misogynistic conduct.

But child pornography is different. The mere fact that it exists means that a crime has taken place. Just by looking at this stuff, or passing it on to others, the pedophile is perpetuating a crime that occurred against a child and is therefore exploiting the child—whether or not he was present at the original crime scene. Like adult-killers Paul Bernardo, Bittaker and Norris, and Lake and Ng, many molesters make their own child pornography, carefully keeping a record of their illegal sexual encounters so they can relive them over and over. Others may be involved in so-called child sex rings, where one or more adults (usually a trusted friend, not a family member of the victims) has a pattern of abuse and exploitation of several child victims, who may be both male and female. But even if child pornography is purchased mail order, off-the-shelf, by someone who's never touched a child, anyone collecting it is guilty of exploitation. It's the same as photos taken of an adult rape victim.

Although the pedophile may think nothing's wrong with using the pornography as fodder for his fantasies, a child is still being victimized. And as with any such paraphilia or fetish, the potential is always there for escalation. There's a danger that there may come a point where the fantasies aren't enough and the pedophile feels the need to act on his desires with a real child—maybe by hiring a child prostitute, molesting a child he knows, or abducting a stranger. While he may draw a distinction between what he rationalizes as sex-for-hire and the abduction and rape of a neighborhood kid, the moment he involves that child, criminal exploitation has occurred. Realistically, we don't need to fear that every guy who has sexual fantasies about children will actually molest a child, but I certainly consider it a red flag to be watched.

I also agree with Ken Lanning that just as not all pedophiles are molesters, not all molesters are pedophiles. A variety of motivations may drive the so-called situational molester. Some may be acting out aggressions they are only able to express against the most vulnerable of victims. These subjects would also be likely to target the elderly, or prostitutes—other relatively easy targets.

A risk with these individuals is that their behavior, too, may escalate. What may begin as an impulsive, isolated event against a child may turn out to be just a trial run if he succeeds without getting caught. Their crimes may grow more violent; they grow bolder as their criminal career progresses, attacking more victims and taking more time with them to act out their fantasies more completely. We saw this type of evolution with the Arthur Shawcross case in Rochester, New York. One of the ways Gregg McCrary figured out how to catch the killer was realizing he was returning to the dump sites to spend more time with the bodies of his victims. And once he was caught, it turned out that his first two victims had been not prostitutes or homeless women, but a young girl and boy.

There are probably a lot more situational than preferential child molesters, although a pedophile who molests will likely molest far more children over the course of his lifetime because that is where his primary sexual urges lie. It's what he's going to be thinking about all the time. It is possible that a situational offender may molest just one child, one time, or it may become a long-term behavior for him.

In *Child Molesters: A Behavioral Analysis for Law Enforcement Officers Investigating Cases of Child Sexual Exploitation,* published by the NCMEC, Ken outlines four types of situational child molesters: repressed; morally indiscriminate; sexually indiscriminate; and inadequate. Repressed types are guys you find abusing their own children because they're most readily available. Not surprisingly, they tend to have very low self-esteem and have sex with children as a substitute for adults they can't approach. This type of subject is more likely to use a lure or con rather than force to get a child to go with him, and the incidents are usually linked to some precipitating stressor in his life.

The morally indiscriminate type would also molest his own children, although he will manipulate, lure, or even use force to obtain other victims. This subject is probably abusive in virtually all areas of his life: he abuses his wife and friends, is a liar and a cheat at home and at work, and he has no qualms about stealing something he wants. Because this type of subject has no conscience, it is not difficult for him to act on impulse.

Both this type and the sexually indiscriminate molester, if asked why they molested a child, might think to themselves, "Why not?" but the sexually indiscriminate molester takes that thought a step further. He abuses children because he is bored and the experience seems new, exciting, and different to him. Ken describes these types as "try-sexuals," meaning that they'll try anything. These guys might pursue group sex with adults, spouse swapping, bondage, whatever—acts which aren't criminal with consenting adults—but then they may involve a child (even their own) in that sexual experimentation. Compared with the other types of situational child molesters, these subjects generally come from a higher socioeconomic level and are more prone to molest multiple victims. Whereas the other types are into child pornography, this type might have a much more diverse collection of erotica.

Finally, the inadequate type of situational child molester is much like the subjects described in other chapters. In fact, in my unit we dealt mostly with the morally indiscriminate and inadequate types. This subject is a social outsider. He'll have few friends his own age as a teenager and may continue to live with his parents or an older relative as he grows older. For this subject, children are nonthreatening, like his other potential targets—the elderly, prostitutes. His victim could be a child he knows well or a stranger he can use as a substitute for a peer he can't approach. The subject is not so much naturally sexually attracted to children as he is sexually curious but insecure around adults. If he collects pornography, it will involve adults, not children. Because he is so withdrawn from society, the danger is that his hostility and anger could build up until he finds an outlet for them.

This subject can be very dangerous, then, if his rage explodes, often leading to torturing and killing his victim.

I dealt with a combination inadequate and morally indiscriminate type in a case I handled in the early 1980s, just when the profiling program at Quantico was getting geared up.

The police department in Dickinson, North Dakota, is proud of the work they do and they should be. In March 1983, they had only one unsolved murder case on their books. But that one case was a particularly gruesome double homicide that was almost two years old. They asked for a profile that might help in their investigation.

As they described it, early in the morning of November 16, 1981, a transient worker staying at the Swanson Motel in Dickinson stopped by the motel office for a cup of coffee, as he did every morning. But this time, he found the body of the manager, fifty-two-year-old Priscilla Dinkel, lying face-down on the floor, bound and gagged, with an electrical cord tied around her wrists and neck. Her nightgown and housecoat had been pulled down, partly exposing her back.

When the police arrived, they noted splinters of wood in her hair and made another horrible discovery: searching the premises, they found Ms. Dinkel's granddaughter, seven-year-old Dannelle Lietz, in the back bedroom, also murdered. Her body was found under the covers on the bed, with another cord around her neck. There were ligature marks on her wrists. Autopsies indicated both victims died as a result of strangulation and Dannelle had been sexually assaulted.

In the year and a half since the crime, investigators had followed many leads but still had nothing concrete.

In evaluating the case, I started with victimology. Priscilla Dinkel had recently moved to Dickinson to take the job as manager of the motel, which catered to transient workers in the area's booming energy industry. Rooms typically were rented by the week, and the motel was located in a part of town whose character had changed quickly with the influx of temporary workers to feed the industry's growth. In fact, the chief of police had warned locals to start locking their doors, a practice previously unheard of up there.

Although there was nothing in her personal background

to indicate Priscilla Dinkel was high-risk, her job, the location of the motel, and the transient nature of the place led me to classify her as a high-risk victim. I felt her granddaughter, on the other hand, was simply at the wrong place at the wrong time. At her young age, she had no control over her life or her environment and I saw her as a victim of opportunity.

The UNSUB in this case had time to tie up both victims and brutalize them. Ms. Dinkel was not sexually assaulted, but was rendered unconscious through blunt-force trauma to her head. The offender also cut her bra and underwear, fulfilling some need of his and displaying hatred and aggression, dominance and control. He struck Dannelle in the head at some point, too, fracturing her skull. Before he left, he also took money from the motel's cash box.

Clearly, he spent quite a bit of time at the scene and appeared to be comfortable there, leading me to profile an offender who knew his victims and the area. It did not appear that he went there that night specifically to kill them, though. More likely, the homicides occurred spontaneously. The crime scene reflected elements of both disorganization and inventiveness; the offender was adaptable, using electrical cords from lamps and a vacuum cleaner to tie up his victims.

A mixed scene of this nature led me to believe that alcohol was a factor that night and that the UNSUB probably had a history of alcoholism. With the level of aggression demonstrated against the older victim, I figured he was one of those Jekyll and Hyde drinkers. Normally a loner—not at all a ladies' man—a louder, more aggressive side of his personality would come out after a few drinks, although he'd only be able to express this to people he felt he could dominate. He would have difficulties in any relationships with women.

Since people don't just jump into double homicide, this subject would have been in trouble with the law before. He might have done time for crimes like assault, robbery, or burglary. Offenders leaving this kind of crime scene are typically of average intelligence, but this guy probably had not finished high school. When he had a job, it would involve physical rather than intellectual work, such as a laborer, mechanic, or truck driver. He would not keep himself neat; he'd appear in need of a bath, shave, and haircut.

Of all the behavioral clues left throughout the apartment, the most significant came from the crime scene in the bedroom with the young girl. When he attacked Dannelle, her grandmother was out of the picture and he could act out his fantasies, easily dominating and controlling her. In his assault he was consuming her, reinforcing his power over the situation. The fact that he covered her up with the bedclothes, however, said a lot about his feelings after the fact. He was trying to eliminate the assault, feeling disgust and distaste over his actions. With this apparent change of heart, he felt some remorse over her death, in contrast to the apparent justification he felt for his actions against her grandmother.

Whenever you have any signs of remorse like that at the scene, there's going to be spillover into the UNSUB's post-offense behavior. He would be compelled to talk to someone, to find out what the police were doing regarding the investigation, he'd increase his alcohol consumption, alter his physical appearance in some way, maybe visit the girl's grave.

The only area of the UNSUB's life that I had trouble with was his age. As I've mentioned, this aspect is often problematic. I've seen subjects like this range in age from the late teens to early fifties, so I advised police to focus on the post-offense behavior and the other elements of the profile instead of looking for an offender of a particular age. I also warned that after the publicity died down, the subject had probably skipped town. As I always do, I told the investigators to give me a call if they wanted to discuss things further or brainstorm on proactive and/or interrogation techniques.

Dickinson police continued the investigation, interviewing nearly thirty suspects. Only one fingerprint was recovered at the crime scene and that turned out to belong to one of the investigators. Later, when DNA testing was available, police went to reexamine evidence and found it had been destroyed when a freezer in the lab malfunctioned. No witnesses were ever found to shed a clue about the events of that night.

However, none of this stopped the tenacious police in Dickinson. At one point, they even consulted a psychic from out of state, sending personal effects of the victims and photos of possible suspects and known sex offenders in the area. She chose one man from among them as the killer. Investigators' suspicions about this guy grew when the sheriff's office in Missoula, Montana, contacted them after he allegedly exposed himself to neighborhood kids. His friends told the sheriff he'd been talking about these murders in Dickinson. Police interviewed this suspect extensively and asked him to take a polygraph, which he refused. They also took a dental impression from him to compare with bite marks on Dannelle's right cheek, but the results were inconclusive.

Jerry Theisman of the North Dakota Bureau of Criminal Investigation, a graduate of the FBI National Academy, contacted us in December 1985 for an evaluation of this man as a viable suspect for the double murder. We explained to him that it would be highly unlikely for someone to deescalate the level of violence in this manner. After having essentially gotten away with a brutal rape and double murder, this UNSUB wasn't going to risk getting caught exposing himself in his own neighborhood. Also, the Dickinson killer had taken money from the crime scene. This guy didn't seem to be hard up for cash.

Still undaunted, Dickinson PD told us there was another suspect who met nearly all the points in my original profile and who was given a polygraph early on in the investigation, which gave indication of significant deception. The problem was, he'd left town and no one knew where he went. His name was William Thomas Reager and he'd lived in the motel at the time of the double homicide. He not only knew the victims but used to baby-sit Dannelle and seemed to have a crush on her mother, Melody. The family noticed that when he visited he would invite the child to sit on his lap, always putting his hand somewhere on her leg, which made them uncomfortable. Just a few nights before her murder, Dannelle had asked her mother not to allow him to baby-sit. The night after the murders, Reager was arrested for drunk driving and was interviewed by police. Now, years later, Dickinson police were searching for Reager's whereabouts.

By 1991, Sergeant Chuck Rummel had taken over the case and contacted us again. I was out of town when he called, so Jud Ray got involved and stayed with the case until its conclusion. Rummel had tracked Reager to Batesville, Arkansas, aided by a National Crime Information Center computer search run by a nearby county. Dickinson officials contacted police in Batesville to let them know Reager was a suspect in a double murder. Interestingly enough, authorities there were working on the unsolved murder of an elderly woman in 1988. In June of that year, the body of seventy-seven-year-old Della T. Harding was found under a bridge in a dry riverbed. The previous day she had been bound, beaten, and strangled in her home after an apparent break-in. At the time of her murder, Reager lived about a mile from Harding.

After tracking his suspect further, Rummel finally got to interview Reager in the sheriff's office in Clinton, Arkansas. He consulted Jud Ray before making the trip. Armed with our prediction that the offender would feel remorseful about the rape-murder of Dannelle Lietz, and with results from the original polygraph which indicated he'd been lying, Rummel and Jerry Theisen kept at him until he finally confessed, providing details on the Dickinson murders that had not been previously released to the public or even known to police, such as the fact that he took more than cash from the crime scene that night.

According to Reager, he'd gone to the office to talk to Mrs. Dinkel about her daughter Melody. He wanted to get to know Melody better, an idea her mother scoffed at. Instead of being discouraged, Reager grew enraged and "went berserk" by his own description, hitting her with a piece of wood from the table. Reager said Dannelle came in from the bedroom while he was tying up her grandmother. As I visualized it, he had to maintain his control of the situation and he did this with his attack on the girl. He admitted that in addition to the money, he took a picture of Dannelle and Melody and a decorative platter from the scene—items not previously reported missing. The killer kept a memento of his crime.

Reager was a white male, thirty-nine years of age at the time of the crime, with a history of offenses that included grand larceny, passing bad checks, burglary, and petty larceny. Of average intelligence, he worked as a laborer, truck driver, dishwasher, and carnival worker. Photos showed he always looked sloppy. He changed his appearance after the murders: he stopped dying his hair and let it go completely gray. He had a history of drinking and a drunk driving arrest, and his difficulties with women included separation from his second wife—whom he wed while still married to his first wife. He was reportedly getting ready to marry a third when he was arrested. The second wife confirmed that he had a "nonfeeling" personality, that they'd had marital difficulties and that he drank frequently. Finally, his version of the events of that night confirmed anger and hostility toward Ms. Dinkel, who didn't take him seriously as a suitor for her daughter.

Along with his arrest in March of 1991 for the North Dakota crimes, Reager was also charged with capital murder in the 1988 Harding case in Arkansas. Investigators in both states noted that he'd traveled throughout the country in the ten years between the Dickinson case and his arrest, and police in Dallas, Texas, announced they were looking into possible ties to the murders of several elderly women there.

We have to be grateful for the Dickinson authorities' dogged pursuit. Over the course of a decade, new people were assigned to the case and each one took up the mantle with dedication and professionalism. Oftentimes, once the initial momentum is lost, old cases appear so stale no one wants to work them and they just sit there. There's no doubt in my mind that Reager would have continued to let his impulses lead him, killing until he was either locked up for another offense, died, or just plain grew too old to do it. But that would have taken a long, long time.

In the Batesville case, Harding was another older, female, vulnerable victim known by Reager, who'd visited her residence before. Like the Dickinson victims, she'd received a blow to the head but died as a result of strangulation. The offender used electrical cords to strangle his victims and took money from both crime scenes. Reager confessed to that killing, as well as the other two, then later waffled over his involvement, although he also admitted his guilt to his fiancée. As fate would have it, laws of nature caught up with

Reager before the laws of man could. After he was charged with the three murders—and after the lead prosecutor in Arkansas, Don McSpadden, announced he would seek the death penalty in the Harding case—Reager had a fatal heart attack. Although you like to be able to bring a guy like this to trial, especially after so many years, appeals in death sentence cases in Arkansas were running at least ten years at the time. For Frank Dinkel, husband of one murder victim and grandfather to another, closure came sooner. At news of Reager's arrest, he was quoted by the *Bismarck Tribune* as saying, "I was hoping it would be solved before I died."

Little Dannelle Lietz was clearly a victim of opportunity—raped and murdered by a situational child molester simply because she was there. Preferential or pedophile child molesters, on the other hand, have a clear sexual and erotic focus on children. They are not driven by situational stress or emotional insecurity; they simply prefer sex with children. They have predictable behavior patterns that they exhibit time and time again. This ritual behavior is a signature, something they have to do as part of their sexual activity, even if it makes carrying out the crime riskier or more difficult, like abducting a specific type of victim using a well-rehearsed script, even if this victim is hard to get without being observed and even if the script will slow his getaway.

They also tend to be of a higher socioeconomic background than the situational molesters. They are constantly driven to molest young people, unlike situational types who might molest a child once in their lifetime. While all preferential child molesters share the same general sexual orientation, they're very specific and individual in their choice of victim, with both gender and age preferences (although more prefer boy victims to girls and the younger the preferred victim, the less preferential the sex of the child becomes—those who look for toddlers tend to be less discriminating as to gender).

Ken Lanning outlines three types of preferential molester, based on the different but predictable behavior patterns they exhibit: seduction, introverted, and sadistic.

When you read in the media about a local teacher charged

with fondling or raping one of his students, or a coach accused of behaving inappropriately with the kids on his team, you're dealing with a seduction-type molester. This subject actually courts his victims with gifts and/or attention, slowly winning their trust, lowering their inhibitions. He is very good at communicating with children and at choosing victims who will be most susceptible to his ploys. A child who receives little affection at home, for example, will be flattered and will appreciate his attention.

This is where your natural instinct can help you protect your kids. If someone seems to be paying too much attention, seems a little too focused on children, and spends a disproportionate amount of time in their company instead of with adults, the warning lights should go on. I'm not saying that every supportive coach or lonely, elderly man on your block is a sexual deviant waiting to prey on your child—far from it. We don't want to become so suspicious of people that we sap all the joy and satisfaction out of human relationships. But be sure to supervise your children's relationships.

You don't have to tell your ten-year-old you think her softball coach might be a pervert, just watch over her, go to the games, and if you're suspicious, don't let her be in a situation where they'll be alone together. Also, try to develop a nurturing relationship so she'll be less easily swayed by attention from someone else. I didn't have a lot of time for my family when I was with the Bureau, which I regret. But I hope my kids felt close to me and understood that if anybody ever did or said anything that made them at all uncomfortable they could come to me or Pam. These guys tend to pick lonely, poorly supervised kids. You don't have to be Supermom or Superdad; just stay aware of who your kid's friends are and pay attention to that little voice in your head.

A lot of these seduction types can be involved with several victims at once—their own personal child sex ring. Victims may be children in his Scout troop, his classroom, or his neighborhood. He spends time with them, listens to them, and knows how to communicate with—and manipulate—them. Because he's an adult, a lot of well-behaved kids will feel they should listen to him and he'll use that authority and status to his advantage. If none of his young victims reports him early on, the tide won't turn until he's ready to end one of his relationships, when a child victim grows up and becomes too old or mature to appeal to him any longer. This is the point when most victims report the exploitation, unless the molester's threats and possibly even physical abuse keep them in line—probably the same means he used to prevent them from leaving or reporting him before he's ready to move on.

Unlike the seduction type, other molesters with the same drive for sex with children simply don't have the interpersonal and social skills to lure their victims. The introverted type is more like the cliché of the creepy stranger in the raincoat in that he's more likely to hang around parks or playgrounds, watching kids. You'll be able to spot him—he may look like he's ready to flash his victims, and at times he'll do that. His sexual activity will be limited to brief encounters and he usually targets strangers or much younger children. He may act out his fantasies by making obscene telephone calls to children, exposing himself, or having sex with child prostitutes. If he can't find any other way to obtain victims, he may even marry a woman with young children or have his own with her; they will then be his convenient victims from infancy.

The most horrifying and physically dangerous preferential child molester, though, is the sadistic type. Like sadistic rapists and killers of adults, they need to cause pain—physical and/or psychological—to be aroused and satisfied sexually. A sadistic type of molester will use either trickery or force to gain control of his victims and then torture them in some way for his sexual gratification. Although there seem to be fewer sadistic molesters, these are the most likely to abduct and murder their victims.

What's also frightening is that there have been cases where seduction-type offenders have turned sadistic. It's not clear whether these guys have had sadistic drives all along which surfaced later, maybe triggered by some stressor, or if they developed over time, gaining confidence and experience from their earlier exploits.

While we can't say the same for situational child molesters, pedophiles exhibit very predictable behaviors, many of which a parent can recognize. As a teenager, the pedophile may have very little social contact with other teens: his sexual interest is already directed toward children. As an adult, he tends to move frequently and often unexpectedly, as suspicious parents or law enforcement in effect run him out of town. If he joins the military, he may be discharged with no reason given. In many cases, the subject will have a long history of prior arrests, including molestation or abuse charges, as well as trouble with child labor laws, passing bad checks, or impersonating an officer. If there are prior arrests for child molestation, he may have been involved with multiple victims—if he molests one child from a neighborhood group, he probably at least attempted to molest others.

Once we can review all his crimes, you'll see that a high level of planning (and risk) went into repeated attempts to lure children. Unlike the situational molester, a pedophile puts a lot of time and energy into developing the perfect approach, which he may practice in order to attain a skillful delivery. His lifestyle will reflect the fact that he prefers children to adult sexual partners. These days, with "returning to the nest" becoming more popular, a twenty-five-year-old single man living with his parents is not unusual. As he grows older, though, he may draw attention to himself if he never dates women. He may also live alone, in a house decorated in a way that will appeal to the age/sex of his preferred victim. Depending on that category, he might have toys or dolls or all manner of games and amusements that he wouldn't have in any other context.

The subject may be in a relationship with a woman but it will be one of extremes: the woman will be either weak and childlike or dominating and much stronger than he is. Although most girlfriends or wives don't want to discuss their intimate lives, if you could interview them confidentially, they might admit that their husband or lover has some kind of sexual problem. He is also a collector of child pornography, possibly including photos he's taken himself. Like the guy I pointed out to Pam at the girls' dance recital, they may be aroused by photos of children who are not undressed or posed in specifically sexual ways. He may take his camera to the park and shoot roll after roll of film, fantasizing about the children once the pictures are developed. Keep in mind that a pedophile can be turned on by the children's section of the Macy's catalogue the same way most normal men enjoy perusing Victoria's Secret.

Although many pedophiles successfully blend into the social fabric—at least for a while—some aspects of their lifestyle do tend to set off warning buzzers. People who seem excessively interested in our children make us distrustful. An adult who hangs around in arcades, malls, and parks, who seems to have no friends his own age appears out of place. A pedophile knows his sexual tendencies must remain secret so it is hard for him to connect with other adults in any meaningful social way. Often, adult friends are also pedophiles since they offer validation and reassurance.

This type of subject generally uses idealized language, referring to children as innocent, pure, and clean, for example. He may also talk (or write) about children as "objects, projects, or possessions." Ken Lanning cites excerpts from letters such as, "This kid has low mileage," or "I've been working on this project for six months."

They will also be very specific in their choice of young friends, though appearance will be more important than actuality; in other words, if a man has a preference for ten-year-old girls, a fourteen-year-old who looks and acts ten is preferable to a ten-year-old who looks fourteen.

Keep in mind that any one of these elements does not make your neighbor a child molester. Taken all together, though, they may indicate some danger. As with any other situation we face as parents, we need to exercise common sense and trust our instincts. The descriptions can help us recognize potential dangers, but they're no substitute for careful, attentive parenting, child safety training, and, in some cases, just plain luck.

There are some cases where the parents cannot protect the child, or at least one parent can't because he is the problem. As hard as it is for the rest of us to imagine, many victims are abused by members of their own family, the same people most children turn to for guidance, love, and support. Incestuous child molesters can fit any of the profiles discussed earlier, from repressed to seduction types. And they can be ruthless and calculating in their pursuit of victims: an introverted pedophile may marry and have sex with his wife solely to produce a child he can molest (which is risky for him because he has no guarantee that the child will be of his preferred gender); a seduction-type molester may marry or befriend women who have children the right sex and age, offering to be a father figure for the children. When the children in the family grow too old to appeal to him any longer, he'll move on to another family situation and start again. These subjects will only have sex with the wife or girlfriend when absolutely necessary, and then must fantasize about children or may ask the woman to dress as a child or talk baby talk.

And it's not only fathers who do this. Peter Banks, director of outreach at the NCMEC, who spent years on the police force in Washington, D.C., investigating child abuse cases, tells of a heartbreaking case where two police sergeants he met—married to each other—were having trouble with their oldest son. It started with bad grades and generally disrespectful behavior, escalating into petty crimes like shoplifting and finally culminated in a crime spree where the teenager went down to Georgia, stole a car, and got caught robbing a convenience store. As he was being led away, cuffed, his mother asked him if there was anything they could do to make sure his younger brother didn't grow up like him.

"Yeah," the boy replied. "Keep him away from Grandpa." The woman's father had been living with the family and apparently molesting her oldest son for years, right under their roof. She effectively lost her son and her father the same day.

Why wouldn't this boy tell his parents the awful truth sooner? Victims of incest have so much to lose by reporting their abuse. If you think about it, our society punishes these young victims in so many inadvertent ways. In addition to the embarrassment, fear, and humiliation, think about what happens to a child who reports one of his family members. In the best-case scenario, where action is taken immediately to protect the child, the molester isn't removed from his environment, the victim is. The child loses his house, his siblings, his friends, his school, his dog—everything. In the worst case, the person he turns to for help is either unable or unwilling to help, reinforcing to that kid that he's not worth the time or trouble to help, psychologically traumatizing the child further by sending the message that the abuser's threats were accurate, and what would happen if he told anyone is true.

It's also very difficult for a child abused by a nonfamily member to report the situation. In the beginning, a victim won't tell anyone because he's flattered by the attention and doesn't know what's coming. Later, that molester is just as expert at keeping the child silent as he was at the initial seduction. With all types of molesters, the child victim may be afraid that he or his family members will be hurt physically by his tormentor.

Other emotions also come into play—embarrassment, confusion. The molester may emotionally blackmail the child. And since many are expert at making sure they always have access to children (as a Little League coach or just the "nice guy" who always takes the neighborhood kids camping or on other outings), they can even use group dynamics to keep their victims in line, using competition or peer pressure to keep recruiting new kids and rotating older ones out without being discovered.

The adult molester is more experienced, older, more resourceful, dangerous, and far more manipulative than a child is. The only real protection your child has is the security and self-confidence you give him and continually reinforce.

Ken Lanning describes the predictable post-accusation stages child molesters go through when faced with the risk of a criminal investigation or prosecution. Not surprisingly, the initial reaction is total denial. He may act surprised, shocked, even indignant upon hearing of the claim against him. He may try to explain the action as something the child misunderstood: "Is it a crime to hug a child?" Depending on his social support structure, he may have family, neighbors, or co-workers to back him up and attest to his character.

If there is cold evidence that makes it impossible for him to deny the charges, he may try to minimize them: maybe he touched one child, or it only happened once, or he fondled the child but never for sexual gratification. Often the molester knows the laws and would rather admit to a lesser offense. In these cases, sometimes victims may inadvertently help the offender because of their embarrassment. Adolescent boys, for example, may deny that sexual acts took place even if investigators have found photos proving that they did. Or victims may play down how many times "it" happened.

Another common offender reaction is justification: the molester may claim that he gives the child more attention than the parents do, so it makes more sense for him to teach the child about sex, or maybe he's been under a lot of stress and/or drinking too much. These guys are constantly trying to justify their urges and actions to themselves—they don't want to believe they're sexually deviant criminals. The most common justification usually blames the victim in some way: the victim seduced him and he didn't know how old she was, or the victim is really a child prostitute. Even if that were so, a crime has still been committed since consent is completely irrelevant when sexual activity involves a child.

Along with the justifications come fabrications, and the cleverer the molester, the more intriguing the lie. There was one pedophile who said some children made a sex video and when he found out about it, he kept it to show to their parents. Less creative but equally desperate molesters may suddenly develop mental illness, or play the sympathy line, hoping that remorse and strong ties to the community will make people feel sorry for a troubled but basically good guy. In a sick, backward way, they will try to defend themselves with their contributions to their community, like volunteer work with kids, which only exist to provide access to children.

There is also always the possibility that the molester will try to cop a plea to a lesser crime to avoid public trial. One advantage is that the young victim won't have to suffer the trauma of testifying in court, but it can be confusing in cases where the offender pleads "guilty but not guilty." He could plead guilty without admitting that he committed a crime, or he could plead not guilty by reason of insanity. In the end, the public may never know what the molester did and the child may wonder why his tormentor isn't considered guilty by the law.

Finally, like a lot of criminals who lose control of their

lives once they're found out, any child molester who's been arrested is a high suicide risk. And since a lot of them come from middle-class backgrounds with no history of previous arrests, if a suicide occurs, it's possible that the police will be blamed for the death—and, again, the child victim or victims will be left confused.

Like the boy abused by his grandfather who got in trouble with the law, many child molesters were themselves victims of some form of abuse as children. While this doesn't excuse their behavior, it illustrates the cycle of victim/victimization we see over and over again. As Peter Banks puts it, walk into a police department and look at the names of children in the abuse/exploitation files. Then look in the files of juvenile delinquents. Finally, look in the files on prostitution and violent crimes. You'll find many of the same names in all three. Although not every abused child ends up in the later files, virtually everyone who does get there started out as an abused child. They may be future victimizers (of children and/or adults) or what we call "professional victims"— women who keep getting involved with abusive men, or turn to prostitution at a young age, for example. As a society, we have to be prepared to reap what we sow. If we see something that's not quite right about a child's living arrangements and we don't try to deal with it today, we're running the risk that we'll have to deal with it down the road.

Richard Allen Davis, the man convicted of kidnapping and murdering twelve-year-old Polly Klaas in Petaluma, California, in October 1993, claimed his bad childhood made him what he is. In closing arguments during the penalty phase of his trial, the defense portrayed the defendant's mother as an emotionally distant woman who once held her son's hand over a flame and virtually abandoned the boy after divorcing his father. In a desperate but unsuccessful bid to avoid the death penalty, the defense also claimed his father was abusive, once severely injuring his son's jaw with a punch.

In contrast to Davis's background, what's particularly heartbreaking about Polly's case is that her parents lost their child from an environment they'd tried to make the safest of all safe havens—her own home. For an abductor, this is a very high-risk crime.

Late one night, Davis quietly broke into Polly's mother's house in Petaluma and abducted the girl at knifepoint in front of two of her friends who were there for a slumber party. At the time, Polly's mother and half-sister were asleep in nearby bedrooms. The abduction was considered so high-risk for the offender that just about everybody working the early investigation suspected it had to be an inside job: the offender had to be someone who had access to the house. Early on, police speculated that Polly's father, divorced from her mother and living elsewhere, may have somehow been involved. The ordinarily sleepy northern California community grew even more shocked and terrified as it became apparent to them and to investigators that he had nothing to do with the crime—a stranger had invaded their home.

Ironically, in the first few hours as investigators were looking into Polly's father as a possible suspect, Davis had a run-in with sheriff's deputies near Santa Rosa, just twenty-five miles north of Petaluma. Investigating a trespassing call, they found Davis trying to get his white Ford Pinto out of a ditch. They questioned him, searched his car, and let him go, unaware of the description of a wanted man put out by the Petaluma police and unaware that Davis had temporarily hidden the girl—still alive—nearby. Davis returned to his victim, strangled her, and left her body in a shallow grave alongside a freeway.

It was another, more successful encounter between Davis and police that eventually led to resolution for the Klaas family. Davis was arrested for drunk driving and police matched his palm print to one left by Polly's abductor. Along with his confession, he provided a description of where he left her body. Later, in the trial, the defense claimed the abduction and murder came as the result of a botched burglary attempt and denied that he tried to assault Polly sexually. Prosecutors, however, presented witnesses who placed him in her neighborhood just days before the abduction, indicating he'd stalked her, which fit with an earlier pattern of assaults against women. In the end, the jury didn't buy his claims.

Clearly, parents can't be expected to stand as armed

guards over their children as they sleep. In this case, it was the justice system that failed to protect the child. At the time of the abduction and murder, Davis was on parole, having served half of a sixteen-year sentence for an earlier kidnapping. His adult life had largely been spent in prison for one crime after another and, like a lot of offenders, Davis had been growing more and more violent with each crime. Instead of being rehabilitated, after release from prison his crimes escalated. Davis's record included convictions for assault with a deadly weapon, kidnapping, and robbery. The prosecution in the Klaas case introduced testimony of some of his earlier victims, still suffering from the terror of their attacks, to reinforce that this horrible crime was just one piece of a larger, dangerous pattern of behavior. In closing arguments, prosecutor Greg Jacobs called the abduction and murder "a grievous affront to humanity" and apparently the voting public of California agreed. Polly's case is considered largely responsible for the state's passage of one of the nation's toughest versions of a "three strikes" law, mandating life sentences for repeat offenders.

In addition to a difficult childhood, Davis's defense team stressed his troubles with alcohol and substance abuse. I can sympathize with a person truly making an effort to overcome these problems and do something positive with his life, but Davis made a conscious choice when he committed his crimes. Fortunately, in Polly's case, the jury held him accountable. Although his defense team tried to convince jurors that his life should be spared because Davis was remorseful, their client brazenly indicated otherwise, making an obscene gesture for media cameras when he heard the guilty verdict. For his conviction of first-degree murder with special circumstances of kidnapping, burglary, robbery, and attempted lewd act with a child, the jury recommended a sentence of death by lethal injection.

The abduction and murder of nine-year-old Amber Hagerman on January 13, 1996, in Arlington, Texas, snatched off her bicycle on the side of a road with witnesses nearby, wasn't quite so daring, but also high-risk nonetheless. In that case, if the perpetrator had been a little more skillful and quicker on his feet, he would have been able to allay the concerns of witnesses who heard the girl's screams by throwing the bicycle in the back of his truck and saying something to the effect of, "All right, that's it, young lady! I'm taking you home." My point here is that if we see conflict in a public place between an adult and a child, we can't necessarily assume that adult is a parent disciplining his or her son or daughter for a tantrum or other misbehavior.

So why is it that some predators of children are content and able to blend into a community, molest the kids in their neighborhood, and never abduct—let alone kill—any children, while others like Davis steal them away at knifepoint? Keeping in mind that every offender has individual needs and impulses driving him, Ken Lanning and Dr. Ann Burgess of the University of Pennsylvania, who collaborated with us on our extended serial killer study back in the 1970s and 1980s, describe some of the differences between molesters who do and molesters who don't abduct children as part of their criminal activity. According to their analysis and research, most abductors are social misfits who are less likely to have had a previous relationship with the child they abduct, in part because they have less contact with children than molesters who don't abduct. With poorly developed social skills, abductors can't get easy access to children like the seducers can. Their lack of social competence also makes it harder for them to develop relationships with women, even as a cover, so they're also usually unmarried. Since they can't manipulate or lure a child away, they often carry weapons which are used more to help them intimidate and control their victims than to physically harm them. And, like other types of offenders, abductors usually showed signs of trouble as a child.

Ken Lanning describes four phases of abduction for the offender: buildup; abduction; post-abduction; and recovery/release. In the buildup, the subject engages in fantasy that creates some need for sexual activity, although it may not start out child-oriented. He validates and rationalizes his fantasy by talking to others who share or encourage it or by looking at pornographic material that fuels it. There could be a precipitating stressor that prompts the subject to act on his fantasies, and then either an opportunity presents itself or the offender plans and creates one. When the subject is ready to carry out the abduction, victim selection becomes key.

Choosing a complete stranger that he can't be linked to is critical to his odds of not getting caught. Ken calls "thought-driven" offenders the ones who plan an MO and stick to it, weighing risks and using opportunities to their advantage, selecting any victim who fits a broad profile. Planning ahead and exercising discipline in victim selection, if he can resist impulsive or sloppy mistakes, gives the abductor a much better chance of getting away clean.

The "fantasy-driven" abductor, on the other hand, is more concerned with his ritual. He might script the abduction with a very specific type of victim in mind and then not be flexible enough to modify or deviate from his plan even if it increases his risks. This compulsiveness, driven by such specific needs, makes it more difficult for him to carry off an abduction successfully.

Post-abduction is where it really starts to get tricky for the offender. If the abduction was motivated by sexual fantasy, the subject has to keep the child alive and hidden long enough to carry out his fantasies. A sadist, for example, needs to keep the child alive, awake, and in a soundproof environment so he can enjoy his power and domination, inflicting pain. A preferential molester might have a "happily ever after" scenario as part of his fantasy, which is impossible in reality and requires extensive planning to attempt: often, the offender sets up a secret room or cage where he can keep his victim.

When the pressure gets too high, either from the media or from the realization that the situation isn't living up to his fantasies, the abductor needs to get rid of the child—dead or alive. Depending on the particulars of the abduction, he might simply let the child go, dropping him off on the side of a road or even close to the victim's home. In cases where a child has been abducted by someone who's not a family member, the child often turns up alive. The longer the victim's been missing, though, the smaller the chances of a positive outcome. In some cases, the abductor also kills himself. Some abductors kill as part of the ritual itself. Or it could be because they can't think of another way out. Richard Allen Davis claimed he didn't plan to kill Polly Klaas, but after driving around with her for a while he felt he had to because he didn't want to go back to prison. It was the only way he could control the situation.

In profiling a child killer, it's critical to analyze the crime scene, which in many cases is the body dump site. Where you find the body, and how quickly you find it, tell us a lot about the killer. Organized killers tend to transport the victims (alive and dead) over distance. They dispose of bodies in places that take longer to find and where conditions may help destroy evidence—in water, for example. Or, they go for drama or shock value, placing the body where it will be found, in a place or condition that will create outrage in the community. As with organized perpetrators of other types of crime, these guys are of average or above-average intelligence and do have social skills. They plan their crimes, targeting strangers indiscriminately (the choice of a child victim could be situational or preferential), and kill to avoid detection, for the thrill, to fulfill sadistic urges, or for other reasons. Organized child killers may well be psychopathic serial killers. They are more aggressive in sexual activity with their victims before they kill them. Disorganized offenders are more inadequate sexually and so are more likely to assault the victim after the child is unconscious or dead. Of lower intelligence, they frequently don't plan the abduction and often kill inadvertently—using excessive force against a small child, for example. Socially inadequate, they tend to choose a victim they know. Rather than transporting the victim, they feel most comfortable abducting and killing close to home. They may not even have the means to transport a body. Their victims are usually left at the crime scene or someplace where they are found more quickly. They will just dump the body somewhere or bury it in a shallow grave.

It's a sad fact that parents can murder their own children and stage an abduction to divert attention, as happened in the Susan Smith case in South Carolina in 1995. The younger the murdered child, the more likely it is that a family member is responsible, although it is then less likely that they also sexually assaulted the child. A tragically typical scenario would be a lonely and desperate single mother who sees her only chance at happiness coming from a man who claims to love her but who has no place in his life for her child or children. Or, even more pointedly, he may tell her he wants to marry her and start a family of "their own."

If the child's body is found, there's a very good chance we'll figure out who did it. Parents aren't usually as detached about disposing of their children's bodies as strangers are— they may wrap the body in plastic and bury it someplace significant to them. If they feel remorse over the murder, they may try to lead investigators in the right direction so the body will be found and buried in a proper ceremony.

With the complicated living arrangements of many families these days, however, we're seeing more nonparent adults responsible for the murder of children in their household. The hideous murder of twelve-year-old Valerie Smelser in Clarke County, Virginia, drew national attention when her mother's live-in boyfriend, Norman Hoverter, was accused of killing the girl after a long history of abusing her and her three siblings.

In January 1995, Hoverter and Valerie's mother, Wanda Smelser, reported the girl missing from a roadside stop. Her body was found the next day, nude, dumped in a ravine. As word got out of the girl's emaciated condition, former neighbors and others came forward to talk of the abuse they'd suspected. The family had been reported to child protection services, but as they relocated and child abuse cases far outpaced growth in budgets and personnel, Valerie and her siblings somehow got lost in the shuffle.

Preparing for trial, prosecutors detailed evidence of the abuse: Hoverter and Smelser made Valerie stay in the basement, sometimes chained, nude, to the door, forced to urinate in an old coffee can and defecate on the floor. She was not allowed to eat with the rest of the family but had to beg for crumbs or steal food at night. She was killed after she accidentally spilled the coffee can on the floor in the kitchen. In the ensuing beating, Hoverter forced her face in the spilled liquid and slammed her head against the wall with enough force to make a hole in the drywall. Although her mother's defense originally planned to claim that she was a victim of Hoverter's manipulation—using the defense of battered woman's syndrome—she eventually pleaded no contest to abduction and second-degree murder. She didn't admit her guilt in the torture and murder of her daughter but acknowledged that there was enough evidence to convict her. Hoverter also pleaded no contest and is serving a life sentence for abduction and first-degree murder.

With the exception of cases where children are killed by their parents (not typically sexual molestation cases), or where women acted as accomplices to stronger, dominating males (like the Bernardo and Hoverter cases), all the subjects of child murder and molestation cases described so far have been men. There are female sex offenders and child abductors, but the overwhelming majority of cases reported involve male offenders. I think most of us in the field who work with crimes against children agree that there are more female child molesters out there than the numbers would seem to indicate. There's a social stigma attached to a male having sex with a young girl (a "dirty old man"), whereas many people still consider sex between a young boy and an adult woman as a "rite of passage."

Cases have been reported of abuse and fondling of infants and toddlers at day-care settings. Here, women traditionally have greater access to young children and their nurturing role involves bathing, dressing and undressing, examining, and touching them. The child victims can't express themselves and it may not be obvious to an outside observer that a caregiver is doing anything wrong. When women molest older children, they generally do so with, or as, an accomplice. These women rarely fit the behavioral patterns and characteristics described for male preferential child molesters; they usually have some other psychological needs and problems driving them. They may have been long-term victims of sexual abuse as children themselves, and/or have a history of domestic abuse as an adult. Women who abduct children (not family members) are driven by different needs than those who molest the toddlers in their day-care. They are not acting on sexual urges but out of a desire to fill a void in their lives: they need to have a child. This need manifests itself in an unusual type of crime: infant abduction.

The NCMEC, working in conjunction with the FBI, the International Association for Healthcare Security and Safety, and the University of Pennsylvania School of Nursing, has launched several studies. The numbers are small—

it is estimated that out of an average 4.2 million births oc-
curring in the United States annually, fewer than twenty
infants are abducted—but we call them "high-impact" cases
because the effect on parents, nurses, and other health care
professionals is tremendous. As with other crimes against
children, though, it's hard to get a handle on reliable figures
since reporting is always an issue. We don't know, for example, how many abduction attempts are thwarted each year.
Hospitals, in particular, have a vested interest in not reporting near-misses to authorities. We do know that it happens throughout the country, in large and small hospitals,
but it is more prevalent in urban areas.

As a parent, it's impossible to imagine going from the
exhilaration and joy of finally seeing your new baby to the
terror and devastation of learning your infant is gone: that
the "nurse" who told you she needed to take the baby to
the nursery for tests or the "hospital administrator" who
offered to take the child for the customary photos disappeared with the infant. New mothers, often exhausted from
the physical and emotional experience they've just been
through, have literally handed over their infants to abductors. Other times, a woman dressed as a nurse has simply
snatched a baby from the hospital nursery and walked out
of the hospital, sometimes hiding the child in bulky clothing
or a large shoulder bag, but other times making no effort
to conceal the baby.

While most of the time the abductors take the child from
the hospital, they've also been known to abduct from the
baby's home. Answering an advertisement in the local paper
for a baby-sitter, for example, they wait for the mother or
other family member to leave the room and simply take
the baby.

Obviously, these offenders don't look suspicious or nobody would hand over a baby to them. From my early work
and by the more recent studies, we can draw a pretty clear
profile of this type of offender. Nearly always female, often
overweight, infant abductors appear perfectly normal. Many
have responsible jobs and most have no criminal record.
We've seen two age group clusters: sixteen to twenty-one
and thirty-two to forty-five. These ages represent the typical
beginning and end of childbearing years, which is apparently

very significant to this type of subject. Infant abductors suffer from low self-esteem and their sense of self-worth may be based on their ability to be wives and mothers. Many have older children from earlier successful pregnancies. Without a young child to care for, they feel inadequate, as though their existence has no value. The crime is tied to these complex emotional needs and not the traditional motives of greed (such as a kidnapping with a ransom demand), sexual gratification, or power.

The precipitating stressors will be different, too. While an inadequate man may murder a child after he's lost his job or been dumped by his girlfriend, a female infant abductor's stresses are more likely related to childbearing: a recent loss of a child through miscarriage, stillbirth, or even abortion; the approach of menopause; a recent hysterectomy; or a threatened end to a relationship that the woman may feel could be saved by a new baby.

These offenders operate with a curious blend of intelligence and denial. A lot of thought and planning goes into the abduction, including months of lying to their husband or lover and family and co-workers as they feign pregnancy. Their act is so complete that they change body size, go to regular "doctor's appointments" (which they may have their partner drop them off for), make preparations for maternity leave, shop for things for the baby, and talk about the upcoming birth. We have seen reports of women going so far as to steal a pregnant woman's urine sample at a doctor's office, or taking someone else's sonogram to show their partner. They can be so convincing people will throw showers for them. Their partner, often someone significantly older or younger than they are and usually somewhat gullible, can get caught up in the excitement of planning as well. The hospital abductor will do research, visiting nurseries and maternity units several times before the abduction to get the lay of the land, figure out which hospital represents the lowest risk for them, and also judge the size of the infant population they'll get to pick from on any given day. They read through birth announcements and baby-sitter-wanted ads to research an abduction from home. In either case, they will lie, impersonate, use trickery and deceit to such an extent that they may believe they are getting their own baby. Some develop symptoms of false pregnancy. All are in denial of the fact that in nearly every case they will be caught. In fact, in many cases, they are turned in by the very loved ones and friends they show off their new baby to when the child is recognized from media coverage of the abduction.

The abduction itself, whether planned for nine months or just a few hours, shows signs of that planning. In a hospital setting, the abductor has nurse's garb to wear, knows where everything is located, and is even able to convince other nurses that she belongs there. Her ruse is often scripted and she knows the names of mothers and infants so she can also impersonate a visiting family member. Abduction from a home is less risky since there are fewer authorities and other people to interfere and protect the infant. Victim selection isn't nearly as important to them as choosing the site and means of the abduction. Because their need is simply to have a child, they're not preferential in their choice of victims as far as sex goes, although most select a baby of their own race (or that of the supposed father).

While most of the time these offenders are not violent, if force is used to obtain the baby it is usually applied in home abductions or outside a hospital. The abductor may take an infant at gunpoint in the parking lot of the hospital, or may use a weapon to overpower a parent at home. The harder it has been for the abductor to obtain an infant (if she's made several attempts which have been thwarted just before the abduction) the greater the likelihood that she will turn to violence and take greater risks out of desperation.

In some cases, the subject will go so far as to murder a parent or other caretaker obstructing her.

Joan Witt, a thirty-year-old new mother, was killed trying to defend her four-day-old daughter, Heather, from an abductor. Nineteen-year-old Wendy Leigh Zabel shot Witt several times and shot and stabbed the baby's grandmother as she abducted the child from the Witts' home in Jacksonville, Florida, in November of 1987. Zabel was desperate to have a baby. She'd been trying for years.

In planning the abduction, she visited the nursery at the hospital where Heather was born. But the hospital was too much of a high-risk setting for her to snatch the child there. Tracking down the Witts days later, she knocked on the door pretending to be in labor and asked to use their phone to call her husband. The infant's mother and fifty-six-year-old grandmother were the only ones home at the time and they acted solicitously toward Zabel, advising her that Heather had just been born at nearby Baptist Medical Center and she should go there. After they let her use the bathroom, Zabel emerged with a gun and a knife and ordered them to hand over the baby.

According to Zabel, what happened next surprised her. She knew the mother instinct was strong but she didn't think she'd actually have to resort to force to get the baby. When she moved toward the baby's crib, however, both women tried to stop her. She stabbed the grandmother and then shot her as Joan grabbed the baby and ran outside for help. There, Zabel shot her once in the leg and twice in the abdomen before grabbing the baby and fleeing.

Zabel's MO coincides with patterns of behavior observed with most infant abductors: the crime took place during the day; she used a verbal ruse to get into the victim's house so there was no sign of forced entry; and the crime scene obviously showed signs of a panicked or hurried retreat. Before the abduction, Zabel and her partner had been preparing for the baby for months, purchasing baby things, telling his co-workers about the pregnancy. Reportedly, no one who knew the couple was suspicious about the infant, despite the fact that Zabel had been "pregnant" about eleven months at the time of the "birth." Although originally charged in the abduction, Zabel's companion was later dropped as a suspect when his alibi for the afternoon of the murder-abduction held and it could not be proven that he knew the baby wasn't really theirs. He also agreed to take, and passed, a polygraph.

Unlike the many infant abduction cases that are solved following tips from the community, Zabel was undone by the gun she used in the attack, which she discarded on the side of the road not far from the victim's home.

Zabel had never previously been in trouble with the law. In fact, her father was a retired highway patrol sergeant in her home state of Wisconsin. In an interview taped about four years after the abduction and murder, Zabel said she'd always suffered from low self-esteem. She felt she was unattractive: too tall, too fat, and not pretty. She reportedly also suffered a false pregnancy, which gave her expectancy more credence with friends and family members.

Wendy Zabel is serving three consecutive life terms earned in a deal that enabled her to avoid the death penalty by pleading guilty to armed kidnapping, first-degree murder, and attempted first-degree murder, without the option of an appeal.

The media is often key to the quick recovery of a missing infant, and the way the case is played in the papers and on television can be critical to the level of care the baby receives from the abductor. The event should not be characterized as a kidnapping or abduction, and the perpetrator should not be referred to as evil. You want to avoid panicking the abductor, causing her to flee and/or harm the infant. Also, instead of stressing punishment to the offender, news statements should emphasize the safe return of the baby. You want to reach out to the abductor's friends, family, neighbors, and co-workers, who will be sympathetic to the victim's family and quite possibly suspicious about the new baby.

One case that was solved following a lead phoned in to police by an anonymous caller was of interest to my unit in part because of how well it followed the elements of a classic infant abduction. Around 9:30 on the morning of June 20, 1988, a woman posing as a hospital nurse visited Renee McClure, a new mother at the High Point Regional Hospital in High Point, North Carolina. The "nurse" told Mrs. McClure that her son, Jason Ray, needed to go to the nursery to be weighed. Shortly thereafter, a real nurse entered the room and figured out what happened. Local police were contacted immediately and the FBI joined the investigation that afternoon.

The anonymous call came in the next day, along with a walk-in witness who corroborated the caller's information. Based on those leads, police and FBI agents arrested Brenda Joyce Nobles for the abduction, along with her daughter, Sharon Leigh Slaydon, who figured out the baby wasn't her mother's but had not turned her in. Jason was found at their home, hidden in a back bedroom closet. His hair had been cut off in an apparent attempt at a disguise but he was otherwise in good condition.

From interviews with Nobles and Slaydon, we learned that Nobles's boyfriend (who was about seventy years of age) would not marry her unless she could have his child. He especially wanted a son. Since she'd had a hysterectomy years earlier, which she didn't tell him, she knew she'd have to find another way to accomplish this. In December of 1987, she told him and other family members that she was pregnant and started eating heavily so her body would transform convincingly. Slaydon had a baby at High Point in May of 1988 and Nobles took that opportunity to familiarize herself with the maternity ward. On June 19, 1988, Nobles visited another relative at the hospital and again stopped by the nursery. When she saw Jason McClure, she decided to put her plan into action.

According to Nobles's boyfriend, on the morning of June 20 she told him she wasn't feeling well and thought she might go into labor that day. When he returned home from work later, he found "his son" in bed with Nobles, who told him she'd given birth that morning in an outpatient clinic in town. He was so excited he invited friends and relatives to come over and celebrate the boy's birth, never questioning her story or the child's true identity. Someone, however, was suspicious enough to make the call, and in the end Nobles received a sentence of twelve years in prison for the abduction.

As both the Zabel and Nobles cases illustrate, these offenders are not particularly criminally sophisticated and they often leave a trail investigators can follow. Despite wearing a nurse's disguise, for example, they show their face to people before and during the commission of their crime—giving police a description they can start publicizing immediately. They often discard parts of their disguise at the crime scene, leaving valuable fingerprints and other forensic evidence linking them to their crime.

They also tend to strike close to home. Investigators can often get quick leads by looking at the hospital's records of recent miscarriages or stillborn births. The abductor may have applied for a job at the hospital or even worked there before. In abductions from a home, often someone can give a description of the getaway vehicle. But the most important leads come from those close to the abductors. Sometimes people get suspicious because the new baby is actually a three-month old, which anyone who's ever been close to an infant can see looks and acts very different from a newborn. An abductor will happily show friends "her" baby, but can provide only sketchy details of the birth. No one knew when she went into labor and she contacted no one—not even the supposed father—in time to let them visit her in the hospital. There is also no birth certificate for the child. These facts, coupled with a good description of the baby and the abductor, circulated quickly over a wide area, often result in a relatively quick return of the infant to the parents.

Although perpetrators of infant abductions are nearly always female, every so often there is an exception. In the summer of 1991, Charles Neil Ikerd and his mother-in-law, Maize D. Hester, called the Aurora, Colorado, Police Department to report Charles's eighteen-year-old wife, Terra Ann, and three-month-old daughter, Heather Louise, missing. Terra had been suffering from postpartum depression, and at first her husband agreed with her therapist that she was probably just trying to get some time away. Still, after discussing things, he and Maize—who allowed the couple to live in her home—were concerned enough about Terra and the baby to file a routine missing person's report.

Things grew less routine about three weeks later, when Terra's body was found in a field thirty miles outside of town by a road maintenance worker. She'd been shot twice in the chest and once in the head. There was no evidence of sexual assault and no sign of Heather. The position of Terra's body and the fact that there were no shell casings located nearby indicated she'd been killed someplace else and transported to the dump site. University of Colorado experts examined the state of decomposition and vegetative growth around the body and determined she was killed shortly after she disappeared, probably within two days.

I've often said that victimology can be key to solving a case like this, and investigators looked into Terra Ikerd's personal life. On the day she disappeared, Terra and Heather had both been at Terra's job at a local sports club, where she'd started work just three days earlier. She got a paycheck that day and took Heather with her to the bank to deposit all of it. Then she went home to change clothes before going out again with her daughter. In a phone call with her mother, it didn't sound like there was anything wrong. Sometime in the afternoon, a neighbor saw her and Heather get into a car driven by a white male. No one saw her alive again.

Her husband, Charles, was an immediate suspect, since they had a less than perfect marriage and he didn't seem as broken up about his wife's disappearance with their daughter as people thought he should be. But he had an airtight alibi for the time of her disappearance—he was hard at work at a local fast-food restaurant—and with his minimum wage job, it didn't seem he had the money or the planning skills necessary to carry out a contract job. As the victim's lifestyle came under closer scrutiny, at least three boyfriends came to light, one of whom had a vehicle that matched the description of the one her neighbor saw Terra get into the day she disappeared. Another boyfriend was also a viable suspect. A drug and alcohol abuser, he'd threatened to kill her if she ever married anyone else. A third boyfriend was in the Air Force and worked as a military police officer in Colorado Springs. He'd been issued a service revolver and ammunition that might match the weapon used to kill Terra. His alibi—that he was attending a funeral out of state when she disappeared—still left him enough time to travel back and kill her.

With multiple leads but no solid information—and still missing the baby—investigators struggled until August 8, when they were contacted by authorities in Topeka, Kansas, who had a lead from their Crime Stoppers hotline. The caller phoned to report an attempted baby sale in Kentucky that involved a baby who matched Heather Ikerd's description. Using information from the Kansas police, Colorado authorities identified the man involved as Ralph Blaine Takemire. In his mid-forties, Takemire was a biker living in Kansas. When members of the Ikerd family were questioned about the man, Terra's father-in-law referred to him as "Uncle Ralph," an old family friend who visited them over the Fourth of July. During his visit, Takemire spent a lot of time with Terra and Heather, buying them Harley-Davidson

T-shirts as gifts. The Ikerds felt that despite the coincidence of the date of his visit and Terra's and Heather's disappearance, Uncle Ralph was an old friend who would never be capable of something as horrible as abduction and murder.

Investigative authorities felt otherwise and the Kansas City FBI SWAT team began surveillance of Uncle Ralph's house that very night. They confirmed that a baby was on the premises and confronted Takemire as he left the house the next morning. They recovered Heather alive and in good health. After confessing to Terra's murder and Heather's abduction, he was arrested on federal charges of kidnapping. A search of his home and vehicle yielded shell casings from the murder weapon, along with bloodstains and Terra's blood-soaked purse, in the vehicle. The gun used in the murder was found at a nearby pawn shop.

When interviewed by the FBI, Takemire indicated that he'd originally been driven to his crimes by many of the same motivations as female infant abductors. He had apparently been unable to impregnate his wife and felt the need to get her a child somehow, especially after they'd had arguments about how he promised to buy her a baby and then didn't. Takemire rationalized his actions by concluding— from just his quick observations over the Fourth of July visit—that Terra was unfit to raise the child.

Another case that was unusual both in its level of violence and in the disorganization of the perpetrator came to our attention in the summer of 1987. On July 23, a very pregnant Cindy Lynn Ray went for a routine prenatal checkup at the clinic of the Kirtland Air Force Base Hospital, just outside Albuquerque, New Mexico. As she left the clinic she was met outside by a woman named Darci Kayleen Pierce, who abducted her from the parking lot using a fake pistol to get the woman into her 1964 Volkswagen Beetle. Pierce had been telling her husband, friends, and family members for the past ten months that she was desperate for a baby and was now pregnant. She drove her victim to a remote area in the Manzano Mountains just east of Albuquerque, where she strangled Ray unconscious using a fetal monitor cord from Ray's purse. She dragged Ray behind some trees, then used her car keys to perform a Caesarean section and bit the umbilical cord to cut it. Leaving her victim in the wilderness, Pierce drove back to Albuquerque and told people she'd delivered her baby by herself on the highway between there and Santa Fe.

An ambulance was summoned and Pierce and the baby were taken to the University of New Mexico Medical Center, where she refused to be examined by a physician. Doctors there surmised the baby had not been born vaginally and confronted Pierce, who then claimed she'd been given the baby by a surrogate mother who delivered with the help of a midwife in Santa Fe. The case came together when a midwife at the Air Force base mentioned that a very pregnant military dependent was missing. After being questioned by police, Darci Pierce finally led investigators to Cindy Ray, but it was too late to save her. She had died from blood loss and exposure.

After learning of his wife's confession, Ray Pierce was shocked by the vicious crime and the truth about his wife's condition. In his interview with Albuquerque police and Air Force special investigation agents, he said that he believed his wife had been pregnant for about ten or eleven months. Darci Pierce was placed in custody at Kirtland and later sentenced to life in prison.

Fortunately, in Pierce's case, suspicious hospital authorities contacted law enforcement immediately, although they had no proof that anything illegal had taken place. Equally important, local police and military investigators quickly formed a solid investigative unit and worked together to bring the case to closure. While we don't always see this type of cooperation with other kinds of crimes, with infant abductions the benefits of early reporting and effective publicity are obvious enough that authorities do come together and get the word out, setting up tip lines so people in the community can quickly report anything or anyone suspicious. And, in the past five years, largely as a result of groundbreaking work done by people such as John Rabun, vice president and CEO of the NCMEC, who's also the author of guidelines for prevention of infant abductions in hospital settings, the incidence of those crimes has been reduced dramatically. Hospitals are now proactively training their employees, instituting greater security measures, and putting immediate response plans in place.

Rabun and the NCMEC have also made guidelines available to parents. These guidelines and more information for parents and health care professionals can be obtained from the NCMEC by calling 1-800-THE-LOST or writing the Publications Department, National Center for Missing and Exploited Children, 2101 Wilson Boulevard, Suite 550, Arlington, VA 22201-3052.

Even when these stories have a happy ending and the infant is returned safe and apparently healthy, there are tremendous and long-term effects on parents and, when abductions occur at hospitals, health care workers. Lawsuits are common, but nurses suffer more from psychological problems like post-traumatic stress disorder than fear of recrimination at their job. Even nurses with long and successful records may transfer or leave the profession altogether after an abduction, so traumatized are they by the feelings of guilt and helplessness from the event. Parents, too, go through a range of emotions throughout the abduction: from the trauma of the initial realization that their infant is gone, through the anxiety and fear of waiting for his or her return. Even after the baby is returned, the parents can never relax. They have to rebond with the child and the child with them, and are often terrified that something else may happen. Parents exhibit signs of PTSD, and at the very least tend to overprotect their child in the future. Often the child, too, while well cared for following the abduction, can suffer nightmares, fears, and flashbacks. And through the offender's criminal trial and any ensuing civil litigation, everyone is retraumatized.

As in all types of crime, I'm always advising people to "study the art," to get inside the offender's identity, but there's one instance in which all we have to look at is a blank wall, and that's the most frustrating situation of all. When an infant or child stays missing, it breaks down the victim's family as well as everyone involved in the investigation. You have no body, you have no crime scene to analyze, so you're stuck working with the most generic of assumptions. When the victim is a child rather than an infant, statistically your UNSUB is probably not a family member, is probably a "he," and is probably motivated by sexual desires. Maybe the way the abduction took place will give us an idea of the sophistication level of the subject, but you're essentially looking at every sex offender—known or suspected—within a radius of a couple of hundred miles. Then you widen your search to include known or suspected abductors of children or adults. It can be a fishing expedition that may lead nowhere. And what makes it even worse is that some of your suspects may be so inadequate they'll confess to crimes they never committed just for the attention and short-lived power. Unless you quickly prove these guys are full of it, you have to spend the time to follow up every lead—however bogus it sounds—because you can't risk missing an opportunity to get the child back alive.

Even years later, when in most cases it's safest to believe the child's dead, families don't move in hopes that the child—or someone—will call, maybe recognizing their loved one from the NCMEC's free Missing Children Web Page. In turn, experts at the NCMEC use computer age-enhancing software to try to picture what the child would look like as he or she matured, hoping the image will strike a spark of recognition in someone, somewhere. In the meantime, investigators try to pull leads from any recent similar cases in the area.

Our world is full of dangers for children, from freak accidents to planned violent assaults by adults. The good news is that just as you can protect your kids by making buckling their seat belts an automatic reflex of getting in the car, you can ingrain other safety skills that will protect them without making them overly fearful. Next we'll discuss what you can do for and with your children to help prevent them from becoming one of the too many faces on NCMEC's wall.

CHAPTER 6

Fighting Back

As we've seen, children can fall prey to a frightening variety of dangerous predators. And the analogy of predator and prey is apt, since children in society, like young, defenseless animals in nature, are in many ways ideal victims.

Little Dannelle Lietz was a victim, as was Christine Jessop, for the same reason other children have become victims: they have no control over their environment. Kids can't pick their family members, baby-sitters, neighbors, parents' friends, or local school. If someone in their household physically or sexually abuses them, if they live in a dangerous neighborhood or attend a school where drugs or weapons are problems (or where a playground bully beats them up during recess every day), they can't just pick up and move. And if they do run away, they become vulnerable to different dangers in their new hostile environment.

But the majority of kids at risk are trapped. Young children, abused or neglected, or even older ones, may not realize that other children live any differently, that their lives are not normal. For example, I had a case of a violent serial rapist. When this offender was a young teen, his father would take him out to bars most nights of the week, where he would pick up a prostitute, beat her or slap her around, then go off to have sex with her within the boy's hearing. Now I'm not excusing what he became—unless we're literally out of our minds, we're all responsible for our actions. But I do submit that it's a lot more problematic developing a respectful attitude toward your fellow human beings, male or female, when this is your role model of how women are supposed to be treated.

Even in the safest and healthiest of home environments, though, aspects of children's very nature can work against them. There are definite characteristics—universal to all children—that make them ideal victims, including that they are curious by nature, they are easy for adults to manipulate and influence, they need affection and attention, and they feel a need to defy their parents in different ways at different stages.

Every parent can attest to a child's natural curiosity. I know I've both cursed and admired the way my kids were always getting into things, sometimes getting hurt in the process, often just on the verge of calamity when Pam or I walked into a room. As my two daughters and son were growing up, I would alternately marvel at their frequent displays of intelligence and resourcefulness and their occasional incredible lapses of judgment. We see a toddler dashing into the street as a scary sign of thoughtlessness or willfulness. She sees it as one new thing to explore enthusiastically and doesn't understand that the scolding or smack on the bottom she instantly receives for her adventurousness is merely her frazzled parent's feeble attempt to correct a suddenly dangerous situation.

The catch-22 for parents is that we don't want to take that curiosity away from our kids because that's what's going to inspire them to learn about the world around them; that's what makes them unique, interesting individuals. It's difficult, because there's such a fine line. If we see a toddler playing on the edge of the pool, just outside the range of watchful eyes for a second, we're so scared of what might have happened if we weren't there that we go ballistic and try to make sure that kid never goes near a pool alone again. But the voice of reason in the back of our minds is also saying, "Wait—you don't want to traumatize him so he's afraid of water for the rest of his life!"

It was, in part, her natural curiosity that cost the life of Megan Kanka. Early one July evening in 1994, the energetic seven-year-old tired of watching TV with her sister and went outside to see if one of her friends in her suburban Trenton,

New Jersey, neighborhood wanted to play—maybe hop-scotch, one of the little girl's favorites. A short time later, her sister went out to join them but found that Megan had never showed up at her friend's house. Almost twenty-four hours later, Megan's body was found just a few miles from home in a local park, placed in a plastic toy container. She had been raped and strangled.

As it turned out, Megan was a victim of her environment, although there was no way parents living on her block would have known it was high-risk before her abduction. The sub-urban New Jersey neighborhood the Kankas lived in was quiet, except for the normal sounds of children at play. No one knew that the three men who lived in the house across the street from the Kankas had all done time in Avenel, a New Jersey facility where sex offenders serve their sentences and receive therapy that's supposed to make them less of a threat when they're released back into society. No one knew until one of these men, Jesse Timmendequas, was arrested for Megan's murder. Timmendequas had previously been convicted of fondling and almost strangling another seven-year-old girl. He had lured Megan to his house by offering to show her his puppy.

Megan's family and others in her community were horri-fied by the crime. Their horror grew to outrage when they learned that her attacker had a history of sex crimes. Their outrage turned to activism and eventually led to the passage of "Megan's Law," which calls for communities to be noti-fied when high-risk, paroled sex offenders move into their area. The 1994 federal crime bill required that states register and keep track of convicted sex offenders for ten years after release, as well as alert law enforcement when they locate in their communities, but it didn't require the information be made available to the public. Passed as a federal statute in May 1996, Megan's Law required this notification in all states. There were already forms of the law on the books in most of them, but the requirements differed vastly from state to state, ranging from those where residents had to contact police to research offenders in the area to others where police had to contact residents, schools, women's shel-ters, and camps, with the name, address, and photo of pa-roled sex offenders.

There has been a lot of controversy surrounding the law, with court challenges in a number of states. Some argue notification is an invasion of privacy that punishes the offender twice by threatening his ability to turn his life around. There is fear of what parents might do once they find out one of these people lives in their neighborhood. Attorneys for offenders argue that once their client serves his time, he should be given a clean slate to start over. In this country, we do like to believe in redemption.

The biggest problem with that argument, though, is that a preferential child molester is not going to stop being attracted to children.

Suppose someone—some higher authority—came to me and said I was okay except for the fact that my attraction to adult women was wrong and perverted. I would find it very difficult to change that, no matter what I did. I'm an educated, middle-class father of three with ties to the community and a heavy "investment" in the system and our societal structure. And yet, even at the risk of all that, I would find it just about impossible to change my sexual orientation to conform to the dictates of what some other authority said I should if I wanted to be acceptable in law-abiding society. The same, I'm sure, would be true of a gay man or lesbian in similar socioeconomic circumstances to mine. Regardless of what you told him or her about how it was "wrong" to be attracted to other adults of the same sex, it wouldn't change their sexual orientation. It may force them underground, as prejudice against homosexuals often has, but it isn't going to change them.

The same is true with preferential pedophiles—only more so, because many of them don't have the same vested interest in the system that most of us do. Many of them are respectable professionals and businesspeople who are, in fact, living this part of their lives in secret. But many more are fringe elements of society, just as murderers and rapists of adults are. And we've learned from our experience and research, we're not going to get them to voluntarily give up their interest in little boys or little girls any more than you're going to get me to give up my interest in adult women or a gay man to give up his interest in other adult men.

But if you can't get him to give up the interest, can't you

at least make him understand that restraining himself is in his own self-interest (so he won't be sent back to jail)? Well, you can try, just as you can try to get serial rapists to restrain themselves even though they get satisfaction out of raping adult women. But I don't think you're going to be very successful at it. As Peter Banks puts it, "You don't just wake up one morning and decide you're going to go out and murder a child. Child molesters don't look at things from the same perspective we do. We look on it as irrational. They look on it as normal."

He echoes the sentiment of a lot of people who work with missing and exploited children and see what he sees: "There are certain things for which we should have zero tolerance. I think that stealing the innocence of a child is in some ways worse than murder."

After my experiences interviewing repeat violent offenders in prison and working with local police to solve their crimes—normally recidivist crimes—I'm afraid my faith in rehabilitation is pretty low. They get arrested, behave themselves in prison, and tell their shrink they're feeling much better, really. But it's all self-reported. They say they're able to control their urges, but how can we know what will happen once they're released? What a lot of people in the psychiatric and judicial communities don't seem to grasp is that *violence is situational.* It has to do with the environment and the opportunity. The mere fact that an individual is a model prisoner has very little to do with what he'll do once he's no longer in a closely observed, highly structured situation.

Arthur Shawcross was a model prisoner during the fifteen years he was incarcerated for the murder of a young boy and young girl in Watertown, New York. Within months of his release, his inadequacy and rage had got the better of him and he was killing prostitutes in Rochester. Jack Henry Abbott, convicted murderer who won fame and the support of much of the literary world for his fine book on prison life, *In the Belly of the Beast,* was such a good prisoner and such a model of rehabilitation that he was released. And unlike most convicts, he had fame, support, a reputation, and the friendship of influential people. Despite this, within a few months of his release he got into an argument with a waiter in a Greenwich Village restaurant, could not control his rage, and killed the young man. Though I haven't heard, I would not be at all surprised to learn that he is once again a model prisoner.

I can't help but wonder if the attorneys of child molesters or other violent offenders are willing to let their own children befriend these guys once they get out. Will they let their own kids be the guinea pigs in some informal child molester rehabilitation study? What makes us think that once they've seen they can manipulate educated, advanced-degreed, mature adults into believing what they want them to believe, that they'll stop using their influence and skills to prey on children, especially children to which they're very strongly sexually attracted? Or, as I've heard from so many victims and their families: Okay, give offenders a clean slate after they've served their sentence—as soon as their victims are physically, mentally, and emotionally made whole . . . or brought back to life.

In Megan Kanka's community, the citizens have taken another, less controversial step to start the healing process. The local Rotary Club purchased the house across the street from the Kankas—where her murderer lived—and paid for it to be torn down. The site will become "Megan's Place," a park where parents will be able to keep watch as the neighborhood children play.

With statutes like Megan's Law and programs at such places as local malls where parents can get their kids fingerprinted, society keeps coming up with new ways to protect children. Walk into any major retailer of children's goods and you'll see what amount to leashes for kids on display amidst the toys, clothing, and other basic supplies. I've even seen ads for battery-operated tracking devices that make beeperlike sounds when parents activate the homing mechanism. I've also heard of at least one time such a device was found near the home of a child who was abducted and murdered, the safety device discarded as the child was taken away.

When my children were born, I was almost afraid to hold them, they looked so fragile. As our kids grow bigger, we become more confident that we won't harm them and more paranoid about all the forces out there that might: we put protective plugs in all our electrical outlets, stash cleaning fluids and medicine out of reach, buy bicycle helmets, and try to think of every way we can to keep them safe. Then we hear about stories like Megan Kanka's, or Cassie Hansen's, or Polly Klaas's, or Amber Hagerman's, or Shawn Moore's, or any number of others, and then we want to keep them within direct view at all times, or lock them in their rooms until they're well into their twenties.

What we have to remember is that like a lot of other dangers to our children, adults who would do them harm are something of a known entity, in the same way automobile accidents or childhood diseases are known entities. As parents, we can learn about the dangers they represent and then translate that knowledge (and fear) into practical means of protection. We know that predators of children use every advantage they have to influence potential victims, and unless a child is prepared, the adult has the edge: he's bigger, stronger, and, according to most parents, adults are to be obeyed. Shrewd child predators will not only use these factors, but may stage the scene to enhance their position of authority. They may impersonate police officers or priests—trustworthy figures they feel the child might have been been taught to follow. In some cases, they will play on a child's emotions, showering him with attention, manipulating him, later threatening and isolating him emotionally from adults who would protect and help him. Or they may lie in wait, looking for an opportunity to make a clean snatch-and-grab.

Now for the good news: you have the means and the weapons at your disposal—already in your own home—to defeat these predators in many instances, or equalize the odds in the others. Before we start getting crazy, let's remember one important thing: the probability is that your child will *not* be abducted, just the potential is there. And that's something you can guard against. Your relationship with your children, combined with some relatively simple safety skills you can teach them, are your best means of protecting your kids.

In the last chapter we talked about seduction-type child molesters who shower kids with affection and attention over a period of time. Peter Banks and others at the NCMEC keep stressing that the single biggest gift you can give your children is *self-esteem*. Kids who don't get enough emotional

168

support at home are much more likely to be targeted by preferential molesters in the first place. They can spot the needy and vulnerable, just like that lion on the African veldt can spot the most vulnerable springbok in the herd drinking at the watering hole.

These offenders will sometimes target single-parent families specifically because the parent may appreciate another adult who's willing to spend time with the kids. Parents have to trust their instincts. If it looks like someone is trying too hard to be there for your child, be suspicious enough to at least chaperone their time together.

All families go through periods where members are alienated from each other; children and adults each go through emotionally difficult times. Even when you're having a rough period, you want to make sure that somewhere inside them your kids know you love them, no matter what. They need to hear you say "I love you" and "You're special." We give them plenty of negative reinforcement when they do something wrong; we need to make sure we keep that in balance with the positive.

Your kids must feel they can come to you if something happens that makes them uncomfortable. This can be hard, especially if a child gets in a bad situation because he's disobeyed one of your rules. It's tough, for example, for a thirteen-year-old boy who's not supposed to watch R-rated movies on cable to admit that he went over to an older friend's house to watch videos and something happened that didn't feel right.

Communication with kids is so important. If they have questions—and they will—you want them to come to you. If your kid gets the impression from you that sex, for instance, is a completely taboo subject, he's not going to be any less curious about it. He's just going to get the information from someone else. Child molesters exploit this and turn it into an opportunity. Sharing information, they can earn a child's trust while lowering his inhibitions and resistance. This doesn't mean that if your child senses you're uncomfortable discussing details of human reproductive science or sexuality that he or she is going to end up being molested by the first pervert who comes along. It just means you have to be aware that as children grow older, the focal points for their curiosity naturally evolve and change. When they're ready for information, ready to ask questions, you have to be there for them, always stressing how much you care about them.

If something bad ever happened, it would be critical for your child to be comfortable coming to you. Remember how hard it is for them to tell someone about being molested in the first place, and then think about the reaction they're likely to get if they press charges. For every child victim willing to report a sex offender, there are any number of people who will discount their version of events. We've all seen articles in the newspaper about a popular teacher, for example, accused of molesting a young student. There are usually quotes from people in the community who love and admire this person, often slamming the child victim. If the pressure gets too great, think about what happens if the child recants the charges: he'll never be believed about anything ever again. Unless he or she knows you'll help to deal with the situation and hold the offender accountable, coming forward with a report of abuse can be a no-win situation for the child. Abusers know this; one of their most effective threats is to tell a child no one will believe him.

Depending on their age and sophistication, children can often be as reliable witnesses as adults, sometimes more so since they seldom have a particular axe to grind. But many times, they're confused by what has happened and may not know how to express it. As in interviewing adult rape victims, it takes someone with the right experience and sensitivity to interview the child victim, to find out what happened from his or her point of view, without undue intimidation or improper influence.

While a major theme here is the need for parents to spend time with their kids, the fact is that we can't be with them twenty-four hours a day. And kids with the best emotional support system in the world can still be in the wrong place at the wrong time. Sometimes, unfortunately, as with Dannelle Lietz, there's really nothing anyone can do to prevent the situation. But other times, self-confident and armed with the personal safety skills you've taught them, kids can minimize the risk that circumstances will be right for a victimizer to choose them.

It's the same thing I used to try to get across back when I worked a bank robbery detail in the Detroit Field Office: We may not be able to prevent bad guys from robbing banks. But we can harden targets so that they're less likely to hit your particular bank. It's common sense that we do this in our home. If you have a burglar alarm, or dead bolt locks, or a barking dog, or a well-lit perimeter, or all of these things, the thief is much less likely to target your house; there are just too many obstacles to justify the risk. Likewise, we want to harden our children as targets, create too many obstacles to justify the risk. And if we all do that, then maybe we can actually begin to cut down on the overall number of crimes against children.

The National Center for Missing and Exploited Children has developed guidelines for parents to follow as they try to keep their children out of potentially dangerous and/or exploitive situations, as well as age-specific "safety strategies" for children. They emphasize that these strategies are designed to help kids react in different situations and make the right decisions to stay safe—not to be afraid or antisocial. They also emphasize that when teaching children anything, it's vital to make sure you're approaching them on their own age-appropriate level. If you give little kids too much information, too many rules at once, they zone out and tend not to remember any of it. If you oversimplify for an older kid, though, you get the same reaction.

With all age groups, the NCMEC stresses protecting children by empowering, rather than frightening them. It doesn't do any good to frighten them with the bad things "strangers" can do. In fact, that not only scares them but gives them a false sense of security with people who aren't strangers.

The NCMEC safety strategies are helpful because they combine skills children should have at various ages (for example, knowing their home phone number and address) with behaviors they should learn at each age. Through the Adam Walsh Children's Fund, the Center put together a program called "Kids & Company: Together for Safety," which features a range of educational materials, including exercises and games for kids in kindergarten through sixth grade. As parents, you can instill the ideas yourself at home, but if you'd like to get more information or to talk to someone about having the curriculum implemented at your children's school, contact the NCMEC directly at 1-800-THE-LOST. A summary of this information, prepared by the Center, can be found at the end of this chapter.

One of the skills which can be presented in a nonthreatening way is the Buddy System, which simply teaches children not to go places by themselves. As adults, we know that kids who are alone are easier targets and so are at greater risk. We don't have to tell them the bogeyman waits for kids walking home from school alone. They just need to learn, in a positive way, to stay with their buddies. And it's easy for kids to remember that they need to stick together—with their parents, sisters and brothers, friends, or classmates. In the NCMEC program, for example, young children learn about the Buddy System through a song.

Another behavior you can teach your children that may help eliminate some situational opportunities for victimization is Check First. Check First is central to the Kids & Company program. The message is simple and nonthreatening for children: just check with me before you go somewhere or do something. Even at a very young age, kids can understand that they have to ask a parent or baby-sitter before they do something. And if you give them positive reinforcement every time they check with you, they'll feel good about themselves.

As Peter Banks states it: "The number one weapon against the child molester is the self-esteem of the child." This can't be repeated often enough.

They'll also learn from you how to make good decisions over time. Child predators often confuse kids by putting them in situations in which they're not prepared to make the right judgment call and then take advantage of their confusion. We know that an adult should not be asking a small child for help unloading groceries, for example, but a child may not immediately recognize that as inappropriate. Their eagerness to help may make them vulnerable. If they know to check with you first, though, you can make the choice and set an example of what's okay and what's not.

You can talk to your kids about when touching is okay and when it's not. Like adults, kids have an inner warning

172

buzzer that goes off when they're in a situation they don't like, but they may need help to become aware of those feelings, and in understanding that they are right to follow their feelings. They know that a hug from grandma feels good and secure, for example, and they'll instinctively feel differently about the wrong kinds of touches.

You can reinforce their feelings by talking to them about the kinds of touches that feel good. As Peter Banks points out, it would be a terrible shame for all concerned if the fear over child molestation prevented all hugging and touching and appropriate signs of affection between adults and children. With a teacher, a coach, or any other adult, it's not difficult to distinguish between hugs, pats, or other touching that seems appropriate and those which do not once the child understands that both kinds exist.

Most kids are taught to be respectful of adults, which is appropriate, but they should know that there are circumstances where they can say "No" to an adult. And when an adult is trying to touch them in a way that makes them feel uncomfortable, confused, angry (or "yucky," depending on the age of the child), it's a good time to say "NO."

I remember my kids each went through a period around age two or three where it seemed like all they could say was "No!" But as they grow older, many kids get more timid, so it's not a bad idea to practice saying "No." You can role-play, describing situations (not too frightening, but clearly times when the right answer is "No") so your child can practice looking you right in the eye, with a serious expression, saying loudly, confidently, and clearly, "No," or "Don't do that!" It sounds like a small thing, but if a potential molester realizes this kid's going to give him a lot of resistance, even simply verbal resistance, he'll most likely move on. It's like having a miniature poodle in your house. The dog is obviously not big enough or strong enough to overpower an intruder, but all that yapping could make a less determined offender pick another, quieter target where he'll be less likely to draw attention to himself.

You want your children to understand that their bodies are their own and no one should touch them in a way they don't like. Make sure your kids know what parts of their body are "private," that they don't have to share those parts with other people, and that they shouldn't be asked to touch anyone else's private parts. If you use the real, anatomic terms for things (penis instead of pee-pee, for example), they'll understand that these are important body parts that deserve respect and they'll feel comfortable talking about them.

There are some times when other people may need to look at their private parts, such as at the doctor's office or when a baby-sitter gives a young child a bath, but they still need a good reason. If your child has to be examined by a doctor, make sure you can stay in the room. And for their own protection and self-confidence, children should learn personal hygiene skills as early as they're ready and should then have responsibility for that themselves. Finally, kids need to know that if someone does try to touch their private parts, it's not their fault. Just as important, if they tell an adult and that person doesn't do anything to help them, they should keep telling until they find someone who does.

Of course, it is important to keep context in mind so that children are not unnecessarily traumatized. Virtually all children play doctor with each other at one time or another in their early development. This is a normal part of exploring themselves and their bodies and the explanation we give them when we "catch" them at it is important to their future development and adjustment. When this activity becomes a serious concern, however, is when there is a large age or sophistication gap between one participant and the other. Then it's not normal childhood development and exploration; then it's sexual exploitation.

For all elementary-school-age kids, the NCMEC has an easy-to-remember phrase that sums up what kids should do in any situation in which they feel uncomfortable: NO-GO-TELL, which stands for saying NO, then GOing and TELL-ing a parent or another adult the child trusts about what happened. Children need to understand that sometimes, even if someone asks you to keep a secret, you still have to tell somebody. Kids & Company differentiates between "swell" secrets, which are fun to keep and don't hurt anybody, and "tell" secrets, which really have to be told to someone. Even if he promised not to tell, if a child has a secret that hurts him, he should understand that it's good to tell a trusted grown-up about it. You should acknowledge that sometimes it's hard to talk about something that's scary or confusing, and that even if they don't tell right away, they can anytime they want to. It is never too late.

You can practice this even with younger children, giving them scenarios and asking them if the secret in the story is a swell secret or a tell secret. For example, if daddy tells you what he got mommy for a birthday present, but says he wants it to be a surprise so don't tell her, that's swell. If the baby-sitter tells you she wants to play a game where you get undressed and touch each other's private parts, that's definitely a tell! Ask them to describe some swell and tell secrets, making sure they understand the concept.

Most of this is a way of organizing common sense, and the NCMEC has done a great job of putting it in words and phrases that are easy for kids to remember and for parents to teach and reinforce. The last part of their program, teaching kids safety strategies for different settings like shopping centers, new neighborhoods, or when they're home alone, deals with something most parents tend to overlook.

We get so caught up trying to keep our kids away from strangers that we forget to identify for them people who are safe to turn to when we're not around. As a child, my parents and all of my friends' parents taught us not to talk to strangers. But practically speaking, there are certain strangers we have to be able to talk to. Think about it: if you're separated from your five-year-old in the mall and you've taught her never to talk to strangers, you've left her stranded! We need to teach children how to choose people who could help them in an emergency: someone wearing a uniform or a name tag or standing behind a counter; a pregnant mother pushing another child in a stroller; bus drivers; school crossing guards; elderly grandmothers. Not only will this give them a safety net, it will boost their self-esteem and confidence because they know what to do if something happens. Am I willing to swear that no pregnant woman or bus driver has ever harmed a child? Of course not, but the chances are very slim and we've got to play the odds. We've got to teach our children to be profilers—to profile who are the safest people to go to when they need help.

Realistically, every parent I know (including myself, I

must admit) has misplaced a child at some point or another. I don't mean that the child's been snatched away, but maybe you're shopping with your three kids and one of them wanders off. Or maybe your child has permission to ride his bike with his friends up and down the block and instead they go one block farther, inside another friend's house to watch TV, and lose track of time. Whatever the reason, you'll probably have at least one time in your life as a parent—for at least a few minutes—where you won't know your child's whereabouts. It'll scare the hell out of you, but if you've prepared your child in advance, you'll feel that at least they know how to act, what to say, and whom to contact if they need help.

If your child is missing for any extended period of time, you can make life easier for yourself and the authorities by always keeping a recent photo and current description handy. By current description I mean keeping track of your kid's height and weight as he grows. Be able to describe his eye and hair color, favorite jacket and sneakers. These things, with a photo of your child that actually looks like him, is what will help you get your kid back quickly in most of those rare instances where you do have to get the police or other authorities involved. Photos are especially important with younger children, who can change dramatically over a period of weeks—think of how different a toddler looks as her hair grows in and darkens and you start to dress her in young-kid clothes instead of frilly baby things.

You need photos and descriptions of older kids, and you need to talk to them in advance about how to handle other situations as they're ready for them. With youngsters who might spend time alone in the house, you need to discuss how they should handle visitors at the door and phone calls. Along with your emergency list of names and phone numbers of people they can call if they need someone, also give them a list of people they're allowed to open the door for (and if someone's not on the list but seems to really need to get inside they should Check First by calling you or a neighbor they trust). On the phone, they should act like there's an adult home even if they're all alone, maybe pretending to go look for a parent before telling the caller the adult can't come to the phone.

All the tips described so far will help build self-confidence in kids of all ages. If they know they have the right to keep their body parts private, if they know how to say "No" to a situation they don't like, if they know how to call home, or how to identify a safe stranger to help them, they feel empowered and are much less vulnerable as potential victims.

You also empower them by letting them help you choose a baby-sitter. Of course, you should ask any potential baby-sitter for references—which you should check yourself—and watch how he or she interacts with your child, but you should also get the child's feedback. The NCMEC advises you to ask if they like and trust the sitter. Once they've baby-sat your children, and after they leave, ask your child what they did while you were away and how they felt while you were gone. Ask this every time you leave your child with someone. When you're checking out a new sitter, ask for references that include not only previous employers, but teachers, friends, neighbors, relatives, or counselors. And really ask them about the person's qualifications. Keep a written record of the sitter's name, home address, phone number, and driver's license number, if they have one. If you're meeting prospects through a baby-sitting service, find out if they run criminal background checks or any other type of screening process on their employees. Again, what we're trying to do here is turn the odds in our favor.

These days, a lot of children spend time in day-care. If you're looking for a day-care center for your child, go beyond taking a tour and watching your child play on-site. The NCMEC notes you may want to meet other adults who will spend time with your child, like bus drivers and janitors. Check with police and social services to see if there have been any complaints or charges brought against the center. Make sure the center is licensed and that it runs criminal background checks on employees. Finally, if you can take the time, volunteer to help out with field trips or any events they may plan so you can observe how the staff and children interact.

I may be old-fashioned, but I think it's also more than parents' responsibility to keep children out of harm's way. I don't mean to minimize their role, or let them off the hook in any way, but if they give parenting everything they have, the rest of us ought to give them some assistance. I'm really dating myself here, but when I was a kid, if I got into trouble somewhere I didn't have to tell my mom when I got home. She already knew. The grapevine of teachers/neighbors/beat cops/concerned adults worked a lot faster than I could run or ride my bike.

I think most of us in law enforcement, and certainly any of us who've spent time at crime scenes where the victim is the same size and age as our kids back home, wish we could get back to the era where people looked out for each other more. Since her murder, Kitty Genovese has become something of a symbol for the way our society works—or doesn't. Everyone says how horrible it was that so many neighbors heard her screams and no one stepped in to help her, but we do much the same thing today.

In fact, the situation is even cloudier now. If my father saw a lost child crying in a store, he wouldn't hesitate to walk up and try to help, maybe even taking the child's hand to comfort him. Today, people are afraid that if they approach a child they don't know, they may be mistaken for an abductor or molester! Even if you're hesitant, how hard is it just to keep an eye on a child from a distance while you report the kid's situation to a store clerk or security guard? When you think about what could be at stake for the youngster, do you really have an excuse not to be a benevolent stranger? And wouldn't you want someone to look out for your child?

Peter Banks, himself a former police officer and detective, puts it most succinctly: "There cannot be an error if you intervene in good faith."

Society is more violent than it used to be; knives and guns have replaced fists in settling arguments. If we hear a child screaming in the apartment next door, and perhaps have seen both the child and her mother bearing suspicious bruises, we may suspect something's not right at home. Some people would argue it's human nature not to get involved; it's self-preservation—what if that man next door gets angry with *me* for reporting him? But it's got to be human nature that we protect each other—especially those who are unable to protect themselves.

Peter Banks tells a story from his days as a cop in the District of Columbia. He overheard the dispatcher answering the phones one night giving a caller a hard time. "Why are you calling now? What do you expect us to do?"

Banks decided to look into it and learned that it was a call from a woman who'd reported a suspicious incident involving a neighbor the week before. Late one night—much later than a seven-year-old should have been up—this woman heard the little girl next door crying and moaning loudly and worried that something was the matter. But the girl lived with her grandmother and the neighbor didn't want to cause trouble for them, so she didn't call the police.

After a few days, the woman's conscience was eating away at her—what if something bad was happening next door and she did nothing to help the little girl? So she called the police, who went to the apartment and found nothing apparently amiss. The telephone call Banks overheard was another call from the woman about the same incident. She knew the police hadn't seen anything suspicious, but she was really worried about the girl.

Banks was incredulous—here someone cares enough to follow up and we're giving her a hard time? He sent officers back out to investigate further and soon had reason to be glad he did. It turned out that this girl was born to a mother who didn't want her. She spent her infancy in the hospital, then went into the foster care system, then went to live with her maternal grandmother, who abused her. She went back into foster care and finally ended up with her paternal grandmother—the woman she was living with at the time the concerned neighbor made the call. This grandmother was holding two jobs, working day and night to make ends meet. The night of the trouble, she came home from work at midnight and found a note from the girl's teacher that she hadn't done her homework. Utterly exhausted and at her wit's end, the woman whipped her granddaughter with a jump rope. When a police official checked the child's entire body, he found she had red marks and black-and-blue bruises on her back, buttocks, and legs, indicating the beating wasn't an isolated incident.

Why didn't the police who originally investigated the incident find anything? For one thing, they probably weren't looking very hard. For another, as much as the little girl obviously didn't want to be beaten, this may have been better to her than other alternatives. This child had been back and forth through so many houses she could hardly even remember all the names. Here, she's finally with a family member willing to take her in; she's not going to let the police find out anything bad happened—they'll take her away.

She wanted to stay with her grandmother and the grandmother was doing the best she could to make it work so she could keep the girl. Is this a bad person? Is this someone who enjoys inflicting pain on children? Of course not. She was working sixteen hours a day and basically punished the girl out of frustration. She didn't know any other way to deal with the situation. Authorities arranged for the girl to be tutored so school wasn't a problem anymore and got the grandmother some help, to try to build a better home and a healthier relationship for both of them. And they did well over time with intervention and counseling. But this never would have happened if the neighbor hadn't gotten involved and stayed on the police when it looked like nothing was being done. Had she not, the child could have ended up as another statistic and certainly would not be as well-prepared to face adulthood. As Peter Banks says, if there's a lesson to be learned from that case, it is: don't be satisfied. If you think something bad is happening, keep calling and calling—or call other agencies until you're convinced that someone is helping the child. And if you're not sure you should, think again of Valerie Smelser, who was horribly mistreated, then murdered by her own mother, Wanda, and Wanda's live-in boyfriend.

Or think of a little girl so special she overcame being born homeless and addicted to the crack cocaine her mother used all through her pregnancy. Little Elisa Izquierdo's story is a tragedy of extremes: the love and protection of her doting, dying father, mixed with periods of brutal, hideous abuse at the hands of her disturbed mother and her mother's vicious husband.

When Elisa was born at Woodhull Hospital in New York City in February of 1989, social workers there contacted the Child Welfare Administration to report the baby's drug-addicted state. Her father, a cook at the homeless shelter where Elisa's mother lived on and off, was immediately granted custody of the baby. Although he hadn't necessarily planned to be a father at that point, Gustavo Izquierdo seemed to relish the role and took his responsibility very seriously. He enrolled in parenting classes at the YWCA and took Elisa to the Montessori preschool at the Y from the time she turned a year old. He fixed his daughter's hair every day, ironed dresses for her to wear, and even rented a banquet hall to celebrate when she was baptized. But Izquierdo had cancer, and after a while it was too difficult to make the payments for her schooling. Elisa was such an exceptional student that her teachers and principal stepped in, introducing her to Prince Michael of Greece, who was a patron of the school. He was so enchanted by the intelligent, lively, and beautiful little girl that he promised to pay for Elisa's private schooling at the Brooklyn Friends School all the way through twelfth grade.

But in addition to this charmed aspect of her life, Elisa had a dark side to face. Her mother, now married and with more children by her husband, maintenance worker Carlos Lopez, fought for, and won, visitation rights. In 1990, social workers vouched for Awilda Lopez, saying she'd turned her life around: given up drugs, settled down with a good provider. Both Lopezes offered to take random drug tests. Elisa began unsupervised visits with them the next year.

From that point on, concerned adults in Elisa's life grew worried as they saw warning signals: the girl complained to adults at school that her mother hit her and locked her in a closet; her father told a neighbor Elisa had begun having nightmares and accidents as though no longer toilet-trained; and she had cuts and bruises on her vagina, making him worry that she'd been sexually assaulted. Elisa's principal at Montessori reported to *Time* magazine that she notified the Brooklyn Bureau of Community Services and called a hotline to report her suspicions. Elisa's father petitioned family court to remove her mother's visitation rights. By 1993, Gustavo Izquierdo had purchased plane tickets to his native Cuba—perhaps in a desperate effort to get his daughter away from those he was afraid would hurt her. Before he was able to make that trip, though, his cancer caught up with him. He died in May 1993.

Elisa's mother filed for, and was granted, permanent custody of the girl following Izquierdo's death. His cousin, Elsa Canizares, along with teachers and the principal at Montessori— even Prince Michael—fought to prevent it, but Elisa's mother had some strong allies. Child Welfare recommended she get custody, saying it had been keeping track of the family for over a year. Lopez's lawyer from the Legal Aid Society had their caseworkers' assertion that they'd visited the home and thought Elisa and her siblings would be happy living together with their mother. And Lopez had won over officials at Project Chance, a parenting program funded by the federal government to help the poor. Although she'd had setbacks, occasionally returning to drugs, Lopez also attended parenting classes and seemed to be committed to working things out.

Either because no one had the time to really check, or the Lopezes did a great job of convincing experts they were working hard to be a model family, Elisa was forced to return to an environment that was questionable at best. In addition to the problems her mother had in the past, her stepfather, Carlos Lopez, had a documented history of domestic violence. In early 1992, one month after Awilda Lopez gave birth to the couple's second child, he pulled out his pocketknife and stabbed his wife seventeen times, allegedly in front of Elisa during one of the child's weekend visits. Elisa's mother spent three days in the hospital and he served two months in prison.

Now, with five other children already in the household, resources (including patience) were already stretched to the limit. Who knows what was going on in the mind of the lonely little girl who was still trying to make sense of her heroic daddy's death? It's agonizing to think of how frightened she must have been to lose him and to learn that now she had to live with adults she so feared that short visits gave her nightmares.

By September of 1994, Elisa's last place of refuge was taken from her: her mother removed her from Montessori and enrolled her in a public school. Soon, officials there reported to the deputy director of CWA in Manhattan that Elisa frequently came to school bruised and appeared to walk with difficulty. They were reportedly told there was insufficient evidence for the agency to act on the complaints. Eventually, even Lopez's allies at Project Chance feared the worst. According to *Time,* Bart O'Connor, who runs Project Chance, contacted Elisa's CWA caseworker and was told he was "too busy" to go check it out. But over time, O'Connor, too, lost contact with the family, who avoided him and anyone else who would try to take the child away.

The day before Thanksgiving—November 22, 1995—

Fighting Back

Awilda delivered her last, fatal beating to the child. The *New York Times* quoted Elisa's aunt, who had a terrible phone conversation with Awilda that night. Lopez told her sister the girl wasn't eating or drinking, hadn't gone to the bathroom, and was "like retarded on the bed." The next day, Lopez called a neighbor for help, who discovered the child was dead. Even then, her mother's behavior was erratic: at first she refused to call police, then ran to the roof of the apartment, threatening to jump.

One NYPD lieutenant called Elisa's death the worst child abuse case he'd ever seen. Her mother confessed to slamming the child into a concrete wall, forcing her to eat her own excrement, mopping the floor with the girl's head. Police investigators reported there was no part of Elisa's body not beaten, bruised, or otherwise injured. She had been sexually violated repeatedly with a hairbrush and toothbrush. Neighbors, many of whom say they tried to contact child protection authorities, confirmed that Elisa's mother had gone back to drugs, once trying to sell a tricycle to raise money for more crack. They said they could hear the little girl pleading for her mother to stop, but her mother believed the child's father had put a spell on the girl that she had to beat out of her.

Child Welfare Administration files in New York City are confidential, so there's no way of knowing how many times people tried to save Elisa, or just how or where the system broke down, though God knows it did. In many ways, however, the bureaucracy is an easy target. Investigating child abuse can be a thankless, depressing, and often dangerous job. While the number of reported child abuse cases is rising—twenty-five percent in the five-year period between 1988 and 1993 according to reliable figures—budget cuts keep bringing down the number of caseworkers to watch over those kids.

Children need all our protection more than ever. If you suspect a child is living in a situation that is abusive, negligent, or dangerous to the welfare of that child, call someone. And keep calling until you find one who's ready to help. If anything ever happened to your child and you couldn't be there, you'd want someone else to make the call. If you're afraid of personal repercussions, call any one of the anonymous tip lines available to report suspected abuse.

In one way or another, we've got to fight back.

In an article written for *Parade* magazine, Prince Michael

sadly observed that in little Elisa's case, as fearful as they were of her mother, he and others trusted the laws to protect the girl. Many times, they can, if someone alerts authorities that a law's been broken.

There is a lot of information on these subjects, as well as tips on how to safeguard your children when they're on the Internet, how to protect them from family abduction, and just about every other area of child protection from crime and/or victimization, all available from the NCMEC. Much is also available on the Internet at: http://www.missingkids.org, or you can contact them using the toll-free number: 1-800-THE-LOST.

The good people at the NCMEC keep the pictures on the wall, and keep circulating computer-enhanced photos by mail and Internet and any other means available, to remind all children that if anything ever happens to them, someone will look for them. They care enough to let innocent little strangers know that they'll look forever if that's how long it takes to find them and make them safe.

The children in your life should know how important it is to you that they be safe and happy, too. As simplistic as it may sound, the words "I love you" and "I'm proud of you" can help insulate your children from a host of evils—from child molesters to peers who might offer them drugs or alcohol. Their confidence and self-esteem, together with our involvement and commitment, can go a long way toward fighting back.

Through the courtesy of the National Center for Missing and Exploited Children and the Adam Walsh Children's Fund, we are reprinting several key guides to child safety. We should all be very grateful to the people who devoted the time and energy to develop them and try to protect all our children.

MY 8 RULES FOR SAFETY

1. Before I go anywhere, I always CHECK FIRST with my parents or the person in charge. I tell them where I am going, how I will get there, who will be going with me, and when I'll be back.
2. I CHECK FIRST for permission from my parents before getting into a car or leaving with

anyone—even someone I know. I CHECK
FIRST before accepting money, gifts, or drugs
without my parents' knowledge.

3. It is safer for me to be with other people when
going places or playing outside. I always use the
BUDDY SYSTEM.

4. I say NO if someone tries to touch me in ways
that make me feel frightened, or uncomfortable,
or confused. Then I GO and TELL a grown-up
I trust what happened.

5. I know it is NOT MY FAULT if someone
touches me in a way that is not OK. I don't have
to keep secrets about those touches.

6. I trust my feelings and talk to grown-ups about
problems that are too big for me to handle on
my own. A lot of people care about me and will
listen and believe me. I am not alone.

7. It is never too late to ask for help. I can keep
asking until I get the help I need.

8. I am a SPECIAL PERSON, and I deserve to
feel safe. My rules are to:

- CHECK FIRST.
- USE THE BUDDY SYSTEM.
- SAY NO, THEN GO AND TELL.
- LISTEN TO MY FEELINGS, AND TALK
  WITH GROWN-UPS I TRUST ABOUT MY
  PROBLEMS AND CONCERNS.

WHAT YOU CAN DO TO PREVENT CHILD ABDUCTION AND EXPLOITATION

Know where your children are at all times. Be familiar with their friends and daily activities.

Be sensitive to changes in your children's behavior;
they are a signal that you should sit down and talk
to your children about what caused the changes.

Be alert to a teenager or adult who is paying an
unusual amount of attention to your children or
giving them inappropriate or expensive gifts.

Teach your children to trust their own feelings,

and assure them that they have the right to say NO to what they sense is wrong.

Listen carefully to your children's fears, and be supportive in all your discussions with them.

Teach your children that no one should approach them or touch them in a way that makes them feel uncomfortable. If someone does, they should tell you immediately.

Be careful about baby-sitters and any other individuals who have custody of your children.

DETECTING SEXUAL EXPLOITATION

Sexual exploitation should not be confused with physical contacts that are true expressions of affection. A warm and healthy relationship can exist if adults respect the child and place reasonable limits on their physical interaction.

Child molestation is often a repeat crime. Many kids are victimized a number of times. The reality of sexual exploitation is that often the child is very confused, uncomfortable, and unwilling to talk about the experience with parents, teachers, or anyone else. But they will talk if you have already established an atmosphere of trust and support in your home, where your child will feel free to talk without fear of accusation, blame, or guilt.

Parents should be alert to the indicators of sexual abuse:

- Changes in behavior, extreme mood swings, withdrawal, fearfulness, or excessive crying.
- Bed-wetting, nightmares, fear of going to bed, or other sleep disturbances.
- Acting out inappropriate sexual activity or showing an unusual interest in sexual matters.
- A sudden acting out of feelings or aggressive or rebellious behavior.
- Regression to infantile behavior.

- A fear of certain places, people, or activities, especially being alone with certain people. Children should not be forced to give affection to an adult or teenager if they do not want to. A desire to avoid this may indicate a problem.
- Pain, itching, bleeding, fluid, or rawness in the private areas.

BASIC RULES OF SAFETY FOR CHILDREN

As soon as your children can articulate a sentence, they can begin the process of learning how to protect themselves against seduction and exploitation. Children should be taught:

If you are in a public place, and you get separated from your parents, don't wander around looking for them. Go to a checkout counter, the security office, or the lost-and-found and quickly tell the person in charge that you have lost your mom and dad and need help in finding them.

You should not get into a car or go anywhere with any person unless your parents have told you that it is okay.

If someone follows you on foot or in a car, stay away from him or her. You don't need to go near the car to talk to the people inside.

Grown-ups and other older people who need help should not be asking children for help; they should be asking older people.

No one should be asking you for directions or to look for a lost puppy or telling you that your mother or father is in trouble and that he will take you to them.

If someone tries to take you somewhere, quickly get away from him (or her) and yell or scream, "This man is trying to take me away!" or "This person is not my father (or mother)!"

You should try to use the Buddy System and never go places alone.

AGE-SKILL CHART

Grade Level	K	1	2
Skill			
Telephone	Know 7-digit telephone number	Review home telephone number Know how and when to call the Operator	Know how to get help in an emergency (parents' work numbers, police, fire, neighbors, Operator)
Address	Know name, hometown, and state	Review home address	Review home address
The Buddy System	Know how and when to use the BUDDY SYSTEM	Know how and when to use the BUDDY SYSTEM	Know how and when to use the BUDDY SYSTEM
Check First	Know when to CHECK FIRST	Know when to CHECK FIRST	Know when to CHECK FIRST
Types of Touching	Recognize "private parts" of the body Distinguish between "OKAY" and "NOT OKAY" touches	Recognize "private parts" of the body Distinguish between "OKAY" and "NOT OKAY" touches Distinguish between "SWELL" secrets and "TELL" secrets	Recognize "private parts" of the body Distinguish between "OKAY" and "NOT OKAY" touches Distinguish between "SWELL" secrets and "TELL" secrets
NO-GO-TELL	Know how and when to use NO-GO-TELL	Know how and when to use NO-GO-TELL	Recognize common tricks Know how to respond to unsolicited attention by someone older
Safety Strategies in various settings	Know how to choose people who could help in an emergency	Safety strategies in stores Know how to choose people who could help in an emergency	Safety strategies in unfamiliar neighborhoods Know how to choose people who could help in an emergency

3	4	5 and 6	Grade Level
			Skill
Know 11-digit telephone number

Know how to make long-distance calls | Know how to use a pay telephone to make local, long-distance, and emergency calls | All safety strategies and skills taught in previous grades are reviewed and reinforced through a variety of projects and activities in grades 5 and 6 | Telephone |
Identify home state and surrounding states on map	Make ID card		Address
Apply the BUDDY SYSTEM in a variety of situations	Apply the BUDDY SYSTEM in a variety of situations		The Buddy System
Apply CHECK FIRST in a variety of situations	Apply CHECK FIRST in a variety of situations		Check First
Review "private parts" of the body

Distinguish between "OKAY" and "NOT OKAY" touches

Distinguish between "SWELL" secrets and "TELL" secrets | Review "private parts" of the body

Review types of touching

Distinguish between "SWELL" secrets and "TELL" secrets | | Types of Touching |
| Recognize common tricks

Know how to respond to unsolicited attention by someone older

Apply NO-GO-TELL in a variety of situations | Recognize common tricks

Apply NO-GO-TELL in a variety of situations | | NO-GO-TELL |
| Safety strategies when home alone or in charge at home

Know how to choose people who could help in an emergency | Safety strategies when home alone or in charge at home

Know how to choose people who could help in an emergency | | Safety Strategies in various settings |

CHAPTER 7

Sue Blue

As soon as he saw her for the first time, John Albert Collins knew that Gertrude Martinus was the girl for him. It was May of 1956 at the White Cannon Inn in East Rockaway, Long Island. Gertrude, or Trudy as she was called, was there for a Young Republican Club dance. Jack Collins and his buddy Ron White were sitting in the cocktail lounge, celebrating having recently gotten out of the Navy. They were savoring a pair of frosty Heinekens when Trudy passed through on her way to the ladies' room. Jack's friend recognized her and called out to say hello. Then he introduced her to Jack.

"Right then and there, as our eyes met," Jack said, "I saw straight into her soul, and I was utterly and profoundly in love."

Trudy wasn't so sure, at least not so quickly. She was with a date that evening who would not be at all appreciative of this other man's attention.

But Jack persisted. He got her phone number from Ron. He called a week later and asked her out. She agreed. During this first date, he asked her to marry him.

Her parents were understandably wary about this fast-lane approach from a young man whose current summertime employment was as a general laborer, occasionally working the garbage detail, for the Department of Public Works in the town of Lynbrook, Long Island. Never mind that he was awaiting autumn entry into Columbia University's Graduate School of English literature.

Still, Thomas Martinus, a bank examiner, didn't have a whole lot of room to talk. He had asked Mamie Johanna Hotze to marry him on the third day after they'd met. So by that standard, Jack Collins was something of a slowpoke. When Trudy's dad died in June of 1994, he and Mamie had been married for sixty-eight years.

For whatever combination of reasons, personal confidence or divine plan, Jack and Trudy Collins each knew what they wanted. They were engaged that August and married in December of 1956. Ironically, Trudy's parents had constantly warned her as a child: "Always do your very best, or you'll end up marrying a garbage man."

After a semester at Columbia, Jack decided a Ph.D. in English might not be the fastest route to providing the kind of life he wanted Trudy to enjoy. She had a very good job as a legal secretary for Caltex—the California-Texas Oil Company—and it was an insult to his sense of 1950s manhood to think of a woman having to support him. So he quit grad school and got a job in the purchasing department of M.W. Kellogg, a major international engineering and construction company. After a year, he had been promoted to buyer and had enrolled in night law school at NYU.

As he got to know his son-in-law, Tom Martinus's continuing concern was that since Jack was Catholic, he'd keep Trudy pregnant all the time, spending her life tending an army of kids. Yet after seven years of marriage, Jack and Trudy were still childless. By this time Jack had graduated from law school, and had decided his career ambitions lay more in diplomacy than in either business or law. He sat for and passed the notoriously challenging U.S. Foreign Service examination, and with Trudy at his side, was sworn in as a foreign service officer on January 2, 1962, in the State Department's Diplomatic Reception Room.

Now living just outside of Washington, D.C., they contacted Catholic Charities of Northern Virginia to try to adopt a child. But since Jack was Catholic and Trudy was Episcopalian, they were considered a "mixed marriage" and told theirs would not be considered a suitable situation for adoption. The Episcopal Church agency told them the same thing. But their passion to be parents had not diminished.

In August 1963, Jack was serving as vice consul at the U.S. consulate general in Aleppo, Syria, responsible for consular and commercial affairs. He had heard of an orphanage called the Crèche in Beirut, the capital of neighboring Lebanon, from which it might be easier to adopt a child.

As it turned out, because Jack's professional responsibilities kept him in Aleppo, Trudy was able to travel there first. The Crèche was run by the Sisters of Charity, a French religious order. She was escorted into a room of about thirty cribs containing children ranging in age from birth to about six months. Just at this time, however, there was an attempted coup in Syria, and the borders closed and telephone lines were down. Being a resourceful diplomatic wife, Trudy waited until the crisis passed, then as soon as she could get a telephone line, she called Jack in Syria and said, "I think we've found a child."

But she didn't want to tell Jack anything about her selection. So as soon as the borders reopened, Jack eagerly undertook the three-hundred-mile journey, driving south to Homs, west to the Mediterranean coast, and then south again to Beirut. He met up with Trudy there, and together they went to the orphanage. Trudy and the orphanage director took Jack into the same room and let him go from crib to crib, getting acquainted with each child. When he had finished the procedure, he told Trudy which child he had selected.

"I think it was the eyes," says Jack.

It was the same choice as hers—a beautiful little dark-haired, dark-eyed six-month-old boy. The director told them they could take the child with them for the next few days while the nuns completed the paperwork. By August 25, the little boy was theirs. The nuns had called him Robert Raja Rabeh. Jack and Trudy wanted to name him Thomas after Trudy's father, but soberly decided that he would inevitably be called Tom Collins, a nickname no child should be saddled with, so they agreed on Stephen Thomas Collins.

They returned to the States when Stephen was a year and a half old, and had him naturalized on November 9, 1964, at the Federal Courthouse in lower Manhattan, amidst a crowd of new American citizens from all over the world. When the time came for him to swear his allegiance to his new country, Trudy raised the baby's right hand for him. A month later the three of them flew to Sweden for Jack's next assignment, with the U.S. embassy in Stockholm, and this time little Stephen traveled on an American diplomatic passport.

In Stockholm, Jack served as deputy scientific attaché. Once they were settled in Sweden, he and Trudy started thinking about another child. They contacted the orphanage in Beirut and asked if they could adopt a little girl this time. But for a combination of reasons, no female children in the age range they were looking for were available, so they kept in touch, hoping the situation would change.

When they returned to the United States in late 1966 and settled in an apartment in Alexandria, Virginia, they still hadn't been able to adopt another child. Around March of 1967, Jack was attending mass one Sunday at Blessed Sacrament parish when he noticed in the church bulletin an item announcing that Catholic Charities had changed its policy on adoption and now only required that one parent be Catholic. When he got home, he excitedly told Trudy the news and the next day they put in their application. An elaborate round of interviews and home visits followed, during which the Collinses sensed their raising of Stephen, now a toddler, was being scrutinized in exhaustive detail.

Finally, by summer, they got a call from the agency saying they had a female child who might be right for them.

She was a year old. Her christening name was Regina Celeste, which the adoption officials told them meant heavenly queen, but everyone called her Gina. When Jack and Trudy saw her for the first time, they thought she was, in Trudy's words, "just as sweet as she could be." But, they also had to admit, it was not really her best day. She had a bad cold, her nose was running constantly, and she wouldn't stop crying. Also, her right foot had been turned in since she was born and she had to sleep each night with a spreader bar that looked like a medieval prison device attached to each ankle to keep her lower legs apart. In spite of that, she was absolutely adorable, with beautiful blond hair and luminous, almost opaque skin. Within another six or eight months they were able to dispense with the leg brace, though she had to wear corrective shoes until she was five. The foot problem must have made a deep impression, though, because as she grew up, she constantly pushed herself at athletics and sports, particularly the sports that involved running.

Her beauty belied her personal history, which was a woeful one. In the year she'd been alive, she'd already been through at least three foster homes. Her birth mother had been young and unwed and had given her up in the hopes of finding a better life for her. She was initially settled with a military family, but when they'd gotten orders to relocate, that foster-home placement fell through. The agency became unhappy with the next family she went with, having some concern that she was being mistreated, so they took her back. She had just returned from a third foster home when Jack and Trudy saw her and fell in love with her. They decided to call her Suzanne Marie, the middle name in honor of Trudy's mother, Mamie. To make sure Stephen didn't feel slighted, they reaffirmed to him that they'd also specifically picked him out to be theirs and how special he was to them, and that now he would have a sister who would be special, too.

They took Stephen with them when they went to pick up Suzanne and bring her home. "We went in hoping for the ideal situation," Jack recalls, "where we'd see our little girl again and she'd run right up to me or Trudy. Instead, we both walked over and she backed away and started crying. We took another step and she backed up another step and cried harder. And then Stephen started walking toward her and she hobbled over and put her arms around him. I think they bonded that minute."

Trudy adds, "With what she'd been through, she was so afraid of big people, I think she was glad to see someone her own size."

As they walked out to the car with Suzanne, she was still sniffling and sobbing, about to be taken away by yet another family. But then Stephen put his arms around her and said, "It's all right, Suzanne. Don't cry. You're our family and we're your family." She stopped crying.

In the car, they heard more sniffling. Then they heard

Stephen whisper to her, and she stopped. This happened several times on the way home, and each time Stephen would whisper to her and she stopped. They never knew what he said, but at that point Trudy turned to Jack and said, "Stephen's in charge."

And when they got home, he was the one who showed her her room and her bed. He was the one who told her what to do. Suzanne looked up to Stephen as her leader and worshipped him from then on.

For about a month after they got her home, Suzanne did anything they asked her to, with no argument and no balking. It was delightful for a while, then Trudy became concerned.

"I thought, 'There's something wrong with this child. She's not normal. She's too obedient.' It suddenly dawned on us that with her background, she wasn't sure if she was going to stay. Stephen talked to her a lot, and once she became convinced in her own mind, 'Okay, this is forever,' she became a normal child."

What Trudy began seeing in her daughter were attributes that would really never change all through Suzanne's growing-up years. She was a blond-haired, blue-green-eyed beauty, utterly charming and always going off in many directions at once. "A true Gemini," says Trudy.

She showed her spunk and adaptability in various ways. Since she'd been a baby, she was hardly ever without her security pacifier. Jack thinks the habit was probably started in one of her foster homes. When she was a little less than two, the Collinses were driving to Bethany Beach, Delaware, for a brief vacation. She must have managed to roll down the rear window and then suddenly they heard Stephen call out, "Mommy! Daddy! Suzanne's lost her plug!"

We've got to get it back, Trudy thought, but Jack said, "I can't stop here."

Suzanne said she thought she could get along without it. Impressed, Trudy said, "Suzanne, you've just grown up. Now you're a big girl and you don't need that."

Jack adds, "And she didn't. She never needed the pacifier again."

For Suzanne, everything in life was so exciting, she wanted to do it all at once. And whatever it was she had her sights fixed on, no amount of advice or threat of punishment could deter her. Every day of her life since she was a very little girl, Suzanne Marie Collins had her own agenda. That remained constant.

Another constant was her unwavering love of her big brother. Even when the four-year-old Stephen started to rethink the benefits of sharing Mom and Dad with a baby sister and sometimes balked at sharing his toys and playing with her, she continued adoring him.

The two children were very different—the intense and darkly handsome little boy with the penetrating eyes and his blond and cuddly, doll-like sister. Stephen was hyperactive, always fussing, wanting to control something or have his own way. Suzanne was more laid-back, sweet, and alluring, just happy to be alive and in a stable, loving environment. Suzanne wanted her way, too, but she seemed to know instinctively how to go around corners to get it rather than taking a direct approach. Or, as Stephen recently put it, he was much more frenetic and intense like his mother, and she was much calmer and more laid-back like her father.

And her father was absolutely smitten with her. Early on, it became clear that Suzanne's favorite color was blue. Jack started calling her Blue Bell after he noticed this. In certain light, he thought, her eyes were the same color as the sky. Sometimes, he shortened it simply to Belle. Trudy called her Sue Blue. Suzanne loved all of the nicknames. The serious-minded Stephen continued calling her Suzanne.

Right from the beginning she showed her curious, independent streak. She had learned how to rock her crib to get it to move and managed to move it over to the bookcase where Jack kept his legal books, and, on more than one occasion, climbed onto it. During a family trip to Chicago when she was three, she wandered off because she saw a set of swings in the distance and thought she could master them. When the terrified Trudy caught up with her, she was playing with about five other children.

"She just never looked back," said Trudy. "She was fearless. I'm not sure Stephen was any better behaved than she was; he just had more reasonable fears which kept him from getting into trouble."

When Stephen was in elementary school and Suzanne was

a five-year-old in preschool, the family moved to Salonika, in northern Greece. It was a big adventure for both kids. Stephen had some residual memory of Sweden, but this was something completely new and exciting for Suzanne.

Before Jack assumed his posting as political officer at the American consulate general in Salonika, there was a week of briefings at the embassy in Athens, during which the family was put up at the elegant King's Palace Hotel. After an initial nap to try to overcome the effects of the nine-hour plane ride, it was time for what Jack and Trudy always referred to as "TFH"—the teeth, face, and hands ritual.

Suzanne was sent into the bathroom first. After what seemed like quite a while, Trudy called in, "Suzanne, are you okay?"

"Oh yes, Mommy," the child declared.

"I hear the water running. Aren't you finished yet?"

"Oh yes," she replied. "I finished my teeth."

"Then would you open the door, please?"

Suzanne had discovered that the cap from an American toothpaste tube fit just perfectly in the Greek sink drain. And once she had the basin filled, she could watch the water cascade over the edge and onto the floor—a rather spectacular show.

They then went to dinner at the hotel's rooftop terrace restaurant, which offered a beautiful view of the floodlit Acropolis. Jack surveyed the menu and translated it into English for the kids, who both responded with disbelief, "What! They don't have hamburgers?"

A short while later, the lights on the terrace suddenly go off. Waiters with trays start crashing into each other. Fearing the worst, Trudy says, "Suzanne, do you have something in your hand?"

She replied, "Yes, Mommy."

"Would you hand it to me, please?" Sure enough, it was the plug for the lights. "She'd just wondered what it was for," Trudy explained.

Unfortunately, their waiter just happened to be the man who had been sent in to unplug the sink in their flooded bathroom.

Their room was on the fourth floor of the hotel. The next day Trudy heard Stephen say, "Mom, she did it again!" and looked up to see Suzanne climbing onto the railing of the balcony. She just had no fear.

Four days later, as they were about to leave the hotel, they stopped in for one final lunch. "In the downstairs dining room," Trudy recalled. "It seemed safer. We'd just finished eating and I'm looking at Suzanne and she's got a glass in her mouth; it was a stemmed wine glass and I guess it was new to her. And I said, 'Suzanne, are you drinking or are you just playing with that glass? Why don't you put your glass down if you're not drinking?'

"So she does, and there's this huge piece missing. I said, 'Suzanne, don't say a word. Nod if you have something in your mouth that isn't food.' She nodded. I said, 'Gently open your mouth and put it in my hand.' Thank God she'd bitten it off in one piece and wasn't bleeding. I said, 'Suzanne, why did you do that?'

"She said, 'We don't have glasses like that back home. I wanted to see how it tasted.' So we tiptoed out of the hotel and never looked back."

Stephen remembers that Suzanne was always a very happy child. "She had a really shiny personality. She was always in a good mood. Because of my father's work, my parents always did a lot of entertaining and Suzanne was invariably the star of the show. She loved the attention. There wasn't anyone who didn't like her."

By the physical evidence, this continued to be true. Jack and Trudy have at least ten or twelve thick photo albums chronicling their children's growing-up years. There is scarcely a picture of Suzanne anywhere without a radiant smile.

She found it easy to make friends. Trudy enrolled her in a Brownie troop, which she loved. She wanted to wear her uniform all the time and couldn't understand why it was reserved for meetings.

Whatever took hold of Suzanne's imagination came easily to her; whatever didn't interest her was like pulling teeth, and that included her studies. When the family was transferred from Salonika to Athens, she and Stephen went to the Ursuline School. In September or October of their second year there, one of the nuns sent a report home saying that Suzanne couldn't seem to master the multiplication tables. So when he got home from work that night, Jack said to her, "You're a smart girl. Why are you having trouble?"

She replied, "Well, I think my brain rotted over the summer."

Jack said, "Could I hear that again?" She repeated her analysis of the problem. So he told her, "We're going to play a game together. We're going to make fun out of the times tables."

"So I just kept drilling her. Whenever I saw her I'd say, 'Eight times two!' or 'Nine times six!' and it became a challenge to her to come up with the right answer. I think it drove Trudy a little mad, but she learned her tables and had fun with it. You always had to challenge her."

Despite Suzanne's lack of interest in school, languages came easily to both children. While English was the first language Stephen learned to speak, from his infancy in Lebanon and Syria he understood a good deal of both Arabic and French. He maintained the French, studied it in college and speaks it fluently. Both children took Greek in school and the teachers remarked how quickly and accurately Suzanne had picked up the proper accent and intonation, even better than Stephen had.

By the time they left Greece, Stephen was thirteen and Suzanne was ten. Actually, Jack was glad to be going home. The final two years of his mission in Greece had coincided with a period of Greek political upheaval, the Cyprus crisis and its aftermath. Several Americans had been killed and he didn't like the trend he was seeing. He was concerned that something could happen where he wouldn't be able to protect his family and he didn't like that lack of control.

From Greece, the Collinses moved to Madison, Wisconsin, in 1976 as part of a new State Department program in which foreign service officers were to learn about government below the federal level so they would be better equipped to explain our grass-roots system overseas. Jack was initially assigned to the governor's office, and then moved on to become special assistant to the director of the Department of Health and Social Services. He and Trudy both considered themselves conservative and traditional and were wary of what they saw all around them in this liberal college town.

They were particularly concerned about the attitudes their kids would pick up in school.

But Madison was beautiful and charming; they made good friends and so did the children. As soon as Suzanne experienced her first McDonald's she decided that American life was okay. And being a pretty blue-eyed blond, she fit in right away with the indigenous Swedish and German stock. She looked as if she had come right off one of the local dairy farms.

Stephen, on the other hand, had the opposite experience, a Middle Easterner in Middle America. His classmates thought he was Mexican and tormented him unmercifully, though Stephen took it stoically. Actually, he was in high school before he confided to his parents how he'd been treated in Wisconsin and both of them felt very guilty for not having recognized the problem and dealt with it. But as a result, Stephen felt he had to excel in school to prove himself and he was an A student from then on. He even joined the school football squad although he was short and stocky and was regularly pummeled by blond giants all around him. Perhaps as a latent result of his first months of life as a foundling in a Lebanese orphanage, Stephen went through life with the attitude that everything has to be earned and fought for.

The next stop on the odyssey was Springfield, Virginia, just outside of Washington, D.C., when Jack transferred back to State Department headquarters. Suzanne was twelve and Stephen fifteen, and if the two of them ever felt as though they had an actual home base, an actual place to be from, it was to be Springfield.

Jeff Freeman met Steve Collins the summer before they both started tenth grade and they quickly became best friends. And he soon became close with Suzanne, whom he remembers at the time as being a cute little tomboy who always wanted to hang around her big brother and his friends. He also remembers that while Steve might have found this annoying or bothersome from time to time the way older siblings inevitably do, he was always tactful and tried extraordinarily hard to include her and make her feel welcome.

While Stephen continued to do well at Robert E. Lee

High School, Suzanne wasn't lighting any academic fires at Francis Scott Key Intermediate. In repeated meetings with the parents, teachers and counselors told them they were being too strict, that both children, but particularly Suzanne, needed a more unstructured life. Jack and Trudy felt that with her inability or unwillingness to concentrate on her studies, less structure was exactly what she did not need. They felt confused and bewildered, as if all the traditional standards and rules had mysteriously changed or evaporated while they were overseas.

For example, to Suzanne it always seemed a telling point in a parental argument or discussion that "the other kids in school are doing it," whatever "it" happened to be—wearing makeup, going to the mall alone, staying out late. The reasoning didn't seem very compelling to Trudy, and that was where the conflict lay. Trudy would do whatever she thought was ultimately best for her children, whether her action turned out to be popular or not. Suzanne would continue to do whatever she set out to do, merely factoring in the discipline or punishment as a price to be paid.

There was the time when Suzanne wanted to sleep over at the house of a girlfriend whose mother had a live-in boyfriend, an absolute taboo as far as Jack and Trudy were concerned. "She had some real problems with that," Trudy remembers.

Trudy also didn't want her daughter wearing makeup to junior high school, despite the fact that many of the other girls were doing it. Jeff Freeman now owns his own home construction and remodeling business. He did a lot of renovation work on the Collinses' house in Springfield before they sold it in 1994. While he was working on a heating vent in the basement he noticed a small package, all wrapped up. He pulled it out and opened it and found a stash of makeup, lipstick, and eyeliner. He wrapped it back up and replaced it where he'd found it, but then called Stephen and described it.

"I'll bet that was Suzanne's," Steve said, recalling that she often went to great and creative lengths to get around her mother's bans. The traditional and proper Trudy didn't approve of wearing jeans to school, so Suzanne would sometimes leave the house for school and change into jeans in the bushes.

"Actually," Steve says, looking back on this period of their lives, "Suzanne was twice as good as I was. I was going out drinking sometimes three or four nights a week. She just didn't mask it as well as I did. I was getting good grades and it's easy to mask a lot of things when your grades are good. Suzanne wasn't getting good grades so she was always under the microscope. They worried more about the decisions she made than mine. I always looked like I was well-adjusted, whereas she couldn't follow the most basic instructions, so she could do something totally dumb."

Jack wasn't as worried about Suzanne's behavior as Trudy was, although he admits that since he was out of town a good deal, she bore the brunt of the monitoring and disciplining. Like Stephen, a part of Jack wished that if his daughter was going to be sneaky about what she wanted to do, that at least she could pull it off so he wouldn't have to know.

"I really didn't think we had a major problem," said Jack, "but as parents, you want everything to be as perfect as possible and when you see something that isn't, you want to do something about it. Maybe it was a test of wills. She was saying, 'I'm growing up now. I'm feeling my oats. I want to stand on my own two feet!' So that's what it became— back and forth. She just dug her heels in. She wouldn't give in and we wouldn't give in."

"Sue often said, 'I want to be mistress of my fate,'" Trudy remembers. "'I want to decide what I'm going to do.' And I would answer, 'Well, there are certain areas where you can't do that yet. You're underage and we're your parents.' Then she would say, 'But I know what's good for me.' I would say, 'Well, that's debatable. And besides, we're in charge.'"

"She'd always be saying, 'Steve gets to stay out this late; why can't I?'" Jeff observed.

Trudy said, "She'd be due home at a certain time and she wouldn't come home and she wouldn't call. So when she did finally come home, the riot act was read. We'd say, 'We told you, so next time we're going to take an hour off.' But of course, that didn't matter. She went out and stayed out late anyway."

Both Steve and Jeff Freeman remember Suzanne frequently being grounded or on restriction for some infraction or other. "She was always getting busted," Steve remembers. "It got to the point where there was nothing more they could take away from her. They set times for her to do her homework and stood over her until she did it. They loved her so much they wanted things to be perfect for her. But all in all, I think her personality was a lot healthier than mine. I always had to do something one hundred percent. Suzanne had much more of a devil-may-care attitude about things."

Whether she intended to or not, Suzanne had a knack for pushing all the right buttons with her parents, both positively and negatively. Trudy took pride in the clothes she bought for her daughter and hated it when Suzanne would continually borrow from and swap with the other girls.

"I'd be doing the wash and I'd say to her, 'Where did this come from?' 'Oh, that's Sara Jane's,' she'd say. And I'd say, 'Haven't we been over this before? You will not wear other people's clothing. You will not let other people wear your clothing.' Well, she didn't mind me a bit. She'd just say, 'Everybody does it, Mom.' Do you know how tired I got of hearing that? But nothing deterred her. She'd just keep on doing it."

But she also knew how to use her charm and naturally affectionate personality. She was always putting her arms around people. Trudy says, "She'd hug me and say, 'I'm so sorry, Mom.' I used to tease her and say, 'Don't try to get around me by giving me a hug. Hugs don't count when you're not doing what I asked you to do!' She'd say, 'They don't count for anything?' And then, of course, I'd have to relent and say, 'Well, they count for something.'"

One basis of the conflict with her parents were her grades in school. "The Collinses' expectations for both of their children was for them always to meet their potential," Jeff observed. "Steve delivered straight As and Suzanne delivered Cs."

Other than science class, academics just didn't turn her

on. Says Stephen, "She just wasn't academically challenged in high school."

She found all the other aspects of high school tremendously engaging. She was elected to student council each year and ran all the school dances. Through the church, she regularly did volunteer work with retarded children and young adults.

Trudy recalls one church social Suzanne helped organize for these disabled young people: "Some of these boys were probably twenty-six but the doctors said that their intellectual and emotional level was about seven. And Sue told me, 'I would make them get up and dance.' She said that seemed to please them and she said it worked out so well. And she said, 'I don't understand why people are afraid of them. You can make their day a little nicer; that's the important thing.' I remember I said to her, 'Well, I admire you, Suzanne. I'd probably be hesitant. I'd be afraid of the reaction I'd get.' She said, 'Well, there's nothing sexual about it, Mom; it's nothing like that. They just want someone to care about them and treat them nicely, and I enjoy doing that.'"

She also loved being around and working with the elderly and had a special relationship with Trudy's parents. She seemed to take great pleasure and satisfaction from giving advice and affecting the lives around her. Suzanne was the school's primary advisor to the lovelorn and was continually getting caught passing notes in class advising her friends on their relationships. Much of this incriminating evidence would end up being sent home to Trudy with letters from the teachers saying, "Instead of her classwork, this is what Suzanne was doing today."

One teacher commented, "If school could be just social arrangements, Suzanne would get all As."

Her room reflected her expansive personality. She had the largest bedroom in the house and filled it with dolls and stuffed animals. After she filled the shelves, she started on the windowsills. Wherever in the world Jack would travel, he'd bring something back for her. "But," as Trudy noted, "it was an effort for her to stop long enough to hang something up or find a proper place for it, so it would just get shoved in the corner and then she'd close the door and nobody else got to see it."

She had also grown from a cute and tomboyish little girl into a gorgeous young woman. "Very, very pretty, the top one percent," in her proud brother's opinion. The opinion was borne out by others. Jeff says, "She blossomed in tenth grade, which gave her renewed self-confidence. I thought she was very cute."

She did some modeling and possessed an excellent fashion sense. All of this also made Stephen even more protective of her. "I always wanted to know who it was she was with when she went out on a date," he admits. "Before she'd go out, the guys and I would try to get with whoever it was and roast him in kind of a kidding way, but send him away with the right attitude. A lot of people were interested in her and I was just trying to look out for her and help her out." Stephen's concerns for his sister were taken quite seriously by anyone approaching her. He was short and stocky, very strong and athletic, and a weight lifter with biceps like tree trunks.

In her own way, Suzanne was just as athletic as Steve. And when she matured, she matured fast and dramatically. She appeared older than her age and so stopped looking like Steve's kid sister. Even when she was still in junior high, she fit in more with his crowd, and before long they would say to him, "Why don't you bring Sue along?" She was very popular. And while there were many aspects of her life which really worried her parents, they always trusted her judgment with boys. On that score, she'd never done anything to alarm them. And besides, they knew Stephen was looking out for her.

According to the time-honored suburban ritual, Stephen got his learner's permit within days of his sixteenth birthday and his driver's license shortly after that, then bought himself a huge used Pontiac. Jack and Trudy hoped they could hold out driving privileges as an incentive to Suzanne to get her grades up.

"Every time she'd bring home a report card, I'd say, 'Gee, Sue, you know you're still sort of far away from what you want. Shouldn't you be thinking about that?'" said Trudy.

Other than social organizing, Suzanne's greatest passion in school was sports. She was a hurdler on the high school track team and an outfielder on the women's softball team.

With her long legs and tall, slender frame, she was a natural athlete. This was particularly gratifying to a girl who had spent the first year and a half of her life having to sleep in a leg brace. Being the perky beauty she was, she'd been approached about joining the cheerleading squad, but that wasn't for her.

"We thought of her as kind of a semi-jock chick," Jeff Freeman remembers. "Suzanne would always prefer to do rather than watch. She'd always rather participate."

"She became her own person early," he adds. "She developed a sense of herself earlier than a lot of kids." And she had to try everything herself. One day in high school, Suzanne and another girl skipped school, obtained a bottle of rum, and proceeded to kill it off between them to see what it would be like. Her next tactical error was showing up for her softball game.

Trudy got a call from the school office: "Your daughter is in a questionable state. We think you'd better come pick her up." As soon as Trudy saw her, it was obvious what she'd done. "She was blotto."

When they got home, Suzanne meekly asked, "Are you mad, Mommy?"

"Let's say I'm very disappointed," Trudy replied sternly.

"Are you going to punish me?"

"No, Suzanne," her mother explained. "Because tomorrow morning you are going to be punished by the good Lord."

"What do you mean?" she asked.

"You'll see," Trudy said.

"The next morning, she was so sick, she turned every color of the rainbow, ending up with green. It was terrible, and the hangover lasted for two days. I would get her a cold compress and she would say, 'Mommy, why are you being so nice to me?' I felt so badly for her.

"When she finally came out of it, she just said, 'I don't like feeling like that.' I said, 'I'm very glad to hear that.'"

The house in Springfield became a focal point for Steve and Suzanne's social circle. Perhaps it was because Suzanne was such an organizer, perhaps it was because Jack and Trudy always welcomed their children's friends and talked to them as intelligent adults. Often, Steve says, there were ten or twelve guys there at one time. Also, there were often friends staying with them. To this day, Suzanne's and Stephen's friends continue to visit Jack and Trudy, and often spend the night whenever they're in town.

When she was in high school, Suzanne commented to her mother that there was a girl in her class named Gina, and that she really liked the name. Trudy told her how interesting that was, since Gina had been her original name.

Suzanne asked, "Do you think it would be possible for me to find out who my birth mother was?"

"I think now because of laws like the Freedom of Information Act, you probably could," Trudy said. "If it's important to you and you'd like us to, we'll help you find out."

"Well, let me think about it," Suzanne said, but she never pursued the matter.

They then asked Stephen if he wanted help learning about his own origins. "Why should I want to know who my original parents were?" he said. "I'm happy with you."

Suzanne was a high school sophomore when Stephen left home for college at the University of Virginia in Charlottesville, continuing as the academic star he had been in high school. He intended to major in fine art. By the end of his first year, he decided he was more interested in commercial art than fine art, so he decided to transfer to Virginia Commonwealth University in Richmond, whose program was more heavily oriented toward commercial art.

Jack thought this was a terrible idea, moving away from such a challenging and nationally prestigious university, but felt it was Stephen's decision to make. He became more actively involved when Steve went down to Texas over the Christmas break to visit a friend, and then announced he had decided to stay there, drop out of school, and look for a job in the oil and gas industry.

Jack told him, "You're making a bad judgment and you're going to be on your own if you do that. We will not bail you out."

Suzanne became extremely upset that Jack and Trudy seemed to be abandoning and throwing out her beloved brother.

"No, Suzanne, I'm not throwing him out," Jack replied. "It's his choice. If he stays in college, we'll do whatever we can to help and support him. But he's making a bad choice and I can't encourage him or support it." They were never sure whether Suzanne approved of Stephen's move or not, but regardless of how she felt and regardless of the conflicts she herself had had with her parents, she couldn't bear the idea of Stephen being estranged from the family.

But the bottom had recently fallen out of the oil market and jobs were scarce. And Stephen started to feel subtle pressures from his friend's family; they were concerned that he intended to live in their house forever. In the meantime, though, he'd met a girl who offered to let him live with her. He got a job working in a local supermarket to help support them. He wrote to Suzanne about her, saying she was blond and pretty and just like his sister.

Interestingly, while Stephen stayed in Texas, his Texas friend decided to go to school in the Washington, D.C., area and stayed for a while with the Collinses. At one point, Stephen decided to come home for a visit and announced he was bringing his girlfriend home with him. Upon meeting her, Suzanne quickly decided she was nothing at all like herself.

Stephen returned to Texas and got a job in the construction business. Jack and Trudy were beside themselves.

"Eventually he called us," says Jack. "He'd been in a car accident, his relationship with his girlfriend had ended, somebody had stolen his wallet with his driver's license, he'd fallen off a building, he'd broken his glasses, and he was out of money. He'd about hit rock bottom."

Jack had foreign service business he couldn't postpone, so Trudy flew down to Texas alone. "I never thought much about the devil and things like that, but when I got down there and saw what was happening, I thought, 'The devil lives in Arlington, Texas.' All these young people who had run away from home. They were merely existing; their lives were terrible. All these young girls would come over to talk to me—you know, I was their mother figure—and tell me their sad tales: how they went with this man who was married but he loved her so much he was going to leave his wife. And they all believed it. It was very sad.

"Anyway, I finally said to Stephen, 'This is your last chance. This is it. You come back with me or you stay here.'

An aerial view of the FBI Academy on the U.S. Marine Base in Quantico, Virginia. Our offices were sixty feet underground, behind the tall building at the lower right. (FBI photo)

My era's Investigative Support Group gathers together one last time at my retirement dinner in Quantico in June 1995. From left, Steve Mardigian, Pete Smerick, Clint Van Zandt, Jana Monroe, Gregg McCrary, Jim Wright, Greg Cooper, me, and Jud Ray. Not pictured are Larry Ankrom, Steve Etter, Bill Hagmaier, and Tom Salp. (Photo by Mark Olshaker)

Special Agent Jim Wright on one of the firearms ranges at Quantico. Despite the "cerebral" nature of the work we do, each member of the Investigative Support Unit is first and foremost an FBI special agent. (Photo by Mark Olshaker)

Special Agent Gregg McCrary, who confronted the unknown killer of Kristen French on national Canadian television, saying, "If you are watching, I want to tell you that you are going to be apprehended. It's just a question of time." (Photo by Mark Olshaker)

Special Agent Jud Ray, who was a soldier, police officer, and detective before joining the Bureau. When police in Alaska told him they had a suspect who fit his profile of the murderer of a woman and her two young daughters in every way except that he didn't know the victims, Jud confidently told them, "You don't have the right man." (Photo by Mark Olshaker)

Cassandra Lynn "Cassie" Hansen was abducted from church in St. Paul, Minnesota, on November 10, 1981. Her body was found in a Dumpster the next morning. Through the combined efforts of the St. Paul police, the FBI, and heroic local citizens, her killer, Stuart Knowlton, was brought to justice.

Stuart Knowlton, convicted killer of Cassandra Hansen. (St. Paul, Minnesota, Police Department photo)

Thirteen-year-old Shawn Moore, whom my colleague Special Agent Jim Harrington described as "a kid who had everything going for him." On Labor Day weekend, 1985, Shawn was abducted near a convenience store close to Brighton, Michigan, by Ronald Bailey, who killed him on Sunday at a friend's hunting cabin.

Ronald Lloyd Bailey, the convicted killer of Shawn Moore, was a young man with a long, bad record before he even committed that crime. (Livingston County, Michigan, Sheriff's Department photo)

Ronald Bailey's recently purchased silver Jeep Renegade, which helped lead to his arrest. (Michigan State Police photo)

Stephen and Suzanne Collins, already best of friends, on their way to the school bus while their father, Jack, was stationed in Greece in 1972. (Photo by Trudy Collins)

Suzanne Collins in her uniform for the Robert E. Lee High School Lancers softball team. (Photo by Trudy Collins)

Suzanne Collins proudly standing in front of her regulation-made bunk bed at Parris Island, August 1984. Her parents saw this as quite a contrast to the way she'd kept her room at home.
(Photo by Trudy Collins)

Lance Corporal Suzanne M. Collins's red Marine Corps T-shirt. Sheriff's deputies found it lying in the grass near her body in Edmund Orgill Park in Millington, Tennessee, on the morning of July 12, 1985.
(Shelby County, Tennessee, Sheriff's Department photo)

The authors with Jack and Trudy Collins at their home in Wilmington, North Carolina.
(Photo by Carolyn C. Olshaker)

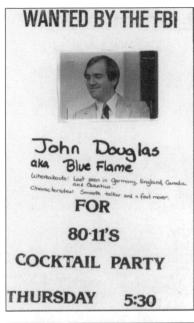

WANTED BY THE FBI

John Douglas
aka Blue Flame

Whereabouts: Last seen in Germany, England, Canada and Quantico.
Characteristics: Smooth talker and a fast mover.

FOR

80-11'S

COCKTAIL PARTY

THURSDAY   5:30

Our work can be pretty grim, so occasionally you have to make an effort to lighten up. In the midst of my intense travels profiling cases in the 1980s, my colleagues at Quantico made up this "official" FBI Wanted poster inviting fellow personnel to a cocktail party in my honor.

Amber Hagerman with her brother at what turned out to be the last Christmas of her life. (Photo courtesy of Richard Hagerman)

WHO KILLED
AMBER HAGERMAN?
REWARD
$75,000

SUSPECT CHARACTERISTICS

SUSPECT CHARACTERISTICS

SUSPECT IS A WHITE OR HISPANIC MALE
AGE 25 TO 40.

SUSPECT MAY CURRENTLY OWN OR MAY
HAVE PERVIOUSLY OWNED A FULL SIZE
BLACK PICKUP TRUCK.

SUSPECT MAY HAVE TROUBLE HOLDING A
JOB.

SUSPECT PROBABLY WORKS IN A JOB THAT
DOES NOT REQUIRE MUCH CONTACT WITH
PEOPLE.

SUSPECT MAY HAVE ANGER CONTROL
PROBLEMS AND TENDS TO BE VIOLENT AT
TIMES.

AMBER HAGERMAN, WHITE
FEMALE AGE 9, 4'6, 80 LBS.,
BLUE EYES, SHOULDER
LENGTH DARK BROWN HAIR,
WHITE SHIRT WITH MULTI-
COLOR HAND PRINTS, PINK
PANTS, BROWN SHOES,
BLACK AND WHITE BOW IN
HER HAIR.

SUSPECT MAY HAVE SUFFERED SOME
TYPE OF STRESSFUL EVENT PRIOR TO
1-13-96.

SUSPECT MAY LIVE ALONE OR WITH
AN ELDERLY PERSON.

SUSPECT MAY FREQUENTLY CARRY A
KNIFE.

SUSPECT MAY HAVE POOR RELATIONS
WITH WOMEN.

SUSPECT MAY HAVE FEW FRIENDS OR
BE A LONER.

ON SATURDAY 1-13-96 AT APPROXIMATELY 3:18 P.M. 9 YEAR OLD AMBER HAGERMAN WAS RIDING HER
BICYCLE IN THE PARKING LOT LOCATED BETWEEN THE ABANDONED WINN-DIXIE BUILDING AND THE
LAUNDRY BUILDING AT THE SOUTH WEST CORNER OF E. ABRAM ST. AND BROWNING DR. (1600 E. ABRAM
ST. ARLINGTON, TEXAS) AT WHICH TIME SHE WAS ABDUCTED. THE UNKNOWN SUSPECT WAS DRIVING A
BLACK PICKUP. THE SUSPECT GOT OUT OF THE TRUCK AND LIFTED AMBER OFF OF HER BICYCLE AND
CARRIED AMBER TO THE TRUCK WHILE AMBER WAS KICKING HER FEET, WAVING HER ARMS, AND
SCREAMING. THE SUSPECT PLACED AMBER IN THE PICKUP AND FLED WEST BOUND ON ABRAM ST.
AMBER'S NUDE BODY WAS FOUND ON WEDNESDAY 1-17-96 AT 11:39 P.M. IN A DRAINAGE DITCH LOCATED
IN THE FOREST RIDGE APARTMENTS WHICH ARE LOCATED ON GREEN OAKS BLVD. A SHORT DISTANCE
WEST OF HIGHWAY 360 IN ARLINGTON, TEXAS. AMBER HAD BEEN SEXUALLY ASSAULTED AND HER
THROAT HAD BEEN CUT MULTIPLE TIMES WITH A KNIFE.

SUSPECT VEHICLE DESCRIPTION: FULL SIZE AMERICAN MADE BLACK PICKUP TRUCK, STANDARD CAB,
CLEAN CONDITION, LATE 1980'S TO EARLY 1990'S YEAR MODEL, STANDARD EQUIPMENT, NO KNOWN
OPTIONS OR AFTERMARKET ACCESSORIES.

SUSPECT DESCRIPTION: WHITE MALE OR HISPANIC MALE LESS THAN 6'0" TALL AND MEDIUM BUILD.

A $75,000.00 REWARD HAS BEEN OFFERED FOR INFORMATION WHICH LEADS TO THE ARREST AND
CONVICTION OF THE SUSPECT OR SUSPECTS WHO KILLED AMBER HAGERMAN. PERSONS PROVIDING
INFORMATION DO NOT HAVE TO IDENTIFY THEMSELVES. THE SUSPECT AND THE NEWS MEDIA DO NOT
HAVE TO KNOW THE IDENTITY OF PERSONS WHO PROVIDE INFORMATION ON THIS CASE. IMMIGRANTS
WHO HAVE ENTERED THIS COUNTRY ILLEGALLY WILL NOT BE DEPORTED AS A RESULT OF CONTACTING
THE POLICE AND PROVIDING INFORMATION ABOUT THE AMBER HAGERMAN CAPITAL MURDER.

CALL CRIME STOPPERS

METRO 469-TIPS

Nine-year-old Amber Hagerman was abducted in broad
daylight on Saturday afternoon, January 13, 1996, in
Arlington, Texas. Her nude body was found the following
Wednesday. She had been sexually assaulted and her throat
was cut. So far, the monster who killed her has not been
caught.

And I got him new glasses, we got him a new driver's license, and I just said, 'We're not funding any more of this. If you want to come back, you come back now.' So he did."

He came back home around Christmas of 1983. This time, Jack said Stephen could not start college right away. "You're going to work for a year and show that you're going to do something with yourself." After that, he was able to get back into the University of Virginia, where he once again excelled in his course work and then graduated with honors in economics in 1987.

Looking back on the experience in Texas, Stephen comments, "I got about ten years of immaturity out of the way in two years." He also admits from this vantage point that his blond and blue-eyed girlfriend there was "nothing like Suzanne."

The way Jeff Freeman sees it, "Suzanne was an anchor for him. When things were tough with their parents, they bonded even closer with each other. And the older Suzanne got, the more advice Steve got from her. It was really incredible how much he loved her."

Suzanne didn't have her brother's academic options. As smart as she was, her grades had never been good enough for UVA, or any other college with any kind of meaningful scholastic standards. And she made it clear she didn't want to go to a local community college or settle for some "rinkydink job," as she put it; she wanted to go somewhere away from home.

The decision to join the Marine Corps came as a surprise to everyone. Recruiters from all the services had visited her high school and one day in March of her senior year she came home and told her parents, "I'd like to join the Marines." Jack doesn't remember ever having heard her mention the military before that.

He was tring to figure out how he felt about this, so he said, "Well, gee, Blue Bell, I'm really curious. You know how proud I was of being a naval officer and you've heard all my stories about serving on ships. I can't imagine why you'd want to go in the Marines rather than the Navy."

She looked at him squarely and said, "Because, Dad, the Marines are the best."

"What could I say to that?" Jack recalls. "So I answered, 'Well, you're the best, Suzanne, so that's fine.'"

When Stephen found out about her decision, he was as surprised as his parents. "I expected her to go to college. I never thought about her not going to school. But I didn't question her decision. The main thing I remember is that I was very, very proud of her."

Jeff Freeman says, "I was surprised. I thought it was a pretty ballsy thing for a woman to do. She said she wanted the challenge and I had no doubt she'd be successful at it."

Jack still had to come fully to terms with it in his own mind. "I'd say to Trudy, 'Is this a good idea? Should we discourage her?' And then I thought, well, let's analyze the whole thing. She hasn't studied well enough to get into college. If she didn't go in the Marine Corps, she won't want to continue living at home. She'd want to get an apartment with another girlfriend, get a job. We'd be nervous wrecks worrying about where she was, where she parked the car, was it dark, would she be alone? I thought, at least I know she'll be safe in the Marine Corps. Someone will be watching her and looking out for her all the time."

Even after Suzanne committed to the Marines, in some ways Jack could not help being a typical father. When she came downstairs to model her prom dress—very bright red and very short, accentuating her splendid figure—Jack said, "Are you sure there's nothing missing?"

"It was definitely not a dress I would have chosen for her. But every time I made that sort of comment, she'd say something like, 'You are going to cut your sideburns, aren't you, Dad?' So we would end up laughing about it."

Suzanne graduated from high school on June 4, 1984, and went into the Marines on June 27. She did her basic training at the Marine Corps Recruit Depot, Parris Island, South Carolina.

Those of us who did their service in the Air Force, or any branch other than the Marines, know how tough by comparison Marine basic training is. The concept is to break each recruit down and then build him or her up in the Marine mold. Suzanne thrived in basic training, pushing her mind and body to each new challenge. She had her long blond hair chopped off short and spent all day long drilling in a uniform. All of the discipline she couldn't accept at home, she accepted willingly and enthusiastically in the Corps. The drill instructor seemed to have it in for Suzanne, perhaps because she was so pretty and from an educated, upper-middle-class background. But Suzanne accepted this as part of the challenge. During the eight weeks of basic training, a number of the women in her platoon washed out, some on the verge of nervous breakdowns. Suzanne knew she needed this kind of structure in her life and loved the sense of direction it gave her.

The letters she wrote home would detail how tough the training was, but never expressed any doubts or reservations. And when they came down to Parris Island for boot camp graduation, Jack and Trudy couldn't have been more proud. She took Jack to the huge rappelling tower and said, "Dad, I did that! Isn't it cool? I did that!" She took almost equal pride in demonstrating to her mother that this daughter who could barely get it together to keep her room from being a total wreck could now make a bunk bed so tight that a quarter would bounce off it.

When recruits enter basic training, they're given their uniforms and caps. When they graduate, they're given the Marine eagle, globe, and anchor insignia to put on the cap. There is a photograph of Suzanne receiving her insignia from the drill instructor who gave her such a hard time. Suzanne has a beaming grin on her face, as if to say, "You said I couldn't do it and I did it!" For her, that was perhaps the proudest moment of all.

Before taking up her first temporary duty assignment at Cherry Point, North Carolina, Suzanne came home on leave. Her parents noticed a difference right away, and so did Steve. She was totally confident, utterly sure of herself. "When she came back," Stephen says, "her attitude was, 'Hey, this is my life. I'm on my own now. You can make suggestions, but I make the decisions for myself now.' "

She also finally got her driver's license and bought herself a car—a used red Pontiac Firebird that had a tendency to break down. But now she could go where she wanted, when she wanted.

Stephen drove her down to Cherry Point and they had a lot of time to talk along the way. At the Marine Corps Air

Station there, she was assigned to the Second Marine Air Wing, a Harrier jet squadron, for five weeks of on-the-job training while awaiting the next scheduled start of avionics technician class. By this time, Suzanne had begun giving serious thought to getting her higher education in the military and trying to become among the first female Marine aviators. The avionics training would be the first step. She set her sights on a fleet appointment to the Naval Academy and began writing letters asking for advice and recommendations. She was convinced that a strong military performance would overshadow her lackluster high school academic record and show she had gained the maturity and leadership capabilities to take on anything the Marine Corps had to offer.

Private First Class Suzanne Marie Collins reported to MATSS-902—Marine Aviation Training Support Squadron 902—at the Memphis Naval Air Station in Millington, Tennessee, on October 20, 1984, to begin Class A avionics school. As proud as her parents had been of her physical prowess and mental toughness at boot camp, they were even more impressed that she seemed willing and able to take on such technical subject matter as wiring diagrams and circuits and flight theory. "Had she had to take that course at Robert E. Lee High School, she would have flunked it; I'm sure of it," says Jack.

At Millington, Suzanne was hard to miss—a tall, blond beauty with a striking figure honed by constant exercise. One of her fellow Marines, James Brunner, wrote, "She had a manner about her that was always so graceful and beautiful. I remember her walking through the mall, turning all the heads, wives nudging husbands and men tripping over themselves. Lord knows, the first time I saw her I walked into a pole."

In March of 1985, Suzanne met the person who soon became her best friend: Susan Hand, who had arrived at Millington on March 11. In fact, the similarities between the two women were remarkable. Aside from their first names, they'd bought similar model cars without knowing each other. Both women were tall, blond, and widely considered to be knockouts; there are photographs in which Trudy can hardly tell them apart.

Though they didn't go through boot camp together, they both entered basic training from comparable backgrounds that were different from those of just about anyone else around them. "Almost everyone else there was either a Southern hillbilly or from a military family," Susan explains. "Neither one of us knew much about the military going in, so we were viewed as being prissy and stuck up, even though we weren't."

Susan was exactly a year and a month older than Suzanne. She was the oldest of five children from Lisle, Illinois, and after two years of college at Northern Illinois University in De Kalb, her parents couldn't afford to continue her schooling. So Susan went into the military to pay for her education. "The Marines were a way out for both of us, a way to get far away from home and be on our own."

Like Suzanne, Susan chose the Marines because she perceived they were the best. She was at Millington for air traffic control school and lived downstairs from Suzanne in the same barracks building.

Life at Millington was only slightly less spartan than boot camp. The barracks held two to four women per room, sleeping in metal rack bunk beds. The floors had to be polished and waxed daily. Suzanne decorated her part of the room with posters of the Chippendales male strippers.

Before too long, the pair of Susan and Suzanne became well-known throughout the base. "Everyone on base knew us," says Susan. "We were always in the spotlight. When we'd wear our bikinis to the post pool, everyone would stare at us, but we didn't care." Both women were five foot seven and 118 pounds with the same build. Suzanne's eyes were greenish blue and Susan's are greenish brown and Suzanne's hair was slightly lighter in color. But they could easily—and did—swap clothes, which gave Suzanne particular satisfaction.

"Suzanne was completely open and friendly all the time, and always fun. But I think we were resented by a lot of the other women there," Susan observes. "We were two tall blonds, more intelligent, better spoken, and better looking than most of the others in the military, especially at Millington. The guys really liked us, and our superiors, too. I know that caused some trouble for Suzanne."

She came in for the particular ire of a staff sergeant and a warrant officer who seemed to resent her looks, attractiveness to men, and easy charm with superior officers.

"These two were really mean to both of us," says Susan. "They were always calling us into their office. Suzanne made them mad all the time with her independence and free spirit. She'd go off post with friends and not come back when she was supposed to. They'd go after her for anything. She really tried their patience. I would try to stay more within the system. If they said we couldn't do something, I'd call the captain and get him to fix it, which made them even madder."

Another thing that got Suzanne into difficulty occurred early on in her time at Millington when she dated an NROTC university student. Though Susan comments that "The people we had most in common with were officers," and though she herself ended up marrying an Army infantry lieutenant, of all the services, the Marine Corps took the dimmest view of fraternizing between enlisted personnel and officers. "I think the other girls were jealous," she says. "It reminded me a lot of high school.

"We would date a lot, but it was innocent. Suzanne was both innocent and outgoing at the same time."

Also, about that same time, Suzanne had been promoted from PFC to lance corporal.

Actually, it was another woman, a friend of Suzanne's named Sue Drake, who introduced her and Susan to their boyfriends. Chris Clarkson and Greg "Gonzo" Gonzowski, both Marine air traffic control technicians, were best buddies from their hockey-playing days in Michigan's Upper Peninsula and co-captained the Memphis Naval Air Station base soccer team. They hit it off immediately and soon the two couples of Susan and Chris and Suzanne and Gonzo would go everywhere and do everything together. Suzanne and Susan were just about the only two girls considered good enough to be invited to play soccer with the guys.

"I never saw her depressed," says Susan. "She was a really good friend—caring, fun, adventuresome when she wanted to be. I was more quiet and reserved. I always wanted to be more daredevil and spontaneous like she was. The one who was really adventurous was Patti Coon, who was one of her roommates, and I think after Suzanne's strict high school years, she was trying to be like Patti sometimes." Next to Susan, Patti was probably Suzanne's best friend. Whenever she was off duty and wasn't around Susan, she was often with Patti.

"She always wanted to go out dancing," Susan continues. "She liked really upbeat music and she was good at improvising. We went to clubs on Beale Street in Memphis, or in Germantown, a Memphis suburb which was considered a little tamer and safer. We tried every food for the first time."

James Brunner, who was stationed with Suzanne at Millington, remembers, "She was such an outstanding Marine, and yet when in civilian clothes and off-duty, she was so charming you couldn't help but like her—a sense of humor that was very cute. I could be depressed all the way and in ten minutes I'd be laughing. She could be such a lady and also one of the guys, yet always a lady, even take a shot of whiskey that would make my eyes water and choke, and still dance me til I would drop."

Being tall and very attentive to their figures, Suzanne and Susan were always worried about their weight. "We didn't like the mess hall because everyone would be staring at us, so instead we'd go out a lot with Chris and Gonzo. We particularly liked Wendy's salad bar. We'd starve ourselves all day, then go pig out on their salad."

The main thrust of their weight control and fitness program, though, was exercise, and they'd frequently go out running together. Susan could handle seven or eight miles at a time, but Suzanne would often go another two or three after that. The base was divided by a highway with a walkway built over it and Suzanne would frequently run around the golf course on the north side of the base, either by herself or with the guys, when she wanted to go longer distances. Suzanne became fanatical about running and would try to get out for a long run almost every day. She also worked out regularly in the gym, and seemed to like the fact that all the men would always watch her work out. Aside from being flattering, it gave her extra incentive to show them what she could do.

Among her greatest accomplishments at Millington was membership in the honor deck. As the official description put it, "Only the most motivated students are selected as members of the honor deck, after being recommended by their troop handlers and maintaining an eighty-five percent academic average. Members of the honor deck participate in Color Guard details, formation runs for charity, and various civil functions throughout the Memphis area."

What this description fails to mention is that before Lance Corporal Collins came to Millington, all members of the honor deck had been male.

Suzanne saw no reason for this and she wanted badly to prove that women could do just as good a job as men. She researched the regulations in the Marine Corps Order, which made reference to appropriate elements of "Marine manpower" for rifle drill and firing. She then convinced the authorities that manpower was a generic term and did not imply "male power." If women were admitted into the Marine Corps, even if their numbers were specifically and officially limited to five percent, then they were part of the manpower, just like the men.

Like Jackie Robinson joining the Dodgers, making the team is one thing, being accepted by your teammates is another. For the first several weeks Suzanne was on honor deck, the men gave her a very hard time. Many of them even admitted as much after the fact, clearly defying her to prove herself. They were convinced she'd been assigned because of her striking good looks rather than her ability to cut it with her peers, and it took her some time to win them over. But win them over she did.

Richard Tirrell, a member of the Millington honor deck, reminisced, "I have to admit that for quite some time after Suzanne joined the honor deck I wondered why she would subject herself to the ridicule and harassment that she experienced from other women Marines and male Marines alike. However, it wasn't long after getting to know her better that I realized that Suzanne had deeply imbedded principles and moral standards that minimized the obstacles in front of her to reach the goals that she set for herself. In all honesty, she brought the best out of me. Her vibrant attitude, zest for life, and sense of humor created an air that was naive and sophisticated at the same time, even though that would seem to be contradictory. For myself, that particular combination helped me to become more effective and more motivated in my work with honor deck."

As it turned out, her fellow Marines were so impressed with her that they added her name to the physical training—or PT—cadence count which enumerated Medal of Honor winners and other Marines noted for their exploits.

To a former Marine friend of Jack's Suzanne wrote, "They have a PT chant about Dan Daley and other famous Medal of Honor winners and such. Well, now they have added a couple of lines down here about Lance Corporal Collins. Our honor deck PT is used almost every day, so I hear that many times a day. Every time I hear it I become more inspired and honored that I was able to join the U.S. Marine Corps." If she hadn't been famous enough around base before, she certainly was now.

While Suzanne was fighting the battles of honor deck equality, Susan Hand was achieving her own independent fame by winning the title of Navy Relief Queen by the largest margin in the base's history. Navy Relief is a charity for enlisted personnel and their dependents and the voting for queen is an annual fund drive and major base event. You vote by contributing a dollar in the name of the candidate of your choice. In 1985, it had been twenty-six years since a Marine had won the title and Captain Nowag was determined that the losing streak was going to be broken this year. He approached Susan and said, "You're going to be the next Navy Relief Queen."

Out of 200,000 votes, Susan received 125,000. Prizes included a four-foot-tall trophy, a gold chain, and $200 for dresses. Suzanne was thrilled for her friend and arranged to get off school two days before graduation to see Susan crowned.

As graduation quickly approached, the only dark cloud on the horizon was that Suzanne had been assigned back to Cherry Point, while Susan was going to be an air traffic controller at El Toro Marine Air Station in California. Greg Gonzowski was going to California, too. Greg loved her and wanted to start thinking about marriage. Suzanne liked him very much, but according to Susan, she was having too good a time to settle down yet.

For the long term, the two women knew they'd always be

close and envisioned ultimately raising their kids together. But they also wanted to figure out a way that they could be together for the short term. The hope seemed to be getting Suzanne transferred to California, and both of them agreed to start working on it as soon as they took up their new assignments. Then, if all went well, they'd both be going to Annapolis together on fleet appointments. After graduation, Susan thought she would transfer into the Navy to become a pilot. Suzanne was convinced the Marines would start letting women fly.

On July 10, Susan's mother and four-year-old sister came down from Illinois for the graduation. The next evening, Susan and Suzanne were going to celebrate by going to dinner with Susan's mother at the house of one of Mrs. Hand's friends in the Memphis suburb of Germantown. But shortly before they were to leave the base, the barracks staff sergeant assigned Suzanne to be Duty NCO for the day, which meant she couldn't go. She told Susan and her mother to go without her. They arranged to meet in an open green on base the next morning before graduation. Susan was upset by this maneuver, feeling it had only happened because the sergeant was jealous and had it in for Suzanne. She never should have been assigned to duty the night before graduation; someone else could easily handle it.

Duty consisted of sitting at a school-type desk behind a painted red line in front of the barracks building, checking out people who went in. Every hour on the hour she was to circle the barracks to make sure everything was as it should be, then enter in the circuit on a log. At best it's tedious and boring and Suzanne probably felt she was being punished for her attributes. Susan says they sometimes assigned her friend to duty, knowing it would mean missing honor deck functions.

There wasn't much Suzanne could do, confined to the base for the evening, but one thing she could do was log out to go running. She'd spent most of the day packing and making arrangements for the next day, so she was restless and itchy for some serious exercise. Shortly after 10:00 P.M., she went to her room, where she saw Patti Coon and her other roommate, Victoria Pavloski. She and Victoria had a minor argument about who was going to clean up the room. Suzanne

218

agreed to clean it up in the morning before graduation. She then changed from her uniform into a red Marine Corps T-shirt and red athletic shorts, put on her white socks and Nike sneakers, a white bandanna around her forehead, and wrapped a blue exercise sweat belt around her waist, then came back out to begin stretching and limbering up for her run. She told Janet Cooper, who had quarterdeck watch duty, that she felt restless and thought she'd run for about a half hour or so. They talked for about ten minutes while Suzanne was stretching and Janet thought she seemed in a very good and happy mood.

She had a lot to be happy about as she went off into the night on her run. She was a beautiful, healthy, and physically fit nineteen-year-old who had proved herself in the toughest regimen a woman can take on in the American military. Her dream of the Naval Academy and becoming one of the first women Marine aviators was well on track, and at Cherry Point she'd get the chance to prove herself yet again. Her parents couldn't have been more proud, her brother worshipped her, she had a best friend and a man who wanted to spend the rest of his life with her. She had worked hard and played hard and a future of limitless potential was out there, hers for the taking.

CHAPTER 8

Death of a Marine

The morning of Friday, July 12, 1985, Susan Hand looked for Suzanne in the base park where they'd arranged to meet before Susan's graduation ceremony. When she didn't show up, Susan became concerned that she might not be feeling well, so after the graduation, she went to Suzanne's barracks to see if she could find her there.

"Some people looked really strange, but no one would say anything to me."

Before long, though, Captain Nowag's aide found her and said the captain wanted to see her in his office. By now it was afternoon, the sun was overhead, and Susan was still in her dress greens. Susan thought it a little strange that the captain had sent for her; she couldn't think of anything she'd done wrong that would occasion a visit to "the principal's office." But Nowag liked her and they'd always been friendly. He probably just wanted to say goodbye personally.

As soon as she was shown into his office, she said brightly, "Hey, what's up?"

"You'd better sit down," he said. When she'd obeyed, he said, "You hang out with Suzanne Collins a lot."

Susan said, "Yeah."

He came over and put his arm on her shoulder. "I don't know how I'm going to say this to you, but your friend Suzanne was found in the park in Millington and she'd been murdered."

"No," Susan responded. It was halfway between a whisper

and a whimper. "No way," she stated more emphatically. "Are you sure?"

Captain Nowag nodded grimly.

Susan had never had anyone close to her die before. The only death she'd experienced was that of her grandmother, whom she used to see about twice a year. "There's no way this could happen to Suzanne," she asserted, now in tears. "She just turned nineteen!"

He pulled up a chair and just sat there with his arm around her.

Steve Collins was home alone in Springfield when the military car pulled up in front of the house in the early afternoon of Friday, July 12. Jack, now retired from the foreign service, was in New York for the day helping his brother-in-law, Ed Wicks, with a patent development issue. By then Trudy's parents were living with them and she had taken them out to a senior citizens lunch. Steve was home recovering from a foot injury he'd sustained over the Fourth of July holiday.

He'd just gotten out of the shower when he saw the car pull up. His first thought was that it must be Suzanne. She was due home either today or tomorrow, and he figured that with his sister's resourcefulness and charm, she must have gotten someone in power to give her a ride.

But then the doorbell rang and when he answered it, two men in uniform were standing there. One was a chaplain.

"Mr. Collins," one of them said. "We have some bad news for you. Suzanne's been killed."

At first, Stephen couldn't completely process the message or deal with the shock. Paul Newton, a neighbor who was a retired Marine colonel, remembers seeing him beating a bush with his crutch and screaming, "No, no, no, no, no, no." Colonel Newton had always been very proud of Suzanne and had told her that when she was commissioned, he wanted to give her his ceremonial sword.

Stephen's first cogent thought was, "My God, my mom's coming home."

A little later, Trudy pulled into the driveway with her parents in the car. When she saw the official car, she also figured that Suzanne must have connived a ride home. But then Stephen came over to her window. "Mom, I need to talk to you."

"Right here?" she said.

"No. Leave Nana and Poppa in the car and come right in."

"Parked on a hill?" Trudy responded. "Leave my Mother and Dad in the car?"

"Yes," he said. "I want you to come right in. Please come right in."

When she got inside, Stephen introduced her to the two officers. One of them said, "Please sit down, Mrs. Collins." And when she had, he said, "Your daughter has been murdered."

Then she went back out to the car, brought her parents in, and sat them in the living room without telling them what had happened. She came back to where Stephen and the two officers were and said, "Let's go out on the back patio where we can talk without them hearing."

Out on the patio, her reaction was the same as Susan's. "You must be mistaken," she said.

"No, I'm afraid not. We'll tell you all we know. So far, what we know is that your daughter was running on base last night. Someone came up behind her and grabbed her, then took her off base, attacked her, and killed her."

Trudy thought to herself, "If I don't write this all down, it's not going to register. I'm not going to remember what they're telling me."

The four of them talked for a while. Trudy remembers the chaplain being sensitive and very nice. "Can I help you?" he asked. "Can I tell your folks?"

Trudy said she should tell them.

"Well, can I go in with you? Can I be with you in there?" he asked.

"Maybe it would be a good idea if you came," she said.

"Mother and Dad just sort of sat there, stunned, unable to comprehend what they were hearing," Trudy recalls. "Then we tried to reach Jack in New York."

When they finally located him, they had him pulled out of a meeting. Trudy said, "Something bad . . . something terrible has happened. Suzanne has been killed."

Jack sat down. "What did you say! How can that be? I

don't understand." He was thinking, "I've got to get home right away."

Before he left, he went back to tell the men he was meeting with what had happened. Two of them, whom he had come to know quite well, were Jewish. Jack said, "In the Christian Church we pray for people's souls when they die. I'm not sure exactly what you do, but if you could just pray for Suzanne and for me and my family, I'd be very grateful." Jack says they were absolutely shattered with grief and shock. They couldn't have been more compassionate or understanding.

Jack's brother-in-law accompanied him on the flight back to Washington, D.C. Around 6:30 P.M., Trudy and Stephen met Jack at the shuttle gate at National Airport. The three of them grabbed each other tightly and silently hugged.

When they got home, Jack immediately got on the phone and called down to Tennessee, trying to find out exactly what had happened. They had a suspect in custody. He was the husband of a Navy enlisted woman and lived on base. But Suzanne had been taken off base and killed in a park in Millington, so there was an overlapping jurisdictional issue between the Naval Investigative Service, the Millington Police Department, and the Shelby County Sheriff's Office. He couldn't even find out where Suzanne's body was.

When Stephen started hearing the details, he said, "It must have been more than one guy. Suzanne was strong. When we wrestled, she could almost beat me. It had to be more than one guy."

"We'll know more tomorrow," Jack was told.

At that moment, Suzanne was lying in the office of the Shelby County medical examiner. The autopsy report, signed by James Spencer Bell, M.D., stated: "Death was due to multiple injuries inflicted by blunt trauma to the head, pressing on the neck and pushing 20½ inches of a 31 inch long, 1½ inch diameter sharply bevelled tree limb up the perineum through the abdomen into the right chest tearing abdominal and chest organs and producing internal hemorrhaging."

At around 6:00 A.M., sheriff's deputies had found her nude body lying face-down in the grass with her head turned to the right, under a tree about 150 feet off the road in Edmund Orgill Park in Millington, just east of the Navy base. Aside from the tree limb forcibly inserted between her legs, there were various other wounds on her body and her face had been so badly beaten that an initial identification was difficult. Scattered nearby were her shirt and shorts, socks, underwear, and exercise belt. Together, they formed a red, white, and blue pattern against the green backdrop.

About an hour before, Patti Coon had discovered that Suzanne's bunk had not been slept in, and worriedly called security. When Suzanne failed to show for morning muster, an all-points bulletin went out to base security, the Millington police, and the sheriff's department.

The overall elements of what had happened were quickly pieced together.

At about 11:00 P.M., Marine Privates First Class Michael Howard and Mark Shotwell were jogging together, heading north along Attu Road on the north side of the base near where buffaloes are kept in pens, when they saw a female jogger matching Suzanne Collins's description running toward them. Just before she reached them, she crossed over to the other side of the street to face traffic. Shortly after she passed them, they noticed a car parked ahead of them on the shoulder with its high beams on. Howard thought it looked like a mid-1970s Ford station wagon, dark-colored with wood-grained paneling on the side and a very loud muffler. Suddenly, the car started, swerved onto the road and began heading south, the same direction as Suzanne.

Shortly after the vehicle passed, Howard and Shotwell thought they heard screams coming from about three hundred yards or so behind them. They turned immediately and took off in that direction. When they'd covered about a hundred yards the screams stopped and they saw the station wagon pull back onto Attu Road, heading toward Navy Road. Just then, another car came by in the opposite direction, and the glare of the headlights prevented them from seeing exactly what was happening.

They continued running after the car but quickly lost it, so they ran to the base North Gate 2 and reported the incident to the guard there, David Davenport. Davenport called base security and reported the possible abduction, adding that he had seen the station wagon exit the base through his gate. The driver was male, and he had his arm around the shoulder of a woman in the passenger seat. Though he hadn't been able to read the license number, he recalled that the car bore Kentucky plates. One security unit went to Davenport's gate to get additional information, while Richard Rogers, the chief of the watch for base Section 2, went out himself to try to find the car after issuing a "Be on the Lookout" to base security, Millington police, and the sheriff's department.

While Rogers was still out looking for the car, he got a call to respond to a fight at the corners of Center, College, and Bethuel streets in the residential area of the base. About ten minutes after midnight, he saw a car matching Davenport's description. It was headed south.

Rogers stopped the car, which was driven by Sedley Alley, a twenty-nine-year-old white male, six foot four, and weighing 220 pounds. He worked as a laborer for an air conditioning company and was living on base as the dependent of his wife, Lynne, who was enlisted in the Navy. Alley agreed to accompany Rogers back to the security office. Lynne Alley was then contacted and brought in for questioning, too. But Lynne looked a lot like the description of the possible abduction victim and it appeared that what they were really dealing with was a domestic disturbance, so the security officers let them both go.

The two joggers, Shotwell and Howard, were in the building at the time giving their own statements. As soon as the Alleys drove away and they heard the loud muffler, they said that this was the same car they had seen and heard.

At around 5:00 A.M., security got a call from Corporal Kimberly Young relaying the information from Patti Coon: that Suzanne Collins had gone out jogging the night before and evidently had not returned. Young provided a description of Suzanne and brought them photographs of her. That was when the investigation was geared up again, quickly resulting in the discovery of her body in Edmund Orgill Park in Millington.

A little after 7:00 A.M., Richard Rogers ordered two of his patrolmen, John Griggs and Gregory Franklin, to apprehend Sedley Alley and bring him in. He then called Navy Captain

Barry Spofford, commanding officer of the base, and Marine Colonel Robert Clapp, Suzanne's commanding officer, and told them what was happening. Dorothy Cummings, the troop handler for Suzanne's section, was brought in to view the body and make a positive identification.

Then, since the abduction had taken place on a federal reservation, they contacted the FBI Resident Agency in Memphis, which sent Special Agents Jack Sampson and Anna Northcutt to the scene.

At the crime scene, police and sheriff's deputies saw that Suzanne's head was covered with blood. There was a large bruise on each shoulder blade and scratches that ran from her shoulders down to her waist. Until it was removed during autopsy, there was no way to tell how far the sharp, thick tree limb had been forced up between her legs, only that about eight or so inches was protruding. When they turned her over on her back, they could see that her left eye was bruised and swollen shut and there were contusions and bite marks on her left breast. The resulting medical examiner's report was twenty-one pages long.

Less than half a mile away, police found a screwdriver matching the description of the one Sedley Alley used to start his car, since it no longer started normally with a key. When the Naval Investigative Service secured and examined Alley's car, they found bloodstains on several areas, both inside and out.

At the security station, Alley initially denied all involvement and asked to see an attorney. On his own, though, he then changed his mind and said he wanted to tell what happened. That was when he told the story of going out drinking and driving, going up to talk to the pretty blond Marine, then accidentally ramming her with his car, carrying her into the car to take her to the hospital, having her wake up and resist him in the car, driving off base to Edmund Orgill Park, where he panicked and hit her to keep her quiet, not realizing he was holding the screwdriver in his hand. He believed that that was what killed her, and it was a complete accident. After that, he panicked even more, at which point he got the idea to stage it to look like a sexual assault, removing her clothes and breaking off the tree limb to insert into her dead body.

What would come out before too long, however, was that with all of the numerous wounds on Suzanne's body, the medical examiner could find none that corresponded to either a screwdriver puncture wound to the head or being struck by an automobile. Then there was also the testimony of three young people out in the park that night who never saw Suzanne or Sedley Alley but who heard what they described as a "death scream" at about the time Suzanne would have died.

Lynne Alley was also questioned. She had been out at a Tupperware party with girlfriends most of the evening. Sedley wasn't home when she came back and she didn't see him again until she was brought in for questioning during the night. In the morning, when she noticed the grass stains inside the car, she assumed they'd been caused by their two dogs, who frequently rode in the car. She also disclosed that her husband had been married previously, in Ashland, Kentucky, and that his former wife had accidentally drowned in a bathtub in their house there about five years before.

Subsequent investigation revealed that this "accident" was a questionable death that occurred on February 28, 1980, three days after Debra Alley filed for divorce. The grounds for divorce were sexual perversion. The nude body of the twenty-year-old woman was found in the bathtub with numerous bruises and strangulation marks around her neck. Alley said she had been out drinking with other men that night, came home drunk, took a bath and drowned. She had been dead for several hours before the police or ambulance were called. The coroner ruled that she had choked on her own vomit and had a french fry stuck in her throat. Alley had a history of violent outbursts against both wives. His four-year-old child by Debra had witnessed him beating her on several occasions.

There were additional details which tied Alley to the general vicinity of the Suzanne Collins murder. Air conditioning maintenance equipment had been stolen from an officer's residence on Friday. When stopped for questioning, Alley had the stolen items in his car.

Sedley Alley was charged with the premeditated first-degree murder of Lance Corporal Suzanne Marie Collins of the United States Marine Corps. Before the day was out, NIS and FBI representatives had consulted with Assistant U.S. Attorney Lawrence Laurenzi, who assured them that if, for any reason, the state charge of murder would not support the death penalty, he was prepared to seek it in connection with the federal crime of kidnapping. That didn't turn out to be an issue, however. As soon as he was apprised of the facts and shown the file, Assistant District Attorney for Shelby County Henry "Hank" Williams had decided he was going for the ultimate punishment. He refused even to entertain inquiries about a possible plea bargain.

At Marine Aviation Training Support Squadron 902 graduation at Naval Air Station–Memphis that afternoon, there was an empty place. The base flag had been lowered to half-mast and the long-awaited ceremony was not the joyous occasion everyone had anticipated.

Jeff Freeman was at school at the University of North Carolina at Wilmington when Steve called with the news that Suzanne had been killed. He couldn't believe what he was hearing. In a tragic coincidence, the brother of his roommate's best friend had just been killed on a motorcycle. Jeff called him the next day to see what he could do, then came back to Washington to be with Steve and prepare for the funeral.

In the midst of their unendurable grief and quest to find out exactly what had happened to their daughter, Jack and Trudy Collins now had to deal with the practical considerations of Suzanne's funeral and burial, even though they were told investigators wouldn't be able to release her body to them for several more days.

Since Jack was a deeply religious Catholic, they considered a church-related cemetery. They were also offered several Marine and Navy burial grounds. And because Suzanne had died while on active duty, she was entitled to be buried at Arlington National Cemetery. It was Stephen who ended up making the final decision, insisting to his parents that Suzanne go to Arlington, the final resting place of the nation's most-honored dead.

"I wanted Arlington because I felt Suzanne deserved the best," he explained, "because she was the best."

Meanwhile, Susan Hand had to drive back to Illinois with her mother and little sister.

"Driving back through Indiana, I cried the whole way," she recalls. "My mother tried to comfort me, but nothing helped. Along the way I got a ticket for going eighty-two. I had no idea what I was doing. I just kept seeing Suzanne in my mind."

Greg Gonzowski was just as devastated. "He really loved her," says Susan. As soon as she got home to Illinois, she called Greg and they began making plans to get to the funeral, for which they'd both have to take leave. Susan wanted to be designated as the Marine to escort Suzanne's remains back to Washington, but the staff sergeant who Susan felt always had it in for both of them designated herself instead. To this day, Susan feels an additional sense of emptiness and loss from not being able personally to accompany Suzanne on her final journey.

On Wednesday, July 17, a memorial service was held for Suzanne at the Memphis Naval Air Station. Colonel Robert Clapp, the commanding officer of Marine Aviation Training Support Group 90, concluded his remarks by saying, "She was an eager and aspiring young lady with demonstrated ability, an observable sense of pride, and a sure knowledge and ready acceptance of the responsibilities she bore as a Marine in the service of her country. . . . She was an achiever, goal-oriented, a winner. She didn't sit around and wait for things to happen—she made them happen. She was very close to realizing yet another success as she was about to graduate from avionics school.

"I think all of us feel it is a great tragedy that Suzanne's talents and ambitions could not be fully realized, for she certainly was a credit to the Corps she was so proudly serving. Perhaps it will help us just a little bit today if we remember that she was a part of us—and that we are still here to carry on, that one is not truly gone until no one remembers—and we will not forget. So her spirit will remain alive in her Marine Corps and will continue—through us—to serve that eagle, globe, and anchor, a service which in its own unique way gives those of us who understand it more satisfaction than most of us can adequately express. She will be a Marine forever, and as someone once wrote:

"She will not grow old as we are left to grow old;
Age shall not weary her, nor the years condemn.
But at the going down of the sun, and in
The morning, we will remember her."

The band played the Marine's Hymn. Then, when the lone bugler played Taps, there was scarcely a hardened Marine in the chapel who could keep his eyes dry.

Because of the disfigurement Sedley Alley's beating had caused, it was decided that the casket would remain closed for the wake and funeral. Still, when it arrived back in the Washington area, Jack and Trudy and Stephen knew they had to see her one last time.

"We had to know, as best we could," says Jack, "everything that happened to her."

But they were hardly prepared for the shock when the casket lid was opened for them. She was in her dress uniform, wearing white gloves.

"My heart cried, my soul cried," he says. "I was screaming inside. I mean, I just couldn't believe that anybody could do something so savage. It didn't look like Suzanne, because he had battered and beaten her face so much they had to reconstruct it. They did the best they could, but it wasn't the Suzanne we knew."

At the wake, the closed casket was accompanied by Suzanne's picture and an American flag.

On the warm and sunny afternoon of Thursday, July 18, 1985, Suzanne Collins's funeral was held in the old Fort Myer Chapel adjoining Arlington National Cemetery. There was not enough room for all the mourners inside and many had to listen to the service from outside the front door.

Susan Hand had caught a military hop to Andrews Air Force Base in Maryland, where Greg Gonzowski picked her up. She'd never been to Arlington before and she said the experience sent chills down her back.

"It was scary. All during the funeral, I was holding back a cry the whole time. Greg and I were sitting toward the back of the chapel. We were both in our dress greens and it was very hot, but that didn't seem to matter to us."

What did matter was when the honor guard brought in

the closed white casket. Susan was overwhelmed by the imagery of the white casket, of the pure and innocent life that had been taken from them.

It was also the second time Stephen cried. He had cried when he'd first gotten the news, but then not again. Even when they viewed Suzanne's body, he was the one who remained dry-eyed and strong for his parents. But this was too much for him.

In the memorial book he had inscribed, "Suzanne, may you rest in peace eternally, Stephen."

Just underneath that entry, Trudy had written, "We will love you always, dear Sue Blue, Mom and Dad," followed by a heart and a long row of Xs.

Suzanne Marie Collins, lance corporal of the United State's Marine Corps, was laid to rest with full military honors in Grave Number 127, Section 50, just off Ord and Weitzel drives, near the western edge of Arlington National Cemetery.

As part of the military ceremony, the flag draping the casket is removed by the honor guard and meticulously folded into a tight triangular shape which is then presented to the next of kin. But after the flag was removed, folded, and presented to Trudy, they brought out another flag, which they proceeded to drape over Suzanne's casket. They then followed the same procedure again, and this one they presented to Stephen. He treasures that flag and will keep it with him until he dies.

The next day, Jack and Bill Shepherd, a close friend from Glen Ellyn, Illinois, drove Susan to Andrews where she was getting a military flight back to Chicago. On the way back, Jack said, "You know, Bill, I think differently about death now."

Bill said, "What do you mean?"

"I no longer fear it the way I used to," Jack said. "Nothing that can possibly happen to me is as terrible as what's already happened to Suzanne. And now I've got something to look forward to when I die: I can see Suzanne again."

It was in the weeks after the funeral that the Collinses began to be able to fill in more of the details of their daughter's life and death. I say "life" as well, because immediately they began hearing from hundreds of people whose lives Suzanne had touched, adding a dimension they always knew was there but of which they now had documentary proof. The letters, tributes, gifts of love and friendship fill many boxes in their house, all attesting to what a special person Suzanne was. Many of the people who contacted them whom they had not even met before still keep in touch and continue to visit Jack and Trudy to this day. Touchingly, many of the letters bring them up to date about their lives and confide in them the way their writers used to do with Suzanne. It seems that just about everyone who knew her has felt the need to keep her alive in their memories and active in their imaginations.

On August 20, Jack and Trudy went down to Memphis and Millington, where they met with the key people involved in Suzanne's case. They insisted on seeing the crime scene and autopsy photos; they wanted to understand just what had happened to Suzanne and how much she had suffered. They had to read the autopsy report and see the close-ups of her face and broken body. The medical examiner, who had been reluctant to burden them with the information, told them it was the worst case he had ever seen.

They insisted on being taken to the scene of her death. "We wanted to stand on the spot where our daughter's body lay," said Jack. "We wanted to stand where she was brutalized and where she bled."

When they went to the Shelby County Sheriff's Office, Sergeant Gordon Neighbours came over to them, introduced himself, and spontaneously hugged Trudy. "I'll tell you what should have happened to that son of a bitch," he said. "I should have grabbed him and killed him on the spot."

Stephen had already expressed similar sentiments that Friday evening as he sat with his parents on the edge of their bed and talked with them into the early hours of Saturday morning.

"I agree with how you feel, Steve," Jack said. "I couldn't agree with you more. But the guy is probably in custody now and we wouldn't be able to get at him. But even if we could, would we really want to become like him—a brute and a savage?"

* * *

What they put their faith in instead was the judicial process, and they couldn't have had a better or more dedicated advocate than Hank Williams.

As it happens, though we didn't know each other then, Hank and I started from a similar place at a similar time. One difference, though, was that he had a law degree. Hank joined the FBI as a special agent in 1969, one year before me. His first assignment was with the Salt Lake City Field Office, then he moved to San Francisco where he worked on the organized crime unit. While there his and his wife, Ginny's, first daughter was born. Knowing how much moving around an FBI career can mean, and knowing that he wanted to practice law at some point, he left the Bureau, moved back home to Tennessee, and went to work as a prosecutor.

Williams was in his early forties. He wasn't falsely or overly theatrical like a lot of trial attorneys, but his seriousness of purpose and sense of mission were always evident. He recalls, "I just thought it was a pathetic circumstance that this girl joins the U.S. military to defend her country, she's on base with all the security around her and this happens. I read the file and said to myself, this is definitely a death penalty case. I wasn't going to plea-bargain this one, and after talking to the Collinses, I was even more resolute in that."

Williams not only prosecuted the case as a counselor at law, he also became a psychological counselor to Jack and Trudy Collins at a time when they desperately needed to rely on a sensitive person within the system. He took it upon himself always to be there for them, to listen to their fears and anxieties and frustrations, and considered himself their advocate as they all waded through the mountain of pretrial motions and procedures.

"When they first came to Memphis," Williams recalls, "they insisted on seeing the crime scene photographs. I was extremely afraid of this, because I felt they needed psychological help and I thought this would be too much for them. But they told me they needed to understand just what had happened and be able to share Suzanne's pain, so I finally agreed. But once you see something like that, you can never forget it."

233

Ironically, the defense tried to have some of the photos suppressed because they could "inflame the jury."

Sedley Alley was represented by Robert Jones and Ed Thompson, two of the preeminent defense attorneys in Memphis, both of whom Williams greatly respects. Despite what he considered the clear-cut nature of the crime, he knew he wouldn't have an easy time with them.

Nor did they have an easy time with their client, as it turned out. I don't mean he completely clammed up and refused to talk; he simply didn't tell them anything relevant or assist in his defense. Going on a year after the murder, Williams and his assistant, Bobby Carter, were pushing for trial.

The defense brought in a psychologist named Allen Battle to examine Alley. When Dr. Battle interviewed him, he got a similar response to what Alley had been giving his lawyers. To any substantive question he'd respond, "I don't remember."

Now, there are only a couple of ways to interpret the behavior of a defendant in a capital murder case who gives investigators a detailed confession just hours after the crime and then, months later, tells a psychologist he doesn't remember anything about the incident. My personal interpretation, barring compelling evidence to the contrary, would be that he's either attempting to save his own skin or just telling the entire system to take a flying leap. A more charitable interpretation—and one that would play a whole lot better from a defense viewpoint—might be that the horrible event of the death of this young woman so traumatized him that he had developed total amnesia about it.

How could this happen? Dr. Battle wondered. After all, on July 12, he told the detectives what he'd done and that he'd killed her. Well . . . how about if *only one personality* remembered? The others didn't, *because they had no part in it!*

That was the explanation Dr. Allen Battle came up with. He then hypnotized Alley and became more convinced.

Candidly, there weren't many other arrows in the quiver at this point. Alley can't very well deny the crime—he's already admitted he killed her and the medical examiner's detailed report is pretty definitive about the way she died.

If you're the defense, you might as well try to place it in a context that at least gets rid of some of the horrible responsibility.

Ten days before the scheduled trial date of March 17, 1986, Jones and Thompson officially raised the possibility of multiple personality disorder. They said they needed more time to study Alley's supposed condition. The trial was postponed to evaluate for mental competency.

Alley was sent to MTMHI—the Middle Tennessee Mental Health Institute. For six months, six therapists of various sorts examined him without coming to any definitive conclusion. Physical tests revealed nothing out of the ordinary. Dr. Willis Marshall, a psychiatrist brought in by the defense, examined Alley under drug-induced hypnosis to help overcome the "amnesia." With this type of attention, Alley was able to remember the night of July 11, 1985.

Under hypnosis, Alley revealed that he had been split into three personalities that night. There was the regular Sedley, there was a female personality called Billie next to him in the car, and there was Death, dressed in a black hood and cape and riding a white horse next to the car as it drove along.

While Dr. Battle stuck with multiple personality disorder, Dr. Broggan Brooks, for the prosecution, specifically ruled it out in his own opinion, saying Alley was a "borderline personality." DSM-III—the *Diagnostic and Statistical Manual of Mental Disorders, Third Edition,* the standard psychiatric reference—characterized borderline personality disorder as "an instability in a variety of areas, including interpersonal behavior, mood, and self-image." It went on to describe intense and unstable relationships, intense anger, and impulsive, unpredictable behavior characterized by wide mood shifts. (We are now up to DSM-IV.) Four other examiners said they weren't sure and required more time to study Alley.

With respect to hypnosis as a forensic examination tool, we've all seen or heard about the nightclub acts in which a hypnotist selects members of the audience and gets them to cluck like chickens, or convinces them they can't raise their arms, or regresses them back to a past life in the court of Cleopatra. There is a tendency for us to think of hypnosis as a combination of infallible truth serum and a state of utter suggestibility, even though when you stop to think about it, those two concepts are mutually exclusive.

The fact of the matter is that hypnosis doesn't work on everyone—I'm not even sure it works on most people—and what it really is, is a technique for helping the subject focus and concentrate on a particular time, place, or idea. That's why it's sometimes helpful to police in getting specific details from witnesses, such as a physical description or a license plate number, though it certainly isn't foolproof any more than a polygraph is foolproof. What this means in real terms is that in some cases the subject might be very suggestible on either a conscious or semiconscious level to what he thinks the hypnotist wants to hear, or, with the heightened state of concentration that the hypnosis provides, he might be even more effective in constructing his own desired account of events. I have seen remarkable control studies in which, under the guidance of the hypnotist, subjects relate extensive details of events which have already been established not to have taken place. I'm not saying hypnosis isn't sometimes effective or useful; I'm only saying it's far from definitive—something many doctors, lawyers, judges, and juries don't understand.

As to multiple personality disorder: from my experience, MPD is a diagnosis that generally emerges post-arrest. In point of fact, it is a very rare phenomenon, so any therapist who tells you he has extensive experience with it ought to be suspect right from the beginning. In the few documented cases in which it is seen, it is much more common in women than in men and almost always arises out of early childhood sexual abuse. And if you're going to see evidence of MPD, you're going to see it early.

Another issue is that while MPD seems to be a psychological response to abuse or violence inflicted upon an individual—who then retreats into another personality to lessen the trauma or fantasize getting back at the abuser—there doesn't seem to be any evidence that MPD has made an otherwise nonviolent person become violent. In other words, there is no literature I'm aware of, or that any of the experts I've consulted are aware of, suggesting that a violent personality ever takes over and does what it wants with the other personalities unaware or unable to control it.

So, to state it plainly: If you're going to make a case for multiple personality disorder—particularly as a defense for a crime of violence—you're going to have to do a pretty good job of documenting the evidence going back to early childhood rather than a sudden appearance around the time of the crime. And if you're going to use it as an insanity defense, you're going to have to show—which I don't think you can—that one personality was responsible for the crime and the others were powerless to stop "him." In Sedley Alley's case, for example, which of the personalities killed Suzanne Collins? Was it Death; if so, maybe he was just doing his job. Or was it Billie—maybe she was jealous of another woman. Or was it regular old Sedley, in which case we can forget about the other two and just try him on the merits. One thing's for sure: some personality or other gave a detailed description of killing Suzanne to the authorities, and I've studied the transcript—there's no mention of Billie or Death or indication of a feminine persona.

Kenneth Bianchi, who, along with his cousin Angelo Buono, was charged with the rape and murder of ten young women in the notorious Hillside Strangler case in Los Angeles in the late 1970s, claimed to be a multiple personality and convinced several psychiatric experts, who ultimately identified ten separate personalities under hypnosis—eight men and two women. In what has become a classic of forensic psychology, Dr. Martin Orne of the University of Pennsylvania revealed Bianchi as a fake and even showed where all of the other identities had come from and the technique Bianchi had used to develop them and call them up. Bianchi withdrew his insanity plea and began cooperating with prosecutors to escape the death penalty. Bianchi is currently serving five consecutive life sentences.

But Drs. Battle and Marshall stuck to their guns. Marshall testified that as a child, Alley was mentally abused by his father, which is where the multiple personalities began. Battle thought that because of a childhood urinary tract problem which required surgical correction Alley developed a female personality to handle the pain. The Death personality, he concluded, was the result of an underlying psychosis.

Meanwhile, the pretrial procedure dragged on.

On June 8, 1986—the day that would have been Suzanne's twentieth birthday—Trudy wrote:

> With the trial of this dreadful man, who is her confessed murderer, having been postponed twice and now, perhaps, once again, we are groping for patience, relief from our oozing wound and solace in knowing that Sue is in God's hands and can no longer be hurt.
>
> The need we have to start the healing by putting this deed in the court so that justice can be meted out, is great and heavy. It is almost an inhuman act to have this final reach for justice postponed and prolonged for reasons of the inadequacy of our justice system. It appears that the criminals have every card in the game of death and the victim has nothing.

Preparing to leave for the trial, Jack and Trudy had put their dog in the kennel and were literally on their way out of the house for the trip to Tennessee when the phone rang, telling them there had been another postponement. Had the call come one minute later, they would have taken on the expense and made the trip for nothing. Among the other tasks Williams took on himself was trying to convince the Collinses that as excruciating as the delays were to them, the judge was doing it right, giving the defense all the latitude they asked for to prove their case.

Still, he admits, "The frustration level was incredible."

After four postponements, the murder trial of Sedley Alley finally got under way in early March of 1987, in Thirteenth Judicial District Criminal Court, Shelby County, Tennessee, with Judge W. Fred Axley presiding.

In the days just prior to the beginning of the trial, Williams and Carter went to interview Dr. Battle. While he insisted that Alley looked like a multiple personality case to him, when the two men pressed him, he admitted that he couldn't say which of the personalities was in control at the time of the murder.

At the request of the prosecution, I flew down to Memphis. I stayed at the River Place Hotel, the same hotel where Jack and Trudy Collins were staying. Jack testified, telling the jury what kind of person Suzanne was.

Williams had originally contacted me at Quantico through Harold Hayes of the Memphis Field Office because he was worried about establishing motive in what might seem to a jury (and was) so senseless a killing. His greatest fear, he said, was that Battle or Marshall would do well and, absent another reasonable motive for the killing, the jury would buy their version. As it turned out, though, they came up with a fine, intelligent jury that didn't.

I had two main purposes in being down there. First, Williams and Carter were hoping Alley would take the stand. If he did, they wanted advice from me on how best to nail him and get him to show his true personality, as I'd helped District Attorney Jack Mallard do during the Wayne Williams (no relation to Hank Williams) child murder trial in Atlanta. Throughout that trial, Williams had come across as a mild-mannered nonentity who couldn't hurt a fly. We knew, however, that he had a huge ego and might insist on testifying. Once he did, I gave Mallard pointers on how he could intrude on Williams's physical and emotional space and get him to lash out emotionally, showing the jury his true colors. The moment when he did was a turning point in the trial, leading to Williams's conviction for murder.

The second purpose was to help the prosecution explain the motive for murder by providing them with analysis from a behavioral perspective that they could explain to the jury. As soon as Williams had described the case to me over the phone, and then I got a chance to review the complete file, I knew that Sedley Alley's version of events didn't make sense. He had said the death was an accident, that he had no intent to injure her. That, in a word, was bullshit.

First of all, this was a generally organized type of crime, similar in some ways to what I'd seen from Wayne Williams. The murder itself was mixed—with elements of both organization and disorganization—indicating to me that in spite of her strategic disadvantage, Suzanne must have put up a hell of a fight. This was a ballsy, resourceful abduction, practically right under the noses of authorities. To disable and neutralize someone in the condition Suzanne was in, even for someone as large and strong as Alley, he'd need the element of surprise so he could quickly blitz her. After that, he just as quickly got her into the car and figured out a way to get her off base, even though two Marine joggers were running after him as fast as they could. He got her past the security gate and took her directly to a place he knew he wouldn't be interrupted. You just don't start out your criminal career creating a crime this brutal. He had to have had prior experience. I was therefore not surprised when Williams told me his suspicions both that Alley had strangled his first wife and that he might be responsible for two other murders in California similar in style to the Collins killing, although he was never charged with these crimes.

Second, the crime was clearly of the category Special Agent Roy Hazelwood and I had defined in an article entitled "The Lust Murderer" that we had written for the April 1980 issue of the *FBI Law Enforcement Bulletin*. Typically, these killings are heterosexual and intraracial in nature and are so defined because they involve mutilation or torture of genital areas. While the abduction itself was clearly a crime of opportunity, there was no way Alley's breaking off the tree limb and thrusting it up between his victim's legs while she was still alive (as the autopsy report showed) was anything other than the premeditated, sexualized rage of a sociopath intent on having his own way.

As we said in the article: "The lust murder is premeditated in the obsessive fantasies of the perpetrator. Yet, the killer may act on the 'spur-of-the-moment' when the opportunity presents itself. That is to say, the murderer has precisely planned the crime in his fantasies, but has not consciously decided to act out those fantasies until the moment of the crime. Consequently, the victim is typically unknown to the killer."

In the article, we divided lust murderers into two broad categories: organized nonsocial and disorganized asocial. Though we don't use the nonsocial and asocial of these terms much any longer, the Collins murder case was the work of the first variety for many reasons, including the fact that the trauma was mainly induced before death rather than postmortem.

There is some confusion with the term "lust murder,"

since it doesn't really involve lust in the way we normally think of it. Sedley Alley hadn't been lusting after Suzanne Collins; as far as we know, he'd never seen her before. And the fact that there may be no actual sexual assault or penile penetration of the vagina doesn't mean this is not a sexualized act. In the criminal mind, sex takes many forms. David Berkowitz, who shot his victims and never touched them, admitted that he would later go back to the murder scenes and masturbate, thinking about what he had done. Both in Berkowitz's case and Alley's, I knew what I was seeing here was a sexualized manifestation of power from an individual who, under normal circumstances, had none. The blood found on Alley's shorts, signifying that he had rubbed up against her genital area after killing her, spoke to that.

While certainly sadistic, Alley was not what we would characterize as a sexual sadist, per se. As opposed to someone like Paul Bernardo in Toronto, he was not sexually aroused from the infliction of pain. Though she was beaten severely with blunt force, Suzanne wasn't burned or whipped so that her attacker could get off on hearing her scream. Though her nipple was bitten as an act of general hostility, her attacker didn't use pliers or other instruments of torture on her as Lawrence Bittaker had done to his victims. Alley's motivation lay elsewhere.

There had been a precipitating event in the killer's life prior to the attack. And the brutality against a total stranger—the pummeling, the stripping, the unspeakable cruelty with the tree limb—all that represented displaced anger, projected hostility against someone else. Since all of these types have inadequate personalities, it also served as a substitute for his inability to approach women in a mature and confident manner. When NIS agents searched Alley's house, one of the items they found in his tool box was a mail-order penis enlarger.

As we wrote of the lust killer: "He would be described as a trouble-maker and a manipulator of people, concerned only for himself. He experiences difficulties with family, friends and 'authority figures' through anti-social acts which may include homicide. It is the nonsocial's aim to get even with society."

James Clayton Lawson, the killer (as opposed to the rapist) of the Odom and Lawson serial murder team, explained in an interview, "I wanted to cut her body so she would not look like a person and destroy her so she would not exist." If he destroys the victim, he becomes, in effect, her sole possessor.

Often in these types of crimes, the instrument used on the victim is found prominently displayed at the crime scene. In the Collins case, it couldn't have been any more prominent.

The assertion that Alley had inserted the stick to stage it as a sexual crime was patently ridiculous. Aside from witness statements about Suzanne's scream, the nature of the damage to internal organs showed that the stick was inserted with considerable force three or four times. You don't do that if you're staging. You put it in and get the hell out.

What I wanted to get across to the prosecution team was that they had an angry and frustrated man with a tremendous amount of rage at life in general and women in particular, who tried to blunt his anger with drugs and alcohol, and who, on that particular night, was not going to put up with any frustration. When this pretty young runner wasn't immediately receptive to him—or if he only perceived that, as she may not actually have had the time and opportunity to reject him—he just lost it. He couldn't handle his rage and lashed out at her.

Had Alley not been apprehended as he had been and had this case come to us as an UNSUB crime, we still would have come up with a profile very similar to the actual killer—a white, blue-collar male in his late twenties to early thirties, without close friends or regular employment, financially dependent on another person, with a history of marital problems and domestic violence, et cetera, et cetera. We would have described the type of pre-offense behavior we expected, as well as post-offense hostility to those close to him, weight loss, substance abuse, absence from work, and preoccupation with the case. He would not feel guilty or contrite that he had taken an innocent life, but would be very much concerned with getting caught. He might have made an excuse for taking a trip out of town. We would have known he was familiar with the base and the surrounding area, which meant he was a local, probably living right on base. Since I would expect him to have no military service himself or a dishonorable discharge, he would likely be a dependent of base personnel. With all of this, I think we would have gotten him before too long.

And it would be a good thing, too. Because while Sedley Alley wasn't the standard variety of serial killer, he had no remorse and, in my view, unquestionably would kill again given the right stressors. This was a crime of power and rage and anger and I don't know any cure for those in their most extreme form.

If he had been an UNSUB and we found him and searched his residence, I would have expected to find pornography and possibly drugs. In fact, when Naval Investigative personnel conducted their authorized search of Alley's home, they found, among other items, drug paraphernalia and a series of photos of Lynne Alley in pornographic poses with another man. In the storage room under the stairs they also found a twenty-inch-long stick wrapped with tape and bearing an unidentified stain.

In those days, we were not yet able to testify on behavioral subjects; the courts had not yet accepted this. So I sat behind the prosecutors, took notes, and discussed the case with them at the end of every trial day.

Just in case the motive was still obscure to any of the jurors, Williams and Carter buttressed their contention that he was rational with the evidence that air conditioning gauges left at the commanding officer's house while Alley and others were there in the afternoon to test the compressor over a period of hours were found in Alley's car. This suggested that perhaps he had killed Suzanne because she had seen him steal them since the house was in the vicinity of the abduction scene. The Collinses actually clung to this explanation for a while since it at least gave them a concrete and easier-to-grasp reason why their daughter had been killed. But frankly, I thought this was a long shot; it didn't account for the specifics of the crime, and it was never Williams's main argument. If Alley was simply pissed off that he had been caught in the act and felt he needed to silence his witness, he wouldn't have punished her as he did. The testimony to this point was harrowing.

On the second day of the trial, Virginia Taylor stated that while she and some friends were at Edmund Orgill Park late on July 11, 1985, they heard what she characterized as a "death scream," which seemed to be coming from an area where earlier she had seen an old station wagon headed.

Alley's tape-recorded statement the afternoon following the murder, in which he asserted that Suzanne's death was an accident, was played in court. Jurors got to hear him insist, "I did not have sex with her at any time. I want to make that clear right now." The jurors heard for themselves that he made no mention, nor was there any suggestion, of either Billie or Death.

What struck me as extraordinary about Alley's confession when I heard it and then read the transcript was the way it all just sort of "happened" in his version. Driving his car in an inebriated state, he just happened to bump into this woman who was jogging. Later, when he had her in his control, he just happened to swing his arm in panic, not even realizing he was holding a screwdriver, which just happened to hit her in the head, penetrate her skull and kill her. (And let's remember that with all the wounds the medical examiner found on Suzanne's body, he did not find one consistent with a screwdriver puncture or impact with an automobile.) After Alley says she was dead, he just happened to reach up and touch a tree limb, which gave him the idea to stage the crime to look like a sexual assault by breaking off the limb and shoving it into her vagina. The "death scream" Virginia Taylor heard must have just been the wind or some animal, because according to Alley's version, Suzanne was already dead at this point. At any rate, the whole thing just sort of magically happens, essentially without Alley's active participation. It is as if he and Suzanne are just two pawns who happen to be in the same place at the same time when these bad things occur.

Of course, that wasn't the last word, because Alley also offered his insanity defense, with Battle and Marshall testifying. When you offer an insanity defense, you open up a lot of avenues for the prosecution to dispute the claim. Williams read letters Alley had written to various relatives in which he very rationally discussed his intention to plead that he was temporarily insane and how that would provide a better outcome for him.

In his own mind, Williams classified the Alley treatment

team and other mental health evaluators into the "dreamers" and the "realists." Leading the realists, he thought, was Deborah Richardson, a psychiatric social worker who was mental health program director at MTMHI. She observed Alley closely for several months and testified that his claims of hallucinations and multiple personalities were inconsistent with what an individual actually suffering these symptoms would experience. More specifically, she noted that his conduct during interviews and evaluations was unrelated to his behavior at other times when he didn't have to "perform." According to her testimony, Billie alternated between male and female. She said that Alley, who she stated had an obsession with violent sex, made a habit of associating with the psychotic patients at the hospital to learn how to mimic their behavior. And she also revealed that Alley told staff members of the hospital that he had lied during the confession so his lawyers would be able to show inconsistencies in his story and "get him off."

Williams brought in Dr. Zillur Athar, a psychiatrist of Asian origin whose intelligence and critical sophistication shone through his sometimes halting English. Athar felt that since Alley wasn't being very forthcoming with any of his examiners, they were getting frustrated and started leading him in their questioning. Being smart enough to pick up on what was important and what the "right" answers were, Alley started giving them back to them. To test his premise, Athar started baiting Alley himself, asking him, for example, if he ever woke up around, say, 3:00 A.M. with scary or murderous images. Alley would then tell a subsequent interviewer that he woke up at 2:50 in the morning with terrifying images.

Dr. Samuel Craddock, another member of the treatment team who was a psychologist at MTMHI, had remained on the fence for a long time about the multiple personality diagnosis. But when he got up on the stand, he testified that "at no time in my presence did Mr. Alley show any compassion for the victim." He thought this didn't quite square, since Alley had claimed to him that Death was the personality that had killed Suzanne Collins and that Alley himself was "the good guy."

And when pressed in court, Dr. Battle could not say which

of the personalities had been in control during the murder. Since his theories were perhaps the linchpin of the insanity defense, it began unraveling quickly. Even if Alley were a multiple personality—and again, I stress there was nothing to support that he was—there was no evidence that any personality other than plain old Sedley was in control during the crime and the interrogation. That was the personality that committed the crime, gave the confession, and was standing trial for murder. It seemed pretty clear-cut to me.

Alley's mother, Jane, tried to bolster the mental health argument, testifying in her son's behalf, tearfully telling the court that "there's always been something wrong with him." After Debra Alley's death, she and her husband had been granted custody of Debra and Sedley's two children. Lynne Alley had left him by the time of the trial. In fact, she'd left town and did not testify.

No one else was able to provide any testimony establishing believable evidence of multiple personalities in Alley prior to his arrest for the murder of Suzanne Collins. As Williams recalled, "No one could come up with anything worth a flip to support him having MPD as a child. What kept coming out instead were examples of his antisocial personality."

In the end, Alley chose not to testify. If he had, there is little doubt in my mind that we could have systematically taken him apart, showing him up for what he really was—a mean and sadistic sociopath who was willing and able to take another human life simply because he was frustrated and felt like it.

By the time of the trial, Alley had slimmed down and cleaned himself up. I've found this to be very common. In fact, I often joked that by the time the case gets to court and you look over at the defense table, it's often difficult to tell which one is the accused killer and which one is the attorney. It's very important for the defense to get across the nonverbal message "Now this doesn't look like a vicious killer, does it?"

Though Alley never spoke before the jury, throughout the trial he sat with his elbows on the arms of his chair, paying close attention and passing notes to his lawyers. He seemed neither cocky and self-confident nor pathetic and ineffectual.

He seemed to be a guy unhappy about being on trial for his life.

During closing arguments, Bobby Carter said to the jury, "You've observed him for two weeks now, and he's been able to control his behavior."

He concluded, "The time has come for the excuses to end and for him to pay for his behavior."

For his part, Robert Jones tried to convince the jury that this must surely be the "act of a maniac." The crime was so horrible that it had to be "an act of a person who's clearly deranged."

While I'd be willing to admit that Alley certainly fits the nonlegal definition of a "sicko," the systematic overpowering and disabling of a physically fit female Marine, transporting her to a more secure location, torturing her, then staging the crime was the act of a brutal and self-centered sociopath, not someone who is deranged. From the testimony of the guard at the base gate, it was clear that after Alley rendered Suzanne unconscious, he sat her in the front seat next to him and rested her head on his shoulder as they drove out to make it seem that they were lovers.

Throughout the trial, my heart went out to Jack and Trudy Collins. They looked devastated, exhausted, lost, dazed, and empty. I knew they'd viewed the crime scene photos and I could hardly imagine parents being able to get through them. I'd heard Jack's testimony and thought it heroic.

When it became certain Alley wasn't going to testify, I prepared to leave Memphis and go back to Quantico. The next morning I took the Collinses to breakfast and we talked a long time. In spite of the testimony and their extensive conversations with Hank Williams and Bobby Carter, they still couldn't grasp the motivation—why would someone do this to their daughter? I tried to explain to them what I thought had happened, just as I'd explained it to Williams's team.

Before I left Quantico to come to the trial, I'd stopped by to see Jim Horn, one of the early members of the Investigative Support Unit who had since, along with Jim Reese, become one of the two top law-enforcement-related stress experts in the Bureau. I asked him what I could do to help the family if the occasion presented itself. Horn is a very sensitive, empathetic guy and he told me the main thing I could do was listen and be sympathetic, something Hank Williams was already doing very well on his own. Jim also suggested I have them get in touch with the Parents of Murdered Children organization and several other support groups and I passed this information along to them. I liked the Collinses right away, but had no way of knowing at the time how pivotal and valuable they themselves would soon become in helping and counseling others who experienced similar tragedy. These were my real soul mates. They were the reason I did the work I did.

While the jury was out deliberating, Jane Alley saw Trudy and came over to her. "I'm so sorry about what happened to your daughter," she said. She didn't go so far as to acknowledge her son had done it, but it was something.

"I'll be honest with you," Trudy replied. "I feel sorry for you as a mother and for me as a mother. Your son has caused two mothers untold grief."

After six hours of deliberation, the jury of ten women and two men found Sedley Alley guilty of murder in the first degree, aggravated kidnapping, and aggravated rape. After two additional hours of deliberation on sentencing, jurors recommended death by electrocution. Judge Axley set execution for September 11.

Jack and Trudy think the world of Hank Williams, as do I. He is one of the true heroes of our legal system. He has equal praise for them.

"They were more involved than any family I have ever dealt with in a case of violence. And they kept up that involvement, becoming leaders in the victims' rights movement."

What none of them knew at the time was that rather than ending and bringing closure with the jury's verdict, the ordeal had only just begun.

CHAPTER 9

The Passion of
Jack and Trudy Collins

In October of 1988, Jack was having a problem with a tooth. He went to his dentist, who examined him and said he needed a root canal.

"Okay, fine," Jack replied, "let's do it," and the procedure was done.

Before he left the office, the dentist said, "You're going to be having some pain from this, so I'm going to give you some medication to take when the novocaine wears off."

Within a few hours, the novocaine had fully worn off and the pain was becoming intense. "Pretty serious, front-line pain," Jack recalled.

Trudy saw how much distress he was in and reminded him that he had the pills the dentist had given him.

"I'm not going to take them," Jack told her. "I want to fully suffer this pain and then offer up the pain for Suzanne."

Trudy asked, "What do you mean?"

Jack explained his reasoning. "As bad as this pain may be—and I hope it gets much worse than this—I'm going to ask God to add it all up and then go back to that night when Suzanne was being beaten and tortured and murdered, and to subtract an equal amount of pain from her so that her suffering will become a little bit less."

"Jack, you can't go back in time," Trudy said.

"Well, yes you can," Jack replied. "God doesn't work in time, he works in eternity."

Trudy had never been as sure of this as Jack, but this practice has become a constant act of devotion for him. "Now, ever since Suzanne died, every distress I experience—pain, tension, frustration, anxiety, loss, whatever—all of those things I offer up for her sake. I ask God to apply their merits back to Suzanne at the time of her final agony and terror so that her pain can be lessened by that same amount."

I asked Jack what, if anything, he felt Suzanne's horrible suffering at the hands of Sedley Alley accomplished.

"In and of itself, it accomplished nothing," he said, and there were tears in his eyes. Eleven years later, this is no easier to talk about. "An innocent girl died because she happened to be in the wrong place at the wrong time when a monster needed to vent his rage. But on another level, it accomplished a tremendous amount. It caused us to become much better people, more caring and compassionate. It also inspired us to become active in a civic and political way—fighting for justice for crime victims and their families. It made us reach out to help others whom we might never have helped before."

I commented that it seemed to me as though they must have been pretty good people to begin with.

"We worked at it, but one can always do better. Now, every time we hear about somebody or something that we can help with, we try to help. Steve had asked me once, 'How could God let something so terrible happen to Suzanne?' and Trudy answered him by saying, 'There's evil in the world. Some people try to deny it, but evil walks in this world and we have to address it. We have to counter it every chance we get.'"

"I really feel strongly about that," Trudy added. "If we let evil prevail, even incrementally, it saps us all. Pretty soon it's up to your nose level, then your eye level, and then you get so used to it you don't even realize it's prevailing."

As Stephen has said, "You'll never find a closer couple than my parents." And the one thing they were determined to do was hang together as a family.

"If we fell apart," Trudy said, "then Sedley Alley's victory would have been more complete. We did not want to let evil win. I didn't know if we were going to win or lose, but I knew we were going to be in that battle all the way."

Like most people who have suffered terrible loss, Jack and Trudy came to grips with Suzanne's death in stages.

Trudy explains, "The first reaction I had was, 'Okay, God. I prayed to you to take care of her. How come you let us down?' But then you get realistic: You know, God didn't do this.

"Other people will tell you, 'Oh, this is terrible; there must have been a reason.' I say, 'No. There's no reason. There was an evil person who wanted to do an evil deed.' "

Her next reaction was one of acute vulnerability. She felt anxious and nervous all the time. She privately committed her thoughts to paper several times in a spiral stenographer's notebook:

> What if Steve is hurt, taken from us, what if Jack gets sick, what if I'm sick—fatally—who will cope? Why has this been visited upon us? Did we care too little, do too little—overlook needs? Or are we the "chosen" to share with Jesus his Cross, and endure regardless? Shame on me for questioning. After all, until now, it was grand, wasn't it?
>
> Was it? Did we have our *share* of hardship? Maybe not enough. Why didn't we think ahead? What of the future? Would retirement fill us with enough for our future? Would being idle be acceptable—bearable—once the "horrible" occurred? Did we once think about the possibility of something so horrendous? Now what's to become of us? What worse occurrence could there be than losing our only daughter? Losing our only son?? If you didn't want us to have them, Lord, why did you give them to us?

She became very protective of all those around her. One of Suzanne's best friends still lived in the neighborhood and used to jog alone after dark. When she came over to see them, Trudy said, "Please, promise me you won't go out jogging—even in our neighborhood—after dark. It's just not worth it; it just isn't. Do your exercise in the morning, or with other people. Please."

Eventually, Trudy says, you have to reach the final stage, and that is acceptance. Still, though, she and Jack knew that the most important thing to them was to "go the entire distance" with Suzanne, and until they can do that, says Trudy, "We have unfinished business."

They want to see the murderer of their daughter pay the ultimate price which the people of Tennessee imposed upon him.

They are religious people and not vengeful; they say they do not even hate Sedley Alley, that he is beneath such a human emotion. Though I personally feel that vengeance within the context of the law can have a useful and morally uplifting power, they are content to leave the issue of vengeance to higher authority than ours. Their interest, pure and simple, is to see justice done for their beloved daughter.

Like many, if not most, people who've been personally associated with or seen close-up the effects of violent murder, the Collinses favor the death penalty. But if there were such a thing as life imprisonment without possibility of parole, that would at least assure society that predators like Alley would never again be able to destroy other lives.

"As long as there was absolutely no parole, no *hope ever* for parole," Trudy says. "But we know in this country, that's ludicrous."

"The so-called life-without-parole laws can always be changed," Jack states, "either by court decision or by legislative action whenever a new set of politicians comes into the statehouse. Also, a governor has the power to pardon or commute a sentence. As it is, even with a death-penalty conviction, we're terrified the conviction could still be overthrown, as long as this thing has dragged on. In any event, the nature of the deed demands a response more severe and definitive than life without parole."

Since the trial and verdict, Jack and Trudy simultaneously and continuously have fought two battles: the battle to keep their lives intact and Suzanne's memory alive and her presence felt, and the battle to see justice done for victims of violent crime and their families. They are not unique in either of these respects; many others have joined the fight and there is ever-growing strength in their numbers. But they are representative of the good people who are beginning to say, in Jack's words, "If society is not serious about responding strongly and effectively to the worst crimes, then how can we expect its citizens to act? How do you expect to have a society with any set of reasonable moral rules and standards about how people should treat each other if the crime is not followed swiftly and surely by meaningful punishment?"

They began counseling other victims of loss, and they became activists. Their message to other families was simple: You will never again be the same and you will never again be whole, but you can get through this, you can go on, your lives can still have real value, and you can keep your loved one's memory alive in a happy and positive way.

"Fundamentally, we share our experience with them," says Jack. "We say, 'We're making it, we're not so special. You can make it too.'

"But it's really not so much what you say; there are no magic words. It's simply letting your compassion show through, and they'll know you understand. You might just put your arm around them and simply say, 'God, I'm sorry,' and give them a hug and look into their eyes. And don't be afraid if tears start falling. We've learned so much about ourselves and about grieving since this happened to us."

Another message they shared was that you get each other through. Couples that have suffered devastating loss can either be brought closer together or torn apart. And it's important to be aware of this.

The anguish was often overwhelming. "There were times when I was devastated and didn't know if I was going to cope," Trudy recalls, "and Jack helped me get back up. And I think there were times when he was really down and I helped him."

Jack adds, "If I did not have Trudy, I think I would be a basket case. As much as my faith means to me, it's not enough to have carried me through. We had to do it together or we couldn't have done it."

While still living in Springfield, Jack and Trudy also participated regularly in a support group for surviving family members of homicide victims. They looked forward to its biweekly meetings, where they could link up with others who had suffered similar losses and share their own grieving experiences, coping tools, and survival techniques. The group's two coordinators—Carroll Ellis and Sandra Witt—became valued and trusted friends to all the members, and true heroes to Trudy and Jack.

At the heart of the group's activities were once-a-month "caring and sharing" sessions. Tears and laughter ran together, joined by a link of trust and understanding. In addition, members frequently provided direct support to one another by attending the constant parade of hearings and trials related to the criminal proceedings against the indicted killers of their loved ones. Members also met with law enforcement officials, judges, prosecutors, defense attorneys, correctional personnel, probation-parole officers, and FBI agents to sensitize them to the specific needs of victims and their families. In time, the group became increasingly media savvy. Members began seeking invitations to testify before legislative committees. Television stations began covering some of their meetings and public activities.

There are now many such groups throughout the country, varying widely in scope and program. From their own experience and travels, Trudy and Jack believe that their "old" Fairfax County group is one of the very best of its kind in the nation, and could easily serve as a model for groups just starting out or ones that would like seasoned advice on program content and approach. Readers interested in more information should contact: Director, Fairfax Peer Survivors Group (FPSG), Victim Witness Unit, Fairfax County Police Department, 10600 Page Avenue, Fairfax, Virginia 22030.

The Collinses became advocates for people like themselves, began appearing on television and radio programs—usually together—saying to anyone who would listen: "Do we realize what we're losing in this country? Do we understand we're losing quality people, like Suzanne, who could be our salvation for the future? Do we, as a society, really care?"

"You see what's happening," Jack says. "The worst thing that any of us can imagine in terms of a crime is the violent, brutal, vicious murder of a loved one. And yet that happens over and over again in our society. And by the cavalier way we deal with those crimes today, through the abuse of the criminal justice system, we're giving out a message that the worst things that can happen in our society are either forgivable or are not worth pushing on to their full and final conclusions. That's why you see kids throwing other kids out of windows in Chicago or killing each other over a leather jacket in New York. Murder is no big deal any more. When do we start getting the true message acrss?"

Jack has spent a lot of time and emotional energy thinking about this, and speaks for the way many of us in law enforcement have come to feel.

"The only crimes people get excited about now seem to be 'societal' crimes—you know: threats to the environment, racism, political incorrectness, inadequate treatment for the poor and homeless. It's all generic; it's all group sins. There's no individual sin anymore, no 'I'm responsible for my actions, I've got to answer to somebody.' There's none of that, no personal responsibility, no sense of one's own accountability. We keep coming up with situations where the bad guys and their lawyers will say, 'Oh, what do you expect in a society like this? How do you expect a kid to act?'

"Well, who is society? Society is people, individuals who have to answer for themselves."

From the day Sedley Alley was charged, the one thing they sought was closure—a word you will hear over and over again from victims of violent crimes and their families. As long as the process remains ongoing, as long as appeals continue and the jury's sentence is postponed, as long as the survivors have to relive the horror and have the scar tissue torn off at every hearing or court appearance or parole board review, there can be no closure.

And throughout the entire process they found that while the defendant was accorded every consideration, the victim of the crime—actually the *victims,* for each crime leaves many—was virtually disregarded by the system.

As Trudy wrote in her notebook:

> Can others look at him with pity when they hear of his rage and what he did to this lovely young girl for no reason? Can society condone this, toler-

ate this behavior? Others need to know it *cannot be tolerated.*

In Tennessee, when a defendant like Sedley Alley is found guilty and sentenced to death, there is an automatic appeal to the Tennessee Supreme Court. The middle level, the Court of Criminal Appeals, is bypassed. It took more than a year, until October of 1988, for the trial transcript to be prepared and for oral arguments in Alley's appeal to be made. By this time, he had a new set of lawyers—Art Quinn and Tim Holton. In August of 1989, roughly two and a half years after the trial and four years after Suzanne's murder, the Tennessee Supreme Court unanimously affirmed Sedley Alley's conviction and sentence.

Quinn and Holton then made the standard appeal to the United States Supreme Court. In January of 1990, the request for certiorari was denied, in effect stating that the court saw nothing in the case record indicating or suggesting a reversible error. Justices William Brennan and Thurgood Marshall—both longtime death penalty opponents—dissented. But it seemed that for all intents and purposes, the long slog through the legal system had run its course. Execution was set for May 2, 1990.

So at that point the Collinses felt this part of the ordeal would soon be over and at least when they visited Suzanne's grave, they could tell her that justice had been administered.

But it wasn't over. In actuality, Jack had been given a foreshadowing of why not, two years before. Back in 1988, he had read a speech by U.S. Supreme Court Justice William H. Rehnquist regarding problems of delay and repetition which he saw in the habeas corpus appeals process in capital cases. When Jack found out what it was all about, he realized that this could present a significant problem in bringing their own case to closure.

The concept of habeas corpus is at the very heart of Anglo-American ideas of law and justice, dating back at least to the fourteenth century. Literally, it is Latin for "you have the body," and was intended to compel whoever was holding a prisoner to present him before a legal magistrate at a specific time and place for a judicial review of his status. It is considered the fundamental weapon and bulwark against illegal detention and false imprisonment—by a ruler without cause or a court without jurisdiction. In effect, it lets anyone in custody petition for a hearing as to the legality of that custody.

In the 1969 Supreme Court opinion in *Harris v. Nelson,* Justice Abe Fortas wrote: "The writ of habeas corpus is the fundamental instrument for safeguarding individual freedom against arbitrary and lawless state action. Its pre-eminent role is recognized by the admonition in the Constitution that: 'The Privilege of the Writ of Habeas Corpus shall not be suspended. . . .' The scope and flexibility of the writ—its capacity to reach all manner of illegal detention—its ability to cut through barriers of form and procedural mazes—have always been emphasized and jealously guarded by courts and lawmakers. The very nature of the writ demands that it be administered with the initiative and flexibility essential to insure that miscarriages of justice within its reach are surfaced and corrected."

No one I know of denies that all this is right, proper, and as it should be. But it must be viewed in its correct context.

The Writ of Habeas Corpus rooted in Anglo-Saxon common law and enshrined in our own Constitution is directed specifically at the unlawful detention of an individual by either an executive authority such as a president, governor, or attorney general or by a court without proper jurisdiction. It is not a privilege intended for persons lawfully sentenced by legally constituted courts.

But in 1867, on the heels of Reconstruction, Congress passed a statute that made this federal writ available to state prisoners already convicted by a state court. Under the terms of this new law, the prisoner had to allege that he was being held in violation of the Constitution or a federal law or treaty. What this federal statute foresaw was a *collateral* review by a federal court of the state court's judicial proceedings. It did not view the writ as a vehicle for re-examining findings of law and fact already determined by the state court. The federal review was supposed to deal with such matters as lack of due process, lack of equal protection under the law, prejudicial conduct by a judge, and the like.

It was the abuse of this latter writ, rooted in the 1867

federal statute, that Chief Justice Rehnquist was concerned about, specifically as it related to death penalty cases. In his view, and in the view of many observers, this federal appeals process was taking far too long, and was allowing too many repetitious and frivolous petitions into the system. The result, they felt, was a loss of credibility for the federal appellate process and the erosion of a sense of finality for court judgments.

One additional element must be mentioned here, too. At the state court level, there is also an appeals mechanism similar to federal habeas corpus. In fact, though technically referred to as "a petition for post-conviction relief," it is often referred to as "state habeas corpus." What this means in capital cases such as Sedley Alley's is that, after the state's highest court has affirmed on direct appeal the trial court's verdict and sentence, the convicted murderer can petition the trial judge to set aside that conviction or sentence on the grounds that there has been a fundamental defect in the trial. If the trial court denies the petition, then that decision, too, can be appealed up the line again to the state's highest court, and so on and so on, using this collateral attack mechanism.

In June of 1988, Justice Rehnquist appointed a special Ad Hoc Committee on Federal Habeas Corpus in Capital Cases. This committee, chaired by former U.S. Supreme Court Justice Lewis F. Powell, Jr., issued its report in August of 1989, proposing a series of statutory provisions to remedy the defects in the system. In its findings, the Powell Committee noted that for the 116 executions which had taken place in the United States since 1976, the average length of time for the total appeals process was eight years and two months, with some dragging on considerably longer. The greatest proportion of this time was consumed not in trial or normal appeals, but in federal habeas corpus proceedings.

Up until 1953, there had not been this great delay. But in the case of *Brown v. Allen,* the Supreme Court ruled for the first time that federal courts in habeas proceedings had the power to review *de novo*—from the very beginning— those issues of federal law already decided by state courts during their full and fair litigation of those issues. This case opened the floodgates for a torrent of new petitions that began to inundate the federal courts. Combined with an increasingly permissive attitude on the part of many federal courts in accepting petitions for review of obviously frivolous, repetitious, or marginal issues and a system in which there was neither a time limit for filing nor a time limit on the courts to decide, what we ended up with was a process marked by excessive delay and abuses.

Defendant advocates and opponents of the death penalty will say that repeated habeas corpus rounds are necessary to assure that each defendant has been given a fair trial, free from errors of omission or commission. Critics will say that the Constitution guarantees each of us a fair trial, not a perfect trial, and as long as any error or omission didn't materially affect the jury's decision, then it is just a delaying tactic to gain the defendant some of the additional years of life he denied to his victim. Also, it clearly prolongs the agony and pain of family members and loved ones of the murder victim and prevents closure to the grieving.

A month before Alley's scheduled execution, his lawyers filed a petition for post-conviction relief, appealing the case on collateral issues having to do with the alleged ineffectiveness of his original counsel. Hank Williams, by the way, had thought his legal adversaries very competent, raising every possible issue and benefit of the doubt for their client. "Jones and Thompson are the number one team for capital defense in Shelby County," he says. "They're both very bright guys, they've got a tremendous organization, and more experience than anyone else."

The fact that the jury didn't buy their arguments had nothing to do with effectiveness of counsel.

But by the time Judge W. Fred Axley decided that there was no merit to Alley's claims in his petition, it was September 1991. Almost another year and a half had gone by. Still, Williams doesn't fault the judge; in fact, he has the highest praise for Axley. He was giving Sedley Alley every possible opportunity so the case couldn't be reversed on any technicality.

But Jack realized that with the tools available through state and federal habeas corpus statutes, Alley's lawyers could postpone imposition of the sentence virtually indefinitely. Alley was more likely to die of old age than electrocution.

As Hank Williams put it, "The Suzanne Collins case is a classic example of how you have no justice. Through the jury the People decided in a matter of hours what they wanted to do. The System has spent the last ten years messing around with that. It becomes a ridiculous game. I'll be frank with you, it is a nightmare."

The more he observed the situation, the longer he tracked Sedley Alley's appeals, the more Jack realized that the heart of the problem was the need for habeas corpus reform.

In his quest for justice for his daughter, he had to face a fundamental philosophical and practical question: Do victims and their families have any standing in the criminal justice system? Much of the system is structured—as it should and must be in a society like ours—to protect the rights of the defendant. The issue then becomes: Are those affected by the crime entitled to any relief from their suffering through that same system? Or: Are the rights of defendants and their victims so opposed to each other that both cannot be accommodated at the same time?

Jack started frequenting law libraries for the first time since his own law school days. He began reading up on the history of habeas corpus and how it had evolved over the decades. Then he went up to Capitol Hill, to the congressional committee libraries, reading transcripts of every hearing on post-conviction procedure he could get his hands on.

"I wanted to see who had testified and how they had testified. Maybe I'm a poor researcher, but I couldn't find a single victim or anyone representing a victim who had ever testified before the House or the Senate on the need for habeas corpus reform. It was always judges or lawyers or jurisprudential experts or academics or legal technicians of one type or another, or politicians, but never victims. And I felt it was important for victims to be heard on this issue."

There was a series of House congressional hearings during the spring of 1990. Jack offered himself to the committees as a witness, but they couldn't understand what place someone purporting to represent victims would have testifying about habeas corpus reform. Still, he kept calling, kept visiting Senate and House offices, and kept educating himself.

Jack's activities came to the attention of Cheri Nolan, deputy director of the Justice Department's Office for Liaison Services. Accordingly, when Phyllis Callos, president of a prominent nonprofit victims' rights organization—Citizens for Law and Order, or CLO, based in Oakland, California—approached the Justice Department's outreach office about how to get their message out on the need for habeas corpus reform, Nolan recommended that they get in touch with Jack and Trudy. So began a relationship that would make the Collinses among the most prominent, persistent, and effective crime victims' advocates in the country. Jack and Trudy quickly became CLO's Eastern Regional Directors. They succeeded in building a coalition of some two dozen victims' advocates organizations across the country, representing more than fifty thousand members, working to give the movement enough critical mass to carry weight and influence.

Frank Carrington was in many ways the father of the victims' rights movement in the United States. A former Marine who went into law enforcement, then became an attorney, Carrington wrote several books on the subject and led or served on virtually every panel or commission related to crime victims' rights. He was a founding board member of the National Organization for Victim Assistance, a chairman of the American Bar Association's Victims Committee, and a member of the 1982 landmark President's Task Force on the Victims of Crime. Carrington was not a crime victim or victim family member himself. He had simply observed the effects of crime on families and what he perceived to be serious abuses in the criminal justice system and wanted to do something about them. He carefully and systematically studied the facts and issues to see what habeas petitions were actually accomplishing and who they were actually protecting from unfair treatment. And he came to what he saw as an inescapable conclusion:

"No person in his or her right mind can seriously argue that the otherwise intolerable effects of habeas corpus abuses can be justified because it results in 'doing justice' by freeing wrongfully convicted defendants. Basically, then, we have a situation in which victims or survivors of horrible, violent, vicious criminal activity must literally put their lives 'on hold' waiting for justice to be done, or at least be perceived to have been done."

Carrington became familiar with the Collins case shortly after Jack and Trudy joined CLO and was deeply moved by it. He urged Jack to publicize Suzanne's story and the realities of the criminal justice system as seen by victims. He also encouraged the Justice Department's Office for Victims of Crime to publish and distribute this story.

Inspired by Frank's caring and concern, Jack produced a pamphlet, working closely with Lee Chancellor, Executive Director of the Judicial Reform Foundation. On the first page was a beautiful color photograph of Suzanne in her Marine uniform, and a description of what had happened to her and the history of the judicial process after the Tennessee Supreme Court denied Alley's appeal. Inside was greater detail of the abuses of habeas corpus, including comments by experts on the subject.

The pamphlet was widely circulated. Tens of thousands of copies were read throughout the United States. It came to my attention after Jack came to Quantico to speak to FBI and National Academy classes. I used to keep a stack on my desk at Quantico, offering it to visitors to my office.

Around the same time the pamphlet was published, in early March of 1991, Attorney General Richard Thornburgh convened what was billed as a Crime Summit in Washington, D.C. Held at the Sheraton Park Hotel and calling together experts and interested parties from all over the country for a three-day conference, the summit featured law enforcement personnel, congressmen, state attorneys general, mayors, officials of rape crisis centers, other victims' advocates and organizations, and about a dozen crime victims and family members. Jack and Trudy Collins were invited to attend. President George Bush came and made a personal statement and Supreme Court Justice Sandra Day O'Connor gave the keynote address, stating her opinion that current habeas corpus procedures represented an endless round of appeals that took place after normal safeguards had been followed and normal appeals exhausted.

At the end of the conference, in a session chaired by Thornburgh, each group was given the opportunity to make a statement summing up its goals and assessing the current state of affairs. Jack was asked to do the summation for victims. The essence of his remarks dealt with the fact that almost to a person, crime victims agree that next to the crime itself, the most painful burden for them to bear is the lack of finality of criminal convictions. "Until we know that the punishment of those who have savaged us—or our loved ones—is final, we cannot begin to put our lives back together."

Two months later, on May 7, 1991, Jack first testified before Congress at a hearing on habeas corpus reform called by the Senate Committee on the Judiciary, chaired by Joseph Biden of Delaware. "I wanted to get their immediate attention, not simply to say, 'Your statutory proposals are horrible,' but make them feel what it means to be a victim, to have them grasp this type of thing. So I started by describing what happened to Suzanne, comparing her savage treatment on the night of her death with the relatively mild discomfort experienced by her brutal killer, who, thanks to abuses of habeas corpus, is allowed to live many years after his sentence even though a jury and court have said he should be executed. In effect, I said, 'Let me tell you about the type of creature that's inhabiting death row.' I used strong language to describe how he ravaged her and made her suffer."

Stephen was there in the hearing room. So was Trudy, along with a full gallery who had come to hear a federal appellate judge, an American Bar Association president, the attorney general of California, and a former attorney general of Tennessee, among others. Before the testimony began, Senators Strom Thurmond and Orrin Hatch came down to greet the Collinses, which Jack found both touching and meaningful, the first tangible evidence he'd seen of concern from any member of the legislature. With them was Manus Cooney, a counsel for the Judiciary Committee, who had been staunchly championing Jack's cause from within the Committee's professional staff.

One of the main messages Jack wanted to get across was that the post-conviction judicial process, particularly habeas corpus, needed to be treated as a victims' rights concern.

"Make no mistake about it," he testified, "habeas corpus

is just as much an issue of victims' rights and revictimization as it is an issue of jurisprudence or federalism."

He laid his feelings on the line when he said, "I am a retired foreign service officer of the Department of State. During my overseas appointments, I and my family actively promoted the merits of our democratic way of life and extolled its many by-products, including the criminal justice system. Mr. Chairman, Committee members, I could not and would not do that today. When I came home and our daughter was murdered, our nation's vaunted criminal justice system showed me and my family its true face. Yes, justice—justice aplenty for the killer, with delays, continuances, reviews, stays, tests, hearings, examinations, rehearings, appeals, and petitions. For us, the victims, neglect, uncertainty, waiting, frustration, more waiting, injustice, and growing sense of despair."

As a result of the hearing, Jack felt the rules of the game had finally begun to change. This was the first time the victims' perspective on habeas corpus had been presented. He had made the issue human and personal and accessible to the average citizen, rather than an arcane matter for legal scholars.

"We served notice that victims were not going to be quiet any longer."

They continued building a national victims' coalition. They contacted small and medium-sized groups throughout the country and got to know the people running them. They asked some of those people who were victims themselves to testify before Congress and publicly relate their personal experiences with the criminal justice system. Senators and congressmen finally began hearing from a wide range of victims on a matter which previously had been reserved for "experts."

In his retirement years, when most people begin winding down and taking it easy, Jack had become a militant. He and Trudy went on television to get their message across, either by themselves or lending their support to others. They appeared on the Maury Povich show with a couple from Kansas City whose daughter had been viciously raped and murdered. The producer told them it would be good to have a psychiatrist or psychologist on with them to explain why killers and rapists behave this way.

Jack had just the person. He recommended the distinguished Washington area psychologist Dr. Stanton Samenow, author of such landmark works as *Inside the Criminal Mind,* who, with the late psychiatrist Dr. Samuel Yochelson, conducted a pioneering study on criminal behavior at St. Elizabeth's Hospital. Along with Dr. Park Dietz of California, Samenow is one of the few mental health professionals who really understands the criminal personality from the perspective we've studied at Quantico. Predictably, many psychiatrists and psychologists who haven't done the research these two have don't appreciate their views or their attitudes toward criminal behavior.

On the program, the Collinses and the other crime victims told their stories. Anyone who could do such things must be sick . . . crazy . . . insane . . . right? No. Call him sick if you wish, Samenow explained, but he is not "insane" because he is rationally faithful to his own ideas and values. The perpetrator of this type of crime differs from the rest of us in his character and thinking. We find it difficult to comprehend that someone would *want to* do something so terrible. But that's the way it is.

As a result of his work on behalf of victims and his impressive performance at the national Crime Summit, Jack was asked by Attorney General William Barr (who had succeeded Dick Thornburgh) to join the Justice Department as special assistant to the director of the Office for Victims of Crime, a job he began in December 1991 and held for two years. His role was to be an official government advocate for crime victims and their families. In that capacity he handled inquiries from victims and victims' organizations, advised on legislative initiatives, prepared a major proposal for better publicizing the office's services, counseled, and in general tried to put a human face on bureaucracy and procedure.

Part of that involved traveling around the country, speaking about the Crime Victims' Fund, a provision of the 1984 Victims of Crime Act, which mandated that criminal fines be placed into a special fund that would be earmarked for direct compensation of victims as well as for various support services. These could include therapy and counseling, battered women's shelters, rape crisis centers, and transportation to court hearings, baby-sitting during those hearings, anything that would support victims as they made their way through the system.

Meanwhile, Jack continued speaking out and testifying before congressional committees as Sedley Alley's collateral appeals dragged on. Hank Williams said, "Jack dedicated himself to keeping Congress on track on this issue."

What kept him going? What kept him and Trudy so focused on taking on an entire system, no matter what it required of them? They said they simply wanted to see justice done, that they would not have the closure they needed until they'd walked that final mile with Suzanne.

Stephen says, "They feel Suzanne is watching their every move and I think they're trying to show her even in death how much she means to them. The more they can fight for her and people like her, the more they can show their love. Suzanne died in the process of becoming a mature woman and they never got a chance to enjoy her as an adult. This is their way of dealing with unfinished business."

Throughout the direct appeals process and protracted collateral review proceedings, Alley's prosecutors were initially batting a thousand. So he petitioned again, this time appealing the lower court's denial of his petition for post-conviction relief, and this time it would go to the state Court of Criminal Appeals, to be heard by a three-judge panel in Jackson, Tennessee, in October of 1992. As they did every time anything important in the process came up, Jack and Trudy went to the oral arguments.

Now Alley's lawyers were arguing not only ineffective counsel, but also that the trial judge should have recused himself from the hearing because, among other things, he had made a supposedly prejudicial statement at a speech he gave to a civic group. What he said, in what might have been considered an unfortunately lighthanded manner, was that some of the prison overcrowding could be solved if they would "just execute some of these people that are already in line for it."

The appeals panel was headed up by Judge Penny White, a well-spoken woman in her late thirties, with impressive credentials. But right from the start, Jack felt they were in deep trouble with Judge White.

"It became evident to us right away from body language, attitude, manner of speaking, everything, that she was very pro-defense. There was a marked difference in her attitude toward them and the prosecution team. There were smiles for the defense and some side comments, almost smirks, to one of the other judges while the prosecution was making its case. She gave relatively short shrift to the prosecution while encouraging the defense to tell her more."

It took the Court of Criminal Appeals from October 1992 to April 1994 to hand down a decision that, in effect, said that the judge should have recused himself so we aren't going to decide all the issues raised—we're going to order a new lower court hearing with a new judge. That hearing took up the time from April 1994 until August 1995. Part of the claim of ineffective counsel was that not enough medical experts were brought in on the issue of Alley's mental state, despite the fact that, on direct appeal, the State Supreme Court had seen no problem here and, in fact, the trial date itself had been delayed three or four times to provide for various medical evaluations.

"Essentially," Hank Williams commented, "they were asking for even more doctors to see what in the world Robert Jones could have possibly missed. In other words, Jones was ineffective for assuming that a bunch of medical experts knew what they were talking about."

In all the years since the trial, by the way, neither Hank Williams nor I have heard one scintilla more evidence of either Billie or Death taking over Sedley Alley's personality again. We haven't heard any evidence of Alley expressing any degree of sorrow or remorse. The defense continued grasping at straws.

In the meantime, Jack could feel himself burning out. He didn't want to give up the fight on the national level, but he knew if he didn't step back and let someone else lead the charge for a while, he was going to lose his effectiveness, and possibly a lot more. He was tired, depressed, his breath was short, and his cholesterol level and blood pressure were high.

Trudy said to him, "You're going under and I'm not far

behind. We have got to get out of the D.C. area. If we don't, this is the way we're going to end our lives."

They looked around, talked to friends, and finally decided on the old and venerable community of Wilmington, North Carolina. They moved there in the summer of 1994. Located along the Cape Fear River less than ten miles from beautiful Atlantic Ocean beaches, it was a long way, geographically and physically, from their New York origins, but it fit the bill.

Once ensconced in their one-level house, surrounded by the mementos of a lifetime of world traveling and many photos of Stephen and Suzanne, they tried to calm down and get their lives in order.

On August 31, 1995, Judge L. T. Lafferty, the new judge brought in because of Penny White's 1994 decision, ruled that there was no basis for the claim of ineffective counsel. In addition, during his own hearing of Alley's petition, he permitted the introduction of a great deal of additional medical testimony from expert witnesses. Suzanne Collins had been dead more than ten years.

A month or so later, a case that already had been in the pipeline was decided by the Tennessee Supreme Court, saying that in certain circumstances, state-funded expert testimony should be allowed during collateral appeals. As of this writing, Alley's defense team appealed Judge Lafferty's decision and has sent in a new written brief to the Court of Criminal Appeals. The Tennessee Attorney General's office has likewise prepared its own response brief and both sides are now awaiting the date for oral arguments. Yet once this issue is dealt with—however long it takes—based on their experience, Jack and Trudy are fearful that yet another issue will be brought up, and another, and another.

The issue of supposedly ineffective counsel comes up a lot. At the same time that our age seems to be characterized by a lack of personal responsibility for anything, we are also quick to palm responsibility off or lay blame on others. Just as with the large number of medical suits clogging the courts, if you don't get the result you want in a criminal trial, why not fault someone else?

Hank Williams has what I think is a good solution to this particular problem. Before a trial begins, there should be a list of about fifty questions, almost like a preflight cockpit checklist. The defense attorney should answer each question, or check off each step, then the judge, as part of his own evaluation, should get the defendant on the stand and ask him if he's satisfied. Then the judge certifies that the defense preparation has been adequate. At the end of the trial, perhaps even before the verdict, he should make another determination as to the adequacy of counsel. All of this would go into the trial record. It may not eliminate all the problems with bogus habeas claims of inadequate representation, but it would go a long way. And in cases where there really was incompetent counsel, the court would be made aware of it at the appropriate time—the beginning of the trial.

Williams thinks it's downright insulting to attack competent and dedicated attorneys after the fact just for the sake of legal maneuvering. "The problem," he says, "is that the anti–death-penalty people feel anything they do is justified because their cause is justified. That's a dangerous attitude in a free society."

There have been significant victories, though. A major piece of legislation providing for habeas corpus reform at the federal level was finally passed by Congress and signed into law by President Clinton on April 24, 1996. Public Law 104-132, the Anti-Terrorism and Effective Death Penalty Act, was designed to put an end to the endless recycling of habeas corpus petitions. Before a successive petition in a given case can be heard by a Federal District Court, its substantive merits must be certified by a three-judge panel of the Federal Circuit Court of Appeals. Given the other provisions of the new statute, that circumstance should prove very rare. And the imposition of time limits on both the filing of a petition and its adjudication by federal courts should go a long way toward eliminating undue delay.

Credit for the passage of the bill must be shared by many people and groups. In my opinion and in the opinion of people like Hank Williams, though, the habeas corpus reform is due in large measure to Jack and Trudy Collins and others like them who, believing in the power of the individual citizen and inspired by devotion to their slain loved ones, decided to march into the nation's corridors of power and demand justice.

Says Jack, "Suzanne's fingerprints are all over that law."

Of course, on a state level, every state must pass its own reforms and Sedley Alley's collateral appeals have not even reached the federal level yet, since so much time has been spent on the process thus far in Tennessee. This type of ordeal is being repeated for other victims and their families throughout the country.

For the last several years of this delay, Jack and Trudy have blamed Judge Penny White, who, since her order that Alley's collateral appeal be reheard, had been appointed to the Tennessee Supreme Court in 1994 by then-Governor Ned McWherter. As in many states, once appointed to this court, judges do not run for reelection, but are voted on in a public approval referendum. They don't run against an opponent in this referendum; it's simply a yes-no vote. And the vote, generally by very low turnout, is almost always yes. Penny White's appointment was to be judged by the voters on August 1, 1996.

Jack and Trudy and their fellow crime victims felt that Judge White was simply out-and-out against the death penalty, despite the fact that it was the law of the land in Tennessee. They had written a letter to Governor McWherter in 1994 urging him not to appoint her to the Supreme Court vacancy. They also felt so strongly that so many of her other decisions were egregious, that she was demonstrably anti-victim, that they made the 1,400 mile round trip to Tennessee to actively support a drive to have her recalled from the bench. In this effort, they worked closely with Rebecca Easley from Burns, Tennessee, a widely respected victims' advocate whose sister had been brutally murdered by her husband in a contract killing in 1977. Her sister's case is still being appealed almost twenty years after that terrible event.

Giving interviews about the "judicial Ping-Pong" they were subjected to, talking to reporters, appearing at press conferences and on television, the Collinses and other victims' advocates took part in a massive statewide drive to highlight what they felt were the problems with Penny White as a State Supreme Court jurist. They helped publicize an extensive position paper detailing the facts of many of her major case decisions. They were opposed by the "People to

Retain Penny White" campaign, which raised more than ten times as much money as the anti-White group.

Judge White's critics cited a number of appellate decisions in which she took part that they said proved her bias against capital punishment and against victims. One involved the 1991 murder of Tennessee State Trooper Doug Tripp.

On May 19, 1991, John Henry Wallen had pulled up next to Tripp as he sat in his patrol car and unloaded twelve or thirteen shots into his head, neck, and shoulder in two separate barrages with a .22 caliber rifle. Tripp's revolver never left its holster. The killer admitted he had "made up his mind" that he would shoot the trooper. There was testimony at the trial that Wallen admitted hating police officers in general and told his girlfriend that one day he would kill Tripp or Tripp would kill him. A jury found Wallen guilty of first-degree murder.

When the case came up before the Court of Criminal Appeals in November of 1995, Judge White declared that there was insufficient evidence of premeditation on Wallen's part and therefore the charge should have been reduced to second-degree murder. The other two judges on the panel disagreed.

"It is impossible to tell from the context whether this decision was reached months earlier or seconds before the killing," she wrote.

This opinion outraged a lot of people, especially law enforcement officers who daily lay their lives on the line, particularly Doug Tripp's brother, David, a detective with the Union County Sheriff's Department. "If that can't be tried for first-degree murder," he said, "then I can't imagine what could be."

And that wasn't all.

The same month that John Henry Wallen killed Trooper Doug Tripp, Richard Odom, a convicted murderer who had escaped from a Mississippi prison, raped and murdered seventy-eight-year-old Mina Ethel Johnson in a Memphis parking garage as she walked to her podiatrist's office. As he was raping her, Johnson pleaded that she was a virgin and tried to diffuse his rage, saying, "Don't do this, son."

"I'll give you a son!" Odom testified he replied. The rape was so brutal it tore her vaginal wall, then he stabbed her repeatedly in her heart, lung, and liver until she died. There were also defense wounds on her hands. Odom testified that she remained conscious until she died. The jury convicted Odom and sentenced him to death.

By the time this case reached the Tennessee Supreme Court, Penny White was a member of that panel. She and one other judge ruled that there was no evidence that the Johnson rape-murder was "especially heinous, atrocious and cruel in that it involved torture or serious physical abuse beyond that necessary to produce death," one of the state's "aggravating circumstances," necessary for imposition of the death penalty. Odom was therefore entitled to a new sentencing hearing.

The Supreme Court opinion, while allowing that, "while almost all murders are 'heinous, atrocious and cruel' to some degree, and we have no purpose to demean or minimize the ordeal this murder victim experienced," stated that this standard "must be reserved for application only to those cases which, by comparison or contrast, can be articulately determined to be the very 'worst of the worst.' " "Otherwise," they piously pointed out, "every murder committed in the perpetration of rape could be classified as a death-eligible offense."

Okay, folks. We can argue the merits of the death penalty all we want. But I'm here to tell you that I've been involved with thousands of rape and murder cases during my quarter century in law enforcement, and to paraphrase Detective David Tripp, if raping a seventy-eight-year-old virgin—making this violation the last experience of her life—ripping over her vaginal wall and stabbing her over and over again isn't "especially heinous, atrocious and cruel," or that it isn't "serious physical abuse," then I can't imagine what could be; and believe me, I've seen some pretty bad stuff.

Ron McWilliams, the lead detective on the case, wept openly when describing its brutality at a news conference.

White's critics saw this ruling as manifest evidence that she simply wasn't sensitive to victims of violent crimes and really didn't get what they actually went through. The Collinses and their allies, including Rebecca Easley, David Tripp, and Mina Johnson's sister, Louise Long, concluded that Judge White was simply against the death penalty and was using her position and power to circumvent the will of the jury.

White's supporters said she was just trying to insure fair trials for defendants and that it was unfair to judge her on only a few decisions, though her critics saw an overall pattern in her judgments. Whatever the overall record, though, I personally happen to believe that saying you shouldn't evaluate a judge on one particular decision is like saying you shouldn't evaluate a person on the commission of one particular crime. In both instances, they tell you a lot about where this individual is coming from.

In another decision, she stated that the ruling by a lower court judge that a convicted child molester must display a sign in his front yard for a certain period of time should be overturned because it "undermined his character and self-esteem."

We could argue this point and I might even agree that such a public proclamation might tend to undermine an individual's self-esteem. But it should also be noted that this sentence was imposed by the judge as a substitute for jail time. And since there is so much talk these days about alternative punishments, this might be a preferable one if the subject in question wasn't highly dangerous. But again, if nothing else, that decision of Judge White's was cited as showing a bias toward a convicted felon and away from the victim.

On Thursday, August 1, 1996, the voters of Tennessee voted No on Penny White by a margin of 55 to 45 percent. It was the first time in Tennessee history that a Supreme Court judge had been recalled. "We got the message to the people and the people were aroused," said Jack Collins.

He saw White's recall as a warning to judges not to sit too high up in their ivory towers. "Once those folks get life tenure, they sit back, they become academic and theoretical about life. They don't whiff the sulfur, they don't taste the blood. They have no idea of the grief and the sorrow involved. And they say, well, that's their role: to be above the battle. Damn it, no! You've got to understand the battle. You may not be in it, but you've got to understand it, to take the time to feel it palpably."

Jack and Trudy believe they face years yet before Sedley

Alley's sentence will actually be carried out, and they only hope they live long enough to see it happen. If it does, they both want to be there, watching as their daughter's killer pays the final price for his savage cruelty. They are haunted by the fact that they could not be with Suzanne when she died, and although this would not make up for it, it would constitute the final steps of walking the entire journey with her.

On June 8, 1996—which would have been Suzanne's thirtieth birthday—Jack and Trudy decided to go out to dinner to celebrate. "She was so joyous and upbeat, we wanted to be happy for her," Jack explains. "It was a wonderful evening. Now, on the anniversary of the day she was killed I doubt very much if we'd be going out to dinner, or the date she was buried. But on the date of her birthday, we said, yes, let's be happy for her. I think we'll do this every year."

They still miss her every day, in ways both large and small. Jack wears on his watchband the tiny gold heart Suzanne had on a chain around her neck when she died. Stephen still carries a high school photograph of her in his wallet. Susan Hand, who went on to become an air traffic controller at El Toro and is now Susan Martin, married to Army Captain Eric Martin and the mother of two children, still gets misty-eyed whenever she hears the song "Don't You (Forget About Me)," by the group Simple Minds. It was one of her and Suzanne's favorites. Among many other things, Trudy misses not being able to go shopping with her, not having her there to say, "Mom, those earrings don't go with this."

Recently, Jack wrote a short story entitled "Elegy for a Marine," a very lightly fictionalized account of Suzanne's death from her own perspective. He wrote it as a catharsis, he says, as another way of trying to come to grips with the tragedy, another way to share her pain and spiritually to be with her in the hour of her death as he couldn't be physically. It is a moving tribute to Suzanne's life and courage, one of the most affecting pieces of its kind I have ever read, and a poignant, deeply revealing insight into a parent's anguish.

On the legal frontier, he and Trudy will continue seeking justice for their daughter and others like her, whatever it takes. But they have also established a living memorial: the

The Passion of Jack and Trudy Collins

Suzanne Marie Collins Perpetual Scholarship, part of the American Foreign Service Association Scholarship Program. The Collins scholarship is awarded to children of foreign service personnel—active, retired, or deceased—to pursue their college educations, and is based solely on need.

Contributions in Suzanne's memory can be made to:

AFSA Scholarship Fund/American Foreign Service Association
2101 E Street, N.W.
Washington, D.C. 20037
Telephone: (202) 338-4045 Fax: (202) 338-6820
(Please specify that your contribution is for the
Suzanne Marie Collins Perpetual Scholarship.)

CHAPTER 10

The Blood of the Lambs

Sometime between the late night of Friday the thirteenth in March of 1987 and mid-morning of Saturday, March 14, thirty-year-old Nancy Newman and her two daughters, eight-year-old Melissa and three-year-old Angie, were sexually assaulted and murdered in their own apartment on Eide Street in Anchorage, Alaska, in one of the cruelest and most brutal crimes the investigators had ever seen. Her sister and brother-in-law, Cheryl and Paul Chapman, were the ones who discovered the horror after Nancy failed to show up for work. In addition to the deadly assaults, there was some evidence of burglary. So appalling was the attack and so concerned were authorities that a viciously depraved or serial killer was on the loose, Anchorage police and the Alaska state troopers immediately formed a joint task force.

In any case that could potentially be seen as a domestic homicide, the spouse is always considered among the earliest suspects. But John Newman, a heavy-equipment operator on the oil pipeline who had come up to Alaska with his family from their native state of Idaho, had been injured on the job three months before and had been down in San Francisco since January 3 for treatment and rehabilitation. And aside from the logistical impossibility of his involvement, it quickly became clear to investigators that he and his wife and children had a model loving relationship without a hint of any problems.

Even had John not been ruled out for these clear and

concrete reasons, as soon as we heard a description of the murders and saw the crime scene photos, we knew he had nothing to do with the attack. Sad to say, some parents do abuse, and some parents do kill, their children. They rape them, they beat them, they burn them, they starve them, they smother them. Sometimes they even stab them. But they don't do what was done to the Newman children. We see personal cause domestic homicides in which a man kills his wife, ex-wife, or ex-girlfriend where there is a tremendous amount of overkill in evidence—multiple stab wounds concentrated around the head and neck. And we see cases in which a man will kill his entire family. But whether it's done with a knife or a gun or any other means, it's much "cleaner" than this. Whatever a man might do to his wife, no matter how hideous the punishment he tries to inflict as he kills her, there is no motive we've ever seen in which a father brutally rapes, sodomizes, and slashes up his two little girls, then leaves their bodies out in plain view for whoever finds them. It just does not happen.

Both the Anchorage PD and Alaska state troopers are first-rate organizations, confident enough in their own mission and capabilities that they are secure asking for assistance from anyone who can help them. As routine practice, APD has an assistant district attorney attached to each homicide team to oversee the investigation right from the start. So the newly formed task force immediately contacted Special Agent Don McMullen, the profile coordinator in the FBI's Anchorage Field Office, who gave them a summary of the kind of individual likely to have perpetrated such a gruesome crime. McMullen is a first-rate agent and was one of the top profilers in the field. We had worked together about three and a half years earlier when he was the case coordinator in the murders committed by Robert Hansen—the Anchorage baker who had abducted prostitutes, flew them out of town in his private plane, and then hunted them down for sport in the woods far from civilization. After giving police his own initial evaluation of the Newman murders, McMullen contacted Jud Ray in Quantico.

Jud had been with the Investigative Support Unit for about two and a half years and brought a unique background and qualifications to his job as a profiler. An Army veteran of Vietnam, he had started his law enforcement career as a police officer in Georgia, quickly working his way up to becoming a homicide detective before joining the FBI. He and I first got to know each other back in 1978 when he was a shift commander with the Columbus, Georgia, Police Department, working the "Forces of Evil" multiple murder case at Fort Benning. We then worked together briefly in early 1981 when he was a special agent in the Atlanta Field Office and I came down from Quantico on ATKID—the Atlanta Child Murders. But as it turned out, we didn't work together too long on that one. As I related in *Mindhunter,* on February 21, 1981, two shooters hired by Jud's wife very nearly killed him in his own apartment. He spent three weeks in the hospital under twenty-four-hour armed guard recovering from his physical wounds. The emotional recovery took a lot longer.

Despite obvious differences between us, such as the fact that I am tall, blue-eyed, and white, and Jud is short, wiry, and black, Jud became probably the closest I ever had to a brother. He was serving as profile coordinator in New York when some slots opened up in the unit and I immediately grabbed him and Jim Wright, who was in the Washington Field Office and had worked the John Hinckley case.

Jud asked McMullen for the crime scene photos and whatever other case materials had been developed thus far. Certain pictures were faxed immediately and a full set arrived at Quantico on Tuesday morning. McMullen told Jud that based on the profiling input the field office had already provided, the police thought they had a good suspect. At this stage, of course, Jud didn't want to hear anything about potential suspects, needing what he refers to as "the freedom of neutrality."

As he sat alone at his desk reviewing the case materials, the first question Jud was asking himself was: Which victim suffered the most damage at the hands of the perpetrator?

The photographs bore gruesome testimony to the fact that all three had suffered horribly. Nancy Newman and both of the girls had been found nude except for nightgowns pulled up high on their chests, and all had been assaulted both vaginally and anally before being stabbed repeatedly. But it didn't take him long to conclude that the most violent assault, the worst mutilation, the greatest sustained rage had been directed against the younger girl, Angie. The three-year-old's throat had been slashed so deeply that her head had almost been cut off. In the hideous autopsy close-up, the gaping ends of the trachea and esophagus are plainly visible, and both the jugular vein and left carotid artery had been completely severed. Angie was covered with blood and there were defense wounds on the fingers of her right hand.

What kind of monster could do this to a three-year-old?

From the crime scene photos, it was clear that the crime had been highly disorganized. From the blood transfer around the scene—the tracking by serological experts of which victim's blood ended up where—police had determined that the UNSUB attacked Mrs. Newman first, then Melissa, then Angie. There was also evidence of some ritual behavior that has no obvious symbolic significance, but which is commonly seen with very disorganized offenders. In this case, the UNSUB had wiped a clean path up the front of Angie's bloody body, from her vaginal area past the top of her abdomen.

Though Nancy was a waitress in a nightclub-bar, nothing in her victimology suggested anything high-risk. Everyone the police interviewed at the establishment said she was loved by all her co-workers and friendly without ever being flirty or encouraging to men. From all evidence, she was completely faithful to her husband, never socialized with customers, and had no involvement with drugs. In short, there was no reason why she or her daughters should be targeted in their own home for such a barbaric crime.

There was one potentially important piece of forensic evidence. After the murders, the killer had washed the blood off himself in the kitchen sink. And on the cloth washrag he'd used (terry cloth is useless at picking up fingerprints), police crime technicians had found lice. Since there was no evidence of lice anywhere else in the apartment, they must have been brought in by the killer. Exclusive of the lice clue, the other thing Jud found significant about the washing itself was that the UNSUB must have felt the need to get the blood off him before he went outside. Why would he spend more time at the scene risking discovery and leaving more evidence, rather than going back to his own place to clean himself up? Well, for one thing, he might not have his own place. These types are often drifters. And if he were familiar with the premises, as Jud surmised he was, it might be a natural reaction for him to do it there. But most importantly, if he took the time and risk to clean up this bloody mess before leaving the murder scene, it probably meant one or both of two things: that he lived with someone else and therefore had to look "normal" when he returned home; and he was afraid of being seen as he left, which meant it was already light out, indicating the murders had taken place on Saturday morning rather than late Friday night.

The case already had a bizarre psychic dimension to it. On the Thursday before the murders, a female mental patient had called Anchorage police, describing a ritual murder which would soon take place in which the killer would drink the blood of his very young female victims and make a sacrificial offering of their bodies. Needless to say, this prophecy freaked out everyone concerned, especially when the news hit the media. The APD had to go back and interview this woman and work through the various aspects of her story, but neither Jud nor the task force could see any real connection. It seemed to be just one of those macabre coincidences that often turn up from nowhere in a homicide case and threaten to throw everyone off track, at least for a while.

After consulting with the Bureau's Anchorage Field Office, the police had set up a blanket canvass and interview regimen designed to surface the type of individual who fit the profile of a classically disorganized violent offender with some previous history of sexual assault. He would be a white man in his early to mid-twenties, disheveled in appearance and nocturnal in habits, high-school-educated at most, no military service, unemployed or underemployed in some menial job, plus other criteria. And the canvass did yield a good suspect—a young man who had recently moved into the neighborhood a couple of doors down from the Newmans. He had no alibi for the time of the murders and the police were encouraged that they had their man.

There was only one problem with him in Jud's opinion. "I kept going back to this little three-year-old," he says. "And what kept tugging at me was that I was convinced this UNSUB truly had to be known to the victims."

The suspect the police had picked up had never met the Newmans.

"In the textbook sense, he does fit our model, but you don't have the right man," Jud stated confidently during a conference call with members of the task force. They pointed out that in every other way except for knowing the family, he was perfect. But Jud stuck to his guns, saying that in this particular case, knowing the family was the key point in the profile; nothing else mattered as much—not age, not occupation, not pre- or post-offense behavior.

Jud advised that it would not be a very good move that early in the investigation to do a confrontational interview. If the guy didn't pan out, it would set everything back and the police would lose both confidence and credibility and the real culprit would have breathed a sigh of relief.

"I couldn't bring myself to accept that a stranger would spend this much time in the home or that the kinds of property he'd taken were the kinds of things a stranger would have taken. There was a certain amount of risk a stranger would have taken to enter the apartment that night, and as we got more and more forensic evidence, I was pretty sure they had the wrong person."

The victims were tied up with cord from the Newman residence. "You don't have to do that if you're just interested in killing someone," Jud explains. "It suggests you want to have some extended interaction with your victim, some sort of negotiation. I did not believe the individual they had in mind as their prime suspect had the sophistication to be up to wanting to spend that much time with his victims. He would have needed better interpersonal skills, a better skill at communicating and negotiating than I felt he had. I was reading a lot of dynamics into that act alone and when I juxtaposed that against the person they wanted to go out to interview, it was sort of telling me, no, no, no."

The wounds didn't support the profile of a sexual sadist, but they definitely showed tremendous rage directed at each specific victim, a key reason to discount a stranger. A stranger just doesn't do this; he has no reason to. There's no motivation for it. It has nothing to do with either MO or any conceivable signature.

Another reason was the types of items that were taken.

A manually operated 35mm camera was missing, and the UNSUB took money from a tin in the kitchen cabinet in which Nancy placed her tips. The tin was not in plain sight, so the UNSUB either would have to have come upon it in a search of the premises, or else known where it was. Now, with as much time as he spent in the apartment, he certainly could have undertaken a search of the entire place. Yet there was no ransacking and very little was out of order, which would be inconsistent with an otherwise disorganized offender. You don't leave the murder scenes themselves looking like a slaughterhouse, then meticulously go through the apartment looking for stuff to steal, perfectly replacing everything you don't want. Professional burglars can do this; disorganized rapist-murderers don't.

In the midst of the two-hour conference call with the task force, one of the detectives said, "Well, what do you think, Jud? This is the best guy we've got going."

Jud reiterated that they had to find a white male in his twenties who knew the Newmans well. Once they did, he said, they would find that this individual had had a particular beef against little Angie, and had experienced some precipitating stressor in his life—probably related to either employment or a failed relationship—in the days immediately preceding the murders.

The detective said, "Well, there is a nephew of hers; actually it's her husband's nephew."

"A nephew?" Jud repeated.

"Yeah, but he's been about five or six hundred miles southwest of Anchorage, and from what I hear, he's just gotten back into town."

Jud said, "That's your man!"

"What do you mean?" the detective asked.

"This the kind of guy you want to look at. He's the one you want to zero in on."

His name was Kirby Anthoney. He was twenty-three years of age and had come up to Anchorage in September of 1985 from Twin Falls, Idaho, in what Alaskans refer to as "the Lower Forty-Eight," and had lived with the Newmans for a time.

"You look into his background," Jud said, predicting

they'd find a bad background. "And you'll find some events in his life that set in motion these killings."

Police investigated Anthoney and discovered that he and his girlfriend, Debbie Heck, who had come up with him from Idaho, had been working on a fishing boat operating out of Dutch Harbor, one of the many bays along the Aleutian Island chain. About two weeks before the murders, Debbie had taken up with the skipper of the boat, who then fired Kirby. Debbie later told investigators Kirby had a bad temper and had hit her on numerous occasions. Kirby believed the skipper had stolen his girl and then thrown him off the job to avoid the competition. He came back to Anchorage angry and dejected.

Jud predicted that Anthoney would be cooperative with police, primarily in an effort to figure out where they were in the investigation and how much they knew about him. If they hadn't charged him, once the level of intensity and publicity died down, Jud said, he'd find a seemingly legitimate reason to get out of town.

Analysis of his behavior after the murders certainly supported him as a suspect. Even though he had lived with John and Nancy (so, for a time, had Debbie), he hadn't gone to her funeral. He had had only perfunctory contact with John when he returned from San Francisco, even though John was clearly grief stricken and in need of emotional support from loved ones. It was also learned that he had a roommate, Dan Grant, and was staying on Eagle Street, about three blocks from the Newmans.

After the conference call with Jud, the Anchorage police and the Alaska state troopers got on him hot and heavy. They interviewed him several times, during which he admitted nothing. Meanwhile, they were working on developing warrants on him, but to Anthoney, it seemed that the investigation was tapering off. That was when he left town, just as Jud had predicted. Expecting that he would try to cross over into Canada, Alaska state troopers notified the Canadian Border Patrol to be on the lookout for him and the Canadian authorities picked him up for driving with an invalid permit.

When they arrested Anthoney and executed their search

warrant, they found Nancy's 35mm camera and when they examined him, he had lice around his genital area.

What had happened by way of background was this: when John left town after his accident, the situation in the Newman household quickly deteriorated. According to Nancy's sister, Cheryl Chapman, Kirby began acting strangely. He was mean to the children. He wasn't working but was hanging around with unsavory characters, not the kinds Nancy wanted around her daughters.

And the reason he was up in Anchorage at all, it turned out, was that he had run into some problems back in Idaho. He'd been the prime suspect in the sexual assault and near murder of a twelve-year-old girl on a lakefront beach. But police couldn't make the case because the girl had been brain-damaged as a result of the attack and couldn't identify her assailant. When Anchorage PD then talked to the chief of police there, though, he said he was absolutely convinced that the girl would have been killed if someone hadn't happened upon them.

Nancy told her sister Cheryl that Kirby was giving her the creeps. Jud also believed there was strong reason to believe that he'd made improper overtures to her. Feeling uncomfortable and unsafe around him without her husband around, she told him to leave the house. That was when he went down to Dutch Harbor with his girlfriend.

So when he loses both her and his job, he drifts back to Anchorage, feeling completely rejected and that everything is stacking up against him. Jud speculated that he must have approached his Aunt Nancy again and tried to get her to take him back, but that she wanted nothing more to do with him.

The likely scenario is that he goes over to the Newman apartment early Saturday morning with the idea of either changing her mind or getting back at her for rejecting her. He sneaks in the same window he had used in the past to come in after hours, which puts him in Angie's room. While she remains asleep, he moves into Nancy's bedroom and confronts her. Perhaps he was friendly or beseeching at first, but it was almost a sure thing that his showing up in her bedroom at 6:00 in the morning scared the hell out of her and only confirmed all of her worst fears about him. So at that point, she wouldn't have welcomed him back into the household with open arms, and probably told him to get the hell out and never come back.

This, of course, would have confirmed for him everything he was feeling about the world being against him and would have been just the trigger he needed to lash out. All the resentment that had been bottled up in him for such a long time was finally given vent and a target. How dare she reject him like that! There would be no more reason for suppressing the lust he felt for her that had so far gone unrequited.

Anthoney had a solid alibi for Friday night. But there was strong evidence that the killings had taken place around 6:30 or 7:00 Saturday morning. Not only was there the behavioral indicator of the offender washing up before he left, there were coffee cups in the bedroom, and by the time the autopsy and lab reports came back, it was known that Nancy's bladder was empty when she died, all suggesting she wasn't killed in the middle of the night as Anthoney's lawyers eventually contended. He had no alibi for that morning.

The task force drew up warrants for three counts of murder, one count of first-degree sexual assault, and one count of kidnapping. A telling detail came when he was picked up and the arresting officer informed him of the charges against him.

Anthoney's reply, rather than the outrage, shock, or "Holy shit!" you'd expect from an innocent man in such circumstances was, "What's this kidnapping all about?" Apparently, he couldn't figure it out because as far as he was concerned, that's one thing he hadn't done.

Technically though, one of the elements of kidnapping in a number of states, Alaska among them, has to do with exerting control over individuals and moving them against their will by force or violence, even if it is only from one spot in the room to another.

Based on how the forensic people had reconstructed the crime scene from evidence such as blood transfer between murder scenes, it was not only possible to determine the order of death, but it also gave Jud a good idea of what had happened.

The rapes and murders were all very violent. And based

on the amount of time the offender had spent with Nancy before moving on to the two girls, Jud theorized that while Nancy's rape was definitely forcible and coerced, there was also an element of cooperation on her part—a desperate attempt to negotiate with him and buy some time. "All right," he imagined her saying, "just don't hurt the girls."

"But unfortunately, once an offender like this commits to an aggravated act like rape, there's no amount of reasoning at that point that would keep him from having to get rid of all the potential witnesses. A stranger would not necessarily have had to do this because he wouldn't have been recognized and identified. He wouldn't have assumed he was going to find materials in the house he could use for control devices, either.

"And I think he really wanted to humiliate this woman," Jud continues. "That's why he tied her up. And I believe some of this activity may have been done to her with the daughters watching."

He had gotten eight-year-old Melissa out of bed and run her down the hallway. That was obvious from the way the body was found and her blood detected in the mother's bedroom. She was found tied as well.

The crime scene photos show little Angie's bloody body lying on the floor of her room with her toys and books scattered around her. Cheryl Chapman reported that Kirby, who used to baby-sit for the girls, considered Angie a "tyrant," and was annoyed, apparently, when she acted like a typical three-year-old.

It's possible that the swath the killer ritualistically wiped across Angie's vaginal area and belly were an indication of some small degree of remorse for having butchered his first cousin. Jud doesn't believe this, though. "He had enough time to clean himself up. He had enough time to look for money and the camera and other things that he took. Certainly he had time to do something at the crime scene, covering up the little girl or any of the things we see, if he had one ounce of remorse. I didn't see any of this. It was just a cold-blooded, brutal killing."

What we saw on the child could have been an ineffective attempt to begin cleaning up so much blood that he simply abandoned the effort when he realized how formidable a task it would be. Or it might have had some significance only to him that the rest of us will never know. The murder weapon was the one item he brought with him, a sharp-edged knife, believed to be one Anthoney often carried.

Looking at the photographs, Jud knew the killer was completely out of control at the height of his savagery. Jud also knew that, given another stressor of similar magnitude, he would find a new target and kill again. Killing a small child is about as cowardly an act as any of us could conceive, and he was obviously displacing his anger against everyone else by assaulting and mutilating her.

"You can't go kick the boss's ass and you can't go kick your ex-girlfriend's butt, and you can't get back at mom, but you really can expend all of this energy against a little child who can't fight back," Jud says. "Kirby wanted to shock the consciousness of whoever found the bodies, knowing Nancy's sister would probably be the person who found them. He'd probably killed these people a hundred times in his mind, given the stresses that were generated in the home and at work. Even if he hadn't murdered these particular people under this particular circumstance, it was just a matter of time before a guy like this would have killed. The fantasy of killing is always sort of lurking in the background."

Anchorage District Attorney Steve Branchflower assigned William H. Ingaldson to prosecute the case. Anthoney was represented by two public defenders—John Salemi and Greg Howard. As soon as he began preparing for trial, Branchflower wanted to know if anyone from the Investigative Support Unit had ever testified on the witness stand as an expert during a case-in-chief (as opposed to merely as a rebuttal witness). The answer was that we had not, since profiling and behavioral analysis were still considered new and experimental and many in law enforcement (not to mention within the FBI) didn't know what to do with them.

Jud came to me and asked whether there was any precedent for this.

No, I told him, we'd never been allowed to give expert testimony before. We called the legal counsel at Quantico, who researched the issue and couldn't find any precedent for us being able to testify on this field of crime analysis that we'd been developing since the early 1970s.

Jud called Branchflower back and told him that while the FBI legal people had no opposition to any of us testifying, he cautioned the DA that we'd never done it.

Branchflower responded, "Well, I think I can get you qualified with your background in police work and having worked homicides for a number of years. At least we want to try it."

Carefully examining the Alaska statutes, he was able to get Jud a preliminary qualification as an expert witness, so Jud flew up to Alaska for the beginning of Kirby Anthoney's trial. Once Jud was actually there, the judge was very cautious about how much latitude he was going to give the FBI. He ruled that Jud couldn't testify on profiling per se, but could testify to post-offense behavioral characteristics. This was the critical issue for the defense, who claimed that their client had not behaved in a manner indicative of a guilty person. Jud, of course, was prepared to claim just the opposite, having predicted what he'd do each step of the way.

Jud's testimony in the Anthoney case became the first time anyone from our unit had been able to testify as an expert on what we did, and in so doing, he helped establish a trial precedent and blazed the trail for the rest of us.

Even before the first day in court, Jud began advising Ingaldson on strategy. "With regard to my direct testimony," Jud says, "I advised him that we should deal strictly with what we believe the defense strategy would be, which was to bring in a lot of people to say that this guy behaved in a certain manner and what did it all mean."

So on direct examination, Ingaldson questioned Jud about his qualifications, how many cases he'd worked, what kinds of behavior he'd seen over and over again, that sort of thing. But on cross examination, the defense began straying away from the strict topic of post-offense behavior, allowing Jud to respond and take in a much broader scope than he would have been permitted on his own. Jud believes that the defense decided not to put on the witnesses it had been planning to have describe Anthoney's behavior, perhaps realizing that armed with Jud's explanations, the jury could easily place a very damaging interpretation on that behavior.

As in many cases in which we consult, one of the main things we're hoping for is that we can get the defendant to waive his Constitutional right against self-incrimination, take the stand himself, and at least show the jury what he's really like. Every day, Anthoney seemed a little cockier and more upbeat, as if he were feeling on top of the world rather than sitting in a murder trial. At times he appeared to be running the defense, telling his two lawyers what to do. In fact, he even had himself declared co-counsel.

This was just the attitude and behavior Jud was looking for. When the defendant is cocky and confident enough to think he can do himself more good than harm, then he's going to insist on taking the stand.

The prosecution was confident about the elements of its case because of the solid forensic work. They had Anthoney's blood and semen, which matched up, plus the lice. But remember, this was a little before the first use of DNA evidence in a courtroom. That would come about a year later in another case in which Jud was involved, a strange story I'll detail in the next chapter. So to have the best chance of cinching a guilty verdict for Anthoney, Ingaldson and Jud wanted to be able to catch the defendant in his own inconsistencies.

When police searched Anthoney's residence, they found Nancy's camera. His explanation was that she'd given it to him. To us and the police, that story was bogus on its face since the camera still had a roll of film in it with the Newmans' pictures from the previous Christmas. If they could just get him up on the stand, they thought they could blow his story out of the water. After reading through the transcripts of interviews with the police, Jud became convinced that while Anthoney might have admired the camera, he had no idea how to use it, which would indicate that Nancy hadn't given it to him.

"I just wanted to get that camera in his hands and let him demonstrate to the court that he didn't know how to use it, because he'd talked so much in the interviews about his knowledge of the camera, how he loved to take pictures and Nancy knew this. APD did a great job of questioning this guy. They really got it down."

Jud had heard from a contact in the media that the black inmates in the jail where Anthoney was being held had threatened to beat him up. "This made no sense to me, but as I learned a bit more about it, what was happening was, he would come back from court each evening and they would shout out, 'Baby killer!' so he would shout ethnic slurs back at these guys.

"So I'm thinking to myself, Hmm, this could be useful. This guy doesn't like blacks and he reacts to blacks in terms of what they do. I thought, let's try to get his ex-girlfriend into court, just in the audience. I think we can get him riled."

Debbie Heck had been put on the prosecution's list of potential rebuttal witnesses if the defense had tried to mount the attack on post-offense behavioral characteristics, so she was there and available.

Jud began sitting in the audience next to Debbie. "This was all very nonthreatening. We were just sitting next to each other. But my strategy was to get his attention, and once I got his attention, I began to lean over and whisper things about the trial to her, asking her what she thought of him. And each time I did something like this, I would get closer and closer. Then I'd put my hand on the back of the bench to make it look as if I were hugging her. And even though I wasn't, I could see Anthoney getting terribly upset. He began whispering to his lead counsel, and I knew what he was saying. So the counsel got up and asked for a recess."

Anthoney and his lawyers went into an anteroom off the court. When they came back about ten minutes later, the lawyers approached the bench and one of them whispered to Ingaldson, "I can't keep this guy off the stand."

Whether he wanted to make an impression with his former girlfriend or simply say, "I'm cleverer than you, black FBI agent," or if he just wanted to do what this type of arrogant defendant generally wants to do—"I can save this"—we can't be sure. But he knew the prosecution had put on a strong case, the defense hadn't put on anything to speak of, and he may have figured he had nothing to lose.

Members of the press appeared to be shocked that he was actually doing this.

Jud then called me back in Quantico and asked me to help him come up with an attack strategy for Ingaldson. Just as I'd advised in the Wayne Williams trial in Atlanta, I suggested that the prosecutor start off slowly and methodically, boosting Anthoney's confidence and letting him think he was winning. Then, little by little, he should move in closer and closer until he begins violating the defendant's sense of his personal space, intrudes on him, then start homing in on his inconsistencies. The key was to take him by surprise.

As I've mentioned, I always like to have a physical object or symbol associated with the murder that the defendant can be made to touch or handle or even stare straight at—something that would have no particular significance to an innocent person, but which would elicit an unmistakable emotional reaction from the perpetrator. In the murder of Mary Frances Stoner, it was the rock Darrell Gene Devier had used to smash her head in. In the trial of Tien Poh Su, it was Deliana Heng's bloodstained panties. And when Jud told me about the camera, I thought this was a perfect object with which to fix the jury's mind on the fact that Anthoney had been lying about everything.

That was just what Ingaldson did. He started off slowly, then moved in gradually for the kill. Abruptly, he stopped his questioning and began talking about the camera. He asked Anthoney how much he'd used the camera, using what he'd said during the police questioning. He described the camera to the jury, then he picked it up and brought it over to Anthoney on the stand.

"How about explaining this to me?" he asked. "What's an f-stop?"

Jud recalls, "Anthoney looked at the camera, and looked at it some more, and then he said, 'I don't know anything about f-stop. I just take pictures.'

" 'Well, what's the quality of the pictures that you take? Good? Bad? What?'

" 'They've been pretty good.'

"You could just see him begin to fold because it was pretty obvious to the jury this guy knew nothing about cameras. He would not have been given that camera because he didn't know how to use it, so it was stolen at the time of the killings. He completely hung himself."

The trial lasted eight weeks. After closing arguments, the jury went out on a Friday. They recessed over the weekend, then resumed deliberating Monday morning. About four hours later they came back with a verdict of guilty on all counts.

Anthoney was sentenced to 487 years in prison. So far, he has lost all his appeals. One of the contentions of the appeals has been the claimed inappropriateness of an FBI agent testifying about criminal behavior. None of the courts has been sympathetic to that contention, nor are they likely to be, as our testimony has become increasingly more widely accepted.

Just before the end of the trial, Jud went on a camping trip with John Newman. They ventured far out into the back country to a pristine lake in the mountains, through areas and onto ground probably few other people had ever walked upon. The two men spent a weekend together.

"We began talking a little bit around the edges of his family life, what it was and what his life had now become. And to watch this thousand-yard stare in his eyes, I could never forget him or what he went through. He had a need to know what happened. He tried to pry out of me all the gory details of what happened to his family in their last moments. I couldn't relate it to him just the way it was; it would have been just too painful. But I certainly understood his need. Even with what's happened to me, I cannot fully imagine what it's like for a man to lose his wife and two daughters like that."

Just as I had experienced in the Suzanne Collins murder case, a powerful feeling came over Jud. "It finally touched me that the ones who loved these people, who are left here on this earth, have to live with this thing daily. And it's happened to me several times since then."

After the trial he tried to stay in touch with John Newman and Cheryl Chapman, offering whatever emotional support he could. This was typical of our unit, and just one of the factors that makes our work at the same time both so stressful and so personally rewarding.

The conviction of Kirby Anthoney was a particularly satisfying moment for Jud, the former cop and homicide detective who was used to dealing in facts and hard evidence and was now called upon to speculate, give opinions, and put himself into the head of his opponent.

"In the time that I'd been with the unit, I'd had some reservations about the ability to sit down with a bunch of photographs and things like that and come up with concepts about what was going on at the scene. But later on I would realize it was not one particular discipline—profiling—that enabled people in the unit to do these kinds of things. Truly, it is a collection of all the disciplines and an understanding and a good depth of knowledge about forensic psychology, forensic pathology, cultural anthropology, social psychology, motivational psychology—all of the things that when they are properly aligned and understood with a sense of investigative technique behind you, you have all these things kind of synchronized. It is not the panacea in homicide investigation, but I don't see how you can effectively work these kinds of cases without those kinds of understanding, all brought to bear upon an analytical process where you walk away saying, 'Hey, I'm reasonably sure that you got the wrong guy, and I'm more than reasonably sure that the guy you're on now is where you want to expend your energy,' as I did in this case."

It's never easy to define what makes a good profiler and criminal investigative analyst. One of the crucial skills is to be able to re-create in your own mind the story of what happened between the two main players in the drama: the victim and the attacker. Jud had been a homicide detective, and a detective's job is to collect as many little bits of information as he can and then work them into a logical, coherent narrative of the crime. That's the reason I've always found good detectives to be among the best storytellers. But I don't think either Jud or I can be sure how much of his extraordinary ability has to do with his extensive police experience, how much of it is just inherent talent and instinct, how much is native street smarts, or whether any of it is related to his having been a victim himself.

By the time he worked the Kirby Anthoney case, it had been six years since his own attack. "Even so," he says, "I still can't isolate my particular event every time I look at a crime scene. Sometimes it's harder than others. I guess it's a little easier when there's been cutting, but it's especially tough when there's been a shooting with wounds and lacerations similar to mine. I think I focus more deeply in those kinds of crime scenes.

"But just having been a victim is another part of the thing that comes into play. Having been near death, I think it gives me a deeper insight into the victimology of a particular crime scene. I bring that kind of awareness, because I *lived* through mine. In a weird kind of way I can almost place myself in that crime scene and kind of project what this woman went through as I look at her. As I look at a photo, I'm almost reflecting back on those seconds and minutes that I struggled through . . . that she *didn't* struggle through. And I use that as I go about thinking about what did happen and what didn't happen, what could have happened, what are the possibilities here? And it all kind of relates to having, in some sense, walked in her shoes, but managed to walk out of the dark that night."

A few years ago, Jud left the Investigative Support Unit and is now chief of the International Training and Assistance Unit, also based in Quantico. In a literal sense, he's moved up in the world. Now his second-floor office has a window, something he never had when he was with us, since our warren of rooms was sixty feet belowground. But even though Jud is now in a more "main-line" FBI job, his faith in and enthusiasm for what he used to do is as great as ever.

"The Bureau has to get involved with this thing bigger than they are. I am absolutely convinced that the answers are there. All the reams of paperwork on these unsolved cases around the world today and especially in this country—it is my sense that they can be solved because the commonalities of these crime scenes are there and it is a matter of the FBI beginning to lead once again to fine-tune the process where they carry this thing to the next level. I think we've only scratched the surface of profiling and crime scene analysis and all the other things we do," Jud asserts. "I think that if we really did more good studies and got back into the prisons and brought in more manpower and really devoted time to what I think is the most pressing problem facing us—violent crime against our citizens—we could make tremendous progress. I think the Bureau has a great role to play here."

CHAPTER 11

Have They Got the Wrong Man?

Carolyn Hamm, a hardworking thirty-two-year-old attorney in the field of historic preservation, hadn't shown up at her office in Washington, D.C., for two days, and this wasn't like her. Normally, she'd call in if she were running five minutes behind schedule, and here she'd missed several appointments without canceling them or following up afterward. At first her secretary didn't panic because she knew Carolyn had been running around for several days trying to get ready for a long and much-needed vacation to Peru. But when she still didn't show up for work after three days, panic set in. She called Carolyn's best friend and asked her to stop by her house and check. It was late January of 1984.

Carolyn's house was a trim white clapboard rambler with contrasting dark shutters on South Twenty-third Street in Arlington, Virginia. When her friend arrived, she noticed the front door was slightly open, allowing snow to drift inside. This was definitely not like Carolyn. Afraid, she found a young man down the street and asked him to go inside with her.

They found Carolyn's nude body in the basement, lying face-down across the doorway into the garage. Her wrists had been tied behind her with a long section of cord ripped from a venetian blind and there was a noose around her neck fashioned from rope that had been used to bind a rolled-up carpet. The rope from the noose was pulled up over a ceiling pipe and down again, then tied to the bumper of Carolyn's Fiat in the garage. They didn't see any blood or bruises on her, but it was obvious she had been dead for some time.

When Arlington police arrived, they were able to determine that the killer entered the house through a basement window where a ventilation hose to the clothes dryer had been removed. On top of the carpet roll where the noose ligature had come from was a six-inch knife, presumably used by the UNSUB to keep her under control. Nothing appeared to be missing from the house except some cash from Carolyn's purse, which was found upstairs with its contents spilled on the floor. A police canvass of the neighborhood revealed nothing. No one, not even the neighborhood watch representative, had seen anything unusual.

During the autopsy, the medical examiner found a lubricant resembling petroleum jelly around the victim's mouth, vaginal and rectal areas, as well as semen in her vagina and on her thighs. There was also evidence of semen on her bathrobe, which was upstairs in the living room. There was a small abrasion on her left instep, indicating that she was dragged across the floor. The time of death was estimated to be after 10:00 on the night of January 22 or very early morning on January 23.

Detectives Robert Carrig and Chuck Shelton began with victimology. Carolyn Hamm, like many well-educated, young professionals in the D.C. metropolitan area, spent much of her time at the prestigious downtown law firm where she worked; she was not well-known to her neighbors. Friends confirmed she was a loner—not the type to pick up men in bars. In fact, she'd had just a few romances. Police found one angry letter from an ex-boyfriend, but he was quickly ruled out as a suspect when his alibi was verified, putting him out of state at the time of the attack.

The two detectives theorized the intruder broke in on the afternoon of January 22 and waited for his victim to return home. What was unclear was how much of the crime was planned: was it a rape/robbery gone bad or had he planned to kill all along? Murders in Arlington were rare, despite the fact that the county is just across the Potomac from Washington, D.C., home to one of the nation's highest murder rates. Arlington averaged just four or five a year, leaving the eight robbery/homicide detectives to work mostly robberies, taking turns with murder cases when they occurred.

Actually, it wasn't Carrig's or Shelton's turn to work a homicide case. The Hamm murder was to be Detective Joe Horgas's, but he happened to be out of town at a family event when the body was discovered. Horgas had sixteen years with the ACPD and it had been two years since he last worked a homicide. When he got back to town about a week later, he couldn't help but look into the case. And when he did, he noticed that two break-ins had been reported within days of the rape-murder, just blocks from Hamm's house. In addition to location, the break-ins shared other characteristics with the Hamm case. In all three instances, the subject gained access through a small rear window.

In one break-in, the subject accosted a single female resident, threatening her with a knife, sexually assaulting her, and demanding money. When she resisted, he slashed her and fled. She gave police a description of her attacker: a black male, about five feet ten inches tall, slight build, wearing a cap, gloves, and mask.

In the second break-in, the intruder apparently grew tired of waiting. He left before his intended victim came back home. But he left some things for her: among other items, pornographic magazines were found on her bed, along with the cord from a venetian blind. To Horgas, the three crimes were obviously related. He also saw a connection to a series of nearby rapes in the past few months.

The description provided by the victim of the one break-in matched a subject known to police as the "black masked rapist." At least nine victims in Arlington County had given the same description of a masked rapist since June of 1983. When Horgas realized the crimes weren't being investigated in connection to the murder, he brought his theory to his supervisor, Sergeant Frank Hawkins, who reminded him Hamm wasn't his case but encouraged him to pursue the break-in connection. Horgas issued a regional teletyped broadcast to departments in northern Virginia, D.C., and Maryland, describing the suspect and a vehicle seen in front of a victim's house. Maybe someone out there would recognize their guy.

In the meantime, Carrig and Shelton came down to Quantico and met with Roy Hazelwood and me to get a profile of the killer and tips on how to interview such a suspect if he was caught. We had crime scene photos and the autopsy report to work with, but virtually nothing in the way of forensic evidence. We were dealing with the case in isolation, not knowing about any potentially related crimes. There was a fair amount of criminal sophistication evident in the scene, indicating someone with experience behind him. And at that time, the rape-murders we were seeing were almost exclusively intraracial. In fact, this is still largely true today; this type of criminal tends to target his own race. Based on that, Roy described a subject who would likely be a white male in his thirties, and I agreed with this assessment. There were signs of both maturity and immaturity at the scene: dumping the purse and taking only cash was immature, while the careful attention to detail in the bindings, with no other bruises or wounds, were signs of a more mature killer. This could indicate two offenders or one killer with two sides to his personality.

Carrig and Shelton tried to match up their notes from Quantico against leads. Meanwhile, Horgas checked the teletype daily, but no responses were forthcoming. Then, on February 6, 1984, Carrig and Shelton arrested thirty-seven-year-old David Vasquez and charged him with the murder of Carolyn Hamm, two weeks before.

Vasquez had recently moved out of a friend's house in Hamm's neighborhood to live with his mother in Manassas, about an hour's drive away. In the days before Hamm's body was discovered, however, two neighbors reported seeing him around her house.

When the detectives visited the house where Vasquez used to live, in his old room they found girlie magazines, mostly of the *Playboy* and *Penthouse* variety, though one magazine had a photo of a woman bound and gagged, with a rope ligature around her neck. Detectives also found pictures he'd taken of women—obviously from a distance and without their knowledge—through their windows and in various stages of undress. It's not unusual to find this type of offender with a large pornography collection, either store-bought or homemade, and while I don't believe there is any reliable data showing that pornography causes men to go out and commit sex crimes, our research does show that certain types of sadomasochistic and bondage-oriented material can fuel the fantasies of those already leaning in that direction. So while there's nothing abnormal about a man wanting to look at naked women in the magazines, the one bondage picture was disturbingly close to the actual crime and the "peeper pictures" showed a willingness to violate another person's privacy on at least a basic level.

Carrig and Shelton picked Vasquez up at a McDonald's in Manassas, where he performed custodial functions, and brought him in for questioning. Over the course of several interrogation sessions, Vasquez confessed to the murder.

He couldn't be linked forensically to semen samples from Hamm's body or bathrobe, but hair samples from the scene had characteristics consistent with Vasquez's pubic hair. And Vasquez's alibi—that he was bowling that night—couldn't be verified. His mother then vouched for him, saying he was with her, but she had changed her story—she first told investigators that she was at work and didn't know where her son was—and could not provide any corroboration.

As suggested by several of the details of his life, such as his job and the fact that in his late thirties he still lived with his mother, Vasquez was not blessed with a high IQ. Investigators therefore believed he must have had a partner in crime—he just didn't seem smart or sophisticated enough to carry it off by himself. In mixed presentations at a crime scene, Roy Hazelwood and I had occasionally seen two offenders working together. Police figured Vasquez could have been the one who left the signs of immaturity. His only known prior run-in with the law was stealing coins from a laundromat as a teenager.

Evidence pointing to the existence of a partner included the semen samples, two sets of shoe prints outside the house, and other aspects of David Vasquez's life that would require him to have assistance, such as the fact that he didn't drive: he was at his job in Manassas the day of the murder and made it back to work on time the next morning at 7:00. There were no buses available to meet that time frame and he had no other means of travel. He would have needed someone to drive him to Hamm's and back. And David Vasquez was not particularly strong. His co-workers told police he had difficulty trying to unload thirty-pound boxes from trucks; Hamm outweighed Vasquez by at least that. He just wasn't physically or mentally capable of acting alone. Investigators and his attorneys tried to get him to reveal the mastermind in the brutal crime but Vasquez wouldn't name any names. His lawyers even had him interviewed under the influence of a chemical "truth serum," but he still implicated himself so they didn't use it in his defense.

The evidence against him included three taped confessions and two independent eyewitnesses who placed him at the scene. In the end, David Vasquez agreed to an Alford plea to a charge of second-degree murder—not a guilty plea but acknowledging that the prosecution has sufficient evidence to try and convict the defendant of a more serious crime. With the plea, Vasquez's attorneys avoided the possibility of the death penalty if he'd been tried and convicted. Instead, he received a sentence of thirty-five years in prison.

Although many believed a partner was still out there, the Hamm case was officially closed.

On December 1, 1987, as the result of a 911 call, Arlington police received a dispatch to "check on the welfare" of a woman whose neighbor was worried that she wasn't answering her door or phone and hadn't been seen in days. Typically, police responding to this type of call find an elderly person who's fallen in the bath or suffered a heart attack. But this time, patrolmen William Griffith and Dan Borelli found a much younger person who'd met a far grislier fate.

The moment they arrived at the two-story, Georgian-style brick, attached two-family home—just thirteen minutes after the 911 call—they found reasons to be suspicious: the back door was unlocked and open as wide as the chair wedged under the knob allowed. Inside, they saw a purse lying on the floor, its contents spilled haphazardly, and instantly smelled the distinctive odor of decomposing flesh.

Upstairs, in her bedroom, they found the body of Susan M. Tucker, lying face-down and naked across the bed, her head hanging over the edge. Her killer had wrapped a white rope tightly around her neck, then down her back to a point where her wrists were tied together, with extra rope wrapped around the binding. A sleeping bag was placed over the middle of her body. The bedroom was ransacked, with clothing, bank statements, and other personal effects scattered throughout.

Although Susan Tucker was married, for the past few months she'd been living alone while her husband, Reggie, was in Wales. A Welsh native, he'd left three months earlier to secure a job and set up house. She was to join him there in a few weeks.

On Friday, November 27, the couple spoke by phone, but then Susan missed a scheduled call on Monday the thirtieth and still failed to answer the phone late that night or anytime Tuesday. Susan was highly responsible, a meticulous creature of habit. When Reggie couldn't reach her at work he grew frantic, calling a cousin of hers in Maryland who promised to check on her the next day. In the meantime, though, one of his calls home had gotten through: Officer Rick Schoembs, a crime scene agent, answered the phone and informed him of his wife's death. Responsibly, Schoembs did not reveal that she'd been murdered since anyone with a relationship to the victim must be considered a suspect early in an investigation.

Initially, the only finds that seemed promising were several hairs taken from the victim's body and sink. Too dark to belong to the redheaded victim or her husband, they appeared to be pubic hairs. Later that week, the neighbor who originally called police located a washcloth Reggie identified as Susan's hanging in a tree near the house.

Schoembs and his partner, John Coale, noted that this was a sophisticated burglar. They checked everywhere it would be possible to lift prints but found every surface the killer might have touched had been wiped clean. He even wiped the washing machine of any shoe prints he may have left climbing in the window.

As in Hamm's case, the subject took only whatever cash the victim had on hand. Collectible coins and credit cards, which could easily be traced, were left behind.

This time it was Detective Joe Horgas's turn to head the murder investigation, and from the beginning it looked to him like Carolyn Hamm's murderer was at work again, even though David Vasquez was still in jail. In addition to the binding, the strangulation, and the position of the body, there were other similarities. The killer entered the home through a back, laundry room window so small it was hard to imagine such a strong killer getting through. Both crime scenes had been wiped clean of prints and in both homes there was some ransacking of belongings, including dumping the victim's purse. Although Tucker's body already showed signs of decomposition, investigators could tell that, like Hamm, this victim put up no struggle—there were no defense wounds. And her home was just four blocks away from Hamm's, nearly visible from the bedroom window.

But this time, the killer had brought his own rope. When Reggie was shown a sample, also found in the laundry room near the point of entry, he didn't recognize it. And the killer was cocky. He calmly ate half an orange at the elegant dining room table, using a long serrated knife to cut the fruit.

Even the victimology was similar. Like Carolyn Hamm, Susan Tucker was a low-risk victim. A white, forty-four-year-old professional—a technical writer and editor for the U.S. Forestry Service—she was known to be reliable at work and something of a loner, although she didn't have any known enemies. She was devoted to her husband and a few close friends, and not likely to pick up or go with a stranger.

Horgas knew that any killer this smart wasn't the type to be observed by neighbors or make other stupid mistakes. He advised Schoembs to take as much time with the crime scene as necessary, figuring the case would hinge on forensics. When it looked like the assailant might have washed his hands or showered on the premises, they went so far as to remove drains and pipes from the sinks and bathtub.

Dr. Frances Field, the medical examiner, later estimated the victim was killed between late Friday and early Sunday. The cause of death was listed as ligature strangulation. Prior to the autopsy, Schoembs used a PERK (Physical Evidence Recovery Kit), standard procedure in any physical assault case, to gather evidence such as semen and other bodily fluids from the victim.

Considering the similarities with the Hamm case, the investigation immediately focused on the never-named, smarter partner David Vasquez may have had in 1984. While investigators dug into the victim's background and interviewed neighbors, Horgas visited Vasquez at Buckingham

Correction Center, one of Virginia's three maximum-security prisons. Rich McCue, one of the defense lawyers who represented Vasquez in 1984, also came along.

Horgas brought Vasquez a cigar, since Chuck Shelton told him he liked them, and soon he began to open up, but not in the way Horgas had hoped. Vasquez cried, saying he'd been assaulted soon after his arrival, and said life in prison was hell. He'd had no visitors in the nearly four years he'd been there. But as desperate as he was to get out, he wasn't able to provide any information that would help him.

Horgas left the prison concerned that they may have locked up the wrong man. Even worse, they had a new murder which might have been committed by the same killer. Horgas set out to reexamine the case that put Vasquez away.

True, Vasquez had confessed several times, but he'd also been interrogated in a method which was inappropriate and which we would have known to be ineffective for someone of his passivity and lack of sophistication. Transcripts and interviews showed they'd used the good cop/bad cop technique on him, raising voices, slamming the table, and surrounding him in a small interrogation room with no windows and full of cigarette smoke. Eventually, he just seems to have broken down. His entire confession seems based on information they'd already given him.

Psychiatric experts for the defense supported Horgas's fears. They had argued that with Vasquez's low mental function, he did not understand the implications of his talks with investigators and was easily confused and overwhelmed.

The evidence that earlier pointed to a second offender began to bother Horgas more now: Vasquez could not drive, so how did he get to Hamm's house? And why didn't the semen match? Were similar hair and some questionable eyewitness accounts enough to convict him?

With no new leads and nothing from David Vasquez on his "partner," Horgas returned to his original theory that the killer was the same subject who broke into two other homes nearby and was responsible for the black masked rapist crimes throughout the county in the six months preceding the murder. He started a careful study of all those crimes.

In one January break-in, a woman called police to report that someone had entered her home through a window in the basement. Nothing was taken except forty dollars in cash and a couple of gold chains. But the burglar left some strange items behind: on her bed was a paper bag containing a carrot, three pornographic magazines, and several pieces of cord cut from venetian blinds. The intruder also left a bucket on the floor at the end of the bed containing marijuana, drug paraphernalia, and a small vial of procaine, a prescription topical anesthetic sometimes used illegally as a sexual stimulant. Investigating officer Rich Alt learned from the burglary victim that a neighbor, too embarrassed to admit it to police, had told her some of the items left at her house were stolen from his home next door, broken into the same night. Their houses were only about two blocks from Carolyn Hamm's.

A week after Susan Tucker's body was discovered, Joe Horgas happened upon what would turn out to be a critical break: a regional message from Richmond PD Homicide. Dated October 6, 1987—two months earlier—it described two murders that occurred around then in Richmond—in September and early October. The description of the attacks read startlingly similar to the Hamm and Tucker murders. Both victims were white women, thirty-five and thirty-two, and both were strangled by an intruder or intruders who broke into their homes through windows. In the phone call he immediately placed to Detective Glenn D. Williams in Richmond, Horgas learned of more similarities: both women were raped and tied up, and in both cases the ME found petroleum jelly around the genital area and anus.

Since the teletype, there was a third rape-murder in Chesterfield County, which adjoined Richmond. Although this victim was younger, just fifteen, she was raped, strangled, and tied in her bedroom like the others. Richmond police weren't sure it was the same perpetrator but they'd sent semen samples from all three to New York, where a lab was analyzing the DNA.

Williams didn't buy Horgas's theory that the crimes in the different counties were related. Rapist-murderers don't commute a hundred miles, and anyway, the guy they were looking for was white. Still, he invited Horgas to Richmond the next day for a task force meeting that would include his department and detectives from Chesterfield.

In Richmond, detectives Glenn Williams and Ray Williams (unrelated but known within the department as "the Williams boys") presented the facts of the two murders in their jurisdiction. As in Arlington, both were shocking in part because of their location: the South Side of Richmond was a quiet, affluent section of town. Most homes were built around the turn of the century, with the exception of some brick, upscale garden apartments from the 1940s. But in Richmond, the murders had received much more play in the media, causing a general state of hysteria, with hardware stores selling out of window locks and entire neighborhoods lit up all night as concerned residents tried to make it impossible for an intruder to slip in unnoticed.

The first Richmond murder had been discovered September 19, 1987, when a man called police to report a strange incident. When he'd gotten home the previous night around 10:00, he noticed a white hatchback parked haphazardly in front of his house with the engine running. He called the police when he realized it was still there, engine still running, the next morning. Police ran the license plates and tracked the car's owner, who lived just yards away in a garden apartment. The investigating officer had the landlady let him into the first-floor, one-bedroom apartment, where he discovered thirty-five-year-old Debbie Davis face-down, dead, across her bed. Like the victims in Arlington, her wrists were tied together: one at her hip, the other at the small of her back. The black shoestring used to tie them ran over her shoulder, so if she moved either it pulled the other tighter.

Naked but for a pair of jean cutoff shorts, earrings, and a bracelet, she had been strangled with a blue knee sock, rigged with a metal vacuum cleaner pipe to form a tourniquet. The ligature was so tight that the medical examiner had to cut it off. The autopsy revealed hemorrhages inside the victim's eyelids, indicating the killer not only strangled his victim, he tortured her: tightening and loosening the tourniquet intermittently for a period estimated between forty-five minutes and an hour. She had also been raped, both vaginally and anally, brutally enough to tear the wall of her vagina. But the only signs of bruising were small abrasions on her lower lip and nose. As in Arlington, there were no defense wounds to indicate she tried to fight her attacker.

But for the scene in the bedroom, there were no signs of struggle in the apartment. The agile intruder gained access through a small kitchen window—only twelve inches wide— that he reached by standing on a rocking chair stolen from a nearby home. Directly under the window on the kitchen counter sat a dish-drying rack full of glasses, left undisturbed by his entry. Police surmised that the offender had tried to flee in Davis's car, but was uncomfortable with the stick shift.

Victimology yielded little, except to confirm that Debbie Davis was not a high-risk victim. A clerk in accounts receivable at the newspaper *Style Weekly,* with a part-time job at a bookstore in a nearby mall, she had the reputation of a homebody. She'd been divorced several years ago and hadn't even dated in a while. All her neighbors, co-workers, and relatives said she was a friendly person who had no enemies and didn't use drugs. She was so well-liked, in fact, that the newspaper offered a $10,000 reward for information leading to her killer's arrest and conviction.

Investigators turned up almost nothing at the crime scene: no fingerprints anywhere in the apartment or on the victim's car. All they had were semen samples on her sheets and comforter, which probably meant the killer masturbated over his victim. They also found incidental hairs: several animal hairs; a facial hair from another Caucasian; and a dark, curly hair.

On October 4, the two Williamses got word of another homicide in the South Side, just a half mile from Davis's apartment. Around 1:30 A.M., a man arrived home and figured his wife, a neurosurgery resident at the Medical College of Virginia, was still at work since he had to unlock the dead bolt on the front door. He showered and got into bed in the dark but realized the bed wasn't made. He turned on the lights to fix the sheets and saw blood on the comforter. When he ran to the closet to throw on clothes and look for his wife, he found her, dead, on the closet floor.

Thirty-two-year-old Susan Hellams lay sideways, facing

the ceiling, barely fitting in the two-by-five-foot closet, her head wedged between a wall and a suitcase. She was naked but for a skirt and slip pushed up around her waist. Her ankles were loosely tied with a purple belt, hands tied behind her with an extension cord, a blue tie wrapped on top of the cord. As in the other murders, the cord was wrapped several times around each wrist: one lay at her hip, the other folded behind her back. She'd been strangled with a red leather belt, made longer by the killer, who attached it to another belt. The autopsy revealed the same kind of petechial hemorrhages found on Davis, but these were more extensive, indicating she'd been tortured and strangled over a longer period of time. The killer was getting bolder, taking his time.

Hellams had no defense wounds, but had abrasions on her lip and nose like Davis, perhaps from being pushed into a wall or other object. Examination of a mark on her right calf revealed a partial shoe print: the killer held her down while he pulled the noose tight. She had been violently raped, vaginally and anally, and a jar of Vaseline with samples of her pubic hair was found on an air-conditioning unit outside a window near the closet. It was through this window—fifteen feet up, on a balcony—that the intruder entered the house without using a ladder. From the balcony, police saw more rope neatly coiled in a planter. Although it would be a difficult climb for most people, the back of the house faced an overgrown alley; someone could slip over the back fence and onto the premises without being seen.

And the killer was able to escape without notice, which took on greater meaning with the victim's body temperature measured at ninety-eight degrees, indicating she probably died between midnight and 1:00 A.M. Perhaps she was found in the closet because the killer was still inside when her husband got home.

Investigators found no fingerprints but did get semen samples from the victim's vagina, anus, and bedding. There were no stray hairs from the killer. Still awaiting DNA results, police had confirmation from their lab that the style of ligature in this case and Davis's was virtually identical.

Victimology gave no indication of what made Hellams a target, except that she was a somewhat stocky white woman with reddish/auburn hair, professionally employed, who lived alone much of the time; her husband was a law student at the University of Maryland who came home only on weekends.

Although the Richmond detectives didn't think it was related, Horgas asked about the rape in the area. That victim was another single white woman in her thirties who lived in a ground-floor apartment in the South Side. November 1, about 3:00 A.M., she awoke to find a black man standing over her with a long knife. The intruder appeared to be in his late twenties, around six feet tall, and wore a ski mask and gloves. A knapsack held rope used to tie her hands. For three hours he raped and sexually tortured her. Around 6:00 A.M., as he started tying her ankles, the victim's sobs got the attention of her neighbors upstairs. He fled when he heard them coming down.

Richmond police did not believe the rapist was the killer they were looking for. This victim was petite, five foot four, and under a hundred pounds, and she was attacked early Sunday morning, not Friday night. The rapist did not tie a noose around her neck, nor did he masturbate on her, and the ropes were not cut by the knife used to cut the rope in the murders. Finally, the task force stood by the original profile and were looking for a white man in his thirties, not a younger black man.

This was the first serial murderer Richmond ever faced and police were trying to learn as they went, taking tips from anyone who'd ever dealt with this kind of animal. The Williamses led a task force which included four extra homicide detectives, an investigator from sex crimes, extra plainclothesmen, even officers from SNAP—the Selected Neighborhood Apprehension Program, formed specifically to fight drug-related violence, primarily in minority housing areas.

The public, in the meantime, formed huge neighborhood watch groups in areas where previously virtually no one was interested in the program. Town meetings were held with local politicians and police. Advice was given and heeded, as neighbors started trimming bushes around windows and doors, keeping lights on, calling one another when they got home. The situation became volatile as people took it upon themselves to protect their turf: in one instance, a resident watched two suspicious-looking men in a car that didn't belong in his neighborhood for an hour before he crept up, put a .45 to the driver's head, and ordered them out of the car. The men in the car turned out to be undercover cops who were lucky not to have been shot by the vigilant civilian.

Jud Ray and Tom Salp from our unit drove down to Richmond and met with Richmond and Chesterfield County Police in a conference room at the commonwealth attorney's office. Jud made the point that although statistics and research supported the subject being a white male in his late twenties, they shouldn't rule out suspects on the basis of race. Given that the killer left no prints or other obvious clues at the scene, Jud profiled an intelligent offender with a prior record of crimes like burglary and sexual assault. And since his victims seemed unable to defend themselves, he must have great upper-body strength.

Jud and Tom also figured the killer had a full-time job, which was why the murders occurred Friday nights. With the type of sexual assault committed, the subject was someone who experienced difficulty with "normal" sex, and likely had difficulty in relationships with women in general. Unlike a lot of violent sexual offenders, he would not be the type to brag about his crime, being much more of a loner.

Quite frankly, the reason we all leaned toward a white offender was that, in addition to the fact that the victims were white, at that point in time we hadn't seen that kind of unique signature aspect among black, Hispanic, or Asian offenders. There were certain acts we were only seeing among whites, such as sexual penetration with sticks or other objects. That was one of the reasons I'd been so confident we were dealing with a white offender in the Francine Elveson murder in New York, a case I worked on with NYPD in 1979, despite the fact that the medical examiner had found a black pubic hair on the body. She had been assaulted with her own umbrella, and I'd just never seen a black or Hispanic do that to a victim. For the same reason, if Sedley Alley had not been arrested so quickly for the murder of Suzanne Collins and police were looking for an UNSUB, I still would have advised them to concentrate their efforts on a white male, based on the way he assaulted her.

It was not until later that we first began to start seeing more unique, weird, and involved signatures in sex crimes perpetrated by blacks and other minorities. George Russell, Jr., an intelligent and sophisticated black rapist-murderer in Seattle, placed his victims in elaborate and degrading poses. One had a rifle inserted into her vagina. This was in 1990. It was important to the prosecution's case to be able to link the murders and prove they were committed by the same individual and I was able to testify on signature, which helped lead to Russell's conviction.

The reasons for this divergence between white and black offenders are still somewhat speculative, just as are the reasons women don't become serial killers as men do. Jud's own theory, based not only on his work in the unit but also on his background as a police officer and growing up in the rural South, is that it has more to do with acculturation than race, per se. "In the interviews we did with rape victims, we just didn't find either things like oral sex or acts of depravity involving foreign objects from nonwhite offenders the way we did from whites. There is a noticeable difference in the psychopathology of black sexual offenders and white sexual offenders regarding the way they each treat the living or dead body." Jud believes that while this will continue to be true among black offenders who remain rural, Southern, uneducated, and/or apart from mainstream American society, those black offenders who have become more acculturated into mainstream society will begin imitating the behavior and custom of their white offender counterparts. "Black predator-type offenders are getting more involved with the depravity we've previously seen in whites," he says.

For that reason, while interracial rapes and murders still are less common than intraracial ones, if we saw "white style" depravity or perversion from a black offender, it would more likely be inflicted on a white victim than a black. On the whole, though, this is one of the many areas Jud referred to in the previous chapter that could benefit from further in-depth and high-quality research.

In late November 1987, the killer struck again. Detectives Ernie Hazzard and Bill Showalter of Chesterfield County outlined the details of the murder there for Horgas and the Richmond task force.

Fifteen-year-old Diane Cho lived with her parents and younger brother in a ground-level, corner apartment in a complex just west of the border between Chesterfield and South Richmond. One Saturday night in late November, the Chos heard their daughter typing a paper around 11:30 P.M. When they got up to go to work at the family store early the next morning, Diane was still in bed. Around noon, they checked with their son, who said she was still asleep. Although they wondered why she was in bed so late, they knew their son did not want to face his sister's wrath by being the one to wake her; they left her alone until they arrived home around 3:00. Mrs. Cho found her daughter, dead, in a horrible scene that seemed to police unmistakably like the Richmond murders.

The room itself looked like nothing was amiss: homework papers in their proper place on the desk, no sign of struggle. But on the bed was Diane's body, nude, her neck and wrists bound. White rope cut deeply into her throat and a heavier rope held her wrists together. The killer had silenced her with a strip of duct tape over her mouth. As with the other victims, there were no wounds or bruising anywhere on her body, except for a fair amount of blood around her pubic region. It was later determined that she was raped so brutally the killer tore a one-inch-diameter hole in her vaginal septum, in addition to tears in her hymen. Both caused bleeding and she was menstruating at the time of the attack. Her fingernails—polished the night before—were perfect, indicating she never had a chance to fight her killer.

In keeping with his pattern, the killer raped her vaginally and anally, leaving some kind of lubricant on the back of her arms and legs. Petechial hemorrhages around her eyes, face, and even shoulders indicated the extent of her torture. There were semen samples in and around the victim, including pure samples on her body and the sheets, indicating he masturbated on her, too.

There were more similarities to the other murders: the killer gained access via her bedroom window, four feet from the ground. Police learned Diane used to remove the screen so she could stick her head out to talk to a friend upstairs.

The killer left no fingerprints or footprints behind and, as usual, the rape-murder took place on a weekend night.

But the killer had branched out into the suburbs, indicating he followed his own press enough to know it would be safer—and more vexing to authorities—to hit new territory. And this time, he struck audaciously when the victim's family members were asleep in the next room. Detectives figured he either broke in while she was asleep and immediately silenced her with the tape or watched from outside, letting himself in while she showered, taking control immediately when she returned to her room. Detective Showalter observed, "This guy had to be watching her for some time to know when the ideal time to strike was."

He also left a bizarre calling card of sorts: on the side of her left leg, above her knee, he'd drawn a figure eight in nail polish. The girl's family had never seen her paint herself, and the polish didn't match the shade on her nails.

Although they figured they'd find nothing, police searched to rule out any other forces at play in the murder. Diane Cho was into the high school chorus and honor society, though, not drugs or pornography or anything else that would make her a high-risk victim. She was a different race than the other victims, and younger, but in some ways she fit their profile physically: her frame, at five foot three, 140 pounds, was much like theirs.

On November 25, serological results confirmed that the semen from the Cho, Davis, and Hellams crime scenes all matched and the two lead detectives from Chesterfield began reporting directly to the Richmond bureau. At that point, the only common link investigators had been able to establish between the three victims—beyond the general physical profile—was Cloverleaf Mall, where receipts showed Cho and Hellams shopped and Davis worked part-time. The task force theorized the subject picked his victims there, following them home to rape and kill. Police could stake out the mall, but how would they recognize him?

In Arlington, Joe Horgas was more convinced than ever that the Hamm and Tucker murders were linked to those in Richmond, and the rapes in Arlington and Richmond were committed by that same perpetrator: the black masked rapist. He formed a task force to investigate Tucker's murder. With his partner, Mike Hill, Horgas was joined by Detective Dick Spalding from burglary and another detective, Ed Chapman, from the sex crimes unit. Within the context of searching for David Vasquez's partner or another perpetrator who might have been involved in both Hamm's and Tucker's murders—say, the black masked rapist—Horgas had them pull all the burglary and rape files for the area from 1983.

Horgas hand-carried evidence from the Tucker crime scene to the Northern Virginia Bureau of Forensic Science in Fairfax County. By December 22, he had preliminary word back from his contact there, Deanne Dabbs (who conveniently had a good friend in Richmond's crime lab), that the semen samples from Tucker contained the same blood characteristics as samples from the Davis and Hellams crime scenes. This would help them nail the offender, since only thirteen percent of the population matched these characteristics. Of course, first they had to have a suspect.

He next began reinterviewing victims of the black masked rapist from 1983. Of the nine, eight agreed to talk to him. As difficult as it was to relive their experiences, once they learned the same man could still be out there, now murdering victims, they felt compelled to cooperate.

The first victim was assaulted in June 1983, in a supermarket parking lot. Around 1:00 A.M., the petite, dark-haired victim, in her twenties, was approached by a thin black man with a knife. About five foot eight, also in his twenties, he'd pulled a T-shirt in which he'd cut eyeholes over his head, and his hands were covered. He forced the victim to drive him around, then had her stop and get out by a wooded area. Threatening her with the knife the whole time, he forced her to perform oral sex and raped her repeatedly. She escaped when he left her in the woods to go back to the car. This victim did not think her assailant ejaculated and was left with the impression that "he's capable of anything. And I mean anything."

The rapist attacked the next three victims in their homes, breaking in as they slept. He matched the same physical description as in the first case, and in each attack he wore gloves and a makeshift mask. The same type of knife was described in each. The pattern of behavior was that he'd start off demanding money, usually making the victim get her purse, then rape her both orally and vaginally. In all three crimes he threatened the women repeatedly with the knife, issuing warnings like "I'm gonna put my dick in you and you'd better come" and "You'll have an orgasm or I'll kill you." To Horgas, it sounded almost as if the subject was working from a script.

In the last of those three attacks, the rapist added two new elements: he duct-taped the victim's mouth and attempted to tie her up. She escaped the apartment as he tried to cut cord from her venetian blinds.

He added still more elements to his next attack. After surprising his eighteen-year-old victim as she got out of her car, he forced her back in the car and had her drive to a secluded location where he duct-taped her eyes and raped her repeatedly: orally, vaginally, and anally. Finally, he tied her wrists behind her back with rope and forced her into the trunk of her car. Miraculously, she was able to escape by kicking the trunk open when she smelled smoke. The rapist had set her car on fire and left her for dead.

In another attack, the UNSUB tied the victim's ankles with stockings and used cord from her venetian blinds to tie her wrists behind her back. The sexual assault was similar to that of the other victims. Looking at the files, it was as if this guy needed to strike every six weeks or so; and he was growing increasingly violent.

Horgas believed the rapist was definitely homicidal by January 1984, and the last rape certainly supported that belief. On January 25, just hours after Carolyn Hamm's friend discovered her body, the rapist broke into the home of the last reported victim. The thirty-two-year-old woman went downstairs to investigate when she heard the door on the side of her house open. There, she found a man matching the same physical description as in the other attacks, from his age and height to his homemade mask and his knife. In a scenario that sounds much like what happened to Hamm, the intruder forced her to bring him her purse. After emptying the contents on the floor he took her cash, then forced her back downstairs where the sexual assault took place. Part of the ritual that night involved an artificial phallus which he brought with him and ordered her to use. When she refused, he beat her about the face, cut her leg, sexually assaulted her again, and forced her outside, where he told her they were going for a ride. She fought back, screaming loudly, figuring if she went with him he'd kill her. Finally he fled.

Investigators learned the sexual device was stolen from the house next door, much as the pornographic magazines and drug paraphernalia had been stolen from one house and left on a bed in the next during the break-in in Carolyn Hamm's neighborhood.

Horgas presented his findings to the task force, which was not overly enthusiastic. It seemed far-fetched that a burglar would escalate to rape and murder. And those on the sex crimes unit thought they knew who the black masked rapist was: they arrested a guy in the summer of 1987 who had a similar MO; they just couldn't prove he had been in action before 1986. By Christmas, Horgas's task force was disbanded.

In the meantime, however, his partner, Mike Hill, came up with two more break-ins that seemed to match the pattern. On January 12, 1984, an attempt had been thwarted when an eighteen-year-old woman woke up her father to have him check on noises she heard outside the house. He found two basement windows damaged and a mailbox placed under a bedroom window, presumably to facilitate entry. Two days later, a twenty-two-year-old woman reported that a black man (of the same description as the man in the rapes, with mask, gloves, and knife) broke into her basement and demanded money or "We'll kill the little girl upstairs." The intruder fled when a roommate made noise coming down the stairs. Both occurred within two blocks of Carolyn Hamm's house.

On December 28, 1987, Horgas boarded a plane bound for New York. He'd gotten approval to have Arlington case samples analyzed at Lifecodes, the lab the detectives in Richmond had turned to for DNA testing. With so many cases seemingly linked, Horgas needed proof. And they had to work fast: just that morning another report came in, this one from nearby Fairfax County, about a seventeen-year-old attacked in her bedroom December 17 by a black man matching the description Horgas knew by heart. Fortunately for that victim her sister walked in the room just as the attacker finished tying her wrists and he fled.

Horgas also knew DNA results would only be useful after he brought in a suspect. So with all the information and behavioral clues he'd amassed, he called the Investigative Support Unit again and said to Special Agent Stephen Mardigian, the profiler whose geographic territory included Virginia, "I'd like to talk to you guys. Can you come over here and sit down with us? I think we've got a homicide up here related to those cases down in Richmond." On December 29, Mardigian and Jud Ray slogged up through the snow to meet with him at Arlington PD headquarters.

In the conference room, Steve and Jud listened as Horgas led them through a major presentation of the evidence. He was organized and methodical. After he presented the Tucker case, he said, "Okay, now do you feel the facts of it could relate to the Richmond cases?"

Steve and Jud were caught in something of a bind. Our unit's effectiveness is based on a high, mutual-trust relationship with each of the police departments and local law enforcement agencies with which we work. We had already conducted an independent case consultation with Richmond, and if the two investigations did end up going off in dissimilar directions, we didn't want to be caught in the middle of a conflict with two important "clients."

But as soon as Horgas completed his review, Steve said, "It was pretty evident to us that these cases were related. From a profiling standpoint, the methodology, the MO were very, very consistent. We said it was our opinion they were probably dealing with the same offender."

Horgas was highly organized. "Now I'd like you to take a look at a homicide that occurred back in 1984," he said. "This is the murder of Carolyn Hamm."

Again, the similarities between the Tucker and Hamm cases were dramatic. "What else was going on in the area at this time?" Steve asked.

Horgas then outlined for the agents the series of burglaries and sexual assaults that had occurred in Arlington in 1983. All the victims were white women, most in their twenties and thirties, attacked by a masked black man with a knife and wearing gloves. In several cases, victims were tied up and venetian blind cords were used as binding. Elements of the sexual assault were similar, and the UNSUB had grown more dangerous with each rape, up to the point of Hamm's murder.

"When you looked at this serial rapist active in the Arlington area at that time and the serial burglar active at the same time, you immediately saw a geographic overlay that also corresponded to the murders under investigation. Jud and I quickly discussed it with each other and said to Joe, 'These are related. There are significant enough commonalities in methodology, escalation, progression.' It all worked out well."

Jud focused on the rapes and the fact that they provided live victims to interview. Therefore, if they were committed by the same UNSUB as the murders, they would have not only the physical evidence from which to draw conclusions, but a tremendous amount of verbal behavior as well. Then he pointed to the painstaking attention to detail in the bindings in each of the Richmond murders and the killing of Susan Tucker. The killer did much more with the ropes than he had to, either to strangle his victim or merely to control her, as seen in the binding from the noose down to the wrists and wrapping extra rope or other binding around the wrists. This wasn't more MO. This was part of the murderer's signature. Looking at the crime scene photos, Jud explained that this UNSUB had a deep need to exert complete control over the situation.

He also declared that the subject was a sexual sadist; he enjoyed torturing his victims, choking them and releasing them, seeing their fear and pain, hearing them beg for mercy.

Steve noted other signature elements: the victims' bodies were all concealed in some way—Tucker with a sleeping bag, Hellams in a closet, Cho with her sheet, and Davis with her shorts. He noted the semen left on the bodies, that all were killed in their bedrooms, and the fact that the killer overwhelmed his victims immediately, leaving them no time to struggle.

This killer was clearly an organized offender who planned his crimes very carefully. He stalked victims, waiting for an opportunity to strike, monitoring their movements, probably for several days. He chose victims who lived alone or would be alone when he attacked. He was sophisticated: he knew if he committed the crimes inside their homes he would decrease the risk that he'd be detected or his crimes witnessed.

Both agents were sure the offender would have a history of crime that went beyond breaking and entering. He may not have been arrested for them, but he practiced with earlier rapes. There was no way he started out with these elaborate murders.

It wasn't just the physical description or disguise elements that convinced Jud and Steve that the rapes and both the Hamm and Tucker murders were committed by the same offender. There was also the psycholinguistics: an aspect of profiling we use extensively in ransom kidnapping cases, hostage situations, extortions, and bombings—in other words, any ongoing situation in which written or verbal communication is our primary behavioral clue. Though we have used it on many occasions with gratifying results, such as in trying to determine a hostage holder's true intentions to know whether, and how much, force should be brought to bear, perhaps the most prominent recent use of psycholinguistic analysis has been in the Unabom case. As we detailed in our book *Unabomber: On the Trail of America's Most-Wanted Serial Killer,* it was the word-by-word, phrase-by-phrase, and idea-by-idea comparison of the Unabomber's published manifesto with other personal letters and writings that led to the identification of Theodore Kaczynski in his remote Montana cabin as the primary suspect in these deadly bombings which had terrorized the United States for more than a decade.

Here, in the cases Joe Horgas had assembled, the rapist's choice of words and his sentence structure were not only consistent from crime to crime, but consistent with the overall personality type we felt would commit this type of crime. This rapist needed his victims to exhibit signs they were sexually satisfied by him to build up his masculinity. His primary motivation was control, exhibited in his insulting language, his use of the knife, and ultimately the binding, torture, and murder of his victims.

Both agents stressed that this type of offender will continue to grow more and more violent with each crime, as he learns and perfects his techniques. Jud showed how the first rape, involving abduction from a parking lot, was high-risk. He learned from that and modified his MO, almost exclusively attacking inside victims' homes from that point on. And his control over his victims also grew over time. Initially, he only used the knife to keep control, but later he began duct-taping victims' eyes and mouths, and tying them up. By the later rapes, he felt confident breaking into houses next door, boldly using props from one in the other. In the later murders, he brought his own rope, demonstrating an even higher degree of planning.

The rapes were practice for the murder: he perfected his method of entry into the homes; he left no fingerprints; and he grew comfortable spending time in the victims' residences, leading them upstairs and downstairs, and raping them in several locations.

In Steve's and Jud's opinion, the killing started when he felt control being taken away. They cited the last rape in Arlington as an example. The rapist quickly escalated his level of violence when the victim refused to use the sexual device as ordered and tried telling him to leave. He perceived her as trying to run the show, to take back control from him, and that enraged him. The later murders were virtually all professional women, achiever personality types, used to being in control of their lives. Since the killer had already overpowered them physically (there were no signs of struggle in any case), perhaps they tried talking to him, verbally resisting. That alone could have been enough to set him off.

After all the presentations, when our guys had essentially confirmed Horgas's suspicions, the detective paused, then said, "Let me explain something. Hamm is actually a closed case, because an individual has been arrested, tried, and convicted." He gave the agents the background on David Vasquez, and told them the theory of the accomplice who was never caught or identified.

"Do you think there's more than one person involved?" he asked.

Steve told him a more thorough review would be necessary than simply looking at all the materials around a conference table, but from what they'd seen so far, he told Horgas that not only didn't they believe someone like Vasquez was capable of Hamm's murder the way it had been described, they didn't buy that he could be part of a two-man team, stressing that this type of crime is committed by lone offenders and that with two offenders there would have been more evidence of divergent behaviors exhibited at the crime scene. From all of the unit's collective experience, it just did not seem that a guy on Vasquez's level would have the intellectual capability or criminal sophistication to commit the crime.

Then they talked about the race issue and the fact that our original profile had predicted a white offender. The agents noted that we hadn't been told about any possible link to the black masked rapist, which pointed up that our product can only be as complete as the input we're given. And, up to that point, with the virtual exception of Wayne Williams in Atlanta, all serial killers had been white. And even Williams had attacked within his own race. But again, Jud and Steve stressed that although statistically rare, it was not impossible that the offender Horgas was looking for was black. Indeed, they agreed that the black rapist and the murderer were likely one and the same, so that was the direction the investigation should take.

So where to begin?

If all of this was part of a pattern, the agents explained, then that pattern should be helpful in identifying the UNSUB. Go back and identify the first rape, they told him; that was the environment in which he felt the most comfortable; that was where he either lived or worked.

"Now, unlike Hamm's, all the rapes are open cases," Steve continued. "No one was ever apprehended. We know from our research that this type of sexual offender doesn't quit on his own. He's either been forced out of the area for one reason or another, or else he's been arrested on another charge."

"Generally speaking, a guy will kill right there where he's been killing until he's flushed out or something else happens," said Jud.

"If he'd been arrested in a rape or related sex crime, he

would have surfaced for consideration in all of these—and he didn't," Steve concluded.

Likewise, if he left the area and began working somewhere else, some other law enforcement agency would have picked up on his pattern and responded to Horgas's published inquiry. And that didn't happen, either. But if the activity ceases, as it suddenly seemed to here, then the chances were good that he'd been incarcerated on some unrelated charge. The only other strong possibility was that he had died, and they could effectively rule that one out since the same offender was apparently now back at work again.

"He was probably arrested as a burglar," Steve stated. "His other profession."

"Look," said Jud, "since you didn't surface a sexual assailant back in the early 1980s but his activity stopped shortly after the homicide of Carolyn Hamm, go back and look for someone arrested for burglary in the environment where the first rape occurred."

A burglary conviction ought to be good for about a three- or four-year sentence, Steve reasoned. The timing worked out. "So if you can identify a subject charged with burglary in northern Virginia, incarcerated for about three years, and then is in some kind of work release down in Richmond, that would be a very high-priority suspect."

Horgas followed the agents' advice. He went back to the first rape—disconcerting in part because if the killer lived in that neighborhood, he didn't live very far from where Horgas lived with his wife and young son, whom he left home alone at all hours because of his job—then pulled the files and reviewed all incidents of individuals arrested for burglary within the appropriate time frame.

In Richmond, where the citizens were in full-blown hysterical alert, the detectives weren't buying his theory—even after he presented them with the same information he showed the FBI agents and even though dark, possibly Negroid hairs were found with several victims.

Immediately after New Year's 1988, Horgas and Hill started reviewing piles of data printed out from the department's computer. They targeted offenders arrested in Arlington in 1984 and released three years later in Richmond. Unfortunately, they weren't able to narrow their search parameters as well as they would have liked: parole records listed offenders from many jurisdictions and they weren't sorted according to the parolee's residence. There was also no indication of the offenders' crimes or when they were incarcerated. So it became a formidable, mostly manual task.

After spending days at this, Horgas refocused. He'd worked the section of Arlington where the first rape occurred and knew a lot of the people there. He tried to remember anyone who would have been the right age to match the description of the rapist. As Paul Mones describes in *Stalking Justice,* his excellent book on the case, the detective drove the streets to jog his memory and finally came up with a first name: Timmy.

Timmy was a local teenager known as a neighborhood troublemaker in the area around the first rape about ten years earlier. Horgas had investigated him then in connection with a burglary, although he was not arrested for that crime. Back then, Timmy had a reputation for having set fire to something—his mother's house or maybe her car, Horgas couldn't recall—which reminded him of how the rapist set fire to the car of one of his victims. Horgas asked around for two days, but no one else in the department remembered this kid. Then, on January 6, 1988, Joe Horgas remembered the teenager's full name: Timothy Spencer.

A couple of computer checks later, Horgas found what he was looking for: Timothy Spencer—a black male just the right age to be the masked rapist—had a history of burglary arrests dating back to 1980, including a conviction in Alexandria, a neighboring jurisdiction to Arlington, on January 29, 1984. Review of his prison history showed he'd been released to a halfway house in Richmond—Hospitality House—on September 4, 1987.

Details of his last conviction were frightening in the context of the crimes for which Horgas and Hill were considering him: he entered the home through a small back window and was arrested with commemorative coins in his pockets, stolen from several homes, along with a pair of dark socks, a small flashlight, and a screwdriver. A five-inch folding knife was found in his car. Several of the masked rapist's victims reported that he wore socks over his hands, that he had a flashlight and pulled a folding knife on them. But the commemorative coins were the clincher. The collectible coins belonging to the Tuckers, though potentially valuable to a burglar, were not taken during that break-in. He'd been sent away once for stealing easily identified coins, and he wasn't going to repeat the same mistake twice. As we'd predicted, he learned from his earlier crime.

According to records, Spencer's permanent address in Arlington was just 200 yards from where the first rape occurred. The halfway house in Richmond was located within walking distance of both the Hellams and Davis homes.

Horgas contacted the halfway house to compare dates of the 1987 attacks with days and times Spencer signed out. None of the test dates ruled him out. Horgas also learned that if Spencer was their man, another part of our theory was correct: he had a day job at a furniture factory during the week.

Horgas tried calling Richmond, but couldn't reach the Williams boys, who were out on the scene of another murder. Initially, it looked like the "South Side Strangler's" work except this victim had been beaten viciously about the head. But later that day, Richmond police responded to a suicide call and found the body of a man who'd dated the murder victim's sister and rented a room from her until she threw him out. It became apparent that the latest murder was the first copycat of the Strangler.

Tension was high January 7, when Horgas and Hill met with the detectives from Richmond. They agreed to surveillance of Spencer, but were still going with the view that their killer was white. But Spencer had put in for another furlough to Arlington that coming weekend and no one wanted to take any chances. In the end, though, his trip to Arlington was canceled by a snowstorm.

There was a setback that Friday when Richmond authorities stopped Spencer outside Cloverleaf Mall, where he was waiting in a car for two women who were observed shoplifting. Although fearful the heat would cause Spencer to leave the area, Arlington police took the incident as proof that he hung out at the mall, where the task force theorized the killer found his victims.

After more than a week of surveillance, Richmond police decided Spencer was doing nothing suspicious, certainly not acting like a serial killer. They announced they were calling off surveillance Monday the eighteenth. With that, Arlington County Commonwealth Attorney Helen Fahey made the decision to go before a grand jury. They went to court Wednesday the twentieth and got an indictment. The arrest warrant was issued and signed that day.

In anticipation of the arrest, Horgas contacted Quantico for interview tips. Steve advised him to be patient and let Spencer do the talking. In his arrest for burglary in January of 1984 he was willing to cooperate with police because he was so glad they knew nothing of his other crimes. Serial killers very rarely confess, Steve warned, but said if Horgas could get him to open up it would be by talking about burglary and not the rapes and murders.

After the grand jury handed down the indictment, on their way to Richmond, Horgas and Hill stopped at Spencer's residence in Arlington. He lived in half of a two-family brick house with his mother and half-brother. His grandmother lived on the other side. Located at the end of a quiet cul-de-sac, near the site of the first rape, the house was within ten minutes' walk of the Tuckers' house.

The detectives explained to Spencer's mother that they were investigating a burglary that took place over Thanksgiving. They told her someone had seen her son in the area and they wanted to check her house for stolen goods. Although they had no warrant, she understood that her cooperation could help exclude her son as a suspect if they found nothing, so she gave them permission to look around.

After a quick search, all they had was a roll of duct tape, not a match to tape used in Cho's murder.

Next, they went to Richmond with tactical squad Sergeant Henry Trumble and another detective, Steve Carter. They arrested Timothy Spencer on burglary charges that evening when he returned to Hospitality House from work. He questioned police, wondering why so many cops were involved in his arrest and why the bond was set so high—$350,000— if he was only wanted for burglary. He gave permission for officers to search his room, which yielded nothing specific, although he did have several screwdrivers and a cap and gloves, whose possession was not that unusual in the middle of winter. But on the bottom side of his mattress someone had drawn the infinity symbol—a sideways number eight—like the one drawn on Cho's leg.

The suspect was talkative and friendly during the drive back to Arlington. When Horgas asked if he would mind providing a blood sample, though, Spencer asked if it was in connection with a rape. Horgas said it was just to check against a burglary; sometimes a burglar cuts himself breaking in. But as Paul Mones reported, Spencer answered, "No . . . if you want my blood, it's got to have something to do with a rape because I didn't cut myself going in no house. I didn't cut myself on no fucking broken window."

When he learned where the burglary took place, Spencer specifically asked if it had anything to do with the murder he read about in the papers, but Horgas kept playing it cool, per his FBI tips. After hours of interrogation by Horgas and other detectives from Arlington and Richmond over a period of several days, Spencer still had not confessed, nor did he ever. He did, however, give a blood sample that was to prove as telling as anything he might have said.

Initial lab results showed that Timothy Spencer's blood was consistent with semen stains on Susan Tucker's nightgown, a match that would only fit thirteen percent of the population. Further, his hair had characteristics matching samples from Tucker's body and sink. But this wasn't enough; they'd need DNA to convict.

We began looking into Spencer's background for hints of what he would become. His parents, both of whom attended some college, divorced when he was seven, after ten years of marriage. His father, a postal employee, reportedly had no contact with the boy after the divorce. His mother worked as a bookkeeper, eventually becoming engaged to a college graduate who had steady work as a bricklayer. Spencer and his mother both stated that family life was good.

But Timmy was always in trouble. At nine, he set a fire in the boys' bathroom and urinated and defecated in various places throughout his school, causing officials to note his anger and hostility and his need to "prove that he is the one in charge of the situation and not the environment," eerily portending future attempts to dominate, show control. He was arrested for larceny at nine and eleven, and by fourteen he'd moved into breaking and entering. In school, he consistently performed below his grade level and was left back after the eighth grade. He did not fit in with his classmates, but resented being forced to study in remedial classes. This was all pretty consistent with backgrounds we'd seen during our interviews with serial offenders. By contrast, his brother, Travis, was a good student and outstanding basketball player at the time.

At fifteen, Timmy had trouble with a hit-and-run and joyriding and was sent to a juvenile facility, dropping out of school for good in tenth grade. By the time he was nineteen he'd been arrested for possession of a concealed weapon, breaking and entering, and probation violation. Throughout the early 1980s he was either serving time for burglary, trespassing, and violation of probation, or living with his grandmother. She felt he made a real effort to change, getting involved in the church and studying for his GED, or high school equivalency diploma.

He had trouble keeping a job, not because he would be fired, but because he would leave after a period of months and move on to another. His work was typically menial: as a janitor or bricklayer. He admitted to regular use of alcohol and marijuana but said he didn't have a problem with either substance.

A psychologist who studied Spencer in 1983 while he was serving time for burglary and trespassing reported he was "mentally intact, not suffering from delusions or hallucinations," but had difficulty following rules. According to the report, he "tends to set his own limits as compared to following those set by others." The psychologist tested his IQ at 89, obviously much lower than Spencer's capabilities.

After his arrest in January 1984, when he was caught redhanded with stolen coins, he still denied his guilt. A presentencing report noted he "rationalizes his behavior and blames others for his involvement in the instant offenses."

And he was a good actor. Even as they were interviewing him, at times investigators found him likable. Like a lot of these guys, except when he lost his temper, it was hard to remember what he was capable of doing. That's why I also stress how important it is to come into these interviews well-prepared and completely familiar with the details of the crimes. Employers characterized him as a friendly loner. His girlfriend, who'd been dating him since the previous October and reportedly saw him every weekend, described him the same way. She denied anything unusual about their sex life—no masks or devices—and did not believe her boyfriend could be a killer. That, of course, was not unusual, either.

Only one ex-girlfriend had anything of potential interest to report. A prostitute, she said Spencer once advised her she could use Vaseline if she ever had trouble with vaginal dryness and admitted to her he enjoyed masturbating, despite his assertion to Joe Horgas that he had "never jacked off," when Horgas confronted him with the fact that semen had been found on and around the bodies. Investigators were never able to establish a relationship between Spencer and any of his victims, although two witnesses could place him on a local bus that went to Cloverleaf Mall. The key to the case was the scientific evidence.

DNA testing took until early March to complete but the results were dramatic: Spencer's blood matched semen samples from the Tucker, Davis, and Hellams crime scenes, as well as one of the early rapes in Arlington. His defense attorneys, Carl Womack and Thomas Kelley, had Cellmark Diagnostics Inc.—a prominent lab in Maryland which would later analyze the samples in the O.J. Simpson murder trial—independently do a blind check on the results of the DNA tests, hoping for a discrepancy. But the experts concurred with Lifecodes's findings. The odds that Spencer's DNA matched another black person's in North America—and police held the wrong guy—was said to be 135 million to one.

In addition to the DNA testing, the local lab in Fairfax processed Spencer's clothing, including a camouflage jacket he reportedly wore every day. Senior forensic scientist Joseph Beckerman matched trace particles of glass from the jacket to glass in one of the basement windows broken by the subject.

On July 16, 1988, Timothy Spencer was found guilty in the rape and capital murder of Susan Tucker. Although they were not considered in the trial, the murders in Richmond could be brought into the penalty phase, and Debbie Davis's father testified on his dead daughter's birthday.

Spencer's mother testified on his behalf, as did the leader

of a community center and a former teacher. Both spoke of his troubled youth. Finally, Spencer briefly told the jury he did not murder anyone and "felt sorry for their families." The jury deliberated three hours before unanimously recommending a sentence of death.

In October of 1988, Spencer was also found guilty in the murder of Debbie Davis. He was convicted in Susan Hellams's murder in January of 1989, and in Diane Cho's in June 1989. The Davis and Hellams cases used the DNA results, but there were no pure DNA samples from the Cho murder scene. Prosecutors in that trial argued the case as a "signature crime," which by law allowed them to introduce evidence from the other murders.

On April 27, 1994, after the failure of several appeals, Timothy Wilson Spencer died in the Virginia electric chair, the first person in the world to receive the death sentence by virtue of DNA identification. Even at the end, he never confessed his guilt. Steve Mardigian drove down U.S. 95 to the state penitentiary in Jarratt, not far from the North Carolina border, to try to interview Spencer shortly before his execution. But Spencer refused to talk or admit anything.

Ironically, despite the state-of-the-art techniques and computers that aided in getting a conviction, the case against Timothy Spencer was truly made by old-fashioned, street-cop detective work. If Joe Horgas hadn't remembered Spencer's name it never would have come up in the exhaustive computer search because of the technicality that Spencer was not considered paroled or released by corrections officials. There would have been no blood to test.

David Vasquez, though, was still in prison, having confessed to the murder of Carolyn Hamm. The two original witnesses would not change their story, the lab samples had degraded too much over time to be definitive, and no one could corroborate Vasquez's alibi.

After his meeting with Jud and Joe Horgas in Arlington, Steve Mardigian had begun the laborious task of analyzing all of the relevant case materials in the Tucker and Hamm murders in Arlington, the murders in Richmond and Chesterfield County, and each separate sexual assault and burglary. All significant data was entered into a computer program to provide a detailed comparison of physical characteristics and verbal behavior.

"That's when the real work started," says Steve. "One of the things we were asking was, 'How do we determine whether the man in custody had anything to do with the Carolyn Hamm case?'"

Mardigian created a grid with such headings as Name of Victim, Jurisdiction, Date, Duration of Crime, Type of Location, Type of Weapon, Type of Binding, Method and Place of Injuries, Initial Contact with Victim, Had Offender Gained Entry Prior to Victim Coming Home?, Location of Assault—Inside, Outside, or in Vehicle, Was Victim Moved Throughout the Residence?, Dialogue and Verbal Behavior in Rapes, Type of Sexual Activity.

Steve then brought the data to me and we each analyzed it independently before coming together for our conclusions. It was clear to both of us that his and Jud's original supposition was correct: there was no question that this was one person acting alone rather than two working together—either two partners such as Lawrence Bittaker and Roy Norris or a sadistic leader and a compliant follower such as Paul Bernardo and Karla Homolka. Vasquez's supposed partner was a ghost.

These crimes—the burglaries, the rapes, and the murders—were all committed by someone with experience, criminal sophistication, and organizational skills. He had the ability to interact for long periods with his victims and took sexual pleasure in manipulating them, dominating them, controlling them, and torturing them. David Vasquez was not a sexual sadist, he didn't have the organizational or interpersonal skills to interact with the victims the way this guy did, and we both felt there was absolutely no way he could have committed these crimes.

It was clear to us that during his interrogations he had been scared and confused, had been given too much information, and, in a pathetic effort to please and cooperate, he had told police of his "dream" in which he had murdered Carolyn Hamm. With all the input he had at that point, he very well could have dreamed it. But that didn't make him a murderer.

Together with Joe Horgas and the Arlington Police Department, we asked Arlington County Commonwealth Attorney Helen Fahey to request Governor Gerald Baliles to grant Vasquez a full pardon. Since he had confessed, that would be the quickest route to getting him out of prison.

On October 16, 1988, we sent Fahey our written report concluding that the murderer of Carolyn Hamm was the same man who had murdered the other victims. The report, in the form of a five-page letter signed by both Steve and me, went with Fahey's petition to the governor.

The pardon process took longer than we expected, as both the governor's office and the Board of Pardon and Parole individually reinvestigated the case and reviewed our analysis. But finally, David Vasquez was released January 4, 1989. He returned to his mother's house and contemplated legal action against Arlington authorities. Eventually, on the advice of several different lawyers, he decided not to sue, and instead received a $117,000 settlement. Frankly, I would have given him a lot more if it was up to me.

But as troubling as David Vasquez's arrest and conviction are—and they are sufficiently troubling that I think they must become an object lesson to all of us in law enforcement—when the possibility arose to Joe Horgas and then to us that this man might have confessed to and been imprisoned for something he didn't do, no attempt was made to sweep a mistake under the rug. Rather, great effort was made to get to the truth of the matter.

As Steve Mardigian put it, "Arlington PD, that same department that got Vasquez arrested, had the willingness to go back and review the case and take the shots they knew would be forthcoming. I think that is a tremendous testament to that department's integrity and dedication."

And as Paul Mones eloquently points out in *Stalking Justice,* "What is unique about the story of David Vasquez is that the people who put him behind bars were also the ones who set him free. No family member, crusading journalist, or civil libertarian banged the drum for David's release. Police and prosecutors did. Ironically, it was Susan Tucker's horrific demise that ultimately became David Vasquez's salvation."

The time and effort my unit spent on the behavioral analysis in this group of cases was the most we'd ever spent on any case up to that time, including the Atlanta Child Murders and Green River. And the bulk of that effort, actually, was devoted not to finding and arresting a guilty man, but to getting an innocent man freed.

CHAPTER 12

Murder on
South Bundy Drive

Practically every decade, it seems, has its own "Trial of the Century." In the 1890s it was Lizzie Borden. In the 1920s it was the Scopes "Monkey Trial" challenging the teaching of evolution. In the 1930s it was the Lindbergh kidnapping case. In the 1940s, the Nuremberg War Crimes Tribunal. The 1950s, the Rosenberg atom bomb spy trial. The 1960s gave us the Chicago Seven. In the 1970s, the Manson Family. The fact that each of these, in its time and place, qualified to someone as the Trial of the Century (and I'm sure we can all think of alternates for each—Dreyfus, Sacco and Vanzetti, Eichmann, Bundy?) speaks to two things. The first is the media's obsession with the moment, of course. The second, I think, has to do with our collective compulsion toward the examination of evil or wrongdoing, or, in the case of politically oriented trials such as Scopes, the Chicago Seven, and, some might say, Sacco and Vanzetti and the Rosenbergs, other people's very perception of truth.

The 1990s Trial of the Century (at least so far) undeniably has been the O.J. Simpson trial in Los Angeles. Perhaps no trial in history was as examined in excruciating detail from outside, or argued from as many points of trivia inside. The only things lost in all of this were truth and, to many people's way of thinking, justice. With as much money and legal resources as were thrown around in this trial, truth became a commodity—to be bought and sold and manipulated in the marketplace of public opinion—and logic became a means to service already-held beliefs.

Millions, if not billions, of words have already been written on the subject and virtually every pundit in the known universe has weighed in with his or her opinion. And like a Rorschach test, that opinion often reveals more about the opinion holder than the case itself. And whatever you say about the criminal trial jury's verdict, you can't convince me the few hours they spent were sufficient time to examine seriously and conscientiously the many months of testimony and such a huge volume of complex evidence. Their own verbal and written commentaries after the fact demonstrated that most of them didn't have a clue what this case was all about.

It's not my intention to pass judgment on the trial itself or the performance of the lawyers or Judge Lance Ito. There's been plenty of that already and if you care enough to have an opinion, I probably couldn't change it anyway. Nor are we going to deal extensively with the physical evidence which, in itself, makes or breaks a case. We're only going to deal with it in its behavioral context, and see how much we can learn about these murders strictly from that perspective.

What I do want to do here is something that, for all the time and money expended in this case, really wasn't done. And that is to examine the double homicide that occurred at 875 South Bundy Drive on the evening of June 12, 1994, from a behavioral perspective and examine what the facts at, and surrounding, the crime scene tell us about the killer from a behavioral point of view. In other words, forgetting O.J. Simpson's celebrity, forgetting the Trial of the Century aspect, forgetting the racial polarization it created, had the LAPD contacted my unit at Quantico for consultation on this particular murder investigation, what could we have told them about who did it? Because if you strip away all of the sensationalism and false issues, the murders of Nicole Brown Simpson and Ronald Goldman are not so different from many other cases we've examined over the years.

Let me remind you that we in my unit are not in the business of solving cases on our own or delivering the names and addresses of UNSUBs. All we can do at this stage of an investigation is help point to the *type* of suspect on which the police should be concentrating. If they already have suspects, we can help them limit and qualify them with our input. And if they are still looking for the UNSUB, we can often help them focus that search.

To pull off this imaginary consultation, we may have to make certain assumptions and stipulations along the way, such as the case not reaching the level of publicity as fast as it actually did. That is to say, we have to assume that I'd have the opportunity to come up with my own objective conclusions before being bombarded by detail in the media. But there's plenty of precedent for that kind of supposition. As a control exercise, those of us in my unit have often examined controversial cases of the past, including those of the Boston Strangler, and Dr. Sam Sheppard, the Cleveland osteopath accused of murdering his wife in 1954, who was found guilty and later not guilty of the crime, and who died before the controversy had quieted. In October of 1988, I took part in an internationally broadcast television special profiling the identity of Jack the Ripper and came up with some interesting and surprising results, as we described in *Mindhunter*. Recently, I was invited to analyze the Lizzie Borden case, one of the most ambiguous in American history.

When the South Bundy murders occurred in June of 1994, I was still chief of the FBI's Investigative Support Unit, which included some of the top profilers and criminal investigative analysts in the world—Larry Ankrom, Greg Cooper, Steve Etter, Bill Hagmaier, Roy Hazelwood, Steve Mardigian, Gregg McCrary, Jana Monroe, Jud Ray, Tom Salp, Pete Smerick, Clint Van Zandt, and Jim Wright. Let me emphasize that, in actuality, we did not consult on this case, nor were we asked.

But if we had been, this is how I think it would have gone. This would be a typical and representative case consultation and analysis.

We would have gotten a telephone call from someone in the LAPD who was designated point man on the case. He probably would have been a detective and he already would have talked to the profile coordinator in the FBI's Los

Angeles Field Office. Let's call him Detective Kenneth Scott so we don't get involved with any of the real personalities in the case.

Unbeknownst to me or my unit at this point, Scott and his investigative team have collected a fair amount of blood and other forensic evidence. But he's not going to tell me about this and I'm not going to want to know, unless it points to behavior. Ultimately, when I finish my analysis, then we'll go over the forensics together and see if they match what I've said. If they do, then we've helped him narrow his investigation and focus with more confidence on a particular type of suspect. If not, then it could point to serious flaws in the case.

Scott begins, "We have a double homicide in Brentwood—that's an upper-middle-class neighborhood not too far from the UCLA campus. When you go several blocks north and get on the other side of Sunset Boulevard, it becomes a strictly upper-class neighborhood. You might say the people living south of Sunset aspire to do well enough to move to the north side. Victims are a twenty-five-year-old white male and a thirty-five-year-old white female. Both died from sharp-force trauma, stabbed multiple times outside the residence of the female victim."

"Have there been any similar crimes lately in the neighborhood?" I ask.

"No, nothing like this," Scott replies.

"How about burglaries or any voyeuristic activities?"

"No."

At this point, I tell him that I want the report of the first officer on scene, a map of the area with sites significant to the crime scene marked, I'll need to see crime scene and autopsy photos, autopsy protocols and the medical examiner's report, if it's in yet, and I'll need as much as he can get me on the victimology—what were these two people like?

What I *do not* want from him is a suspect list (if he's developed one) or any theories about who it could be. I don't want to be influenced by what he's already decided or leads his task force has already pursued.

If this were a major "hot" case—one in which the UNSUB seemed to be active, with danger of new victims at any moment—I might fly out to Los Angeles to give on-scene help and analysis. But in the hours and days following the murders, there haven't been any others with similar MO, so unless the situation changes, I'll continue doing my analysis from Quantico, so I don't get too far behind in my administrative responsibilities or the hundred-plus other cases on which my unit is working.

The Brown-Goldman case materials arrive by overnight mail and I take most of the morning reviewing them, trying to put myself in the place of both victims and perpetrator, trying to discern the "subtext" of the scene. The key thing I'm asking myself is: *Why were these particular people the victims of this violent crime?* Before we can know the *Who?* we must understand the *Why?* And in trying to come up with the answer to that question, I'm asking myself if there is a connection between these two victims or is it simply that one of them was in the wrong place at the wrong time.

By the time I finish, it's just before lunch—morning on the West Coast. Scott is in his office and can arrange a conference call with other key members of the task force.

"The killing is at close range and confrontational. The weapon is a knife, which tells you this is a very personal type of crime. The crime scene is a *mixed* presentation," I begin. "There are both organized and disorganized elements to it, which we'll get to shortly. But I would say the killer was basically organized, which leads me to believe he is a mature individual with intelligence and sophistication and that some planning and intent went into the crime. He wore a cap and gloves and brought a weapon to the scene. The killing of the female victim is efficient and almost military-style, along with a tremendous amount of 'overkill.' At the same time, there are disorganized elements that suggest it didn't go quite the way he planned, and that though he is mature, he has little, if any, experience in crime. There is an obvious lack of control relating to the male victim and evidence of panic when things didn't go quite his way. So you may see some domestic complaints on the offender's rap sheet, possibly minor altercations or fights in a bar, but certainly nothing like a murder and he hasn't done time. So don't expect a police record to lead you to the guy. The mere fact of leaving a cap and glove at the scene and wearing shoes which leave a distinctive footprint speak to a lack of criminal sophistication and experience. He also cut himself, probably as he comes around her throat, and there's a cut in the glove found at the crime scene, which shows he wasn't prepared for that level of fight with Ron Goldman.

"The homicide took place at Nicole Brown Simpson's residence," I continue. "That alone is strong evidence to suggest that she was the primary target. We also know that Goldman was there because Brown's mother had left her glasses earlier in the day at the restaurant where Goldman worked. Nicole had called the restaurant, they'd found the glasses, and Ron had volunteered to drop them by. So his being at Bundy at that particular time was happenstance. Unless the killer actually followed him, he could not be considered the primary target. And if he was being followed, it makes no sense at all that the killer would wait until he was with another person and near potential eye- or ear witnesses. But let's look at some of the other facts:

"As you said, the ME's report says that both victims died of multiple stab wounds. And Goldman's got diffuse multiple defense wounds on his hands and arms. She's found in a fetal position at the bottom of four concrete steps leading up to her condominium door. Her black dress is hiked high up on her thigh, but this looks like it's due to the shortness of the dress and the way she fell rather than any attempt to lift the dress or expose her. This is confirmed by the fact that her panties are in place and there's no evidence of sexual assault and no evidence of staging.

"But there is a lot of bleeding and she bled out on this last step, which was probably where the fatal assault took place. Her throat is cut so deeply she's practically decapitated. The other stab wounds are much more concentrated and directed than they are with Goldman. The killer didn't have trouble controlling her as he did with Ron. He stabbed her repeatedly, not because he 'had' to, but because he 'wanted' to. And this is another reason I say the woman was the primary victim, not the man: the attacker knew her, and knew her well."

"Why do you say that, John?" one of the detectives asks.

"As we've noted, there's no sexual assault, so this isn't a scenario where she pissed off a rapist. This kind of overkill represents rage directed at a particular person, especially since so many blows were directed at the neck. This is not a stranger murder. He did not have to do what he did simply to kill her. He was making a statement. He was punishing her.

"The wounds on the male victim are different. Goldman put up an incredible struggle, one hell of a fight. The types of wounds on him—the defense wounds on the hands and arms and the deeper thrusts to the body—show that the UNSUB was doing what he had to strictly to kill him. He wasn't interested in punishing him or making a point. He was just trying to neutralize him. That's what I mean when I say it didn't go quite the way the attacker planned. He didn't plan for another man to be there. That messed up his organization real fast."

"But as you know, we found a glove and a dark knit watch cap at the scene, John. Couldn't that belong to someone who came to rob?"

"Sure it could," I say. "But nothing was taken. In fact, the UNSUB never entered the house."

"But you said yourself that he was surprised by Goldman being there. Maybe it was his intent to rob and he never got to it." I don't think the investigator really believes this. He's probably playing devil's advocate with me, which is fine, since I should have to support the logic behind everything I say. I'm not necessarily telling them things they don't know or haven't figured out on their own, but it's important to go through my take on the events before we start sharing information.

"First of all, you told me you weren't having problems with burglars in this neighborhood," I say. "But more to the point, a burglar doesn't generally bring a knife with him to the scene. He either brings a gun or no weapon at all. A burglar has two goals: the first is to get in and out without a confrontation and without being seen. If he can't achieve that and he does find himself in a confrontation, his second goal is to get the hell out as quickly as possible. He won't stick around to hurt anyone unless he feels that's his only option for escape. A gun might help him do that; a knife isn't going to do the job. It's too up-close-and-personal and too labor-intensive a way of killing. It is possible, however, that the offender planned on going inside to commit the crime, but was sidetracked when he saw Nicole and Ron together and probably thought there was a romantic relationship between them. She had candles lit all over the house—the kitchen, the bathroom—in spots that could be seen through the windows. This had always been a romantic ritual with her. So someone who knew the meaning of this ritual, who had participated in it himself, might be enraged if he presumed that she was preparing it for someone else.

"We don't know for sure whether or not there was a relationship beyond friendship between Brown and Goldman, but we do know at the very least that they weren't planning anything that night because Goldman was scheduled to meet several of his buddies after he dropped off the envelope containing the glasses."

"So you think he was in the process of attacking her when Goldman happens to show up at the scene?"

"That's possible," I acknowledge. "But I don't think so, because it appears that he began with her, went to him, then back to her. What I think happened was: the UNSUB sees the two of them together; he's been watching, he's been stalking her. He doesn't like what he sees. So he comes out and confronts them. She recognizes him. Goldman probably does, too, so he puts out his hands, palms up, like, 'Hey, stay cool, man. Nothing going on here. I just came to return her mom's glasses.'

"But the offender whacks her on the head with blunt force—boom—probably the butt of the knife, probably sufficient to knock her out.

"He then goes to Goldman, who is about five or six feet away, near a palm tree growing up through the ground. This is maybe two or three seconds later and Ron is caught off guard by the attack on Nicole. He's trapped in this small area—a four-by-six-foot space with a fence behind him—and he's blocked by this palm tree. Instinctively, he goes into a pugilistic stance—we can tell this from the defense wounds—and he's also stabbed in his left thigh and left abdomen. There's a struggle between the two men. The shirt Goldman's wearing is twisted around his body so that when he's stabbed and stabbed again the holes don't seem to line up with the stab wounds when the body is examined later.

"Now, the defense wounds are primarily concentrated on

the fingers of his left hand, and the palm of that hand. What I think happened is that he reached out as the attacker was stabbing with his right hand. Goldman reached out and pulled the left glove off, which is the one found at the scene.

"By this point the offender has worked himself up into a frenzy. As soon as he's got Ron neutralized, which is not easy, he goes back to Nicole, lifts her head from behind, and cuts her throat, slicing right through her voice box, nearly taking her head off.

"The UNSUB then goes back to Goldman because he has to make sure he finishes him off. We know he goes back because her blood is found on the bottom of one of Goldman's shoes. Now, this is very, very important, because it tells you that the offender is not a professional killer. This is not a hit man. He doesn't know exactly what it takes to kill this guy. He has to come back and check on him. He sees that Goldman is dying and he goes back and stabs him multiple times. In fact, he's actually stabbed more times than Brown, even though the personalized sort of attack is reserved for her. That's because even though she's the one he's out to punish, to revenge himself on, the male is the greater physical threat. That's another reason we know the crimes were committed by a single offender. Two or more killers would have been able to control the situation better. You wouldn't have the evidence of such a struggle on Goldman's body."

Even if it didn't happen exactly this way, even if Ron came upon the scene as the offender was already attacking Nicole, that doesn't change my assessment of the type of individual responsible for the crimes or what his motive would have been.

"So you don't think this could be a drug killing, then, John?"

I don't. "Was either victim involved in the drug scene?" I ask.

"Not really. They may have tried recreational drugs. A lot of that crowd does. But there's nothing in the tox screens and both of them took pride in their bodies. Certainly neither of them had ever sold."

"Then who butchers two people who aren't any threat to a dealer's commerce? You expect a drug murder to be very symbolic, like the 'Colombian necktie' in which the victim's throat is cut and his tongue is brought out through the wound. Something like that. It would be done in some symbolic place, not the victim's home. And as I said, it would be done by professionals who would have been better prepared to subdue the male victim. Or, if they weren't, upon finding him at the scene they would have been dispassionate enough to walk away and try again at a more opportune time."

It is very important at this stage to try to classify the type of homicide we're dealing with. If this isn't a rape-murder or a burglary gone bad, if it's not a drug killing, an insurance murder, a criminal enterprise murder, or what have you, what is it? I was lead author on a book entitled *Crime Classification Manual,* which was published in 1992. After years of research and consultation on thousands of cases, some of us at Quantico felt the need for a system of classifying— and thereby explaining—serious crimes that would have the same rigor and organization that DSM—the *Diagnostic and Statistical Manual of Mental Disorders*—has on the psychiatric side. The result was the volume which has come to be called CCM. Outside the Bureau, Dr. Ann Burgess of the University of Pennsylvania and her husband, Allen, a professor of management at Northeastern University in Boston, served as co-authors and oversaw the compiling and organization of the voluminous data. Virtually all the special agents in the Investigative Support Unit and many in Behavioral Science also contributed. For example, Jud Ray headed up the Personal Cause Homicide classification committee and worked with Jim Wright on the Group Cause committee.

In CCM, we classified homicide, arson, and rape and sexual assault according to motive and elements and told police and investigators what the components and investigational considerations of each should be. The first of the homicide categories, Criminal Enterprise Homicide, is broken down into eight sub-groups and four sub-sub-groups. Personal Cause Homicide is broken down into two sub-groups, Erotomania-Motivated Killing and Domestic Homicide. Domestic Homicide, in turn, is broken down into Spontaneous and Staged classifications. None of these are arbitrary or subjective categories. They're based on extensive research and experience.

Because of the type and severity of the wounds, as I've said, and because it is clear to me that the woman rather than the man was the primary target, I do not believe this is a stranger murder. Nor is it what we refer to as a Group Cause Murder. The Manson Family cult killings, for example, were group cause. And a cult murder or a Group Excitation Murder are the only types of group cause that could possibly fit, the others being variations on Extremist Murders—political or paramilitary, religious or hostage.

While the brutality of the Brown murder might seem similar in certain ways to the Tate–LaBianca murders, for example, a close examination reveals major and significant differences. In a cult situation, you would expect to see a lot of symbolism at the scene, such as when Manson family members scrawled "Helter Skelter" and other slogans on the walls with the victims' blood. In the Atlanta Child Murders, despite widespread insistence that a Klan type white supremacist group was behind the crimes, I knew this wasn't the case. There was no symbolism attached to the bodies or the dump sites and it was quite clear to me that a single individual was involved.

As I looked at the Brown-Goldman crime scene materials, there was ample reason for me to believe only a single individual was involved there, too. Aside from the disorganization apparent as a result of having to deal with a second victim, all of the wounds on both victims were consistent with a single weapon. Two or more people in this situation wouldn't share one knife, particularly when one of Nicole's own kitchen knives was lying on the kitchen counter in plain view.

What was it doing there? My feeling is that she was anticipating some kind of threat. Earlier in the day, or even days before, something happened that made her feel concerned. Her intercom wasn't working. She didn't have a gun; the best weapon she could come up with was a knife. We know she was expecting Ron Goldman to come over and return the eyeglasses her mother had left at his restaurant that day. But that's not who she was afraid of.

"You have to go back to the victimology," I say. "There's nothing in Goldman's life or background that sets him up as the target of a vicious attack. I'm not saying he couldn't have been mugged, or even murdered in a homosexual attack (it would have to be homosexual—women don't kill this way). But that isn't what happened here.

"Brown, on the other hand, has been through a very nasty divorce, and she's continued to have an on-again, off-again relationship with a very controlling-type husband up until a couple of weeks ago."

"That's right," Scott says. "A couple of weeks before the murder, she was sick and Simpson went over to the house with food and took care of her. He gave her a beautiful necklace. Sometime after she was well, they got into another fight and she threw the necklace at him."

"So he may have felt she was giving him mixed signals," I say. "And we have evidence that Simpson had been stalking her in the weeks before the murder, driving by places she was eating or meeting friends, looking in her windows, watching her with other people. There's no evidence Goldman was being stalked by anyone or had any enemies in the world."

"So you're saying it's the ex-husband, O.J. Simpson," Scott declares.

"What I'm saying," I clarify, "is that we see a lot of cases like this one, and whoever did it was not a professional or experienced killer, acted alone, knew the female victim well, and had a tremendous amount of rage toward her."

"Well, we haven't come up with anyone else who meets that description," one of the detectives says.

"And by the time this all breaks publicly," another one predicts, "every minute detail of these two lives is going to be subjected to scrutiny. If there was anyone else in Nicole's life who fit that mold, he won't remain hidden long."

(This, of course, did happen, and despite massive efforts by entrepreneurial reporters and, presumably, Simpson's own investigators, not to mention the police, no one of this nature has ever surfaced or been identified.)

"Look," I continue, "we've seen enough of these things to know there's always a pattern, always a motive of some kind. Some monster doesn't just show up from nowhere and butcher two people and then disappear again into thin air."

"Some folks are starting to suggest maybe this is the work of a serial killer. Glen Rogers's name has been mentioned because he traveled a lot and worked in several different states and jurisdictions."

Glen Rogers is an alleged serial killer who police believe may be responsible for at least six murders throughout the United States, in California, Louisiana, Mississippi, Ohio, Kentucky, and Florida. At one time, he was boasting as many as seventy victims. He was apprehended after a high-speed chase in Kentucky in 1995. Because of his wide swath and variety of victim types, he seemed a convenient "universal suspect" for alternate theories of virtually any contemporaneous violent crime.

"The MO and signature are wrong," I point out. "Rogers would pick up women in lower class bars and spend the night with them. It's just grasping at straws to think that this guy is suddenly going to turn up in Brentwood and change the entire way he goes about committing crimes. And this type of sustained aggression that we see toward Nicole Brown, we see that virtually exclusively in situations where a significant relationship already exists between the attacker and the victim."

"So you're saying this wasn't a crime of opportunity. Nicole Brown was definitely the intended victim."

"Definitely. We know there's premeditation and planning. We have the knife, the glove, the cap. The offender selected his weapon of choice. He's got a lot of rage, a lot of hostility, and he wants this to be personal."

"Well, John, we do know from talking to her friends that Nicole was very scared of knives, much more so than of guns."

"Then that's another factor that would suggest the killer knew her well. You know, the method of kill, getting her from behind and slicing through her neck—that's like a military commando thing, particularly when you add the gloves and the watch cap. Was Simpson ever in the military?" I ask.

"We don't think so, but he just recently finished a pilot for a TV series in which he plays a Navy SEAL."

"And those guys are trained to be experts at close-up, silent kills," a detective who was himself in the Navy offers.

"Well, the killer approached the scene thinking he had everything under control," I say. "He thought he could get in, do what he intended, and get out without being seen or heard. And I'll tell you another thing I've been thinking about. Based on what I've seen over and over again in personal cause domestic homicides, I believe the offender was planning to stage the crime to look like a sexual assault."

"What do you mean?"

"If he hadn't been surprised by Goldman's presence—the added factor he hadn't planned on—he would have had the time to try to cover some of his own behavior by making it look like a rape-murder. If he'd been able to do that, you would have found Brown's body with her dress up and panties pulled down or off. Drawers would have been ransacked and something obvious would have been taken. But ultimately, that wouldn't have mattered, because we're better at uncovering staging than amateurs are at doing it. For example, it's unlikely he would have raped her or masturbated on her after she was dead and he would have taken care to place her somewhere where the children wouldn't be the ones to find her. Then, of course, you have to figure that rapists work close to where they feel comfortable, and in that neighborhood, then, a rapist would have to be an upper-middle-class resident—unlikely—or a gardener or maintenance man or someone, and we've got no one like that working the area. But most important, he still wouldn't have been able to control the rage that created the kinds of wounds that strangers wouldn't leave. Nicole Brown was in good shape and she could be a fighter when she had to, so it might have been difficult for a rapist to control her and that might have pissed him off. But then you would have seen more blunt-force trauma, rather than all the stab wounds. A rapist isn't going to mind assaulting a woman who's all beaten up, in fact the sadistic type is going to enjoy it, but he's not going to rape a woman who is bleeding to death."

"John, what we've told you about the events of the day of the murder—does that square with your profile?"

"Absolutely. There's generally a triggering mechanism to these kinds of crimes, some kind of inciting incident in the hours, days, or weeks before. We know that there had been a lot of strife and conflict between O.J. and Nicole in the weeks leading up to this, and the day of the murder, he feels she's snubbed him at their daughter, Sydney's, dance recital.

We also know that his girlfriend, Paula Barbieri, the one who's supposed to help him get over Nicole, is annoyed at him for not letting her go to the recital with him and leaves him a lengthy message on his answering machine saying she wants to break off the relationship. Now, deep down, he probably didn't want her to go because he wants the best of both worlds. He wants to maintain that relationship, plus he wants to maintain the relationship with his ex-wife. There's evidence he's making calls to Barbieri from his residence and from a mobile phone practically up until the time Brown and Goldman are killed. But he's never able to get through to her. So it's still on his mind."

"What if the call had gotten through?"

"It's an interesting question," I respond. "If the call had gotten through, would he have continued on his 'mission'? It's a possibility he might not have, although he's got a tremendous amount of rage built up already. He's getting it from both sides. He's got two women rejecting him and he's not used to being rejected. In my view, he sees Nicole as a possession. When they met, he was an internationally known celebrity and she was a high school virgin.

"We can see how control-oriented he is and how much image means to him. As he divorced his first wife he stipulated that he would give her money but he got to keep the house. He doesn't want people to perceive that he's lost. Even though he may be paying a lot of money in alimony and child support, he can say, 'I didn't lose. I got the house. She had to move out!' The same thing happens again when he breaks up with Nicole: 'She had to move out. I got the house!'

"Then, when he sees Nicole with another man at her own place, this younger white guy, that could be the final trigger he needs."

"What's your feeling about the blood?" Scott asks. "As you saw in the crime scene photos, there's a tremendous amount of blood at the scene. In the Bronco there are several drops, but it's not covering the seats or anything and even though we've got the socks at the Rockingham residence, we don't have a huge amount anywhere else. I suspect this is going to raise questions in some people's minds."

"First of all," I say, "the bloodiest wound—the one to

Brown's throat—was delivered from behind so you wouldn't expect to see a lot of blood on the attacker's person. But if he's anticipating a murder with a knife and he's thinking at all clearly, he has to figure he might get some blood on himself. The fact that we know he brought gloves and a cap with him indicates he was planning ahead, so I would expect him to be wearing some kind of jumpsuit or outer garment that he could take off and discard soon after he changes out of it. If he was able to stop along the way from the crime scene, he'd get rid of it there. Since the murders took longer than he anticipated and he was in a hurry, I'd actually expect to see the bloody clothing discarded later, perhaps at the airport."

One of the detectives says, "The only thing that bothers me in this behavioral discussion is, we're not talking about anyone; we're talking about O.J. Simpson, a major celebrity. A lot of people knew about his marital problems. As he's thinking about doing something like this, isn't he going to stop and think, 'Wait a minute. I'm the obvious guy. As soon as they find her dead, they're going to come looking for me'?"

"You would think so," I reply. "But from my experience, killers—whether they're first-timers or multiple—don't figure on getting caught. Had this unexpected man not appeared on the scene and slowed him down and thrown him off, he would have gotten back home in plenty of time to pull off his alibi and be on the road to the airport for his flight to Chicago without anyone being the wiser. What he might have planned was to be able to get to the airport in plenty of time, then call a friend of his and say, 'I'm worried. I've been trying to call Nicole all evening and I can't reach her. Could you go over and check to make sure she and the kids are okay?' That not only establishes his alibi but also prevents the children from finding their mother.

"And remember that, in addition to being a world-famous football player, he's also naturally very charming and experienced as an actor. He knows how he has to behave to throw suspicion off him, like conversing amiably with people and signing autographs like he always does. In his mind, he's obviously justified the crime. 'She forced me into it.' So he's already got a certain amount of peace with it."

"What about a polygraph if we can get him to submit to one?"

"You'd better be careful. People who've justified the crime in their own mind often come out at least inconclusively on polygraphs. And I'll tell you something else: the further we get from the crime, the better he'd do. By next year at this time, no matter what's happened in the intervening time, I'd bet he could pass."

I'd also suggest to the police that they surveil and monitor Nicole Brown's grave site. As I've mentioned, we've often found that killers not only return to the scenes of their crimes, but also to their victims' graves, as well. The purported reason for the highly publicized "slow-speed chase," which many observers believed showed an intent to flee, was to visit Nicole's grave. I felt right from the beginning that he might return to the grave to apologize, or, more likely, justify himself or berate her for having made him do it. Actually, in recent months reports have emerged that O.J. Simpson did, in fact, visit his ex-wife's grave. No surveillance was undertaken, though I would have been quite interested in the results if it had been.

The next thing we'd talk about would be interrogation techniques. By the time this imaginary profiling consultation would have taken place, Detectives Thomas Lange and Philip Vannatter had already interviewed Simpson, through his own consent, without a lawyer present. Some useful information came out of the session, such as that Simpson admitted having cut himself before the incident where he claimed to have cut himself slamming down a glass in his hotel room in Chicago when he heard from the police that Nicole had been killed. But the interview wasn't nearly incisive enough and didn't go on long enough. If anything, I believe the police were too solicitous of Simpson.

"I was shocked he'd talk to the police," Jud Ray commented. "But from a practical point of view, guys like that are used to beating the system. He must have actually felt he could beat it by doing that, and in a sense he did."

"There's nothing you can do about that at this point," I would say to the task force, "and I'd be very surprised if his lawyers let you at him again, particularly without one of them in the room. But if you do get the chance, it's very important that you get him in a nonthreatening setting where you're able to take as much time as you need, build up in his own mind how much compelling evidence you have, tell him his blood is found at the scene, and then offer him some face-saving scenario."

The same technique that I've used with child killers—suggesting that he didn't want to strangle the little girl but that she "forced him into it"—is often useful with murderers of adults, too. If the crime somehow can be justified in the killer's mind and he believes the police understand this—that's your best shot at a confession. Since Detective Mark Fuhrman had answered a domestic disorder call between O.J. and Nicole some years before when he was a uniformed patrolman, he could be used in the scenario, saying that he knew there had been trouble between the two of them and he saw how she could have provoked him.

You can also use the split personality scenario as I employed when questioning Larry Gene Bell. Though he wouldn't admit that the Larry Gene sitting before me had killed Shari Faye Smith, he finally acknowledged that the "bad Larry Gene Bell" could have. It was as close to a confession as we ever got from him.

We focus on the post-offense behavior, and here there are a number of key indicators. On the most basic level, we examine when LAPD Detective Ron Phillips reached Simpson in his Chicago hotel room on June 13, 1994, and informed him that his ex-wife had been killed. According to prosecutor Christopher Darden in his book *In Contempt*, Simpson not only didn't ask how she'd been killed, he didn't ask which ex-wife! Jeffrey Toobin, in his own book, *The Run of His Life*, states that Phillips did mention Nicole's name, but that Simpson never asked how she had died and whether it was the result of an accident or a crime. In either case, this is very telling. Reacting as if you've not previously heard the news can be thought of as a form of staging—and if you aren't experienced at it, it's difficult to carry it off in a manner believable to a trained observer.

On a general level, I tell the task force, Simpson's behavior is not consistent with what you would expect from an innocent person, particularly an innocent person used to being in control and enjoying constant public adulation. You would expect an innocent person accused of such a crime to respond with outrage, to deny it with every fiber of his being.

"If you think I could kill my wife, you're fucking nuts!" would be an expected response. *"And if you found my blood or hair or fingerprints or anything of mine on the scene, then someone fucking planted them there!"*

This was not the response observed in the days following the announcement that O.J. Simpson would be charged with the murders.

Some, like Simpson counsel Alan Dershowitz, have suggested that Simpson was so overwhelmed with grief and so depressed that he could not muster this kind of outrage. I don't buy this reasoning for a minute. If a man is truly grieved over the loss of his wife (or even ex-wife), it is absolutely crucial to him to defend her memory and their mutual honor with more than a perfunctory denial of involvement. Being innocent and not being outraged in such a situation, in itself, would be very out of character for a personality of this sort.

"Are we looking at a suicide risk, John?"

"When a heavily control-oriented person suddenly loses control, there's always a risk of suicide. But I would think that with this narcissistic a subject, what you might be more likely to see is a feigned suicide attempt, a plea for attention and sympathy. I think he might threaten to kill himself with a knife or a gun, but I don't think you're going to see him slit his own wrists or blow his brains out or anything painful like that. If he does actually make an attempt, expect it to be with pills, and before it's too late he will have called a close friend who could rescue him in time and give him a lot of favorable publicity in the bargain."

As we subsequently learned, Simpson did compose and "publish" a suicide note and held a gun to his head during the Bronco chase. If that's not an attempt to gain publicity, I don't know what is.

At this point in the consultation they'd tell me about their non-behaviorally-oriented forensic evidence, primarily the blood. The preliminary tests link O.J. Simpson to the crime scene. That is to say, the forensic evidence and the behavioral evidence square and support each other. As an investigator, this is the position you want to be in.

"Then I'd say you've got your guy," I conclude.

Weeks later, we will learn that the blood DNA, which has the individuality of fingerprints, also matches, leaving the defense with only one possible scenario of deniability—that the police planted the blood to incriminate their suspect.

Here again, profiling and our brand of investigative analysis can come into play.

If we had been consulted on the initial crime, it would not be unusual for us to be called in again as the prosecution was preparing its case, as we had been many times before, such as in the trials of Wayne Williams, Sedley Alley, and Cleophus Prince. One of the key things we would do is develop an effective prosecutorial strategy if the defendant decides to take the stand in his own defense. With someone as smooth, charming, and controlled as O.J. Simpson, we would be figuring out what the prosecutors could do or bring up in cross examination that would show the jury what they believed him to be capable of doing—that is, brutally killing his ex-wife and her friend.

Since just about everyone, including the jurors, had heard the celebrated 911 tapes of Nicole being threatened by O.J., I would probably use that as a basis of attack, pressing the defendant to prove that that isn't what he's really like. In the course of so doing, I think we could get that aspect of his personality to emerge. We certainly had enough material on his personal life to press some of the right buttons.

A fact which, I'm sure, was not lost on Robert Shapiro and Johnnie Cochran, Simpson's two main attorneys, who insisted he not take the stand. In our legal system, each defendant has an absolute Fifth Amendment guarantee against self-incrimination, and I would not encroach upon this right in any way. The jury is normally instructed to draw no inference one way or the other from the defendant's assertion of that right. In fact, they are told, he need not put on any defense at all. The burden of proof is strictly on the prosecution, as it must and should be.

At the same time, I must say that I think it is somewhat ingenuous on the part of all concerned not to expect normal, reasonably intelligent adults not to at least wonder at someone who, given the chance to help prove his innocence, would think his testimony would do just the opposite. I don't think I've ever been involved with a trial in which someone I thought might possibly be innocent chose not to testify and get that point across.

As Vincent Bugliosi, the extremely able and articulate attorney who prosecuted the Manson case for the State of California, put it, we'd have a pretty wretched system if most of the people charged by the police, brought up before a grand jury, then extensively investigated by prosecutors turned out to be innocent.

So the linchpin of the defense case turns out, to no one's surprise, to be the possibility of a police frame-up of Simpson by elements of the Los Angeles Police Department. To the defense attorneys, this seems to be a pretty good tactic to use since the jury is predominantly black and no one with any sense of reality can argue that, over the years, the LAPD has not had a rather deplorable record when it comes to insensitivity, intimidation, and out-and-out police brutality against minorities, blacks especially. Bugliosi, who is in a position to know, cites several examples of probable police homicides of unarmed subjects. The issue is further complicated by the pivotal role of Detective Mark Fuhrman, the man who found the bloody glove behind Simpson's residence, whose antipathy toward minority groups is well-established.

The defense doesn't have to prove this frame-up. All they have to do is establish reasonable doubt; they must merely show that it could have happened.

Under these circumstances, the prosecution has two choices: ignore the suggestion and press on with their case, or try to disprove it, to neutralize it as a defense.

If I'm giving advice on prosecutorial strategy to district attorneys Marcia Clark and Christopher Darden, I'm telling them that with this jury, they ignore or minimize the issue at their peril. They've got to prove, beyond a reasonable doubt, that a police frame-up didn't happen. Since negatives are difficult to prove, what they've got to do, it seems to me, is show, through behavioral analysis, that, reasonably, it *couldn't* have happened. And the way you do that is to take the jury through the scenario as if it *had* happened.

First of all, we've got to suppose several things: one is that certain LAPD members were of a mind to frame a subject of the stature of O.J. Simpson. Well, maybe they were. After all, we have reason to believe Mark Fuhrman hates blacks.

But we've got a couple of problems here. A number of black police officers and citizens are willing to testify that they never saw any evidence of racial hatred or prejudice from him. He was known to have black friends, and at one point, in fact, he had a black female partner.

Okay, so maybe he hid it and what came out on the notorious "Fuhrman tapes" was the real Mark Fuhrman. So we've got to have a more reliable behavioral indicator of whether a guy like Mark Fuhrman would take it upon himself to frame a guy like O.J. Simpson for murder. And here's where we run into another behavioral inconsistency with the frame-up theory. We know as an undisputed fact that several years earlier, as a patrolman, Fuhrman answered a domestic complaint at the Simpsons' home. I mean, here he sees evidence that this black man has beaten up this white woman, so if he's at all prone to bust this guy's chops, here's his gold-plated opportunity. No one would utter a word of protest if he ran Simpson in on a domestic battery charge. But he doesn't. In fact, he's rather in awe of him. So given this, a couple of years later, how logical is it that Fuhrman suddenly changes his behavior and decides to plant evidence?

You also have to consider the behavioral precedent. As Vince Bugliosi points out in *Outrage,* his penetrating and hard-hitting analysis of the Simpson trial, while the idea of police brutality, unfortunately, is well within the experience of too many black citizens of Los Angeles, the idea of a police frame-up is not. It's too complicated and elaborate and far from foolproof. Even at their worst, this is not the way rogue elements of the LAPD settle their scores. And group behavioral dynamics tend to be as consistent, if not more so, as those of individuals.

Then you have to accept another set of suppositions if you're going to accept the frame-up theory.

To frame Simpson, these cops all have to get together and agree among themselves that they're going to do it. If one of them dissents, they're all screwed. Then they have to agree among themselves that they're going to let the real killer go free. If they've put Simpson on ice as their prime suspect and the UNSUB kills again, they and the LAPD are going to be in some deep shit; there's no way around this.

And even if they're willing to let the real killer go free, they've got to know what at that point is unknowable—that Simpson doesn't have an ironclad alibi for the time in question. If he happens to have been at one of his frequent charity benefits or public appearances that night, then the shit just gets deeper and deeper and these fellows are all not only out of a job, they're contemplating the view across the Golden Gate from a bayside window at San Quentin. No matter how they feel about minorities, after the Rodney King case, could any of them possibly not think they'd get crucified in court and in the media for symbolically beating up on a black man who is not only a lot more prominent than Rodney King, but is adored by most of the country, black and white?

Take a detective like Philip Vannatter. He only has a couple of months to go before retirement after a distinguished career with a spotless record. I've spent twenty-five years dealing with cops—good cops, great cops, not-so-good cops, and bad cops—on a daily basis and I know how their minds work. There is no way in hell that a Phil Vannatter is going to risk his pension and his freedom—in other words, is going to lay the rest of his life and his family's welfare—on the line for something as silly as this, particularly this close to retirement. There just ain't anything in it for him.

And for this frame-up to have taken place would have required a massively widespread conspiracy. I've been around institutions and bureaucracies long enough to know that it's virtually impossible to get anything done on a large scale, particularly spontaneously, without someone else finding out.

So, for a frame-up to have occurred, two sets of detectives from different divisions who didn't even know each other had to meet at the crime scene and spontaneously decide that since one of the victims was O.J. Simpson's ex-wife and since O.J. is black, then they'd just frame him for the murders and ignore the real killer, have confidence that everyone from the lab they'd have to bring into the conspiracy would support them, have faith in the fact that Simpson didn't have an alibi that would blow them out of the water, and risk everything they'd worked for all those years on a cop's salary just to sink a guy who everyone loves and who one of them, given the opportunity to arrest him several years before when he had probable cause, had not done so.

On television, Alan Dershowitz suggested the possibility that perhaps the police really did believe Simpson to be guilty and merely planted the evidence to help their case along. Okay, and maybe Alan Dershowitz took on Mr. Simpson as a client because he genuinely believed him to be innocent and was appalled at the way he was being railroaded by the police and the L.A. County prosecutor's office. But I doubt it. Say what you will about these detectives; they're not naive or stupid. They know what it takes to make a case, and if they believed Simpson to be guilty and saw with their own eyes how much blood evidence there was right in front of them, they had to have reasonable expectation that that blood evidence would link him sufficiently.

All this comes down to one thing: behavior is consistent. Even in its inconsistencies, it's consistent. None of the evidence, behavioral or forensic, not one shred of it, suggested another theory of the case but that the ex-husband of the female victim was responsible for the murders at 875 South Bundy Drive on the night of June 12, 1994.

This is what I would have told the police and prosecutors had they called on me. Whether it would have made any difference in the eventual outcome is another matter.

CHAPTER 13

Crime and Punishment

No matter how noble our notions of truth and justice may be, no matter what lofty phrases we couch them in, our criminal justice system has but two basic aims: exonerate the innocent (and those who cannot legally be proven to be culpable) and penalize the guilty.

Traditionally, there have been five basic goals to our correctional system and they shift in emphasis and importance according to current values and vogues in criminology. These goals are rehabilitation, retribution, isolation from society, vengeance, and punishment.

Rehabilitation is predicated on the premise that we can take someone who's done something seriously wrong and antisocial and by placing him in the proper environment, exposing him to the right experts, getting him to examine and understand his own past behavior, and compensating for missing aspects of his life (such as education or vocational training), we can turn that person around and make him into a contributing, law-abiding member of society. The concept of rehabilitation is inherent in the very term "correctional." When a parent disciplines a child, the underlying idea is that through the punishment, the parent hopes to "correct" the child's behavior. In most states, the name given to the prison system is Department of Corrections.

When rehabilitation works, there is no question that it is the best and most productive use of the correctional system. It stands to reason: if we can take a bad guy and turn him into a good guy and then let him out, then that's one fewer bad guy to harm us. This, of course, is a rather naive and simpleminded way to state the case, but in certain circumstances, it can work. If a person is stealing because he has no job and no training and he can be given training that will lead to a job, then perhaps he will gain self-respect and not feel the need to steal. If a person is stealing to support a drug habit and he can be gotten off drugs, then we can move on to the next step and get him the job and self-respect. The fact of the matter is that in many, if not most, cases, this doesn't work and the offender is back at his old crimes again before too long. But I'm not going to say that it isn't worth the time or effort or money to try to get certain types of offenders onto the straight and narrow, because I think there is hope.

Where I do not think there is much hope—and this is based on years of research and even more years of experience—is when we deal with serial killers and sexual predators, the people I have spent most of my career hunting and studying. These people do what they do not because they need to eat or to keep a family from starving, or even to support a drug habit. They do it because it feels good, because they want to, because it gives them satisfaction. You can certainly make the argument, and I will agree with you, that many of them are compensating for bad jobs, poor self-image, mistreatment by parents, any number of things. But that doesn't mean we're going to be able to rehabilitate them.

My colleague Gregg McCrary uses the analogy of the cake. You've baked this chocolate cake which smells great and looks terrific, but as soon as you bite into it you realize something is very wrong. Then you remember, "Oh yeah, in addition to the eggs and flour and butter and cocoa (and whatever else you put into a cake recipe), I recall mixing in some axle grease from my workshop in the garage. That's the only problem with the cake—the axle grease! If I can just figure out a way to get the axle grease out of the cake, it will be perfectly fine to eat."

This is the way my co-workers, associates, and I view rehabilitation of sexual predators, particularly serial sexual predators. The fact of the matter is that in the vast majority of cases, the urges, the desires, the character disorders that make them hurt and kill innocent men, women, and children are so deeply ingrained in the recipe of their makeup that there is no way to get out the axle grease.

The case of author and murderer Jack Henry Abbot, mentioned earlier, is just one example of many. I recall one particularly heartrending story which also makes the point. Back in the early 1990s, a child molester-killer who had escaped from prison was featured on the television program *America's Most Wanted.* This individual happened to see the program himself, and realized that others who knew him in his assumed identity would undoubtedly see it as well, that they would finger him, he'd be rearrested, and the jig would be up. Knowing this, and knowing his remaining time in freedom would be short, he left home, set out in his car, and kidnapped, molested, and killed another child before the police got to him. He knew that he would be going back in the slammer permanently, where he wouldn't have access to any little children, so he'd better do something while he had the chance.

The other analogy that comes to mind is the fable of the frog and the scorpion. A scorpion comes up to a frog and asks the frog to take him across the pond on his back.

"No," says the frog. "Because if I do, you'll sting me, and then I'll die."

"Think logically," replies the scorpion. "The reason I want the ride is because I can't swim. If I sting you and you die, then I die, too."

The frog mulls this over for a moment and decides the scorpion has a point. "Okay," he says, "hop on."

So the scorpion climbs onto the frog's back and the frog swims out from shore. But then, as they're about halfway across the pond, the scorpion stings the frog.

In his agonizing death throes, the frog gasps, "Why'd you do that? Now we're both gonna die."

And as the scorpion sinks below the surface of the pond on the way to his own death by drowning, he simply shrugs and says, "It's in my nature."

I'm afraid that at this point, none of us—not police officers or detectives, or FBI agents, or lawyers, judges, psychiatrists, or priests—have any real idea how to change that nature once it's gotten beyond the formative stage. That's why people like former Special Agent Bill Tafoya, Ph.D., for a long time Quantico's resident "futurist," feels that recognition of serious behavioral problems in kids and intervention at an early age are absolutely vital. This is the man who considers Project Head Start to be the single most effective crime-fighting weapon in the American arsenal. So clearly, Tafoya states and I agree, we need to take a big-picture view of crime and its causes. As we tell anyone who'll listen, if you're relying on us—the FBI and local police—to solve the crime problem, you're going to be very disappointed. By the time it makes a blip on our radar, it's too late; the criminal personality is already well established.

And this, unfortunately, is the reason rehabilitation often does not work.

So the next approach is isolation from society. If we can't "correct" or "cure" these predators, then we've just got to warehouse them to keep them off the street and keep the rest of us safe. Little need be said about this subject; its uses and drawbacks are self-evident. Many men who are violent and very dangerous in the outside world do okay in prison where life is highly structured and they don't have the opportunity to be harmful to innocent people. But some of them do have the opportunity to be harmful to other prisoners and prison guards and support personnel. And if anyone out there thinks our maximum security prisons, both federal and state, are not rough and dangerous places in which to live, take it from someone who's spent a lot of time visiting them—life in there is pretty damn precarious and threatening.

Of course, these are all bad guys in there, so who cares if they prey on each other? Well, that is the attitude most of us take; we resent all the tax money that goes into prisons and maintaining prisoners as it is. Don't get me wrong, I don't think rehabilitation works in a lot of cases and I am in favor of long-term isolation of the most dangerous offenders. But if we're going to allow the dangerous situations currently operating in our prisons to continue, just don't expect anyone coming out to be a much better person than he was when he went in. Probably, the opposite will be true. It's not an atmosphere conducive to rehabilitation; neither is it one in which you can simply warehouse and not worry about the consequences. I don't want more people let out of prison, but I don't want prisons places where you take your life in your hands, either.

Which brings us to the final view of sentencing, and that is punishment. We can try to rehabilitate, we can isolate them as long as we have to, but what about this goal? Is there any value in making a person suffer because of something he's done to someone else, and can that suffering deter anyone else from committing the same kind of crime?

Let me say at the outset that throughout the ages, the data on punishment as deterrence is not very encouraging. We've all heard the stories of pickpockets operating at the medieval public executions of felons convicted of pickpocketing. And on a level more basic and close to home, how often does spanking a child prevent his repetition of spankable offenses? Deterrence is great if it works, but to make punishment justified and worthwhile, it would seem that it needs some value beyond that.

And I think it has that.

In both this book and *Mindhunter,* I related some of my encounter with Charles Manson and my study of the gruesome crimes committed under his auspices back in 1969. And now, I'm gratified to read that former Manson family members Leslie Van Houten, Susan Atkins, and Patricia Krenwinkel, upon reflection of twenty or so years in prison, regret their roles in the murders of Sharon Tate, Abigail Folger, Jay Sebring, Voytek Frykowski, Steven Parent, and Leno and Rosemary LaBianca. At their periodic parole hearings, their attorneys testify to the women's repudiation of their former guru, their sincere contrition for their crimes, and the certainty that they would no longer be dangerous if released back into society.

I believe them. I really do. I believe they now see Manson realistically and for what he was and still is. I believe they are truly sorry for what they did those two horrible nights back in the summer of 1969. And as one who has studied violent offenders and dangerousness for many years, I believe they probably would not commit another serious crime if let out. They might even become "productive" members of society, teaching others through the errors of their own ways.

But I have also studied the case and all its details. I have gone over all the autopsy protocols and medical examiner's reports. I have seen the hideous crime scene photos of all seven victims, including the eight-months-pregnant Sharon Tate, who pleaded in vain with her attackers for the life of her unborn child. I have used these raw images in my lectures to FBI agents and National Academy police fellows and they never fail to elicit a gasp from these hardened professionals. So, seeing what I have seen and knowing what I know, I'm just old fashioned enough to believe that though these three convicted offenders may now be sorry, though they may no longer be dangerous, the idea of punishment alone is satisfactory justification for keeping them in prison at taxpayers' expense. And in my mind, there is no way they can be sufficiently punished for the monstrousness of what they did.

Does not a civilized and enlightened society believe in redemption? As opposed to rehabilitation, which is a more practical notion, I see redemption as belonging in the spiritual realm and so is a different kind of idea. But here I would argue, as Jack Collins has, that until we take seriously the most serious of crimes, we have no right to call ourselves civilized or enlightened. There are certain crimes that are simply too cruel, too sadistic, too hideous to be forgiven. We owe at least that to those seven innocent victims of the Manson family who had every right to live.

But when I talk about punishment, aren't I really talking about vengeance—the biblical eye-for-an-eye concept? Maybe I am. Which brings up the next question: Does vengeance have a place in punishment?

Should punishment, as administered by the correctional system, be used as a therapeutic or cathartic tool for crime victims and their families? We all want them to have closure, but are they legally (as opposed to merely morally) entitled to it?

Jack and Trudy Collins don't use the words "revenge" or "vengeance" to describe what it is they and others like them seek. "Though I don't disagree with the classic dictionary definition, 'to inflict deserved punishment for an injury,' for most people, they've now become emotionally loaded words with a connotation of personal malice, and their use ends up hurting the victim," Jack explains.

What they want, they say, is "retribution," which the *Oxford English Dictionary* defines as "recompense for, or requital of, evil done."

"It's a way of society balancing the scales," says Jack, "giving the victims and their families a feeling of satisfaction for what was done to them, to make them whole as far as possible or restore integrity—the quality or state of completeness—to both the people and the system. Nothing will ever bring Suzanne back to us. But even if this retribution doesn't bring complete closure, it shows us that society, the jury, and the entire criminal justice system care enough about us to see to it that our daughter's killer receives his appropriate punishment. It lets us know that they did right by us as far as they could."

It seems to me that for serious crimes, retribution through punishment is the only just and moral action that we, as a society, can take. This is not, however, a universal opinion.

As Jack Collins states, "Victims need to put the horror and trauma of the crime behind them as soon as possible and get on with their lives. Victims have a right to expect that defendants will be tried promptly so that, if convicted, their punishment can begin speedily. We've been trying to sensitize people to the fact that victims should not be considered outsiders in the criminal justice system. They have a stake; they should be in the forefront. We deserve and demand a place at the table."

When it comes to the next level of the criminal justice system, he says, "It seems to many observers of appeals courts, including ourselves, that too many of its judges consider the appellate function an academic and theoretical exercise that has more to do with intellectual sleight-of-hand and verbal dexterity than seeing that basic justice is done to victims and punishment meted out to wrongdoers. They appear to fancy the pose of being far above the fray, unaffected in any way by the blood, sweat, tears and violence which started the case's journey to their very chambers."

What the Collinses seek, of course, is the execution of their daughter's murderer in accord with the sentence handed down by his jury and judge.

Capital punishment is one of those issues like abortion. Not many of us are ever going to change anyone's opinion about it, one way or the other. If you are against the death penalty on moral grounds, I think a case can be made for putting away the worst of these monsters for life with no possibility they will ever be let out or paroled. But we know that there is no such thing. And frankly, in certain cases, I don't think it's enough.

As Steve Mardigian put it, "The tremendous devastation against victims warrants that we do something appropriately serious. In my view, we have no reason to keep people capable of inflicting this kind of horror alive."

Some would argue that capital punishment is "legalized murder" and therefore an immoral act on the part of society. My personal feeling is that these offenders have made a choice to remove themselves from society and therefore it is a moral statement to say that society will not tolerate the perpetrator of this kind of horrible act in its midst.

Asserting that capital punishment is legalized murder does a tremendous injury, in my opinion, to the very concept of right and wrong, in that it trivializes the crucial distinction between the victim of the crime and its perpetrator—the innocent life and the one who chose for his own vile reasons to take that innocent life.

If you ask me if I'm personally prepared to throw the switch that would legally end the life on earth of Sedley Alley, Larry Gene Bell, Paul Bernardo, Lawrence Bittaker, or others of their ilk, my answer would be a resounding "Yes!" And for those who talk of forgiveness, I'll tell them I am sympathetic to the concept, but at the same time I do not feel I am authorized to forgive; it's not my place.

Had Sedley Alley *merely* (and I use this word with some trepidation) raped, beaten, and tortured Suzanne Collins, but left her alive and her mental faculties intact, then she, and only she, would have been in a position to forgive him if she so chose. And as far as I'm concerned, she remains the only one capable of forgiving him, but because of what actually did happen, she can only do so now *after* his jury-imposed sentence has been carried out.

That, I think, is what the Collinses mean by retribution rather than revenge.

Now, on the subject of deterrence, I admit that there can be little doubt that as presently administered in the United States, the death penalty is not a general deterrent to murder in many, if not most, situations. Common sense should tell us that if you're a young urban criminal making your living off the drug trade where there are huge amounts of money at stake and your business competition is out there trying to kill you every day, the dim prospect of a possible death sentence and execution somewhere at the end of a fifteen year procedural morass—that is, if you get caught, if you don't plea bargain, if you draw a tough judge and a tough jury, if you don't get reversed, if they don't change the law, et cetera, et cetera—isn't much of a deterrent, or a risk, for that matter, compared to the occupational hazards you face on the street every day of your working life. So let's be realistic about that aspect of the argument.

If the death penalty were applied more evenly and uniformly, and if the period of time from sentence to execution were reduced to a reasonable matter of months rather than a protracted period of years or even the decades that people like the Collinses have had to endure, then perhaps it would become more useful in dissuading would-be offenders in certain types of murders. But frankly, this theoretical speculation doesn't concern me all that much. Meted out fairly and consistently, perhaps the death penalty could become a general deterrent; I'm not certain and I wouldn't be optimistic about it.

But of one thing I am certain: it is, by God, a specific deterrent. No one who has been executed has ever taken another innocent life. And until such time as we really mean it as a society when we say "imprisonment for life," I, and the families of countless victims, would sleep better at night knowing there is no chance that the worst of these killers will ever again be able to prey on others. Even then, I personally believe that if you choose to take another human life, you ought to be prepared to pay with your own.

Our justice system is imperfect. Some monsters can be rehabilitated and go on to live useful and productive lives. Nathan Leopold, who partnered with Richard Loeb in the 1924 thrill killing of young Bobby Franks in Chicago, was paroled in 1958 and went on to finish out his years respectably and productively as a social worker and lab technician, volunteering for studies in malaria research. But you know something? I don't think that would be the case with a Lawrence Bittaker, and I'm not anxious to keep him around long enough to find out. Once you've done something this horrendous, you forfeit your claims to rehabilitation.

Then there's the argument that rather than killing these guys, we should keep them alive "for study." I'm not sure what people mean by this; I don't think they know, themselves. I suppose they mean that if we study enough of them long enough, we'll figure out why they kill and what we can do to stop them.

Now as it happens, my colleagues at Quantico and I are among the few professionals who actually have studied these people. If anyone has a stake, therefore, in keeping them alive for intellectual reasons, it's us. And here's my response to that: If they're willing to talk to me at all, there is plenty of time during the protracted appeals process. If they're only willing to talk—as Ted Bundy ultimately was—as a bargaining chip for staying alive longer, then what they tell me is going to be tainted and self-serving anyway. When you tell me we should keep someone like Bundy alive to study, I say, "Fine, keep him alive six hours longer; that's all I need." I really don't think we're going to get much more beyond that.

I don't hate these people. Some of them, I even kind of liked. I happen to like Ed Kemper, for example. I got along with him well and we enjoyed good rapport. I respect his mind and his insight. Had he been given the death penalty, I would have been personally sorry and sad to see him executed. But I certainly wouldn't have been willing to argue the point with the families of any of his victims, because I know what they've gone through and continue to go through. Compared to their feelings, mine are irrelevant.

But no responsible discussion of the death penalty can fail to include reflection on the fact that our legal system is imperfect and there is always the chance that the wrong man will be convicted. Inevitably, in any consideration of capital punishment, we must confront the example of David Vasquez. And much as we may hate to admit it, his copping of an Alford plea might have saved his life.

The fact that this was a rare, odd type of case in which the defendant actually confessed, not once, but three times, should not give us too much comfort or reassurance. At the same time, I don't think this is a valid argument for scrapping the death penalty altogether.

What I think it is a valid argument for is the insistence on an overwhelming amount and degree of proof. And while some might argue that you can never be absolutely sure, I think in the kinds of cases I'm talking about, you can be sure enough that innocent people like Vasquez will not go wrongly to their deaths.

The types of offenders I most want to see face the ultimate penalty are the repeat, predatory, sexually motivated killers. By the time we catch them there is generally a mountain of solid, behaviorally consistent, forensic evidence against them. As with Cleophus Prince, if he did one of the murders, he did all of them. If there isn't a sufficiently formidable mountain of evidence, then don't execute. But if there is, as there was against Bell, as there is against Alley and Bernardo and Bittaker and so many others, then do what needs to be done.

As Steve Mardigian puts it, "I would hope that the proof is overwhelming, that there would be no question of being able to support the guilt. From this unit's perspective, in Vasquez, there would have been questions. They didn't have the solid physical and lab evidence, and the confession from this type of individual under these circumstances was not enough."

But I'm confident that the legal minds who have expended so much time and energy on other fine points of our criminal jurisprudence system can come up with a standard that will separate out the David Vasquezes from the Timothy Spencers. It's also possible that murder could be made exclusively a federal crime, which would make standards of prosecution and proof more consistent. On the other hand, it would probably involve revamping the entire judicial system, because federal courts simply would not be able to handle the volume of cases and trials they'd have to take over from the states.

So how do you prioritize all our concerns and all the things we might wish the criminal justice system to be? To me, it's innocent potential victims first, victims of violent crime and their families second, and defendants and their families last. First and foremost, I'll do anything I can to see to it that someone does not become the victim of someone who has already committed a similar crime. Failing that, I want to bring victims and their families to the forefront of the system, to give them the due that is rightly theirs. And then I want to make sure that defendants get a fair trial and convicted felons receive appropriate sentences for their crimes. None of these need be mutually exclusive.

Does this mean I think we need a police state? Of course not. It means simply what it says—that we need to keep our priorities straight if we hope to be a just and civilized society.

Ultimately, no matter what we do with our criminal justice system, the only thing that is going to cut down appreciably on crimes of violence and depravity is to stop manufacturing as many criminals. The courts have a role in this, the police have a role in this, the schools have a role, and so do the churches and synagogues and mosques. But the real struggle must be where it has always been: in the home.

As Sedley Alley's prosecutor, Hank Williams, observes, "The federal government spends billions of dollars to fight crime, and they have to. But the only real answer is for mommas and daddies to raise their kids right."

This is easier said than done, but it's the only factor that's going to make a real difference.

At the very beginning of this book, I explained that to do what I do and what the people I've taught do, you have to be able to put yourself in the head of both offender and victim. When your work on a case is done, you try to get out of the offender's head as soon as you possibly can. But the fact of the matter is that you never fully get out of the victim's head, and a part of every victim whose case I've ever worked is always with me.

That's why I feel the way I do and that's why I'm always trying to get others to make that journey into darkness with me, at least a little bit of the way.

Index

JOURNEY INTO DARKNESS

Proof-of-Purchase

1503